Early Childhood Psychopathology

Karen R. Gouze • Joyce Hopkins
John V. Lavigne

Early Childhood Psychopathology

Developmental Models and Treatments

Springer

Karen R. Gouze
Northwestern University Feinberg School of Medicine
Ann & Robert H. Lurie Children's Hospital of Chicago
Chicago, IL, USA

John V. Lavigne
Northwestern University Feinberg School of Medicine
Ann & Robert H. Lurie Children's Hospital of Chicago
Chicago, IL, USA

Joyce Hopkins
Department of Psychology
Illinois Institute of Technology
Chicago, IL, USA

ISBN 978-3-031-68876-8 ISBN 978-3-031-68877-5 (eBook)
https://doi.org/10.1007/978-3-031-68877-5

This Springer imprint is published by the registered company Springer Nature Switzerland AG
The registered company address is: Gewerbestrasse 11, 6330 Cham, Switzerland

To our children, each of whom, in their own way, inspired our life's work

Preface

In 1960 Philippe Aries wrote *Centuries of Childhood: A Social History of Family Life*, in which he argued that it was not until after the Middle Ages that childhood was conceptualized as a separate phase of life. Later, with the advent of schooling and the industrial revolution, laws to protect children firmly established this period of life as separate and worthy of study. At the turn of the twentieth century, G. Stanley Hall, often considered the father of developmental psychology, initiated the first systematic psychological studies of children. Working at the same time, Sigmund Freud highlighted the importance of events occurring in early childhood as the precursors of adult psychological distress. In 1909, the first child mental health clinic in the United States, the Institute for Juvenile Research, was established in Chicago, Illinois. Nevertheless, it was not until many decades later that the field of developmental psychopathology was born, and the social, emotional, and behavioral difficulties of young children were seen as worthy of study in their own right.

There were many reasons why the emotional and behavioral difficulties of young children were not always recognized as important. While the tantrums and noncompliance of preschoolers were difficult for parents to tolerate, they were behaviors that many professionals believed the child would eventually "grow out of." Similarly, at one time, the anxiety that preschoolers experienced ("there's a monster in my closet") was uniformly trivialized as "just a phase" and the possibility that a preschooler might experience depression was not even considered.

After years of research, however, our understanding of early childhood psychopathology and its implications for the individual's development into middle childhood, adolescence, and adulthood has expanded dramatically. For some children these problems do, indeed, dissipate relatively quickly; for others they persist well into adolescence and beyond. Given the growing burden of increasing mental illness on individuals, families, and society, it is essential that we understand how, when, and why some individuals struggle so much more than others with depression, anxiety, and behavioral regulation. Understanding continuities and discontinuities in symptoms over the life span, along with identifying the risk and protective factors that exacerbate or ameliorate these symptoms, is essential to improving the mental health and life chances of all individuals.

The authors of this book became interested in understanding the developmental trajectories of young children struggling with a range of symptoms as a result of over 25 years of clinical experience addressing the struggles, and accompanying pain, of emotional and behavioral problems that lead to functional impairment in children presenting in clinical settings. We recognized that effective early prevention and intervention efforts, at the individual, family, and societal levels, required a better understanding of the risk factors contributing to early and ongoing struggles with emotional and behavioral symptoms. Our interest in studying young children, specifically, stemmed from the knowledge that, often, preventing emotional and behavioral problems is easier than fixing them once they have emerged, that many psychological problems begin in early childhood and persist over time, and that frequently, children and parents are more responsive to intervention efforts when children are young.

Although there are a substantial number of papers published in refereed journals that identify various risk factors—ranging from those associated with the child's socioeconomic situation to characteristics of parents including their mental health and parenting styles, and the child's characteristics—most of this research focuses only on the association of a few of those factors with the child's behavioral or emotional difficulties. While each of these studies is important in elucidating specific associations, our clinical experience made us aware that it was important to take a more comprehensive approach, one that involved looking at a wider range of risk factors and the pathways by which they influence the development of different types of emotional and behavioral symptoms. We expected that relevant pathways might be numerous and varied and could help us put the relative contributions of these risk factors into perspective. We further hoped that this perspective might improve our understanding of the development of emotional and behavioral difficulties during early childhood and, additionally, might inform decisions about designing treatment programs to address children's mental health needs.

It was these efforts and a desire to improve the lives of all children and families that drove this research. In that context, we think it is important to say a few things about the use of language in this book. Although, ultimately, our interest is in promoting the mental health and well-being of children, we believe that we cannot do that without understanding what happens when children and families struggle with emotional or behavioral challenges. Although words like "psychopathology" and "disorder" can sometimes feel negative and pejorative, we maintain that it is important to name the struggles that children have and to recognize them, not as something wrong with the child but as something that interferes with their daily life and compromises healthier development and their life chances. As such, it is essential that we bring these struggles to light and address them as we would any other health problem; the stigma attached to mental health problems has gone on for far too long. That said, the struggles we are studying in this book are different in many ways from physical health issues and applying a medical model, the predominant model used in clinical psychology, is not always illuminating. It is partially for this reason that we view the emotional and behavioral symptoms children are struggling with dimensionally, that is, as continuous rather than categorical. For instance, we believe that children do not have or not have anxiety; rather, anxiety exists on a continuum for all children and manifests with greater intensity or frequency as a function of many factors, many of which are explored in the models in this book. It is only when the anxiety interferes with the child's ability to "engage in the work of childhood," that is, when their anxiety prevents them from functioning well in their environment and with other people, that the anxiety becomes a problem. Furthermore, the term anxiety, like all mental health terms, is bound up in a myriad of social and cultural norms, many of which differ from place to place and from one historical moment to the next. As such, it is important to realize that we use the terms "developmental psychopathology," "normal development," and "emotional and behavior disorders," among others, throughout this book for clarity of language and to acknowledge that mental health struggles are real. Our intention is not to assert a reified notion of what is normal and what is not but, rather, to understand the subjective experiences of children and families whose ability to function well in the endeavors that are important to them, or vital for healthy development, is compromised. In constructing the models in this book, we thus sought to understand which factors at different levels and in different contexts contribute to risk for emotional and behavioral difficulties. We were interested in how combinations of risk factors and the mechanisms through which they operate lead young children to experience struggles in daily functioning, struggles which, at times, set the stage for cascading difficulties that profoundly affect their ongoing development and well-being, and the well-being of those around them. We want to stress that variations in child development are strongly impacted by culture, the historical moment, and the social milieu in which children and families live, learn, work, and play.

This book is the culmination of 20 years of research in which we made a significant effort to advance our understanding of the risk factors and mechanisms that impact mental health and family functioning during early childhood. Our goal was to take a more comprehensive approach than previous research by examining a wider range of risk factors and the pathways by which they have their influence on the development of different types of emotional and behavioral symptoms. Clearly, this effort is not exhaustive; we could not possibly examine all the variables we thought might be relevant. However, we expected that relevant pathways might be numerous and varied, and hoped the research would help us put the relative contributions of these particular risk factors into perspective—a perspective that might improve our understanding of the struggles experienced by so many children and families with whom we have worked clinically over the years. Ultimately, our goal was to gather information that could help in the development of more effective early prevention and intervention programs and in understanding the mechanisms whereby we might improve the life chances of young children.

This book is a true collaborative effort, and thus, the authors are listed in alphabetical order, not according to their relative contributions.

Chicago, IL, USA

Karen R. Gouze
Joyce Hopkins
John V. Lavigne

Acknowledgments

The research described in this book was supported by a grant from the National Institute of Mental Health (grant MH 063665), Principal Investigator John V. Lavigne.

As with any endeavor, there are many individuals who made invaluable contributions to the PACT research program and the writing of this book.

We are deeply grateful to Dr. Fred Bryant whose expert consultation in navigating the complex statistical issues of this research was essential to its success. His positive attitude and feedback were a source of encouragement that always lifted our spirits.

Our thanks to Dr. Susan LeBailly for her attention to detail and skill in managing the myriad aspects of conducting a large-scale research project.

Our heartfelt appreciation to our dedicated graduate students who served as invaluable research assistants. Their tireless efforts and willingness to "go the extra mile" by traveling far and wide to the participants' homes to collect the research data significantly contributed to the success of this research program.

We also want to thank the Chicago Public Schools Department of Early Childhood Education, along with participating school principals and lead teachers, and the pediatric practices in the Pediatric Practice Research Group who provided the means to recruit the participating families.

We are indebted to the families with young children, who generously gave us their time and welcomed us into their homes, and to the children themselves whose strengths and challenges were a constant reminder of why this work mattered to us.

Last, but certainly not least, each of us is immensely grateful to our spouses, without whose support, advice, and patience, this book would not have come to fruition. Words do not suffice to thank you.

It really does take a village.

Contents

About the Authors

Karen R. Gouze, Ph.D., is Professor Emeritus of Psychiatry and Behavioral Sciences at Northwestern University Feinberg School of Medicine and, formerly, a psychologist in the Pritzker Department of Psychiatry and Behavioral Sciences and the Center for Childhood Resilience at Ann & Robert H. Lurie Children's Hospital of Chicago. For over 35 years she was the Director of Training in Psychology at Lurie Children's Hospital (formerly Children's Memorial Hospital) in Chicago where she also worked as a researcher and clinician. Her research addresses risk and protective factors related to healthy child development, particularly in early childhood, and the dissemination and implementation of prevention and intervention practices in community settings. As a clinician, she supports increased understanding of psycho-social stressors, cultural diversity, and developmental psychology to complement the use of empirically based treatment approaches with children and families.

Joyce Hopkins, Ph.D., is Professor Emeritus in the Psychology Department at Illinois Institute of Technology and, formerly, a Psychology Professor in that department for 29 years. She also served as Associate Director and Director of Clinical Training. Prior to that she was the Co-Director of the Parent-Infant Development Service in the Child Psychiatry Department at the University of Chicago Medical Center. Her research focuses on risk and protective factors in early childhood mental health, with a particular emphasis on the role of attachment and parenting. She was President of the Illinois Association for Infant Mental Health, served on that Board for several terms, and currently is a member of the Research Committee. Her other interests include maternal mental health issues during pregnancy and the postpartum periods. Her clinical work focuses on early intervention with young children and promoting maternal mental health during pregnancy and the postpartum period.

John V. Lavigne, Ph.D., is currently Professor of Psychiatry and Pediatrics at Northwestern University Feinberg School of Medicine and a Diplomate of the American Board of Examiners in Clinical Psychology. For almost 40 years he was the Chief Psychologist at the Ann and Robert H. Lurie Children's Hospital of Chicago (formerly Children's Memorial Hospital). For the last 25 years he has been conducting research related to the development of psychopathology in young children. His other interests have included psychological aspects of pediatric chronic illness, unexplained medical symptoms, and ways to improve the provision of psychological services for children and adolescents in primary care pediatric settings.

Chapter 1
Developmental Psychopathology: The Emergence of a Discipline

It is easier to build strong children than to repair broken adults.

Adaptation-Frederick Douglass

Current rates of mental illness are increasing throughout the life span (World Health Organization, 2022b), with some of the most alarming increases occurring during childhood and adolescence (Lebrun-Harris et al., 2022). Understanding the conditions leading to these alarming statistics is critical for designing early prevention and intervention programs that can change the developmental trajectories contributing to these negative outcomes. Yet, this is no small task. Early attempts at understanding psychopathology in children were derived heavily from conceptualizations of psychopathology in adults and, much like pre-Renaissance paintings that depicted children merely as miniature-sized versions of adults, this view ignored the many differences between children and adults. While there were notable exceptions, the early study of child psychopathology, like adult psychopathology, emphasized the role of underlying emotional and psychological conflicts in the development of psychopathology. In doing so, these studies tended to ignore other factors important in child development, such as the impact of physical, cognitive, emotional, and social development on child well-being. At the time, these factors were being studied actively, but completely separately, within the field of developmental psychology (Cicchetti, 1984; Sroufe, 2009). However, with the emergence of developmental psychopathology as a specific discipline in the 1970s, a stronger developmental perspective was incorporated into the study of child psychopathology. Questions such as "What does anxiety look like in a 3-year-old and how might that differ from how it appears in a 10-year-old? Can a 4-year-old be depressed? What factors contribute to extreme oppositional behavior at age 8 and what does this mean for adult functioning?" replaced assumptions about the similarities between child and adult mental illness. Understanding and exploring the risk and protective factors leading to continuities and discontinuities in adaptive functioning throughout the life span defined the work of the developmental psychopathology researcher.

K. R. Gouze et al., *Early Childhood Psychopathology*,
https://doi.org/10.1007/978-3-031-68877-5_1

The Emergence of the Field of Developmental Psychopathology

Essentially, in the last 50 years, developmental psychopathology emerged as a discipline in response to the need for a greater understanding of the emotional and behavioral difficulties observed during the first 18 years of life and for clarity regarding psychiatric diagnosis during this same period (Achenbach, 1974). As diagnostic systems for the classification of psychiatric disorders became integrated into general classification systems for diseases, such as The International Classification System of Diseases (World Health Organization, 2022a, b) and, in the United States, were increasingly codified into the DSM classification system (American Psychiatric Association, 2013), it became clear that many questions remained regarding the manifestation of emotional and behavioral disorders in children. Among others, these questions include the following. Are these emotional and behavioral manifestations in childhood continuous with adult disorder? Do the same atypical behaviors have the same meaning and impact at different ages and how do we understand these in the context of normal developmental phenomena? How do earlier problems in development impact later development? Do the same behaviors or emotional presentations have the same meaning in different cultures or at different times in history? In other words, how is psychopathology organized and how does it manifest at different ages, in different settings, with different external conditions, in different cultures, and during different historical periods?

The emergence of developmental psychopathology as a discipline constituted an integration of many other disciplines, principal of which were the fields of developmental psychology and adult psychiatry. Psychoanalytic theory, which dominated psychiatry from the 1890s through the mid-twentieth century, particularly in Europe where it began, was based heavily on the concept that psychological conflicts developing early in life have a profound impact on the later development of psychopathology. This understanding, however, was based primarily on work with adult patients and their retrospective reports of their childhoods. In contrast, behaviorism, which gained a foothold in American academic psychology and emerged as the dominant force in the American academic psychology of the 1950s and 1960s, emphasized a focus on patterns of observable behavior shaped by very specific environmental inputs (e.g., various types of reinforcement). As such it was not concerned with non-observable events (cognitions, emotions) or with patterns of adaptation and processes of development that became hierarchically organized over time. Both these fields of study neglected to address, in an integrated fashion, the increasingly robust body of knowledge emerging from developmental psychology, which addressed cognitive, emotional, and behavioral aspects of functioning in childhood at multiple levels, biological, individual, and societal, over time and in different contexts. The primary goal of the nascent field of developmental psychopathology was to develop a robust theory of development that brought together these strands of psychiatric, behavioral, and developmental thought into a coherent understanding of typical and atypical development of children and adults longitudinally across the lifespan, in different environments, and at multiple, hierarchically integrated levels. Initially, the field was concerned not so much with the classification of childhood disorders as with understanding the processes by which these disorders emerge, the extent to which they are continuous with and, in turn, impact normal development, and how they become integrated over time to manifest in later mental disorder.

Historically, the field of developmental psychopathology began with the work of Thomas Achenbach in the 1970s (Achenbach, 1974). Achenbach maintained that the primary goal of developmental psychopathology was to establish a framework that could guide the study of development in a number of spheres—physical, cognitive, social-emotional—with particular attention to milestones and how development progresses over time. To accomplish this task, he asserted the need for a greater understanding of age- and sex-based norms against which clinicians and researchers could measure unusual or atypical behaviors and emotional presentations. Achenbach did not view these unusual behaviors as discrete or encapsulated entities but rather as continuous with normal developmental presentations, which might become problematic when occurring at certain ages or depending upon their frequency or intensity. This led to the development of the Achenbach Child Behavior Checklist (Achenbach, 1991), a factor-analytically derived measure of symptom clusters arrayed along a continuum of frequency of occurrence in a community sample. Initially normed on a community sample from the Washington, DC area, it was later re-normed on a nationally representative sample of children aged 4–16 in the United States and derived from empirical research on what constitutes typical behavior at different ages (Achenbach et al., 1995). Achenbach and colleagues later developed another checklist for younger children aged 1 ½–5 years, also based on a nationally representative sample (Achenbach & Rescorla, 2000). These instruments not only provided normative data for the classification of childhood problems in the context of age and gender but also facilitated an understanding of the ways in which developmental psychology provides a context for identifying critical discontinuities in development and, hence, those childhood emotional and behavioral presentations that should be a cause for concern. Achenbach's beginning explorations of continuity versus discontinuity in development and his premise that understanding atypical development or adaptation required an understanding of normative development sowed the seeds for the advancement of the field of developmental psychopathology. In its earliest iteration, however, it lacked nuance beyond understanding age and sex differences in development.

Further elaboration emerged from the work of Michael Rutter and Alan Sroufe (Rutter & Sroufe, 2000). They expanded Achenbach's conceptualizations of continuity and discontinuity in development to include the importance of etiological or causal factors that were potentially non-linear and included conceptualizations of the child as a developing organism that actively shapes their environment. These concepts include the notion that a given construct in early development is not necessarily directly related to that identical construct in later development but might, as a function of bi-directional or multiple ongoing influences, be more strongly related to some other construct. For example, early difficult child temperament manifesting in oppositionality might interact over time with parenting attitudes and practices such that the ultimate outcome for that child is adult depression rather than conduct problems. The extent to which the child shapes their environment and how these changes further impact child outcomes is an example of non-linear causality and of the importance of the child as an active organism in their own development (Sroufe, 2009). Rutter and Sroufe posited that understanding normal developmental processes in the context of complex biological and environmental influences and ongoing transactional interchanges that become hierarchically integrated into new patterns of behavior over time is critical to understanding the emergence of maladaptive behaviors or psychopathology. As Sroufe (2009) maintained, psychopathology is not inherent in people; rather, it develops over time due to ongoing interactions between the individual and the environment forged in the service of adaptation. Each new adaptation is foundational and sets the stage for later adaptations. Sroufe emphasized the role that genes, environment, and personal history all play in future development. This conceptualization of developmental psychopathology required prospective longitudinal study in different contexts that allowed for consideration of the pathways leading to later mental health presentations. It further emphasized the importance of studying children at very young ages since early foundational experiences were posited to be critical in determining, or at least contributing to, future outcomes.

Consequently, early conceptualizations of psychiatric risk seen exclusively in diagnostic and categorical terms were viewed increasingly as inadequate to explain any number of empirical findings over time. For example, it became apparent that early psychiatric diagnoses were not necessarily isomorphic with later psychiatric diagnoses, that early risk factors led to psychopathology in some children but not others, and that the same early risk factors, including particular early psychiatric diagnoses, might manifest in different mental health or diagnostic outcomes in different children under different environmental conditions. This led to an expansion of developmental psychopathology theory and research to include an understanding of protective or buffering factors as well as risk factors. Additionally, developmental psychopathology researchers sought to account for maladaptive childhood behavior patterns that were not necessarily captured in current psychiatric categories. Over time, this burgeoning field of study developed a set of guiding principles that are perhaps best described in Ann Masten's 2006 article, "Pathways to the Future" (Masten, 2006).

Principles of Developmental Psychopathology

Masten (2006), like her predecessors, conceived of developmental psychopathology not as a singular theory but as an integrative field of study that encompassed theory and empirical study from a range of other disciplines. True integration requires a planful, well-thought-out, and coherent set of principles that, taken together, create a framework for past and future work. Clearly emerging from and consistent with the work of those who preceded her, Masten established seven core tenets that both defined the field of developmental psychopathology and became guiding principles for the design of future research. These core tenets included the following: (1) the developmental principle; (2) the normative principle; (3) the systems principle; (4) the multi-level principle; (5) the agency principle; (6) the mutually informative principle; and (7) the longitudinal principle. In designing the research described in this book, we considered all these principles to be critical to understanding the risk factors contributing to the development and maintenance of poor mental health outcomes across three developmental periods: preschool, kindergarten, and formal school entry. Each of these principles is elaborated on below, and a discussion of their application to the research follows.

The Developmental Principle

The developmental principle, perhaps, is the most basic principle established in developmental psychopathology. As noted above, the field of developmental psychopathology emerged largely from the field of developmental psychology. The developmental tenet maintains that developmental psychopathology must adhere to the theoretical and empirical principles that guide its "sister" discipline. Among these principles is the fundamental notion that development is gradual and sequential, that it becomes increasingly complex and hierarchically integrated over time, that the significance of behavior changes over time, and that there are sensitive periods during which fundamental building blocks of development are established. For the most part, development is seen as continuous, with early and later influences acting in concert to produce behaviors that lead to healthy or unhealthy outcomes.

The Normative Principle

Emerging from the developmental principle, the normative principle posits that aberrant or less adaptive development can be understood only in the context of an understanding of normal development. This understanding does not rely on diagnosis or categorical determinations of normality and non-normality but, rather, on the principle that developmental outcomes manifest along a continuum. How can you know, for example, if a child's tantrums at age 3 are worthy of concern unless you know more about the range in which the intensity, frequency, and appearance of tantrums occur for most 3-year-olds, and perhaps, more specifically, for most 3-year-olds in that child's culture, at this point in history, and under these circumstances? Developmental psychology research promotes the understanding of those norms and provides a guidepost against which less adaptive behavior can be measured. As Masten (2006) notes, developmental tasks are more or less important at varying times depending upon such factors as development, culture, and context.

The Systems and Multi-level Principles

The third tenet, the systems principle, and the fourth tenet, the multi-level principle, operate together to capture the importance in developmental psychopathology of understanding that multiple systems at different levels work together to create hierarchically integrated and interactive processes leading to developmental outcomes. In other words, individuals are formed by a complex, transactionally integrated set of systems, ranging from biological to societal levels. Early developmental theorists such as Sameroff and Chandler (1975) and Bronfenbrenner (1977) first addressed the importance of understanding the transactional nature of these interacting systems. Since then, understanding that interacting systems of development ranging from the smallest biological cell (which might be turned on or off depending upon a range of circumstances) to the larger influences of culture and society has guided the fields of developmental psychology and developmental psychopathology. Organisms do not develop and exist in isolation; they are part of much larger systems that interact bi-directionally across levels. A full understanding of the development of less adaptive behavior requires an understanding of the biological influences a child brings to the table and the influences of the environment in which the child lives. For example, we know that a child who is behaviorally inhibited can become more or less anxious over the course of their early development depending upon the anxiety level of their primary caretaker, the actual behaviors that are encouraged or discouraged, and the expectations generated by the culture in which they live (Fox et al., 2005). Although their propensity towards anxiety might be genetically based, the response of their environment at the family level, i.e., parental response, and on up to the societal level (children in some cultures are encouraged to be more independent at an earlier age) can greatly impact the outcome for that particular child.

The Agency Principle

The agency tenet posits that children are active players in their own development—that they engage the environment in ways that alter the environment's influence upon them. This transactional process, between the child and the environment, can lead to profoundly different outcomes for different children. We are reminded of a story we heard many years ago about the fraternal twin daughters of a colleague. This colleague relayed that her older daughter had asked her mother to bring her toddler twin sisters to her third-grade class for show and tell. During this event, the mother was struck by the extent to which the difference in the toddlers' temperaments impacted how the event unfolded. One twin was temperamentally more outgoing and risk-taking; she engaged the world openly and adventurously with large smiles for anyone who greeted her. The other twin was naturally more reticent, particularly if there was a lot of noise and excitement. During this show and tell, the more engaging twin was actively engaged with the children in the class, while the more reticent twin was much less responsive to the children who were calling out her name and saying hello. The mother reported that over time the children in the class completely ceased engaging the more reticent twin and spent all their time engaged with the more outgoing twin, who was laughing and giggling and responding with delight to the classmates. This story illustrates how, in the tiniest of ways, what a child brings to the world influences what they get back from it. Over time, one might hypothesize that these two girls will have significantly different experiences of the world, develop a different schema regarding what the world is like, and develop in significantly different ways.

The Mutually Informative Principle

The sixth tenet, the mutually informative principle, posits that understanding developmental outcomes, both adaptive and non-adaptive, requires a deep understanding of both normal and non-normal development. This, in fact, was one of the first principles of the field of developmental psychopathology, and along with the normative principle, it emphasizes that we cannot know what is problematic unless we understand the very broad range of normal development. The mutually informative principle extends the normative principle to an understanding of both developmentally-expected and developmentally-unexpected behavior. As noted earlier, developmental psychopathologists tend to view behaviors and emotions as occurring along a dimensional axis rather than as categorically "normal" or "abnormal." The mutually informative principle requires understanding the interactions between more and less adaptive functioning. For example, research reveals that there is a range of compliance to caretaker commands during the preschool years, with most children adhering to about 70% of their parents' commands (Johnson et al., 1973). To assess whether an individual child is non-compliant or oppositional at a level that warrants concern, it is critical to understand that typical functioning does not yield 100% compliance. Furthermore, the mutually informative principle suggests that evaluating the less expected aspects of this behavior (e.g., non-compliance closer to 100%) also requires understanding this "abnormal" behavior. For example, is it a function of the loss of a parent, a recent trauma, or another disruptive event that renders the behavior more expected? Without understanding how the developmentally expected and unexpected behaviors interact, it is impossible to determine whether intervention is indicated to right this developmental trajectory. In considering this principle, it is critical to recognize that what is "normal" development is partially determined by cultural norms. Thus, when applying the mutually informative principle, it is critical to understand not just normal development more universally but also the nuances of development in different cultures and sub-groups.

The Longitudinal Principle

Finally, a study of developmental psychopathology requires adherence to the longitudinal principle. The longitudinal principle states that a true understanding of risk and protective factors and developmental outcomes necessitates studying development over time. Without a longitudinal perspective, it is easy to posit assumptions or form inaccurate or misleading conclusions. An understanding of the temporal order of events and their impact and causality can only be accomplished by studying phenomena at multiple timepoints across many periods of time. In contrast, retrospective reports are subject to several biases, including recall bias, positivity bias, social desirability bias, and mood bias (Bell & Bell, 2018). These reports, in which adults recall past events, were more common in the field of child psychopathology prior to the emergence of the field of developmental psychopathology and may have resulted in spurious associations that are no longer apparent when groups of children are followed prospectively. Such associations can suggest outcomes and a need for intervention based on variables that are part of normal oscillations in development or wash out over time. In a well-known study (Offer et al., 2000), male adolescents who were assessed at age 14 and asked about a wide range of contemporaneous experiences were re-interviewed about the same experiences at age 48. The findings revealed considerable differences between the experiences reported in real time at age 14 and the memory of those experiences later in life. Although other studies have revealed somewhat better recall, with moderate correlations between reports collected contemporaneously and those reported retrospectively in certain areas (e.g., the effects of family environment) (Bell & Bell, 2018), differences in recall depending upon the nature of the information being assessed are found. In their article, "On the 'Remembrance of Things Past'…" Henry and colleagues (Henry et al., 1994) found that in a large sample of 18-year-olds asked to report retrospectively on a range of variables that had been collected prospectively throughout their childhoods, the agreement between retrospective report and prospective data, particularly regarding psychosocial and family environment variables was very poor. Such findings drive home the importance of the longitudinal principle's emphasis on research being conducted longitudinally and prospectively when feasible to get a clear picture of the factors impacting developmental trajectories and better versus poorer outcomes.

Developmental Psychopathology Principles Applied to Research: Critical Concepts

Based on these tenets of developmental psychopathology, we set out to design a study of the development and maintenance of both general and specific emotional and behavioral outcomes over the preschool years and early school entry. In doing so, we took into account several concepts critical to sound developmental psychopathology research. These concepts included a longitudinal design, attention to multi-level transactional effects, an interest in cascading effects over time, and a search for understanding outcomes from the perspective of both multifinality and equifinality. Each of these concepts is addressed below.

The importance of a longitudinal approach was clearly elucidated in the discussion of the longitudinal principle of developmental psychopathology. Several issues were considered when designing a longitudinal study. First, what developmental period were we interested in studying? The period between preschool and early school entry was selected because there is considerably less research on children younger than 6 years of age than on those between the ages of 7 and 18. This dearth of information is particularly concerning from a developmental psychopathology perspective because, within this framework, early development is seen as foundational to later development, with early building blocks contributing to later development in a sequential way that becomes hierarchically integrated over time. Sensitive periods, in particular, refer to the phenomenon whereby particular variables exert a stronger influence on developmental outcomes when they occur during certain periods rather than others. Perhaps the best example of this is the concept of parent-child attachment. The formation of a secure attachment during the first year of life gives rise to multiple developmental sequelae in the areas of social development, cognitive development, and mental health (Sroufe, 2005). The inability to form a secure attachment during this sensitive period can have long term negative consequences, particularly in the context of additional risk factors (Sroufe, 1985). Furthermore, one of the critical issues in understanding developmental outcomes in mental health involves the point at which mental health variables are first measured. For example, if certain risk factors are identified as contributing to symptoms of anxiety at age 10, it is important to know whether those anxiety symptoms were present prior to the occurrence of these risk factors. If so, then continuity of symptoms must be considered as an important factor in the development and maintenance of anxiety over time. Issues of continuity and discontinuity in development, as well as a clear understanding of risk factors, can only be obtained by studying children over time, beginning early in their development.

Bi-Directionality and Transactional Effects

Another critical question in developmental psychopathology research is the extent to which effects and outcomes are bi-directional or transactional, i.e., to what extent do ongoing, dynamic interactions between the child and their environment influence each other reciprocally over time to generate particular outcomes? An outcome that appears static when studied at a later age might be better understood if the earlier transactional nature of influences can be seen. Take, for example, the experience of the third-grade twins observed at a "show and tell" event that was cited earlier. A researcher might wish to study the factors leading some children to be socially skilled and engage in a lot of extracurricular activities and others to be shy, spend a lot of time alone, and develop depressive symptoms. Were that researcher to design a study examining a single early risk factor, perhaps, early temperament, for such behavior, she might attribute these personality differences solely to that difference in temperament. Such an understanding would negate the impact of the transactional effects over time, the fact that the early temperament of each twin, *in interaction with the responses they received from the environment,* led to differential outcomes. Identifying the environmental influences will be as important as understanding the temperament differences to fully understand the developmental sequence and design interventions.

Cascading Effects

The concept of cascading effects is somewhat more complicated and describes a process whereby developmental factors at one or more timepoints influence subsequent developmental risk or protective factors, which, in turn, contribute to particular developmental outcomes that do not appear, on the surface, to be related to the initial developmental antecedent. Developmental cascade models can vary, but all such models examine the developmental consequences of interactions of risk factors across and within domains and the ways in which their effects can manifest in other seemingly unrelated areas of development. Such designs have the potential to contribute to our understanding of the comorbidity of different types of psychopathology (Masten & Cicchetti, 2010).

To test for cascading effects, it is critical to measure several areas of behavior that are hypothesized to be related over at least three time points. This design controls for within-time covariance across domains while assessing change in each of the individual domains over time (Masten & Cicchetti 2010). This design, one in which researchers test change over at least three points while measuring multiple variables hypothesized to impact one another at each time point, is rare in developmental psychopathology research despite the richness of the information it can impart (Masten & Cicchetti, 2010). For example, developmental research supports the finding that early secure attachment leads to the development of better cognitive skills and better peer relationships during early childhood (Sroufe, 2005). Better cognitive skills at school entry then relate to more positive engagement with academic tasks, which, in turn, leads to higher achievement. Similarly, better peer relationships lead to engagement in many activities, which build skills and may protect against later depression. Thus, the effects of early secure attachment "cascade" through their impact on later important developmental achievements. There is not necessarily a direct relation between secure attachment and academic achievement in third grade. Rather, this outcome is a result of forces that operate through their impact on other developmentally important tasks. To fully test these relations, it is important to examine a developmental model that assesses all these variables at multiple points in time, considering that certain factors might mediate or moderate relationships that otherwise appear to be directly related. Furthermore, theoretical concepts critical to developmental psychopathology such as stage theory, sequencing, and hierarchical integration over time suggest that selecting nodal transition points in development for study is likely to be most illuminating in promoting our understanding of the impact of risk and protective factors. In the example just provided, failure to achieve earlier developmental tasks is going to be problematic at school entry when the demands on the child change in such a way that having achieved the earlier skills is critical for success. Although the model described in this book does not fully meet the criteria for a "strong" cascade model (because it does not measure all variables at each data-collection time point), it does meet many of the criteria needed. Specifically, it examines the pathways by which multiple risk factors, within and across domains, lead to the development of child behavioral and emotional disorders in a longitudinal design that includes critical points of developmental transition such as school entry. As such it comprises a more robust developmental psychopathology model than much of the extant research.

Equifinality and Multifinality

Concepts of equifinality and multifinality are also critical to theories of developmental psychopathology and to understanding outcomes over time. Equifinality refers to the notion that different factors can contribute to the same outcome over time while multifinality refers to the idea that the same risk and protective factors can lead to different outcomes over time. So, for example, three different risk factors, insecure attachment, hostile parenting, and poor peer relationships, might lead to depression at a later point in development (equifinality), while insecure attachment and negative child affect might lead some children to develop depression, others to develop anxiety, and still others to be symptom free (multifinality). In our work, equifinality and multifinality were explored by examining the same risk factors in different domains over time in relation to different outcome variables, including both internalizing and externalizing symptoms.

The Omitted Variable Problem

Finally, much of developmental psychopathology research is limited in its scope, and even, at times, misleading due to the omitted variable problem. The omitted variable problem (Tomarken & Waller, 2003) refers to the concept that many of the psychosocial factors that an investigator might choose to study in developmental psychopathology share variance with one another. For instance, suppose there are three psychosocial variables that are intercorrelated with one another, and all three are also correlated with a developmental outcome of interest. If the investigator conducts an analysis in which two of those psychosocial factors are examined as predictors of the outcome factor, the variance they share with the omitted and the third factor will be included in estimating the strength of their relations to the outcome. This could mislead researchers to believe that a particular variable has more impact than it actually does. A case in point is the literature on parent depression. Studies that examine the relationship between parental depression and child depression have consistently shown that parental depression is a risk factor for child depression (Brody & Forehand, 1986; Ghodsian et al., 1984; Weissman et al., 2016; Wolkind et al., 1980). However, studies that include other variables such as parenting reveal that it might not be parental depression per se, but rather the particular parenting skills or attitudes of depressed parents that impact child depression outcomes. In a single variable study, the parent depression variable might carry the variance for hostile parenting or parental withdrawal, thereby obscuring the impact of the actual parenting attitude or practice. Conversely, in a more robustly designed study that includes multiple variables, these effects might be teased out to provide a more precise picture of what contributes to particular outcomes. This question is important because it has implications not only for our understanding of risk factors theoretically but also for potential choices about intervention. In a study where it is believed that parental depression per se is the critical risk factor, intervention might include only medication and therapy to address the parent's depression. In a model that recognizes the impact of parental withdrawal or hostility, teaching specific parenting skills, such as following the child's lead or spending 30 min in play with their child per day, along with treatment of the parent's depression, would be the preferred intervention. There is always a tension in research between parsimony and complexity. It is frequently considered best to choose the most parsimonious, that is, the simplest, most straightforward, and least complex explanation of a phenomenon. This concept has guided the philosophy of science more generally and research in psychology specifically for many years (Boehner, 1975). However, it is critical to understand that calls for parsimony often misstate the goal of parsimony: providing *the simplest explanation that can account for the facts.* If the explanation does not adequately account for the facts or the world is, in fact, more complicated, then parsimony becomes misleading (as in the example above) rather than informative (Meehl, 1993).

The omitted variable problem (Tomarken & Waller, 2003) in psychology addresses the need to be sensitive to the complexity inherent in human development and develop testable models that are, in fact, more complex. Developmental psychopathologists, in their call for models that are multi-level, multi-domain, and attend to underlying latent continuity in variables that appear less continuous on the surface (e.g., early secure child-caregiver attachment as it manifests in later peer attachments), acknowledge the need for a more complex understanding of the multiple influences on development as it unfolds over time. Thus, in developing a testable model for understanding the development and maintenance of mental health outcomes during the preschool years, this research group struggled to find a balance between parsimony and complexity. In doing so, the first task was determining what outcomes were specifically of interest and how they should be measured.

References

Achenbach, T. M. (1974). *Developmental psychopathology*. Plenum.

Achenbach, T. M. (1991). *Manual for the child behavior checklist/4–18 and 1991 profile*. University of Vermont Department of Psychiatry.

Achenbach, T. M., & Rescorla, L. A. (2000). *Manual for the ASEBA preschool forms & profiles*. University of Vermont Research Center for Children, Youth, and Families.

Achenbach, T. M., Howell, C. T., McConaughy, S. H., & Stanger, C. (1995). Six-year predictors of problems in a national sample of children and youth: I. Cross-informant syndromes. *Journal of the Academy of Child and Adolescent Psychiatry, 34*(3), 336–347. https://doi.org/10.1097/00004583-19995030000-00020

American Psychiatric Association. (2013). *Diagnostic and statistical manual of mental disorders* (5th ed.). American Psychiatric Association.

Bell, D., & Bell, L. (2018). Accuracy of retrospective reports of family environment. *Journal of Child and Family Studies, 27*, 1029–1040. https://doi.org/10.1007/s10826-017-0948-5

Boehner, P. (1975). *Ockham's philosophical writings*. Thomas Nelson and Sons.

Brody, G. H., & Forehand, R. (1986). Maternal perceptions of child maladjustment as a function of the combined influence of child behavior and maternal depression. *Journal of Consulting and Clinical Psychology, 54*(2), 237–240. https://doi.org/10.1037/00022-006X.54.2.237

Bronfenbrenner, U. (1977). Toward an experimental ecology of human development. *American Psychologist, 32*(7), 513–531. https://doi.org/10.1037/0003-066X.32.7.513

Cicchetti, D. (1984). The emergence of developmental psychopathology. *Child Development, 55*(1), 1–7.

Fox, N. A., Henderson, H. A., Marshall, P. J., Nichols, K. E., & Ghera, M. M. (2005). Behavioral inhibition linking biology and behavior withing a development framework. *Annual Review of Psychology, 56*, 235–262. https://doi.org/10.1146/annurev.psych.55.090902.141532

Ghodsian, M., Zajicek, E., & Wolkind, S. (1984). A longitudinal study of maternal depression and child behaviour problems. *Journal of Child Psychology and Psychiatry, 25*, 91–109.

Henry, B., Moffitt, T. E., Caspi, A., Langley, J., & Silva, P. A. (1994). On the "remembrance of things past": A longitudinal evaluation of the retrospective method. *Psychologaical, 6*(2), 92–101. https://doi.org/10.1037/1040-3590.6.2.92

Johnson, S. M., Wahl, G., Martin, S., & Johansson, S. (1973). How deviant is the normal child? A behavioral analysis of the preschool child and his family. In R. D. Rubin, J. P. Brady, & J. D. Henderson (Eds.), *Advances in behavior therapy* (Vol. 4, pp. 37–54). Academic Press.

Lebrun-Harris, L. A., Ghandour, R. M., Kogan, M. D., & Warren, M. D. (2022). Five-year trends in US children's health and well-being. *JAMA Pediatrics, 176*(7), e22056. https://doi.org/10.1011/jamapediatrics.2022.0056

Masten, A. S. (2006). Developmental psychopathology: Pathways to the future. *International Journal of Behavioral Development, 30*(1), 47–54. https://doi.org/10.1177/0165025406059974

Masten, A. S., & Cicchetti, D. (2010). Developmental cascades. *Development and Psychopathology, 22*, 491–495. https://doi.org/10.1017/S0954579410000222

Meehl, P. (1993). Philosophy of science: Help or hindrance? *Psychological Report, 72*, 707–793.

Offer, D., Kaiz, M., Howard, K. I., & Bennet, E. S. (2000). The altering of reported experience. *Journal of the American Academy of Child and Adolescent Psychiatry, 39*(6), 735–742. https://doi.org/10.1097/00004583-20000-6000-0012

Rutter, M., & Sroufe, L. A. (2000). Developmental psychopathology concepts and challenges. *Development and Psychopathology, 12*(3), 263–296. https://doi.org/10.1017/s0954579400003023

Sameroff, A. J., & Chandler, M. J. (1975). Reproductive risk and the continuum of caretaking casualty. In F. D. Horowitz, M. Hetherington, & S. Scarr-Salapatek (Eds.), *Review of child development research* (Vol. 4, pp. 187–244). University of Chicago Press.

Sroufe, L. A. (1985). Attachment classification from the perspective of infant-caregive relationships and infant temerament. *Child Development, 56*(1), 1–14.

Sroufe, L. A. (2005). Attachment and development: A prospective, longitudinal study from birth to adulthood. *Attachment & Human Development, 7*(4), 349–367. https://doi.org/10.1080/14616730500365928
Sroufe, L. A. (2009). The concept of development in developmental psychopathology. *Child Development Perspectives, 3*(3), 178–183. https://doi.org/10.1111/j.1750-8606.2009.00103.x
Tomarken, A. J., & Waller, N. G. (2003). Potential problems with "well fitting" models. *Journal of Abnormal Psychology, 112*(4), 578–598. https://doi.org/10.1037/0021-843X.112.5.578
Weissman, M. M., Berry, O. O., Warner, V., Gameroff, M. J., Skipper, J., Talati, A., et al. (2016). A 30-year study of 3 generations at high risk and low risk for depression. *JAMA Psychiatry, 73*(9), 970–977. https://doi.org/10.10001/jamapsychiatry.2016.1586
Wolkind, S. N., Zajicek, E., & Ghodsian, M. (1980). Continuities in maternal depression. *International Journal of Family Psychiatry, 1*, 167–181.
World Health Organization. (2022a). *International classification of diseases* (11th Rev.). https://icd.who.int/
World Health Organization. (2022b). *Mental disorders*. https://www.who.int/news-room/fact-sheets/detail/mental-disorders

Chapter 2
Building a Model of Risk Factors for Psychopathology in Early Childhood

The starting point for understanding psychopathology at any age involves finding a way to characterize the symptoms a person might experience. This includes finding ways to identify patterns of co-occurrence of symptoms and describing their intensity and frequency of occurrence. In psychology and psychiatry, the need to characterize symptoms and their inter-relations has involved two different approaches, a taxonomic and a dimensional approach. The taxonomic approach is more consistent with medically driven nomenclature that emphasizes the need for clear diagnostic categorization, while the dimensional approach is more closely aligned with the theory and tenets of developmental psychopathology.

The Taxonomic Approach

The classification of mental disorders occurred much later than the classification of physical disorders. In fact, it was not until the 6th edition of the International Classification of Diseases (ICD-6) (World Health Organization, 1949) that mental disorders were included in this classification system, thereby introducing a common international language for classifying and counting mental disorders throughout the world (Clark et al., 2017). The *Diagnostic and Statistical Manual of Mental Disorders* (DSM) was designed for similar use in the United States. By the second edition of DSM (DSM-II) (American Psychiatric Association, 1968) and the 8th edition of ICD (ICD-8) (World Health Organization, 1967), the broad categories of mental disorders were nearly the same and included psychoses, neuroses, and personality disorders (Clark et al., 2017). With the introduction of ICD-8, the intended function of the manuals evolved from being used to count disorders for epidemiological purposes to serve as practical guides for assigning clinical diagnoses.

Clinical use of DSM-II was limited, however, by its reliance on describing disorders based on psychodynamic theory and lack of attention to the disorders of

K. R. Gouze et al., *Early Childhood Psychopathology*,
https://doi.org/10.1007/978-3-031-68877-5_2

childhood and adolescence. The third edition of DSM, DSM-III (American Psychiatric Association, 1980), introduced a marked change in approach, with a move away from a theory-driven definition of disorders to a more objective, symptom-based approach. Consistent with this approach, a primary goal of DSM-III was to operationally define symptoms and note symptom frequency and duration thresholds as criteria for making a diagnosis to improve interrater reliability. Subsequent editions, including the currently used DSM-5 (American Psychiatric Association, 2013), continued to make efforts to refine these diagnostic categories.

Two important assumptions guiding the taxonomic approach are that mental disorders (a) can be dichotomized as present versus absent; and (b) are discrete entities that are reasonably distinct from one another. In a well-developed taxonomic system, some co-occurrence of disorders is expected simply because it is possible for an individual to have two or more unrelated disorders simultaneously (e.g., pneumonia and rheumatoid arthritis). If two disorders, A and B, are truly independent, then we would expect their co-occurrence to occur at the rate that is the product of their rates of disorder (e.g., if the prevalence of disorder A is 5% and that for B is 10%, they should co-occur in 0.5% of cases).

Among psychiatric disorders, comorbidity refers to the tendency for symptoms of different disorders to co-occur (Clark et al., 2017). The co-occurrence of more than two disorders, none of which is considered primary, is also sometimes termed "multimorbidity" (Langan et al., 2013). In this book, we refer to both comorbidity and multimorbidity as comorbidity. Psychiatric comorbidities are common in both children and adolescents, raising the question of whether these diagnoses really are categorically discrete. Studies reveal that the co-occurrence of psychiatric disorders is much more common than expected throughout the lifespan, with perhaps twice the expected rate in children (Caron & Rutter, 1991; Clark et al., 2017).

The many limitations of the taxonomic approach as it has been applied to the DSM system are described well elsewhere (Clark et al., 2017). We will note just three that are germane to this book. First, the high rates of comorbidity raise the possibility that other diagnostic approaches may better characterize the nature of psychopathology and the relations between different types of symptoms than a taxonomic system. Second, many individuals may display most of the symptoms of a DSM disorder but not enough of them to meet diagnostic criteria. They may have, for example, only three relevant symptoms when four are required. This is particularly true for young children who may then receive a diagnosis of "NOS" (not otherwise specified disorder) or no diagnosis at all. Research with young children (Lavigne et al., 1998) shows that individuals who occupy this "subthreshold" status are likely to contribute to the instability of the diagnostic category because they are reasonably likely to change from "does not meet criteria" to meet criteria" for a particular diagnosis at different points in time. The fluidity of diagnoses suggests that a dimensional approach to the classification of psychiatric disorders might be more useful than the current taxonomic approach.

Finally, and perhaps most relevant to the subject of this book, there are no developmental considerations in the symptom criteria for the disorders. For example, one of the symptoms listed for Oppositional Defiant Disorder is frequent temper tantrums. As noted in Chapter One, frequent tantrums, depending upon frequency and intensity, may be considered relatively normal at age 3 but not at age 6.

Despite the many drawbacks of the taxonomic approach, adopting the taxonomic DSM diagnostic classification system has served as an organizing principle in conducting research over an extended period of time. This was particularly true regarding federally funded research on the treatment of psychopathology. In such studies it became necessary for participants to meet objective diagnostic criteria for a DSM-defined disorder to be enrolled, thereby excluding individuals with "sub-threshold" levels of symptoms who might also be affected significantly. To a lesser but still significant degree, the DSM approach shaped studies on the etiology and risk factors associated with types of psychopathology, likely leading to more studies that focused on symptoms associated with a particular DSM-defined disorder rather than with broader groups of problems such as internalizing or externalizing disorders, or with other important concepts such as adaptive functioning. As noted in Chapter One, this approach also neglected to take into account a range of factors important to high-quality developmental psychopathology research, including: (a) the meaning of different symptoms at different points in development; (b) the role of context and culture in defining and understanding the meaning of adaptive functioning; (c) cascading effects; and (d) other factors impacting our understanding of the relation between risk and child and adolescent outcomes.

A Comment on the DC:0-3R Classification System

DSM-III was an advance over previous iterations of the DSM in that it introduced a specific category for child and adolescent disorders that was not present previously. Yet, it did not systematically attend to developmental differences in the nature of psychopathology or incorporate a true developmental psychopathology perspective. The absence of a developmental focus was most apparent in its lack of attention to very young children. With the development of the DC: 0-3 (ZERO TO THREE, 1994) and its second revision in 2016 as the DC: 0-5™ (Zero to Three, 2005), an attempt was made to develop a classification system for children from birth to age 5. For our purposes, two points can be made. First, both the DC:0-3R and the DC 0-5 are fundamentally taxonomic systems with the same strengths and weaknesses as the DSM approach, other than the lack of sensitivity to early developmental presentations. It is likely that the same problems related to comorbidity and subthreshold cases in the DSM system will emerge in this early childhood classification system. While comorbidity in the DC: 0-5 classification system itself has attracted little attention, it is quite clear that comorbidity in children younger than age 4 who were assigned an ICD-10 diagnosis is common (Koch et al., 2021). These high levels of comorbidity, along with the problem of young children shifting in and out of "meeting diagnostic criteria" status based on symptom counts, lead to a dimensional approach to identifying diagnostic outcomes.

Dimensional Approaches

The emergence of the field of developmental psychopathology, which highlighted the need for a better way to characterize children's behavioral and emotional problems, coupled with the inadequacies of the early versions of DSM, led researchers to seek an alternative approach to describing and characterizing these problems. As noted in Chapter One, during the 1960s and 1970s, early developmental psychopathology researchers such as Thomas Achenbach began to develop a classification system for children by utilizing factor analyses of early behavior problem checklists. Although there had been prior factor analytic efforts, notably that of Quay and Peterson (Quay & Peterson, 1967), the approach of Achenbach in the 1970s (Achenbach, 1991) was particularly influential, probably because the Child Behavior Checklist (Achenbach, 1991) that he and colleagues developed was widely adopted for clinical and research use.

In their approach, Achenbach and colleagues identified two broad-band symptom factors, or dimensions, labeled internalizing (including symptom types such as anxiety and depression) and externalizing (including symptom types of ADHD, conduct problems, and oppositionality). These factors constituted sets of behaviors occurring across a continuum of normality that had different meanings at different ages. These broad-band internalizing and externalizing factors were widely adopted in research with children and, more recently, in research with adults. Many studies have demonstrated that these two factors are not completely "orthogonal" (i.e., unrelated); rather, they are moderately correlated with one another. Over time, two-factor models of the structure of psychopathology that include an internalizing and an externalizing factor that were allowed to be correlated have come to be described as a "correlated factors" model.

Bifactor Models and a General Psychopathology Factor

An alternative approach to a correlated factors model is the bifactor model. First described approximately 30 years ago (Gibbons & Hedeker, 1992), its application to models of psychopathology in children, adolescents, and adults has increased in the last 10–15 years. In a bifactor model of psychopathology, a general psychopathology factor (general p, a term that parallels the concept of a "g" factor associated with general intelligence) loads on each of the measures of symptoms or symptom types in the first level of the model. In addition, there are internalizing and externalizing factors that load on specific subgroups of symptoms. With two factors (general p and either internalizing or externalizing) loading on each specific symptom type, it follows that these are "bifactor" models (see Chapter Nine).

While the taxonomic approach focuses on specific diagnoses, these models, which focus on factors that subsume various symptom types or specific diagnoses, are often referred to as transdiagnostic. These approaches are important alternatives to taxonomic approaches for several reasons. First, they help explain why comorbidity across different DSM diagnoses is so common: if there is a general p factor or internalizing and externalizing factors linked to more than one diagnosis, it follows that individuals might exhibit comorbidity rather than being diagnosed with just a single symptom type.

Second, a transdiagnostic classification system with either a correlated or bifactor structure to psychopathology may fit well because it helps explain why many of the individual diagnoses share transdiagnostic risk factors (Clark et al., 2017; Lahey et al., 2017) (See Chap. 9 for a fuller discussion). Clark et al. argue that most forms of comorbidity may be attributable to shared transdiagnostic mechanisms and that research is needed to determine the extent to which they account for similarities in syndromes and symptom types. Studying transdiagnostic risk factors in relation to dimensional correlated factors or bifactor models may improve our understanding of the etiology of psychopathology across the life span, as well as help to explain constructs of equifinality and multifinality (see Chapter One) in developmental psychopathology research. Consistent with a developmental psychopathology approach, Caspi et al. (2014) noted the importance of a longitudinal approach to studying the structure of psychopathology, while Kotov et al. (2017) noted that structural taxonomies of psychopathology using a dimensional approach may vary with age. The transdiagnostic emphasis on issues of multifinality and equifinality, longitudinal changes, symptoms that fluctuate and have different meanings in different contexts and at different ages, and potentially cascading effects is much more consistent with the tenets of developmental psychopathology than is the traditional taxonomic approach.

Despite the greater alignment between these models and the tenets of developmental psychopathology, there are limitations to the clinical usefulness of dimensional systems. Clinical applications often require decision-making, and those decisions are dichotomous. Does this child have a disorder or not? Should this child be treated with psychotherapy or not? Should this child be started on psychotropic medication or not? The need to make such dichotomous decisions is one reason taxonomic approaches to psychopathology gained more currency than dimensional approaches for clinical purposes. To be able to apply a dimensional classification system to clinical situations requires a way to apply that system to clinical decision-making. That could include, for example, establishing empirically-based cutoff scores that provide guidelines for deciding when a problem is clinically significant enough to require intervention (Kotov et al., 2017). While establishing a clinically useful dimensional classification system may be possible in the future, the dimensional classification systems show less promise for clinical applications but greater utility in helping us understand how psychopathology is organized and what factors might contribute to its etiology and stability.

Dimensional, Categorical: Can There Be Integration or a Rapprochement?

Surely, there must be some way to resolve the debate between proponents of the taxonomic approach with its use of discrete categories and proponents of the dimensional approach with its preference for continuous measures. Pickles and Angold (2003) sought to reframe the "either dimensional *or* categorical" distinction to focus on determining the circumstances in which psychopathology should be conceptualized as dimensional and those in which it should be considered categorical. In their discussion of diagnostic classification systems for use in early childhood, Egger and Emde (2011) second the Pickles and Angold approach.

One way to integrate these two approaches is to identify specific disorders that follow a continuous presentation and those that actually follow a dichotomous presentation, i.e., a disorder for which nature truly has "carved close to the bone" (Pickles & Angold, 2003). Unfortunately, there is no evidence for the existence of a mental disorder that has been established as a categorical entity (Kotov et al., 2017). Given this situation, this approach to integrating taxonomic and dimensional approaches does not look promising.

An alternate approach involves statistical comparisons of categorical and dimensional approaches. This approach was taken in a study of young children in the 1990s (Arend et al., 1996). In that study, consensus DSM-IV diagnoses provided by two clinical child and adolescent psychologists (who had achieved good interrater reliability) were correlated with continuous scores on dimensions of the Child Behavior Checklist. These correlations were consistently low to, at best, moderate in magnitude. It was not possible to discern any diagnostic category that matched well with any of the continuous measures. Again, integration of the two systems using this approach was not promising.

Another challenge to the true integration of these two approaches arises from professional differences. Physicians are trained in a medical profession that emphasizes disease taxonomy; psychologists and other social scientists are trained in professions that emphasize continuous scale construction and population measurement. As a result, the differences in perspective between these professions can be profound. Perhaps the best hope is not integration but rapprochement, with a dimensional approach leading the way regarding studying most aspects of symptom/diagnostic types and their risk factors and the taxonomic approach taking the lead regarding practical matters like assigning a diagnosis, deciding whether treatment is indicated (yes/no) and, at times, counting cases to better understand the epidemiology of disorders.

In our approach to building a multi-domain model of risk factors associated with early child psychopathology, we primarily utilized a dimensional approach since our goal was to advance a developmental psychopathology model to help understand the factors that contribute to the occurrence and maintenance of symptom clusters associated with emotional and behavioral difficulties in early childhood. We were less interested in specific diagnostic outcomes than we were in potential risk for specific types of symptom clusters associated with these disorders. The final decision regarding which symptom clusters to examine was guided by our theoretical understanding of developmental psychopathology and our interest in clinical utility. At the time we designed our study, NIMH issued a specific request for research proposals addressing the development of Oppositional Defiant Disorder and co-morbid depression in young children. It was in response to this request that we proposed the Parents and Children Together (PACT) (Lavigne et al., 2009) study to examine the genesis of the outcome variables specified in the request for proposals, along with symptoms of ADHD and anxiety, which occur commonly in young children. The development of the PACT proposal follows.

Building a Multi-domain Model for Risk Factors Associated with Early Childhood Psychopathology: The PACT Study

As stated in Chapter One, in responding to the NIMH request for proposals, we were committed to designing a study that was theoretically robust, adhered to the tenets of developmental psychopathology, and focused on a longitudinal understanding of the preschool through entry to the elementary school period. The advantages of conducting research from within a theoretical framework are well-known. Scientific fields in which there are well-developed theories, like physics, tend to advance more rapidly than fields lacking such theories. Further, theories may point in the direction of phenomena that need to be understood but have not yet been recognized in research. In addition, theory-driven research is less likely to result in chance findings. The decision of our research group to examine risk factors beginning in the preschool period for symptoms of disorders at school entry emerged from a strong belief in the importance of these early foundational experiences and a commitment to designing a study with clinical utility. In addition to understanding developmental risk factors, we aimed to gather information that could be useful in guiding the development of early prevention and intervention programs.

When we began the process of reviewing the literature to determine what we knew about early childhood psychopathology and, specifically, how oppositional behaviors might be related to symptoms of depression and anxiety, we were aware that we would not find anything as comprehensive as a genuine, all-encompassing theory. We did hope, however, that we would find a reasonably comprehensive model of psychosocial risk factors associated with any or all of the major types of psychopathology that could guide our research with young children. We were disappointed that our search did not identify such a model.

Rather, we identified two different types of work. The first consisted of very broad models such as Bronfenbrenner's ecological model (Bronfenbrenner, 1977), which tend not to specify how specific variables might be related to one another. For example, based on Bronfenbrenner's model, it is not possible to determine if a research model should examine if family stress is associated with anxiety in young children because it contributes to maternal depression, affects some aspect of parenting, or has a direct effect on the child. Thus, the utility of such general models is limited.

The second, quite voluminous, body of work consisted of studies conducted in the past few decades that identified the relation between a specific psychosocial factor and a specific type of symptom or diagnostic outcome. Although these studies greatly enriched our understanding of the risk factors associated with psychopathology throughout childhood and adolescence, they have many limitations. First, for both cross-sectional and longitudinal studies, only a small number of risk factors were examined simultaneously in any particular study. These studies served the useful function of identifying whether there is *any* association between those risk factors and a symptom type. However, when studied in isolation, there is a high likelihood that the magnitude of the association, i.e., the effect size, between a given risk factor and an outcome, will be overestimated. This problem emerges because risk factors may be correlated with one another. If risk factor A and B are correlated and share some variance, but only risk factor A is included in a regression analysis predicting outcome C, while risk factor B is not, then the shared variance will be attributed to the effects of risk factor A. This can lead to inflating the significance levels of the A → C relation and inflating the estimated effect size (Cicchetti & Curtis, 2007; Tomarken & Waller, 2003). As noted in Chapter One in the discussion on parsimonious versus complex models, this is referred to as the "omitted variable" problem. The omitted variable problem can be reduced, and a more accurate estimate of the effect sizes assessed if more relevant variables are included in the model. For almost two decades, consistent with the tenets of developmental psychopathology, researchers have called for studies examining the pathways by which factors across multiple domains influence important child outcomes (Cicchetti & Curtis, 2007; Goodman et al., 2011; McMahon et al., 2003). As a result, we committed to developing a longitudinal, testable developmental psychopathology model that was more complex, had fewer omitted variables, and considered multiple pathways within and across domains.

The approach we took is consistent with that espoused in some recent articles on theory building in psychology (Borsboom et al., 2021; Haig, 2005; Hawkins-Elder & Ward, 2020); however, we began our efforts to develop a testable model before some of these papers were published. This approach is based on an abductive theory of scientific method (Haig, 2005). Typically, the approach to teaching the scientific method is based on a hypothetico-deductive model. Hypothetico-deductive models begin with the construction of the theory. Following the theory, hypotheses are then generated and tested. Although this is the usual approach to teaching the scientific method, Haig argues that, in practice, scientific inquiry typically proceeds in the opposite direction—i.e., it applies a "bottom-up" approach. In this approach, the process begins with identifying empirical phenomena that require explanation, followed by constructing an explanatory theory or model to explain them.

Before describing the application of this approach to the research described in this book, we need to discuss terminology, particularly what constitutes a theory in contrast to a model. Finding a clear, comprehensive description of what constitutes a theory is not easy; even the reports describing theory building cited above do not provide a clear definition of theory. Generally, theories are described as broad explanatory statements about some phenomena of interest, and the implication is that they comprehensively explain all aspects of the etiology of those phenomena across multiple levels. In contrast, models tend to be explicit representations of the factors associated with particular phenomena. These models can be tested but may not be comprehensive in the same way that is implied in discussing theory.

In describing the process of theory construction regarding psychopathology, Hawkins-Elder and Ward (Hawkins-Elder & Ward, 2020) describe a model as a representation of a phenomenon. A simplified model may represent a phenomenon without explaining a phenomenon. An explanation is achieved in a model if it represents all the extant explanatory knowledge for a particular phenomenon. With regard to psychopathology, no single model will suffice. Rather, multiple models focusing on different explanatory levels (e.g., biological, cognitive, psychosocial, etc.) will be needed. Known as model pluralism (Hawkins-Elder & Ward, 2020), this multi-model approach is considered a promising way to advance our understanding of highly complex phenomena, such as the factors associated with the development of psychopathology beginning in early childhood and advancing across the life span.

In their 2021 report, Borsboom and colleagues (Borsboom et al., 2021) describe a practical approach to developing explanatory theories/models, Theory Construction Methodology (TCM). In their 2019 paper, Hawkins-Elder and Ward (2020) describe an approach they term the Phenomena Detection Method for Theory Construction (PDM-TC). Both approaches rely heavily on the abductive theory approach described by Haig (2005). We now illustrate how we applied the TCM and PDM-TC approaches to describe the development of the psychosocial model of risk factors associated with different symptom types in the PACT study.

Identify Relevant Explanatory Targets and Phenomena

Explanatory Targets The process begins by identifying the explanatory targets and relevant phenomena we wish to explain. Our explanatory targets (Hawkins-Elder & Ward, 2020) were the types of early childhood psychopathology that we wanted to model to increase our understanding of the factors that contribute to their development.

We settled on four explanatory targets, each being a symptom type recognized as occurring in early childhood. These included the symptom types of Oppositional Defiant Disorder, Attention Deficit/Hyperactivity Disorder, anxiety, and depression. In defining these four targets, we chose to focus on the symptom types associated with these disorders as described in DSM-IV (American Psychiatric Association, 2000). Hawkins-Elder and Ward (2020) argue that it is problematic to target DSM disorders because there are conceptual problems associated with those disorders and the DSM classification system, many of which were discussed earlier in this chapter. In contrast, Hawkins-Elder and Ward posit that appropriate explanatory targets are individual symptoms, not clusters of symptoms or symptom types as identified in the DSM classification system. While that may be true for some diagnostic entities such as the eating disorders that were the focus of their work, we felt that the empirical literature on emotional and behavioral problems in young children supported the selection of these four symptom types and that a focus on individual symptoms was not necessary. That evidence included reasonable Cronbach's alphas for these symptom clusters as measured by the early childhood version of the Child Symptom Inventory and the symptom count measures of an age-appropriate structured diagnosis interview. This was born out by our earlier work which demonstrated that at least some of these diagnoses are clinically meaningful, relatively stable over time, and reliably associated with prospective prediction of other types of disorders (Preschooler's Project) (Lavigne et al., 2001). Further confirmation of the utility of these choices comes from the CFAs (Strickland et al., 2011) of the early childhood diagnostic groups identified in this study sample.

These four symptom types represent both internalizing (anxiety, depression) and externalizing (ADHD, ODD) symptom types, a decision consistent with previous work (Achenbach, 1991, 2020) and one that proved useful in our later studies of bifactor models in this age group (see Chap. 9). They include the most common diagnostic entities identified in early childhood (Lavigne et al., 2009).

It is important to note that, even though we focus on the symptoms associated with four DSM disorders, we describe these entities as "symptom types" rather than diagnoses. We do so because, consistent with our developmental psychopathology approach, we both conceptualized and measured these variables as continuous without clear clinical cutoffs rather than as dichotomous as in "disorder present" versus "disorder absent."

The reader will note that we did not include an important type of symptom. We excluded autism spectrum disorders because the prevalence of these disorders, although increasing, was too low to allow us to collect a sufficiently large sample of children with ASD even in the relatively large sample that the PACT study was able to obtain.

Empirical Phenomena Once we established targets, it was critical to identify the phenomena that might help explain those targets. In this context, phenomena include stable, general features related to the outcomes, i.e., the emotional and behavioral symptom clusters we sought to explain. The emphasis here is on empirically supported, demonstrable relations between symptom types and other characteristics of the child and the world in which the child is embedded.

To identify relevant phenomena, we searched the literature for studies of risk factors associated with each of the explanatory targets related to anxiety, depression, ADHD, and ODD. These included searching for studies that were either cross-sectional or longitudinal. We identified studies that examined (a) direct relations between a risk factor and a symptom type, e.g., maternal depression and child depression; (b) associations between risk factors, e.g., family conflict and maternal depression; and (c) mediational processes, e.g., mediators or indirect effects, e.g., whether stress might be associated with child anxiety because stress impacts maternal depression which, in turn, impacts child anxiety. As much as possible, we sought risk factors that were cross-cutting and were associated with more than one type of symptom, e.g., stress, maternal depression with child depression and either oppositional, anxiety, or ADHD symptoms. The literature to support these decisions, i.e., which risk factors to explore, is described in Chaps. 3, 4, and 5. The process by which we decided to include particular risk factors is described below.

Developing a Prototheory to Explain Risk Factors and Outcomes in Early Childhood

A prototheory is an initial explanatory model often derived via abductive reasoning (Borsboom et al., 2021; Haig, 2005). Initially, the abductive approach is substantially "bottom-up." Typically, it begins with recognizing specific phenomena and then deriving an initial theory that involves a conceptualization of the causal mechanism(s) that might explain them. Abduction may then become "top-down," with the application of the prototypical mechanisms guiding the development of a plausible model that can be tested.

The development of that initial model might also be guided by principles or models derived from other areas. In this regard, we adopted principles derived from Bronfenbrenner's (1977) bioecological model, the ecological transaction model of Cicchetti and Toth (1998), and the Smeekens et al. (Smeekens et al., 2007) multi-domain model of child psychopathology. Bronfenbrenner's model posits that the child develops in response to a complex series of interacting environmental influences that range from more proximal (e.g., the child's temperament) to more distal (e.g., the family, society). Cicchetti and Toth's transactional model takes this concept further by conceptualizing child development as evolving over time through the ongoing bi-directional interactions both within and across multiple co-occurring levels. As in Bronfenbrenner's theory, these levels range from more proximal to the child to more distal. Furthermore, Cicchetti and Toth posit that at different developmental periods, the relevant risk factors may vary in their strength and in their influence on later outcomes. Finally, we adopted two elements of the multi-domain model of psychopathology described by Smeekens et al. First, we adopted their terminology for four domains of risk ranging from more distal to more proximal. Three of these are ecological domains including: (a) contextual characteristics (e.g., stress); (b) parental characteristics (e.g., psychopathology); and (c) parenting (e.g., hostility). The fourth domain is not ecological but is the most central and complex domain (d) the child domain, which consists of the various systems internal (cognitive, affective, etc.) to the child (e.g., temperament) as well as those that have become internalized from ongoing interactions with the environment over time (e.g., attachment security). Further, in developing this model, we strove to remain true to the core guiding principles of developmental psychopathology described in Chap. 1, including the notion that the transactional aspects associated with the multi-domain risk factors could be quite complex and might be characterized by cascading processes that evolve over time from the cumulative consequences of the interplay between risk factors in different domains across developmental periods (Masten & Cicchetti, 2010). This model posits the possibility that multiple pathways involving etiological processes can lead to the onset of symptom types, their stability and change over time, or their remission. Thus, there might be direct effects of individual risk factors on symptom development or maintenance. There might be complex indirect effects of distal factors that may well operate via their influence on more proximal factors (e.g., family stress might influence parenting attitudes or behavior; parenting may have a direct effect or operate indirectly through child characteristics). To go beyond enumerating risk factors and examine how they operate to effect symptoms, a multi-domain model was needed to articulate these varying pathways.

Developing a Formal Model

Based on these principles, we developed a psychosocial multi-domain model that sought to integrate the various psychosocial phenomena linking risk factors to symptoms and linking one risk factor with another when there were empirical findings to connect those risk factors. We then extended the pathways between the risk factors between and within domains that made conceptual and psychological sense and had previous empirical support. In the context of multi-pluralism, the model is psychosocial rather than biological, genetic, or neuroscience-based, even though it does include child temperament factors, and temperament is assumed to have a biological base. Our focus was on delineating the direct and indirect pathways between risk factors at multiple levels that might help us understand how they affect each symptom type, as well as other risk factors (e.g., caretaker depression may impact anxiety through its effect on the X aspect of parenting and not the Y aspect of parenting).

In addition to adhering to the tenets of developmental psychopathology in building a testable model of prominent, core symptom types that manifest in early childhood, we combined elements of both taxonomic and dimensional approaches. Furthermore, we used a structural equation modeling approach (Kline, 2011), a technique often used in theory construction (Borsboom et al., 2021), which allowed us to examine the overall goodness of fit of the model and the direct and indirect pathways across and within domains whereby these risk factors might influence symptom types. As noted earlier, we initially chose symptom types (outcomes) consistent either with specific types of disorders identified in the DSM system (e.g., Oppositional Defiant Disorder and Attention Deficit Hyperactivity Disorder or with broader categories of disorders identified in the developmental psychopathology literature (e.g., anxiety and depression). Ultimately, our approach decidedly emphasized a continuous, dimensional approach. We chose measures to assess these four types of symptoms and the broader categories of externalizing and internalizing outcomes that allowed for a dimensional analysis. In testing the models, we emphasized identifying risk factors and mediational pathways that were cross-cutting and had empirical support in relation to these symptom types.

In choosing risk factors to examine, the multi-domain model that we chose included, from most distal to the most proximal domains: three factors in the contextual domain (socioeconomic status, stress, and family conflict); one factor in the parent domain (parent depression); three factors in the parenting domain (parental hostility, support-engagement, and scaffolding skills); and five in the child domain (sensory regulation, attachment, temperamental effortful control, and temperamental negative affect. The decision to include each of these risk factors was based on a conceptual understanding of developmental psychopathology and the extant literature reviewed in the ensuing Chaps. 3, 4, and 5.

References

Achenbach, T. M. (1991). *Manual for the child behavior checklist/4-18 and 1991 profile*. University of Vermont Department of Psychiatry.

Achenbach, T. M. (2020). Bottom-up and top-down paradigms for psychopathology: A half-century odyssey. *Annual Review of Clinical Psychology, 16*, 1–24. https://doi.org/10.1146/annurev-clinpsy-0711119-115831

American Psychiatric Association. (1968). *Diagnostic and statistical manual of mental disorders* (2nd ed.). Author.

American Psychiatric Association. (1980). *Diagnostic and statistical manual of mental disorders* (3rd ed.). American Pychiatric Association.

American Psychiatric Association. (2000). *Diagnostic and statistical manual of mental disorders* ((4th ed.). American Psychiatric Association.

American Psychiatric Association. (2013). *Diagnostic and statistical manual of mental disorders* (5th ed.). American Psychiatric Association.

Arend, R., Lavigne, J. V., Rosenbaum, D., Binns, H. J., & Christoffel, K. K. (1996). Relation between taxonomic and quantitative diagnostic systems in preschool children: Emphasis on disruptive disorders. *Journal of Clinical Child Psychology, 25*(4), 388–397.

Borsboom, D., van der Maas, H. L. J., Dalege, J., Kievit, R. A., & Haig, B. D. (2021). Theory construction methodology: A practical framework for building theories in psychology. *Perspectives on Psychological Science, 16*(4), 756–766. https://doi.org/10.1077/1745691620969647

Bronfenbrenner, U. (1977). Toward an experimental ecology of human development. *American Psychologist, 32*(7), 513–531. https://doi.org/10.1037/0003-066X.32.7.513

Caron, C., & Rutter, M. (1991). Comorbidity in child psychopathology: Concepts, issues and research strategies. *Journal of Child Psychology and Psychiatry, 32*, 1063–1080.

Caspi, A., Houts, R. M., Belsky, D. W., Goldman-Mellor, S. J., Harrington, H., Israel, S., Meier, M. H., et al. (2014). The p factor: One general psychopathology factor in the structure of psychiatric disorders? *Psychological Science, 2*(2), 119–137. https://doi.org/10.1177/2167702613497473

Cicchetti, D., & Curtis, W. J. (2007). Multilevel perspectives on pathways to resilient functioning. *Development and Psychopathology, 19*, 627–629. https://doi.org/10.1019/S0954579407000314

Cicchetti, D., & Toth, S. L. (1998). The development of depression in children and adolescents. *American Psychologist, 53*, 221–241.

Clark, L. A., Cuthbert, B., Lewis-Fernandez, R., Narrow, W. E., & Reed, G. M. (2017). Three approaches to understanding and classifying mental disorder: *ICD-11*, *DSM-5*, and the National Institute of Mental Health's Research Domain Criteria (RDoC). *Psychological Science in the Public Interest, 18*(2), 72–145. https://doi.org/10.1177/1529100617727266

Egger, H. E., & Emde, R. N. (2011). Developmentally sensitive diagnostic criteria for mental health disorders in early childhood: The diagnostic and statistical manual of mental disorders-IV, the research diagnositc criteria--preschool age, and the diagnostic classification of mental health and development disorders of infancy and early childhood--revised. *American Psychologist, 66*(2), 95–106. https://doi.org/10.1037/a0021026

Gibbons, R. D., & Hedeker, D. R. (1992). Full-information item bi-factor analysis. *Psychometrika, 57*(3), 423–436.

Goodman, S. H., Rouse, M. H., Connell, A. M., Broth, M. R., Hall, C. M., & Heyward, D. (2011). Maternal depression and child psychopathology: A meta-analytic review. *Clinical Child and Family Psychology Review, 14*, 1–27. https://doi.org/10.1003/sl10567-010-0080-1

Haig, B. D. (2005). An abductive theory of scientific method. *Psychological Methods, 10*(4), 371–388. https://doi.org/10.1037/1082-989X.10.4.371

Hawkins-Elder, H., & Ward, T. (2020). Theory construction in the psychopathology domain: A multiphase approach. *Theory & Psychology, 30*(1), 77–98. https://doi.org/10.1177/09593543198S93026

Kline, R. B. (2011). *Principles and practice of structural equation modeling* (3rd ed.). Guilford.

Koch, S. V., Andersson, M., Hvelplund, C., & Skovgaard, A. M. (2021). Mental disorders in referred 0-3-year-old children: A population-based study of incidence, comorbidity and perinatal risk factors. *European Child and Adolescent Psychiatry, 30*, 1251–1262. https://doi.org/10.1007/s00787-020-01616-2

Kotov, R., Krueger, R. F., Watson, D., Achenbach, T. M., Althoff, R. R., Bagby, R. M., et al. (2017). The hierarchical taxonomy of psychopathology (HiTOP): A dimensional alternative of traditional nosologies. *Journal of Abnormal Psychology, 126*(4), 454–477. https://doi.org/10.1037/abn0000258

Lahey, B. B., Krueger, R. F., Rathouz, P. J., Waldman, I. D., & Zald, D. H. (2017). A hierarchical causal taxonomy of psychopathology across the life span. *Psychological Bulletin, 143*(2), 142–186. https://doi.org/10.1037/bul0000069

Langan, J., Mercer, S. W., & Smith, D. J. (2013). Multimorbidity and mental health: Can psychiatry rise to the challenge? *British Journal of Psychiatry, 202*, 391–393. https://doi.org/10.1192/bjp.bp.112.123943

Lavigne, J. V., Arend, R., Rosenbaum, D., Binns, H. J., Christoffel, K. K., & Gibbons, R. D. (1998). Psychiatric disorders with onset in the preschool years: II. Correlates and predictors of stable case status. *Journal of the American Academy of Child and Adolescent Psychiatry, 37*(12), 1255–1261.

Lavigne, J. V., Cicchetti, C., Gibbons, R. D., Binns, H. J., Larsen, L., & DeVito, C. (2001). Oppositional defiant disorder with onset in preschool years: Longitudinal stability and pathways to other disorders. *Journal of the American Academy of Child and Adolescent Psychiatry, 40*, 1393–1400.

Lavigne, J. V., LeBailly, S. A., Hopkins, J., Gouze, K. R., & Binns, H. J. (2009). The prevalence of ADHD, ODD, depression and anxiety in a community sample of 4-year-olds. *Journal of Clinical Child and Adolescent Psychology, 38*, 315–328. https://doi.org/10.1080/15374410902851382

Masten, A. S., & Cicchetti, D. (2010). Developmental cascades [Editorial]. *Development and Psychopathology, 22*(3), 491–495. https://doi.org/10.1017/S0954579410000222

McMahon, S. D., Grant, K. E., Compas, B. E., Thurm, A. E., & Ey, S. (2003). Stress and psychopathology in children and adolescents: Is there evidence of specificity? *Journal of Child Psychology and Psychiatry, 44*(1), 107–133. https://doi.org/10.1111/1469-7610.00105

Pickles, A., & Angold, A. (2003). Natural categories or fundamental dimensions: On carving nature at the joints and the rearticulation of psychopathology. *Development and Psychopathology, 15*, 529–551. https://doi.org/10.1017/S0954579403000282

Quay, H. C., & Peterson, D. R. (1967). *Manual for the behavior problem checklist*. University of Illinois.

Smeekens, S., Riksen-Walraven, J. M., & van Bakel, H. J. A. (2007). Multiple determinants of externalizing behavior in 5-year-olds: A longitudinal model. *Journal of Abnormal Child Psychology, 35*, 347–361. https://doi.org/10.1007/s10802-006-9095.y

Strickland, J., Keller, J., Lavigne, J. V., Gouze, K. R., Hopkins, J., & LeBailly, S. A. (2011). The structure of psychopathology in a community sample of preschoolers. *Journal of Abnormal Child Psychology, 39*, 601–610. https://doi.org/10.1007/s10802-008-9236-6

Tomarken, A. J., & Waller, N. G. (2003). Potential problems with "well fitting" models. *Journal of Abnormal Psychology, 112*(4), 578–598. https://doi.org/10.1037/0021-843X.112.5.578

World Health Organization. (1949). *International statistical classification of diseases, injuries, and causes of death, 6th revision*. Author.

World Health Organization. (1967). *International statistical classification of diseases, injuries, and causes of death, 8th revisions*. Author.

ZERO TO THREE. (1994). *Diagnostic classification: 0–3: Diagnostic classiffication of mental heath and developmental disorders of infancy and early childhood*. National Center for Clincal Infant Programs.

Zero to Three. (2005). *Diagnostic classification of mental health and developmental disorders of infancy and early childhood: Revised edition (DC: 0-3R)*. Zero to Three Press.

Chapter 3
Contextual Risk Factors: Impact on Early Childhood Mental Health

Children grow up embedded in multiple systems and environments, all of which have an impact on who they are, how they function, and whether they will develop different types of emotional and behavioral problems. Researchers may differ in their approach to describing such systems, but there is general agreement on at least two essential points (Bronfenbrenner, 1977, 1979; Masten & Cicchetti, 2010). First, elements of the systems, often described as domains, differ in how proximal or distal they are from the child, and within each domain, there are a variety of psychological factors affecting the child's risk for developing emotional or behavioral problems. Second, there is an interplay between these factors both within and across domains that can lead to the development of symptoms of psychopathology. In the multi-domain system we examined in the PACT study, these domains, ordered from most proximal to most distal, include the contextual, parent and parenting, and child domains. This chapter focuses on contextual risk factors, Chap. 4 on parent and parenting factors, and Chap. 5 on child factors.

Contextual Domain

At the most distal level, there are factors related to the community and society in which the child lives and the family environment in which they are raised. These comprise the contextual domain and include, among other variables, socioeconomic status, family conflict and stress.

K. R. Gouze et al., *Early Childhood Psychopathology*,
https://doi.org/10.1007/978-3-031-68877-5_3

Socioeconomic Status

While there are different ways to conceptualize exactly what socioeconomic status (SES) refers to, in general, SES refers to a measure of a family's access to resources, including material resources (e.g., financial resources, neighborhood resources), non-material human resources (e.g., education, medical care), and social resources (e.g., social contacts) (Bradley & Corwyn, 2002; Peverill et al., 2020). It is likely that there are differences in the relations of each component of SES to child psychopathology and, perhaps, to different symptom types. Although researchers focusing on the role of SES-related factors in psychopathology argue for measuring each component separately, much research on the relation of SES to child development relies on one of several different general indicators. In fact, these indicators have yielded several important associations with behavioral and emotional symptoms.

SES: Direct Effects on Child/Adolescent Psychopathology

Direct effects refer to a relation in which one variable directly impacts another variable without any intervening factors. Several important findings emerged in a recent meta-analysis of the relation of SES and child psychopathology in population-based studies in the United States (Peverill et al., 2020). First, different measures of SES (family income, poverty status, subjective ratings of SES, and general indicators) yield statistically significant differences in their associations with child psychopathology and general indices, such as the Hollingshead-Redlich Index of Socioeconomic Status (Hollingshead, 1975), also show significant associations with measures of child psychopathology. Second, the association of SES and child psychopathology is not limited to the lower (more impoverished) end of the SES continuum. That is, there are associations between SES and child psychopathology and other health outcomes across the full income spectrum. Third, there is a small but significant association of a variety of socioeconomic indicators with both internalizing and externalizing symptom types. The magnitude of the association is statistically significantly larger for externalizing than internalizing symptoms, but the difference is relatively small.

SES: Indirect Effects

Indirect effects, or mediational processes, refer to relations in which a variable has an influence on a second variable via an intervening variable. Writing in 2002, Bradley and Corwyn (2002) noted that the mechanisms or mediational processes by which SES influences child functioning and well-being have not been adequately explored and, while progress has been made in this regard, there is still much to learn. Possible mechanisms by which SES may be linked to child functioning fall into two categories: (a) environmental resources/constraints, which include access to nutrition, housing, health care, cognitively stimulating material, etc., and (b) psychological influences. The latter includes exposure to stress and conflict in the family, parental psychological problems, and differences in parenting styles. For example, SES effects may be mediated by harsh discipline, poor family support and conflict, and maternal depression (Grant et al., 2006). Longitudinal studies of the stress associated with poverty reveal that negative parenting is a partial mechanism accounting for the relation between poverty and both internalizing and externalizing symptoms (Grant et al., 2003, 2014). Although many studies show an association between SES and one or more of these factors (e.g., between SES and parent psychopathology, SES and parenting, etc.), the number of studies that link SES to child psychopathology across domains of parent psychopathology, parenting, and child factors is still limited and requires further exploration.

Two useful mediational models linking SES and child psychopathology across multiple domains have been proposed and examined. One such model, the family stress model (Conger et al., 2000), suggests that the association between SES or economic stress and child psychopathology is mediated by some combination of parental psychopathology, parental conflict or stress, and/or parenting, particularly harsh, uninvolved, or inconsistent parenting (Benner & Kim, 2010; Conger et al., 2002; Linver et al., 2002; Soltanus et al., 2004). Although specific pathways differ across studies, collectively they provide important findings related to possible direct and indirect effects of SES on child psychopathology across multiple domains of family context.

A second model, also derived from the family stress model, focuses less on the negative aspects of low SES family environments and parenting (e.g., harsh, hostile parenting) and more on the advantages that higher family income plays by allowing parents to make greater investments in their children's development (Conger et al., 2010; Peverill et al., 2020). This investment leads to both instrumental advantages such as better housing and nutrition and also to emotionally and behaviorally based advantages, such as more parental stimulation of learning and better scaffolding ability as the child is coached to take on challenging tasks (Bradley & Corwyn, 2002).

Despite these research findings, important gaps remain in our understanding of the pathways by which SES and other measures of economic hardship are associated with child psychopathology across multiple domains. First, to our knowledge, these multi-domain studies are primarily cross-sectional in design. Thus, they advance our understanding of the pathways by which SES and child psychopathology are associated at a single time period. Still, they do not help us understand how these associations evolve over time. Additional research is needed to determine how such multidimensional factors connect SES with different types of child psychopathology longitudinally.

Second, these studies do not examine the ways in which SES is associated with specific aspects of the child's temperament or personality across domains. We do not know, for example if the pathway by which lower SES is associated with parent depression, parent conflict, and hostile parenting leads to an increase in child internalizing behaviors via the child's temperament or via some other pathway. To fully understand this connection, studies need to include child factors as one of the relevant domains. In the PACT study, we examined the effects of SES longitudinally and its effects on child temperament.

Finally, existing studies all include a single parenting factor, usually hostility, in their models rather than examining multiple parenting factors in the same model. Because of the omitted variable problem discussed in Chaps. 1 and 2, this can lead to an inflated estimate of the strength of this pathway. If understanding these pathways is to contribute to the development of better interventions and policies, multi-domain models that include SES are needed to examine multiple relevant pathways to child psychopathology simultaneously.

Stress

Stress: Direct Effects

While a substantial number of studies address the adverse effects of stress on children, a clear, consistent definition of stress is lacking. To fill this gap, McLaughlin (2018) provides a working definition that characterizes early life stress as (a) environmental circumstances that deviate considerably from the expected environment; (b) are either severe or chronic (i.e., ongoing over time; and (c) require significant adaptation by the typical child.

An association between stressful life events and both internalizing and externalizing child psychopathology in older children is well documented (Grant et al., 2004). In their 2004 report, Grant et al. reviewed 60 papers that examined the relation of stress to the subsequent development of psychological problems in children and adolescents (Grant et al., 2004, 2014; McLaughlin, 2018). They found relations between stress and both internalizing and externalizing disorders, but the association between stress and internalizing disorders was greater than the association between stress and externalizing disorders. This difference, however, may result primarily from the fact that there are a larger number of studies that examine the association between stress and internalizing disorders (Grant et al., 2014).

Researchers have devoted less time to studying the role of stress in psychopathology in young children. For the young child who is only beginning to develop a life outside of the home, a primary source of stress centers on the life stresses that parents experience, the extent to which the child is exposed to these in the home, and the extent to which the home environment itself is stressful for the child (e.g., in cases of parental abuse). Prior studies indicate that parental stress is elevated in mothers of young children with externalizing problems (Baker & Heller, 1996; McMahon et al., 2003) and Oppositional Defiant Disorder (ODD) (Ross & Blanc, 1998), and ongoing stress is associated with stability of an ODD diagnosis (Campbell et al., 1996; Lavigne et al., 1998) suggesting bidirectional influences that interact over time. Recent evidence (de Maat et al., 2022) also reveals that early life stress predicts early childhood behavior problems.

Stress: Indirect Effects

The processes or pathways by which family stressors and stressful life events contribute to the development of symptoms of child psychopathology are not as well understood as the processes linking SES and child symptoms. The approach to developing a model of these pathways depends on whether it is assumed that (a) different types of stressors to which the child is exposed may differ in intensity but are all similar in that they lead to the development of childhood psychopathology via a single, common neurobiological or psychosocial pathway; or (b) different types of stressors contribute to the development of psychopathology by having different effects on the development of the child. The cumulative risk approach assumes that the total number of stressors the child is exposed to is more important than the differences between stressors and that all stressors will have an impact on the development of psychopathology along a common pathway (McLaughlin, 2018). An alternative approach suggests that there is some specificity associated with different types of stressors. As a result, McLaughlin argues for a dimensional approach that assumes there may be some specificity to the underlying processes by which different stressors exert their effects. Her dimensional approach recognizes potential differences between stress that includes a threat dimension (e.g., events that might harm the child, such as abuse, parental divorce, etc.) and those characterized by a deprivation dimension. The latter involves a reduction in the inputs typically expected from the environment, including factors such as a reduction in cognitive and social stimulation that might characterize parents who are overly stressed.

One of the implications of the dimensional approach to early life stress is that a model of the effects of stress should include multiple indicators of different types of stress (McLaughlin, 2018). We follow that approach in the PACT research program, looking at different effects of SES, family stress, and family conflict and their interplay with parent, parenting, and child factors in determining how each of these might affect different symptom types.

The types of mediational processes accounting for the relation between stress and child psychopathology include factors in the parent (e.g., parental depression), parenting (e.g., support), and child domains (e.g., negative affect). However, the number of studies examining each type of mediational process is still quite limited and many have been conducted with older children. In the parent and parenting domain, Doan and colleagues (Doan et al., 2012) found that maternal responsiveness did not mediate the relation between cumulative risk and either internalizing or externalizing symptoms, while Dhondt et al. (2019) report that parent-child conflict mediated the association between stressful life events and adolescent psychopathology. In the child domain, emotion regulation appears to mediate the longitudinal relations between child maltreatment (Alink et al., 2009; Grant et al., 2014), stressful life events (Dhondt et al., 2019), cumulative risk (Doan et al., 2012) and child psychopathology.

Given the limited number of studies of mediational processes associated with stress, further research is needed to advance our understanding of the pathways between stress and child psychopathology. First, the range of potential mediators previously studied is limited and must be expanded. Second, studies generally focus on a single mediator at a time, possibly overestimating the mediational process‘s effect size due to the omitted variable problem. For this reason, we designed a model in which multiple mediators were explored simultaneously, thereby allowing for a greater understanding of the specificity of effects. Third, we designed a model consistent with Grant and colleagues' (Grant et al., 2014) admonition that it is important to study multilevel models to understand the more complex patterns of relations among different levels or systems that link stress to child psychopathology. Additionally, it is important to study the effects of different types of stressors on different types of emotional and behavioral outcomes (Grant et al., 2003). Finally, there are relatively few studies that explore the mediational processes linking stress with child psychopathology in younger children. A recent study (de Maat et al., 2022) revealed that early life stress predicts higher levels of externalizing and internalizing problems at age 6 and that child temperament can buffer these associations. These findings reveal that further study of these mediational processes in early childhood is likely to be fruitful in furthering our understanding of the pathways whereby early stress contributes to later child psychopathology.

In designing the PACT study, we committed to advancing our understanding of these processes by (a) modeling multiple stressors, including economic stress (SES), family conflict, and stress, to examine the specificity of stressors; (b) examining pathways from stress to later psychopathology through a multilevel model that assessed several possible mediators including parent, parenting, and child characteristics and (c) examining differences in the effects of stress across different symptom types, as well as in relation to broad-band internalizing and externalizing factors and general psychopathology.

Conflict

Conflict: Direct Effects

The important role that family conflict, and specifically inter-parental conflict, might play in the child's psychological adjustment has been recognized since the 1930s. Often, the focus of such research was on parental conflict so severe that it was accompanied by divorce or child maltreatment, but this is no longer the case (Harold & Sellers, 2018). There is now extensive evidence that parental conflict itself, even if it does not lead to divorce, is a risk factor for emotional and behavioral problems in school-age children and adolescents (Harold & Sellers, 2018). Furthermore, studies in young children (preschoolers and kindergarteners) reveal that parental conflict is strongly related to both internalizing and externalizing problems (Davies et al., 2004, 2016).

Conflict: Indirect Effects

As we saw for both socioeconomic status and stress, research on the mechanisms by which the contextual factors related to conflict contribute to the development of emotional and behavioral problems in children is lacking. One proposed psychosocial pathway suggests that parents' hostility to one another "spills over" and leads to increased hostility in parenting, which subsequently contributes to negative child outcomes (Harold & Sellers, 2018). Other than hostile parenting, little is known about other aspects of the parent-child relationship that might mediate the relation of family conflict to child psychopathology. One exception is the study of adolescents by Fauber et al. (1990) in which they identified a direct path from parental conflict to child externalizing problems, an indirect path in which psychological control (guilt induction) mediated the association between parental conflict and internalizing problems, and another indirect path in which rejection/withdrawal (i.e., parental hostility) mediated the relation between conflict and externalizing problems. There is no equivalent study in young children, so it is unclear whether parent hostility serves as a mechanism linking parent conflict and these symptoms during an earlier developmental period.

Other research reveals that emotional security in young children may be one mechanism whereby parental or caregiver conflict leads to internalizing and externalizing symptoms (Davies & Cummings, 1994; Davies et al., 2023; Thompson et al., 2020). In this conceptualization, parental conflict serves as a source of threat that undermines children's sense of safety and well-being in their families. This decrease in emotional security subsequently leads to emotional and behavioral problems.

Even less research addresses the child factors that might be influenced by parental conflict, or that might potentially mediate the associations between parental conflict and mental health outcomes. It is possible, for example, that parental conflict has an indirect effect on the development of child psychopathology via its effect on child temperament (e.g., by having an impact on the child's emotion regulation, inhibitory control, or intensity of negative affect). Recent evidence that this may be the case emerged in a study conducted by Thompson and colleagues (Thompson et al., 2020). These researchers examined whether effortful control served as a mechanism linking parental conflict and psychopathology in preschool children. They found that higher levels of conflict led to lower levels of child effortful control, which, in turn, led to more externalizing problems, thus providing evidence that the child temperament variable of effortful control mediates these associations. As with other contextual variables, however, the role of conflict has not yet been studied as a risk factor in a multi-domain model that includes the impact of factors from other systems on this aspect of family functioning.

Thus, our focus in examining the impact of parent and family conflict in our multi-domain model was on tracing its influence on child psychopathology in pathways not only via parental hostility but also via other aspects of parenting (supportive parenting, scaffolding), as well as through several child characteristics such as child attachment and temperament. With that in mind, the next chapter focuses on a discussion of how two systems closer to the child than contextual factors, namely, parent psychopathology and parenting, influence children's risk for psychopathology.

References

Alink, L. R. A., Cicchetti, D., Kim, J., & Rogosch, F. A. (2009). Mediating and moderating processes in the relation betweeen maltreatment and psychopathology: Mother-child relationshhip quality and emotion regulation. *Journal of Abnormal Child Psychology, 37*, 831–843. https://doi.org/10.1007/s10802-009-9314-4

Baker, B. L., & Heller, T. L. (1996). Preschool children with externalizing behaviors: Experience of fathers and mothers. *Journal of Abnormal Child Psychology, 24*(4), 513–532.

Benner, A. D., & Kim, S. Y. (2010). Understanding Chinese Americal adolescents' developmental outcomes: Insights from the family stress model. *Journal of Research on Adolescence, 20*(1), 1–12. https://doi.org/10.1011/j.1532-7795.2009.00629.x

Bradley, R. H., & Corwyn, R. F. (2002). Socioeconomic status and child development. *Annual Review of Psychology, 53*, 371–399. https://doi.org/10.1146/annurev.psych.53.100901.135233

Bronfenbrenner, U. (1977). Toward an experimental ecology of human development. *American Psychologist, 32*(7), 513–531. https://doi.org/10.1037/0003-066X.32.7.513

Bronfenbrenner, U. (1979). *The ecology of human development: Experiments by nature and design*. Harvard University Press.

Campbell, S. B., Pierce, E. W., Moore, G., Marakovitz, S., & Newby, K. (1996). Boys' externalizing problems at elementary school age: Pathways from early behavior problems, maternal control, and family stress. *Development and Psychopathology, 8*, 701–720.

Conger, K. J., Rueter, M. A., & Conger, R. D. (2000). The role of economic pressure in the lives of parents and their adolescents: The family stress model. In L. J. Crockett & R. J. Silbereisen (Eds.), *Negotiating adolescence in times of social change* (pp. 201–223). Cambridge University Press.

Conger, R. D., Wallace, L. E., Sun, Y., Simons, R. L., McLoyd, V. C., & Brody, G. H. (2002). Economic pressure in African American families: A replication and extension of the family stress model. *Developmental Psychology, 38*(2), 179–193. https://doi.org/10.1037/0012-1649.38.2.179

Conger, R. D., Conger, K. J., & Martin, M. J. (2010). Socioeconomic status, family processes, and individual development. *Journal of Marriage and the Family, 72*, 685–704. https://doi.org/10.1111/j.1741-3737.2010.00725.x

Davies, P. T., & Cummings, E. M. (1994). Marital conflict and child adjustment: An emotional security hypothesis. *Psychological Bulletin, 116*(3), 387–411.

Davies, P. T., Cummings, E. M., & Winter, M. A. (2004). Pathways between profiles of family functioning, child security in the interparental subsystem, and child psychological problems. *Development and Psychopathology, 16*, 525–550. https://doi.org/10.1017/S0954579404004651

Davies, P. T., Martin, M. J., Sturge-Apple, M. L., Ripple, M. T., & Cicchetti, D. (2016). The distinctive sequelae of children's coping with interparental conflict: Testing the reformulated emotional security theory. *Development and Psychopathology, 52*(10), 1646–1665. https://doi.org/10.1037/dev0000170

Davies, P. T., Pearson, J. K., Cao, V. T., & Sturge-Apple, M. L. (2023). Family-level antecedents of children's pattersn of reactivity to interparental conflict: Testing the reformulation of emotional security theory. *Develoment and Psychopathology, 59*, 99–111. https://doi.org/10.1037/dev0001497

de Maat, D. A., Schuurmans, I. K., Jongerling, J., Metcalf, S. A., Lucassen, N., Franken, I. H. A., Prinzie, P., & Jansen, P. W. (2022). Early life stress and behavior problems in early childhood: Investigating the contributions of child temperament and executive functions to resilience. *Child Development, 93*(1), e1–e16. https://doi.org/10.1111/cdev.13663. Epub 2021 Aug 27.

Dhondt, N., Healy, C., Clarke, M., & Cannon, M. (2019). Childhood adversity and adolescent psychopathology: Evidence for mediation in a national longitudinal cohort study. *British Journal of Psychiatry, 215*(3), 559–564. https://doi.org/10.1192/bjp.2019.108

Doan, S. N., Fuller-Rowell, T. E., & Evans, G. W. (2012). Cumulative risk and adolescent's internalizing and externalizing problems: The mediatring roles of maternal responsiveness and self-regulation. *Developmental Psychology, 48*(6), 1529–1539. https://doi.org/10.1037/a0027815

Fauber, R., Forehand, R., McCombs, T., & Wierson, M. (1990). A mediational model of the impact of marital conflict on adolescent adjustment in intact and divorced families: The role of disrupted parenting. *Child Development, 61*, 1112–1123.

Grant, K. E., Compas, B. E., Stuhlmacher, A., Thurm, A., McMahon, S., & Halpert, J. (2003). Stressors and child and adolescent psychopathology: Moving from markers to mechanisms of risk. *Psychological Bulletin, 129*, 447–466.

Grant, K. E., Compas, B. E., Thurm, A. E., McMahon, S. D., & Gipson, P. Y. (2004). Stressors and child and adolescent psychopathology: Measurement issues and prospective effects. *Journal of Clinical Child and Adolescent Psychology, 33*(2), 412–425. https://doi.org/10.1027/s15374424jccp3302.23

Grant, K. E., Compas, B. E., Thurm, A. E., McMahon, S. D., Gipson, P. Y., Campbell, A. J., Krochock, K., & Weserholm, R. I. (2006). Stressors and child and adolescent psychopathology: Evidence of moderating and mediating effects. *Clinical Psychology Review, 26*, 257–283. https://doi.org/10.1016/j.cpr.2005.06.011

Grant, K. E., McMahon, S. D., Carter, J. S., Carleton, R. A., Adam, E. K., & Chen, E. (2014). The influence of stressors on the development of psychopathology. In M. Lewis & K. D. Rudolph (Eds.), *Handbook of developmental psychopathology*. Springer. https://doi.org/10.1007/978-1-4614-9608-3_11

Harold, G. T., & Sellers, R. (2018). Annual research review: Interparental conflict and youth psychopathology: An evidence review and practice focused update. *Journal of Child Psychology and Psychiatry, 59*(4), 374–402. https://doi.org/10.1111/jcpp.12893

Hollingshead, A. B. (1975). *Four-factor index of social position*. Yale University Department of Sociology.

Lavigne, J. V., Arend, R., Rosenbaum, D., Binns, H. J., Christoffel, K. K., & Gibbons, R. D. (1998). Psychiatric disorders with onset in the preschool years: II. Correlates and predictors of stable case status. *Journal of the American Academy of Child and Adolescent Psychiatry, 37*(12), 1255–1261.

Linver, M. R., Brooks-Gunn, J., & Kohen, D. E. (2002). Family processes as pathways from income to young children's development. *Developmental Psychology, 38*(5), 719–734. https://doi.org/10.1037/0012-1649.38.5.719

Masten, A. S., & Cicchetti, D. (2010). Developmental cascades [Editorial]. *Development and Psychopathology, 22*(3), 491–495. https://doi.org/10.1017/S0954579410000222

McLaughlin, K. A. (2018). Early life stress and psychopathology. In K. Harkness & E. P. Hayden (Eds.), *The Oxford handbook of stress and mental health* (pp. 45–74). Oxford University Press. https://doi.org/10.1093/oxfordhb/9780190681777.013.3

McMahon, S. D., Grant, J. E., Compas, B. E., Thurm, A. E., & Ey, S. (2003). Stress and psychopathology in children and adolescents: Is there evidence of specificity? *Journal of Child Psychology and Psychiatry, 44*(1), 107–133.

Peverill, M., Dirks, M. A., Narvaja, T., Herts, K. L., Comer, J. S., & McLaughlin, K. A. (2020). Socioeconomic status and child psychopathology in the United States: A meta-analysis of population-based studies. *Clinical Psychology Review, 83*. https://doi.org/10.1016/j.cpr.2020.101933

Ross, C. N., & Blanc, H. M. (1998). Parenting stress in motherss of young children with oppositional defiant disorder and other severe behavior problems. *Child Study Journal, 23*(2), 93–110.

Soltanus, T., Leinonen, J., & Punamaki, R. L. (2004). Children's mental health in times of economic recession: Replication and extension of the family economic stress model in Finland. *Developmental Psychology, 40*(1), 412–429. https://doi.org/10.1037/0012-1649.40.3.412

Thompson, M. J., Davies, P. T., Hentges, P. T., Sturge-Apple, M. L., & Parry, L. Q. (2020). Understanding how and why effortful control moderates children's vulnerabillity to interparental conflict. *Developmental Psychology, 56*(5), 937–950. https://doi.org/10.1037/dev0000909

Chapter 4
Parent and Parenting Risk Factors: Impact on Early Childhood Mental Health

In the previous chapter, we discussed the importance of distal and contextual factors, specifically SES, stress, and family conflict. These factors contribute to the general foundational context within which a child lives and likely have an impact on influences that are more proximal to the child. In a multi-domain model, this more proximal level comprises the parents' own psychological functioning and parenting attitudes and behaviors. Previous research reveals that both parent functioning and parenting skills and behavior significantly influence child adaptation and maladaptation. Thus, in developing a model for understanding child mental health outcomes in early childhood, it is critical to understand the roles of parental psychopathology and parenting attitudes and behaviors. Particularly during the early years of life, when the intimacy and primacy of the parent-child relationship are the strongest and the impact of parenting attitudes and behaviors may be most influential, it is possible that parent psychological functioning and parenting attitudes and behaviors are particularly powerful in contributing to child outcomes.

Parent Depression

In determining what aspects of parental psychological functioning to examine, the PACT team chose depression for several reasons. The first consideration was the prevalence of maternal depression, particularly among mothers of young children. In a given year, approximately one in five children live in a home with a depressed mother (Child Trends, 2017). Furthermore, these figures are typically higher for mothers living in poverty and in historically marginalized communities, as well as for single parents or those with less education (Ertel et al., 2011). Of those mothers living with depression, it is estimated that between 5% and 70% have depression that can be characterized as severe or very severe, possibly leading to significant impairments in home, social and/or work life (McDaniel & Lowenstein, 2013).

K. R. Gouze et al., *Early Childhood Psychopathology*,
https://doi.org/10.1007/978-3-031-68877-5_4

Those suffering from depression are characterized by at least some of the following symptoms—affective disturbance in the form of ongoing feelings of sadness, anger or irritability; disruptions in daily functioning including loss of interest in things that previously brought pleasure; withdrawal from work or other activities; hopelessness regarding the future; low energy and sleep disturbances. As one contemplates the demands of young children, it seems clear that the symptoms of depression are likely to interfere directly with positive parenting. Young children require large amounts of energy, patience, good parental affective self-regulation, and the ability to engage with them in an empathic and reflective manner. As one examines the list of symptoms that characterize depression, it is impossible to imagine even a moderately depressed parent being able to bring their "A-game" to the table.

While deciding to include parent depression in the multi-domain model, we also made the decision not to include other factors. Research shows that parental anxiety is associated with child anxiety (Burstein et al., 2010; McClure et al., 2001; Schreier et al., 2008), but we did not include parental anxiety in the model for two reasons. First, the correlation between anxiety and depression is high, so many of the effects of parental anxiety on child psychopathology were likely to be captured by modeling one internalizing disorder in the parent in the form of depression only. Second, the inclusion of both anxiety and depression meant that we would be removing the variance shared between these two parenting factors and studying their independent effects on parenting and child psychopathology, which was not our interest. We also considered other factors such as substance abuse among parents. Given that we were studying a community sample of families, we felt the rate of substance use problems would be low and thus unlikely to be useful in the model.

Parental Depression: Direct Effects

In a classic review of the impact of maternal depression on children, Gelfand and Teti (1990) posit several plausible theoretical explanations for why depressed parents might negatively impact their children's well-being. Calling on cognitive theories of depression, they note that the negative cognitions of depressed parents (Beck, 1967) might lead to negative attributions of their child's behavior or character. Such negative attributions are likely to impact how children view themselves, leading to increased negative affect. Furthermore, later research demonstrated that, over time, parental depression results in children's increasingly pessimistic attributions about the world (Sutherland et al., 2019). Additionally, Gelfand and Teti posited that these depressive parental cognitions might generate feelings of inadequacy, leading parents to question their ability to regulate their child's behavior or manage their child's emotional or cognitive needs. As a result, they might fail to expend the effort needed to do so. Other theories of depression focus on how depression impacts social interactions and suggest that depressed parents might withdraw from their children, thereby leaving children feeling isolated or unloved. Theories of social cognition (Bandura, 1977) posit that children learn largely through observation and modeling, thereby suggesting that children of depressed parents might learn to imitate their parent's negative affect, low frustration levels, and irritability. It is likely that, for different parent-child pairs, one or more of these factors has explanatory power for the associations found between parent depression and child emotional and behavioral outcomes.

In addition to psychosocial explanations for the association between parent depression and child outcome, it is possible that the transmission of genetic vulnerability for depression from parent to child is a powerful mechanism leading to depressive outcomes in children. Natsuacki and colleagues (Natsuaki et al., 2014) addressed this possibility directly in a study specifically designed to isolate the effects of genetic versus environmental risk. Based on their findings, these researchers concluded that maternal depression is largely an *environmental* risk factor for emotional and behavioral problems in children and that genetic factors are not primary in accounting for these relations. A recent meta-analysis concluded that a differential susceptibility model in which gene-by-environment interactions account for either better or worse outcomes in early childhood depending upon the sensitivity of the environment carries the most explanatory power for associations between risk factors and child psychopathology (Pinto et al., 2015). For this reason and because psychosocial factors are more likely to respond to early prevention and intervention efforts, we decided to focus on psychosocial aspects in the PACT research.

The association between parent depression (frequently focusing on mothers as the more common primary caretakers) and emotional and behavior problems in young children was first documented during the 1980s (Brody & Forehand, 1986; Ghodsian et al., 1984; Wolkind et al., 1980). Subsequently, in a 30-year, long-term follow-up study, Weissman and colleagues (Weissman et al., 2016) noted a two- to three-fold increase in poor mental health outcomes in children of depressed parents compared to controls. Other researchers (Baker et al., 2020; Whittenburg et al., 2023) replicated the finding of an association between maternal depression and both internalizing and externalizing problems, specifically in preschoolers. In general, meta-analyses support the finding of small, but consistent, relations between maternal depression and child internalizing and externalizing outcomes that range from effect sizes of 0.10 to 0.26 (Beck, 1999; Connell & Goodman, 2002; Goodman et al., 2011). In the most recent meta-analysis, Ivanova and colleagues (Ivanova et al., 2022) asserted that the findings of small effect sizes establishing a relation between depression in parents and both internalizing and externalizing outcomes in children are largely consistent across studies.

Factors Impacting the Parental Depression/Child Psychopathology Association

The consistent but only small to moderate effects between parent depression and child psychopathology raise the possibility that other factors impact the link between parent depression and child psychopathology. These other associations warrant careful scrutiny.

Methodological Factors

Methodology varies greatly in studies examining the association between parent depression and child outcome. Among these methodological variations are the temporal nature or time lag between measurements of parent depression and child outcome, whether the study is cross-sectional or longitudinal, whether strength and/or chronicity of depression is measured, whether outcomes are measured dimensionally or categorically, and whether the reporter of parent symptoms and child outcomes is the same or different. In the ideal study, the design would be longitudinal with measurements of parental depression and child outcome that are both contemporaneous and time-lagged, and symptom reports for parents and children would be provided by more than one reporter (e.g., parents and teachers or parents and self-report). Furthermore, although data suggest that these associations are stronger for both internalizing and externalizing symptoms when they are measured dimensionally (Connell & Goodman, 2002), other researchers found stronger associations for categorical measurement of internalizing symptoms (Kane & Garber, 2004), but not externalizing symptoms. Examining all of these methodological questions in their meta-analysis, Ivanova and colleagues (Ivanova et al., 2022) found that cross-sectional associations were stronger than longitudinal ones for both internalizing and externalizing disorders, that the longitudinal associations were stronger when children were older, that the larger the temporal lag between measurement of parent depression and child outcome, the weaker the association, and that informant bias exists with associations being stronger when the reporter of parental depression and child outcome is the same. We designed the PACT study to address at least some of these concerns. Parental symptoms were assessed dimensionally, and measurement occurred across two time points. Unfortunately, the age of the children made it impossible to obtain symptom information from more than one informant because participants in the study were too young to report on their parents' symptoms.

Multifinality

The developmental psychopathology tenet of multifinality (Goodman et al., 2011) suggests that parental depression might lead to different symptom pictures or different emotional and behavioral outcomes for different children. The meta-analyses examining the associations of parental depression with child outcomes, described above, support the notion that parental depression manifests in multifinality, with parental depression associated with both internalizing and externalizing symptoms. While the strength of the associations between parent depression and child outcomes might differ in magnitude for internalizing versus externalizing symptoms, with some researchers finding the former association to be stronger (Kane & Garber, 2004) and others finding the latter to be stronger (Goodman et al., 2020), the difference is not statistically significant (Goodman et al., 2011). Studies that examined only anxiety and depression symptoms in children as outcome variables, rather than internalizing symptoms in general, found that maternal depression predicted both higher anxiety and higher depression scores in children across several time points from ages 5 to 15 (Daundasekara et al., 2021) and, also, from ages 4 to 6 (Gouze et al., 2022; Hopkins et al., 2020). Other studies that examined associations between maternal depression and child outcomes for children who were already considered vulnerable (e.g., those with ADHD) showed that for children with ADHD, maternal depression during the preschool years led to child conduct disorder at school entry (Chronis et al., 2007). Several researchers found transactional effects between child ADHD and parental depression (Cunningham & Boyle, 2002) consistent with developmental psychopathology theories regarding bidirectional influences between parents and children. Overall, the research is quite robust in showing that parental depression is associated with poorer child mental health outcomes of many different types. The questions that remain to be answered, and which the PACT study was designed to address, are, "What are the pathways between parent depression and child outcomes?" and "Are there intervening variables that help explain these associations and which provide information useful in designing prevention and intervention studies?" One such intervening variable might be parenting attitudes and behaviors.

Parental Depression and Indirect Effects on Child Psychopathology via Parenting

Understanding the methodological and demographic variables that are related to maternal depression and child outcomes does not help us understand the mechanisms through which these associations develop, nor do they explain how they are maintained over time. As noted in Chap. 1, development is not a static process: cascading effects over time lead to different outcomes depending upon several intervening variables. What, for example, explains the consistent associations between parent depression and poor child outcomes? Will we see better child outcomes simply by treating parent depression or are there other factors that must be addressed, along with the depression itself, to reduce later internalizing and externalizing symptoms?

Although there is some evidence that alleviating maternal depression alone leads to better child outcomes (Cuijpers et al., 2015; Shaw et al., 2009), many developmental theorists and researchers suggest that the impact of parent depression on child outcomes operates through parenting. As noted earlier, symptoms of depression include lack of energy, high levels of irritability, negative outlooks and attributions, and withdrawal, all of which have the potential to impact a parent's ability to provide guidance, positive regard and mirroring, and unconditional love and availability critical to healthy parenting. As Ahun and colleagues (Ahun et al., 2018) point out, mothers struggling with depression are more likely to be angry and critical with their children and less likely to be tuned in to their children's emotional needs. In a recent meta-analysis, Goodman and colleagues (Goodman et al., 2020) found that negative parenting, positive parenting, and a composite parenting measure consisting of both aspects of parenting helped explain the association between maternal depression and child internalizing and externalizing symptoms, although the effect sizes were somewhat larger for externalizing behaviors. Other emotional aspects of parenting found to mediate the association between maternal depression and child mental health symptoms include less sensitivity, less warmth, and less responsiveness (Daundasekara et al., 2021; Jaser et al., 2005; Lovejoy et al., 2000) and greater hostility and more frequent and intense criticism (Gravener et al., 2012; Hentges et al., 2021; Lovejoy et al., 2000; Panaccione & Wahler, 1986; Riley et al., 2009). Negative parenting and parental psychological aggression also mediate the association between caretaker depression and child symptoms, particularly externalizing ones (Daundasekara et al., 2021; Foster et al., 2008; Henry et al., 2018; Kuckertz et al., 2018; Lovejoy et al., 2000). However, it is important to note that many of these studies are based on research with older children, not preschoolers. In the PACT study we strove to address this gap in the literature by examining three parenting variables: hostile parenting, supportive parenting, and scaffolding. We further strengthened the study by using a mixed methods approach, that is, assessment with both questionnaires and observations, to measure these parenting factors. A better understanding of the mediating effects of positive parenting attitudes and practices is critical because it lends hope for ameliorating these effects through the implementation of parenting interventions (Goodman & Gotlib, 1999), along with treatment for parent depression.

Parental Depression: Indirect Effects via Child Attachment

The child's attachment security is another variable clearly impacted by maternal depression. Secure attachment is based on sensitive, responsive parenting (Madigan et al., 2024). Consequently, since depressed mothers frequently show decreased sensitivity to their infants' emotional signals (Bernard et al., 2018), it is reasonable to expect insecure attachment in babies with depressed mothers. As secure attachments have been shown to be associated with positive developmental trajectories in a number of areas (Sroufe, 2005), it makes sense that the associations between parent depression and poor adjustment, particularly in younger children may be mediated by the lack of a secure attachment relationship. Cicchetti and colleagues (Cicchetti et al., 1998) found that prolonged postpartum depression disrupts the development of secure attachment relationships, while Gravener and colleagues (Gravener et al., 2012) found that insecure attachments in children of depressed mothers were mediated through the mother's criticism towards self and child.

Two meta-analytic studies (Atkinson et al., 2000; Martins & Gaffan, 2000) documented small, but significant, effect sizes for the association between maternal depression and attachment security, with infants of depressed mothers being more likely to be insecurely attached. In somewhat more fine-grained analyses, others found that only major depression or major depression accompanied by comorbidities were associated with insecure attachment in toddlers; milder forms of depression were not (Carter et al., 2001; Sliwerski et al., 2020). Consistent with developmental psychopathology theory, parents' inability to positively reflect their child's affective state or to help the child co-regulate uncomfortable emotions leads to less secure attachment; depressed mothers are more likely than non-depressed mothers to have difficulty with this affective mirroring and support. As insecure attachment leads to poorer psychosocial outcomes (Verissimo et al., 2014), these pathways warrant further examination. Conversely, researchers posit attachment as a protective factor that confers resilience on children even when exposed to stressful environments (Masten, 2021).

Consistent with this notion, a recent study by Whittenburg and colleagues (Whittenburg et al., 2023) found that attachment security moderated the impact of extended depression in mothers such that children of depressed mothers with secure attachments did not show the same high levels of internalizing problems as did insecurely attached children of depressed mothers. This moderating effect did not manifest in the associations between maternal depression and later externalizing problems in children. Other researchers (Munson et al., 2001) also found that the security of attachment did not mediate the association between maternal depression and externalizing disorders. It may be that less sensitive parenting, which leads to less secure attachment, is more of a risk factor for internalizing problems in children than for externalizing problems because poor attachment generates increased anxiety about the world as well as greater negative affect. In the PACT study, we deliberately explored pathways from maternal depression through attachment to child outcomes to determine whether insecure attachment might further help explain the associations over time between maternal depression and child internalizing and externalizing behaviors or help illuminate the differences in these pathways.

Parental Depression: Indirect Effects via Child Temperament

Finally, although child temperament is frequently conceived of as a more biologically based construct, most theorists and researchers (Rothbart & Ahadi, 1994; Thomas et al., 1968) conceive of temperament as a set of characteristics that evolve over time as a result of interactions between the child's biologically based propensities and their experiences. As such it is reasonable to assume that a depressed parent, particularly one who is emotionally unavailable or emotionally dysregulated (e.g., more irritable as a function of their depression), might impact the development of a child's negative affect or emotion regulation capacity. The pathway from parental depression to child internalizing and externalizing difficulties might thus operate indirectly through child temperament. Although Goodman and Gotlib (1999) suggested an explanatory model over twenty years ago in which child temperament was hypothesized to be one of many variables that mediate the pathway from parental depression to child disorder, little research has explored this possibility. Two studies documented the role that inhibitory control plays in mediating this relation (Choe et al., 2014; Hermansen et al., 2022); both established an indirect pathway from maternal depression to child externalizing disorder through poor child inhibitory control. Other studies examined indirect pathways from parental emotion regulation (but not depression specifically) to poor socioemotional outcomes in children through child emotion regulation (Crespo et al., 2017; Maughan et al., 2007) and from maternal negative affect to child internalizing problems via child temperament (Fang & Gagne, 2018).

The role of child temperament in mediating the effects of early maternal depression on later child outcomes is thus inadequately understood and was included in the modelling in the PACT study because it clearly warranted further study. Given the strong relations between maternal depression and child outcomes and between child temperament and mental health outcomes, we expected that parental depression might well affect both child negative affect and self-regulation, so we included indirect pathways from depression to child outcomes via these aspects of child temperament.

Parenting: Direct Effects

In addition to serving as a mediator through which parent depression impacts child mental health outcomes and well-being, it is reasonable to expect that parenting, itself, has direct effects on child outcomes. After all, particularly when considering the developmental trajectories of preschoolers, it is reasonable to assume that parents exert the most significant psychosocial influence on children. Children often spend the largest amount of time in family contexts at young ages, and parents are relatively active in shaping and influencing their children's development. Explorations of the associations between parenting and child internalizing and externalizing symptoms focus on two different approaches to parenting: a dimensional approach and a categorical approach. The dimensional approach examines the associations between specific parenting attitudes and behaviors along both emotional and behavioral dimensions and child outcomes. For example, parental warmth, including behaviors such as acceptance, positive regard, nurturance, and positive affective engagement, is an important emotional factor in child outcomes, as is parental hostility. Along a more behavioral continuum, parental granting of autonomy, behavioral control, overcontrol, and coercive discipline are commonly explored to determine their impact. In contrast, the categorical approach examines constellations of parenting behaviors that constitute parenting styles. Interestingly, even though one would expect parental influences to be strongest during preschool, many researchers examine the 5–11 age range or adolescence when attempting to understand associations and/or pathways between parenting and the development and/or maintenance of child internalizing and externalizing disorders. This is somewhat less true for externalizing symptoms than for internalizing symptoms, perhaps because externalizing symptoms are more common than internalizing symptoms during the preschool years (Egger & Angold, 2006; Keenan et al., 1997; Lavigne et al., 1996, 2009), thereby leading more researchers to design studies in an attempt to understand parenting influences on these behaviors.

Parenting: Dimensional Approach

The following section describes research findings on the associations between parenting behaviors and child mental health outcomes broadly across childhood and adolescence to identify generalizable relations and those that require further research and exploration. Primarily, these general findings are derived from meta-analyses that collate and aggregate data. In presenting these findings, however, it is important to note that many of the studies in these meta-analyses examined older children, captured cross-sectional rather than longitudinal findings making it hard to understand the direction of effects and, in the case of longitudinal findings, neglected to account for levels of internalizing and externalizing symptoms already present. We attempted to address at least some of these gaps in designing the PACT study.

Parental Hostility For the most part, researchers find that relations between parenting and child outcomes are stronger for externalizing symptoms than for internalizing symptoms (Foster et al., 2008; McCarty et al., 2003), although this depends to some extent on the particular parenting dimension being explored. For example, overreactive, harsh, and angry parenting has long been associated with externalizing behaviors (Barrios et al., 2017; Campbell et al., 2000; Eiden et al., 2007; Maccoby, 2000; Rothbaum & Weisz, 1994; Shaw et al., 2003; Waller et al., 2012), although associations between overreactive, harsh parenting and parental criticism are found with internalizing disorders as well (Barrios et al., 2017; Callahan et al., 2011; McLeod et al., 2007a, b; Pinquart, 2017; Rose et al., 2018; van der Sluis & van

Steensel, 2015). In a trajectory analysis examining the role of harsh parenting on both internalizing and externalizing behaviors at ages 3, 5, and 9, Wiggins and colleagues (Wiggins et al., 2015) found that harsh parenting only contributed unique variance to externalizing symptoms over time, while other researchers found that highly critical parenting led to both increased externalizing and increased internalizing symptomatology (Gravener et al., 2012). It is possible that exposure to harsh parenting, particularly when children are young, contributes to a lack of emotional and behavioral regulation and to modeling negative responses to others, which ultimately manifests in externalizing symptoms, including oppositional behaviors with adults, coercive behaviors with peers, and excessive expressions of anger in the form of age-inappropriate temper tantrums. In contrast, internalizing symptoms may result from children's increasing sadness and anxiety over their lack of emotional and behavioral mastery which affects their daily lives across multiple domains. These feelings of sadness and anxiety may also develop in response to the negative reactions of others generated by their externalizing behaviors. The hostility directed towards these children by their parents and the negative responses they get from others may lead to an internalized sense of themselves as unworthy, thereby leading to higher levels of depression. Viewing the world as hostile and threatening may lead, as well, to a heightened sense of vigilance and fear resulting in anxiety symptoms (Negreiros & Miller, 2014). Over time, co-occurrence of externalizing and internalizing behaviors likely increases as seen in how frequently internalizing and externalizing symptoms co-occur (see Chap. 9 on transdiagnostic outcomes); some of this may be due to developmental psychopathology concepts of multifinality; that is, parental hostility can lead to both externalizing and internalizing symptoms over time.

Parental Warmth Parental warmth, responsiveness, and positive regard are also associated with externalizing and internalizing problems, although with small to moderate effect sizes (McKee et al., 2008; Moller et al., 2016). The research that focuses on internalizing problems and meta-analyses that examine internalizing symptoms as a group find consistent associations between high parental warmth and low levels of internalizing symptoms (Pinquart, 2017), with somewhat differential findings for anxiety and depression when they are studied independently. Although low parental warmth is associated with both anxiety and depression concurrently (effect sizes of −0.15 and − 0.029, respectively), associations with anxiety do not hold longitudinally, while they remain relatively strong over time for depression symptoms (effect size, −0.20) (Yap et al., 2014) . Similarly, Fox and colleagues (Fox et al., 2023) found a clear association between parental warmth and child depression but more mixed results for anxiety symptoms. It is likely that low parental warmth leaves children questioning their self-worth and whether they are, in essence, "lovable" while its effects on anxiety might be more related to whether a child has initially high levels of anxiety or other factors yet to be explored.

Clearly, more research is needed to understand these relations. Some researchers attempted to get a better understanding of these mixed results by studying two parenting variables together. For example, Fox and colleagues (Fox et al., 2023) found that low levels of maternal warmth and high levels of overcontrol together predicted high levels of child depression in elementary school-age children but did not impact anxiety symptoms. There is less research on the relationship between parental warmth and externalizing disorders (much of this work looks at parental hostility as the affective component of parenting), but in one study warm parenting at 27 months led to low levels of externalizing behavior at age 6–7 as reported by teachers (Reuben et al., 2016). McKee and colleagues (McKee et al., 2008) found a relation between lower warmth and increased externalizing symptoms across a range of studies in their review. Additionally, they demonstrated that there is little evidence for specificity of an association between parental warmth and one type of outcome versus the other. In the PACT study these affective aspects of parenting were examined through the inclusion of both a hostile and a supportive parenting variable.

Parental Over-Control and Respect for Child Autonomy In addition to examining the affective aspects of parenting, researchers have studied behavioral aspects of parenting dimensions related to the encouragement of independence. On the one hand, this involves the extent to which parents are overly controlling or overly intrusive, and on the other, the extent to which they appropriately grant autonomy. Whereas the research on overcontrol, excessive discipline, and intrusive parenting addresses both externalizing and internalizing symptoms, appropriate autonomy granting has been examined almost exclusively regarding the development of internalizing disorders, specifically anxiety. It seems reasonable that excessive parental control imposed on preschoolers while they begin to assert independence and develop an emerging sense of self might evoke a response from the child that manifests in oppositional behaviors. Conversely, depending upon the child, overbearing parent behavior or parental over-control might lead to the development of anxiety. Parental overcontrol can encourage an excessive sense of dependence by conveying to the child that they are not capable of making decisions regarding independence, thereby affecting their self-confidence and leading them to question their ability to safely explore the world. It is possible, as well, that parental over-control might manifest in depressive symptoms, which emerge in response to the stifling of the child's emerging sense of self. Researchers have documented that low behavioral control is associated with both externalizing and internalizing problems (McKee et al., 2008), while overcontrol is robustly associated with internalizing symptoms in general (Fox et al., 2023; Rose et al., 2018; van der Sluis & van Steensel, 2015) and, more specifically, with depression (McLeod et al., 2007a) and anxiety symptoms (McLeod et al., 2007b; Negreiros & Miller, 2014). In contrast, one meta-analysis (Moller et al., 2016) found that overprotection, but not overcontrol, was related to anxiety symptoms during the early childhood period. These authors hypothesized that, whereas overprotection gives the child implicit messages about an unsafe world that can lead to anxiety, overcontrol is more of a factor for older children and adolescents when they are trying to assert their independence and individuate from their families. Age-appropriate autonomy granting, in fact, appears to be robustly associated with lower anxiety symptoms (McLeod et al., 2007b; Pinquart, 2017), although Moller et al. (2016) did not find an association between autonomy granting and anxiety in younger children. Clearly, the dearth of research on younger children, specifically regarding these parenting practices requires further research; this is partially what inspired the PACT study to focus on 4- to 6-year-old children.

Differential findings for overcontrol and overprotectiveness suggest that these are different aspects of parenting and should be examined independently. Although the need to narrow down the number of variables studied led to the decision not to include a specific measure of parental control in the PACT study, this variable was among the parenting variables captured in the observational parent-child interaction task. Ultimately these parenting variables were reduced (based on a factor analysis) to the scaffolding variable, but because of past research, the specific variable of "respect for child's autonomy," rather than the scaffolding variable, was used in the multi-domain models predicting anxiety.

Parenting: Categorical Approach

Research that examines categorical styles of parenting such as authoritative or permissive parenting reveals that authoritarian and neglectful parenting is associated with increased internalizing symptoms. In contrast, authoritative parenting is related to lower internalizing symptoms (Pinquart, 2017). Overall, there appears to be a clear relation between parenting styles and child outcomes and between parenting attitudes and behaviors and child outcomes. However, these associations are remarkably small given the extent to which children, especially young children, are dependent upon and influenced by their parents. Effect sizes tend to be small; during the preschool years, moderate effect sizes are found most often for the relation between autonomy granting and anxiety (Pinquart, 2017) and for parenting behaviors and externalizing symptoms (Barrios et al., 2017; Campbell et al., 2000; Maccoby, 2000; Rothbaum & Weisz, 1994; Shaw et al., 2003; Waller et al., 2012), but few studies explore developmental models that include large samples examined over time and include important contextual variables and multiple domains of analysis.

Parenting: Indirect Effects via Child Temperament

Based on previous research, parenting clearly has an effect on the development of children with both internalizing and externalizing symptoms, but the small size of these effects suggests that there are indirect effects mediated through other variables, such as child temperament. Studies of bidirectional effects between parents and children make it increasingly clear that children impact their parents' attitudes and behaviors and vice versa (Bell, 1968; Sameroff, 2009). It is thus reasonable to examine both the bidirectional effects that parenting and temperament have on child outcomes over time, and the indirect effects that parenting has on child outcomes via temperament. The notion that parenting and child variables such as temperament interact in some way over time to contribute risk or confer protection on children, which then manifest in different outcomes, is consistent with diathesis-stress or differential susceptibility models of psychopathology, as well as with general tenets of developmental psychopathology which posit transactional interactions over time at multiple levels across contexts (see Chap. 1). Not only are child temperament variables likely to buffer or exacerbate associations between parenting and child outcomes; but it is also true that certain child temperaments might make children easier or harder to parent or might elicit different emotional reactions from parents. In general, a review of the literature (Kiff et al., 2011) reveals complex bidirectional and transactional relations between parenting and child temperament. It supports mediating effects of child temperament on the associations between parental behaviors and child outcomes.

Specific aspects of child temperament found to mediate the association between parenting and child internalizing and externalizing symptoms include negative affect and the various aspects of effortful control (e.g., emotion regulation, impulsivity). Both child negative affect and child effortful control mediate the association between parental discipline and communication and externalizing outcomes in the form of aggression (Carrasco et al., 2020). Child temperament variables such as poor frustration tolerance, low effortful control, and high impulsivity additionally mediate the associations between negative parenting and externalizing behaviors (Bates et al., 2012; Kiff et al., 2011). Furthermore, inhibited temperament indirectly impacts associations between negative parenting, both affective and behavioral, and increases in internalizing problems in preschoolers. For girls, the mediation is strongest for the associations with emotional parenting, and for boys, the mediation is strongest for negative parenting practices (Hastings et al., 2015). Other authors also found sex differences in the mediating and moderating effects of temperament, with girls apparently more sensitive to the affective aspects of parenting and boys more sensitive to the behavioral control aspects of parenting (Kiff et al., 2011). Similarly, these mediation effects might differ depending upon the developmental stage during which they operate, just as certain aspects of parenting appear to have stronger associations with child outcomes at certain ages than others. In general, there is little consistent early childhood research that models the indirect effects of parenting on child internalizing and externalizing symptoms via child temperament. This was one of the primary goals in designing the developmental psychopathology model tested in the PACT study. That is, although there is a great deal of research on the impact of parental depression and various parenting factors on child outcome, the PACT study was one of the only studies to examine both the direct effects and multiple indirect pathways leading from parental depression and parenting through child temperament to internalizing and externalizing symptoms across three important developmental periods.

Modeling Parent Depression and Parenting in the Multi-domain Risk Factor Model

In the PACT study's multi-domain model, decisions needed to be made about how to model direct and indirect effects for parent depression and parenting. Some decisions were straightforward. Evidence is strong that depression is associated with child psychopathology via parenting and child temperament and that the association of parenting can be both direct and indirect via the child's temperament. These paths are included in the multi-domain model. How to best model the relation between maternal depression, parenting, and child attachment was less clear-cut. With child attachment reflecting the internalized representation of the child's sense of security in their relationship with a parent, it can be modeled as a child characteristic closely linked to both parent depression and parenting. It is also a characteristic likely to affect the child's ability to regulate emotions and other aspects of effortful control. Further, the development of attachment is likely to begin in infancy and be well-established by age 4, the age at which the multi-domain model was implemented. For those reasons, we elected to model attachment as a child factor at age 4, with an indirect effect via effortful control measured at age 5 to age 6 psychopathology. Further discussion of child attachment and temperament as risk factors and the modeling of these variables in the PACT study occurs next in Chap. 5.

References

Ahun, M. N., Consoli, A., Pingault, J. B., Falissard, B., Battaglia, M., Boivin, M., Tremblay, R. E., Cote, S. M., & Bouvard, M. P. (2018). Maternal depression symptoms and internalising problems in the offspring: The role of maternal and family factors. *European Child and Adolescent Psychiatry, 27*(7), 921–932. https://doi.org/10.1007/s00787-017-1096-6

Atkinson, L., Paglia, A., Coolbear, J., Niccols, A., Parker, K. C., & Guger, S. (2000). Attachment security: A meta-analysis of maternal mental health correlates. *Clinical Psychology Review, 20*(8), 1019–1040. https://doi.org/10.1016/s0272-7358(99)00023-9

Baker, C. E., Brooks-Gunn, G. J., & Gouskova, N. (2020). Reciprocal relations between maternal depression and child behavior problems in families served by Head Start. *Child Development, 91*(5), 1563–1576. https://doi.org/10.1111/cdev.13344

Bandura, A. (1977). *Social learning theory*. Prentice Hall.

Barrios, C., Bufferd, S. J., Klein, D. N., & Dougherty, L. (2017). The interaction between parenting and children's cortisol reactivity at age 3 predicts increases in children's internalizing and externalizing symptoms at age 6. *Development and Psychopathology, 29*(1–13), 1319. https://doi.org/10.1017/S0954579417000293

Bates, J. E., Schermerhorn, A., & Petersen, I. (2012). Temperament and parenting in developmental perspecive. In M. Zentner & R. L. Shiner (Eds.), *Handbook of temperament* (pp. 425–441). Guilford.

Beck, A. T. (1967). *Depression: Clinical, experimental, and theoretical perspectives*. Harper and Row.

Beck, C. T. (1999). Maternal depression and child behaviour problems: A meta-analysis. *Journal of Advanced Nursing, 29*(3), 623–629. https://doi.org/10.1046/j.1365-2648.1999.00943.x

Bell, R. Q. (1968). A reinterpretation of the direction of effects in studies of socialization. *Psychological Review, 75*, 81–95.

Bernard, K., Nissim, G., Vaccaro, S., Harris, J. L., & Lindheim. (2018). Association between maternal depression and maternal sensitivity from birth to 12 months: A meta-analysis. *Attachment & Human Development, 20*(6), 578–599. https://doi.org/10.1080/1416734.2018.1430839

Brody, G. H., & Forehand, R. (1986). Maternal perceptions of child maladjustment as a function of the combined influence of child behavior and maternal depression. *Journal of Consulting and Clinical Psychology, 54*(2), 237–240. https://doi.org/10.1037/00022-006X.54.2.237

Burstein, M., Ginsburg, G. S., & Tein, J. Y. (2010). Parental anxiety and child symptomatology: An examination of additive and interactive effects of parent psychopathology. *Journal of Abnormal Child Psychology, 38*(7), 897–909. https://doi.org/10.1007/s10802-010-9415-0

Callahan, K. L., Scaramella, L. V., Laird, R. D., & Sohr-Preston, S. L. (2011). Neighborhood disadvantage as a moderator of the association between harsh parenting and toddler-aged children's internalizing and externalizing problems. *Journal of Family Psychology, 25*(1), 68–76. https://doi.org/10.1037/a0022448

Campbell, S. B., Shaw, D. S., & Gilliom, M. (2000). Early externalizing behavior problems: Toddlers and preschoolers at risk for later maladjustment. *Development and Psychopathology, 12*(03), 467–488.

Carrasco, M. A., Delgado, B., & Holgado-Tello, F. P. (2020). Children's temperament: A bridge between mothers' parenting and aggression. *International Journal of Environmental Research and Public Health, 17*(17), 6382. https://doi.org/10.3390/ijerph17176382

Carter, A. S., Garrity-Rodous, J. D., Chazan-Cohen, R., Little, C., & Briggs-Gowan, M. J. (2001). Maternal depression and comorbidity: Predicting early parenting, attachment security, and toddler social-emotional problems and competencies. *Journal of the American Academy of Child and Adolescent Psychiatry, 40*(1), 18–26.

Child Trends. (2017). https://www.childtrends/org/publications/5-things-to-know-about-parental-depression

Choe, A. M., Shaw, D. S., Brennan, L., Dishion, T. J., & Wilson, M. (2014). Inhibitory control as a mediator of bidirectional effects between early oppositional behavior and maternal depression. *Development and Psychopathology, 24*(4 Pt 1), 1129–1147. https://doi.org/10.1017/S0954579414000613

Chronis, A. M., Lahey, B. B., & Pelham, W. E. (2007). Maternal depression and early positive parenting predict future conduct problems in young children wiht attention-deficit/hyperactivity disorder. *Developmental Psychology, 43*, 70–82. https://doi.org/10.1037/0012-1649.43.1.70

Cicchetti, D., Rogosch, F. A., & Toth, S. L. (1998). Maternal depressive disorder and contextual risk: Contributions to the development of attachment insecurity and behavior problems in toddlerhood. *Development and Psychopathology, 10*(2), 283–300. https://doi.org/10.1017/S095457948001618

Connell, A. M., & Goodman, S. H. (2002). The association between psychopathology in fathers versus mothers and children's internalizing and externalizing behavior problems: A meta-analysis. *Psychological Bulletin, 138*(5), 746–773. https://doi.org/10.1037/0033-2909.128.5.746

Crespo, L., Trentacosta, C., Aikins, D., & Wargo-Aikins, J. (2017). Maternal emotion regulation and children's behavior problems: The mediating role of child emotion regulation. *Journal of Child and Family Studies, 26*, 1–13. https://doi.org/10.1007/s10826-017-0791-8

Cuijpers, P., Weitz, E., Karyotaki, E., Garber, J., & Andersson, G. (2015). The effects of psychological treatment of maternal depression on children and parental functioning: A meta-analysis. *European Child and Adolescent Psychiatry, 24*(2), 237–245. https://doi.org/10.1007/s00787-014-0660-6

Cunningham, C. E., & Boyle, M. H. (2002). Preschoolers at risk for attention-deficit hyperactivity disorder and oppositional defiant disorder: Family, parenting, and behavioral correlates. *Journal of Abnormal Child Psychology, 30*(6), 555–569. https://doi.org/10.1023/a.1020855429085

Daundasekara, S. S., Schuler, B. R., Beauchamp, J. E. S., & Hernandez, D. C. (2021). The mediating effect of parenting stress and couple relationship quality on the association between material hardship trajectories and maternal mental health status. *Journal of Affective Disorders, 290*, 31–39. https://doi.org/10.1016/j.jad.2021.04.058

Egger, H. E., & Angold, A. (2006). Common emotional and behavioral disorders in preschool children: Presentation, nosology, and epidemiology. *Journal of Child Psychology and Psychiatry, 47*, 313–337.

Eiden, R., Mink, E., & Leonard, K. (2007). A conceptual model for the development of externalizing behavior problems among kndergarten children of alcoholic families: Role of parenting and children's self-regulation. *Development and Psychopathology, 43*, 1187–1201. https://doi.org/10.1037/0012-1649.43.5.1187

Ertel, K. A., Rich-Edwards, J. W., & Koenen, K. C. (2011). Maternal depression in the United States: Nationally representative rates and risks. *Journal of Women's Health, 20*(11), 1609–1617. https://doi.org/10.1089/jwh.2010.2657

Fang, H., & Gagne, J. R. (2018). Young children's behavioral inhibition mediates the association betwen maternal negative affectivity and internalizing problems: Observations, parent-report, and moderation of associations by age. *International Journal of Behavioral Development, 42*(2), 284–293. https://doi.org/10.1177/0165025417690261

Foster, C. J. E., Garber, J., & Durlak, J. A. (2008). Current and past maternal depression, maternal interaction behaviors, and children's externalizing and internalizing symptoms. *Journal of Abnormal Child Psychology, 36*(4), 527–537. https://doi.org/10.1007/s10802-007-9197-1

Fox, J. K., Sital, M., Halpern, L. F., & Ryan, J. L. (2023). Elucidating the roles of maternal overcontrol and warmth in the development of childhood anxiety and depression: A moderated mediation framework. *Child Psychiatry and Human Development, 54*(2), 609–622. https://doi.org/10.1007/s10578-021-01274-8

Gelfand, D. M., & Teti, D. M. (1990). The effects of maternal depression on children. *Clinical Psychology Review, 10*, 329–353.

Ghodsian, M., Zajicek, E., & Wolkind, S. (1984). A longitudinal study of maternal depression and child behaviour problems. *Journal of Child Psychology and Psychiatry and Allied Disciplines, 25*, 91–109.

Goodman, S. H., & Gotlib, I. H. (1999). Risk for psychopathology in the children of depressed mothers: A developmental model for understanding mechanisms of transmission. *Psychological Review, 106*(3), 458–490. https://doi.org/10.1037/0033-295x.106.3.458

Goodman, S. H., Rouse, M. H., Connell, A. M., Broth, M. R., Hall, C. M., & Heyward, D. (2011). Maternal depression and child psychopathology: A meta-analytic review. *Clinical Child and Family Psychology Review, 14*, 1–27. https://doi.org/10.1003/sl10567-010-0080-1

Goodman, S. H., Simon, H. F. M., Shamblaw, A. L., & Kim, C. Y. (2020). Parenting as a mediator of associations between depression in mothers and children's functioning: A systematic review and meta-analysis. *Clinical Child & Family Psychology Review, 23*(4), 427–460. https://doi.org/10.1007/s10567-020-00322-4

Gouze, K. R., Lavigne, J. V., & Bryant, F. B. (2022). A multi-level longitudinal model of risk factors for generalized and separation anxiety symptoms in a community sample of 6-year-olds. *Child Psychiatry and Human Development, 53*(3), 405–417. https://doi.org/10.1007/s10578-021-01132-7

Gravener, J. A., Rogosch, F. A., Oshri, A., Narayan, A. J., Cicchetti, D., & Toth, S. L. (2012). Maternal expressed emotion, toddler behavior problems and attachment. *Journal of Abnormal Psychology, 40*, 803–813. https://doi.org/10.1007/s10802-011-9598-z

Hastings, P. D., Helm, J., Mills, R. S., Serbin, L. A., Stack, D. M., & Schwartzman, A. E. (2015). Dispositional and envirnmental predictors of the develoment of internalizing problems in childhood: Testing a mulilevel model. *Journal of Abnormal Child Psychology, 43*(5), 831–845. https://doi.org/10.1007/s10802-014-9951-0

Henry, L. M., Forehand, R., Watson, K. H., Gruhn, M., Bettis, A. H., McKee, L. G., & Compas, B. E. (2018). Parental depressive symptoms and parenting: Associations with children's coping in families of depressed parents. *Parenting: Science and Practice, 18*(4), 281–296. https://doi.org/10.1080/15295192.2018.1529453

Hentges, R. F., Graham, S. A., Plamondon, A., Tough, S., & Madigan, S. (2021). Bidirectional associations between maternal depression, hostile parenting, and early child emotional problems: Findings from the all our families cohort. *Journal of Affective Disorders, 287*, 397–404. https://doi.org/10.1016/j.jad.2021.03.056

Hermansen, T. K., Syrstad, K. E., Roysamb, E., & Melinder, A. M. D. (2022). Child internalizing and externalizing behaviors: Interplay between maternal depressive symptoms and child inhibitory control. *Journal of Child Psychology and Psychiatry, 2*(4), e12107. https://doi.org/10.1002/jcv2.12107

Hopkins, J., Gouze, K. R., Lavigne, J. V., & Bryant, F. B. (2020). Multidomain risk factors in early childhood and depression symptoms in 6-year-year-olds: A longitudinal pathway model. *Develoment and Psychopathology, 32*(1), 57–71. https://doi.org/10.1017/S0954579418001426

Ivanova, M. Y., Achenbach, T. M., & Turner, L. V. (2022). Associations of parental depression with children's internalizing and externalizing problems: Meta-analyses of cross-sectional and longitudinal effects. *Journal of Clinical Child & Adolescent Psychology, 51*(6), 827–849. https://doi.org/10.1080/15374416.2022.2127104

Jaser, S. S., Langrock, A. M., Keller, G., Merchant, M. J., Benson, M. A., Reslund, K., Champion, J. E., & Compas, B. E. (2005). Coping with the stress of parental depression II: Adolescent and parent reports of coping and adjustment. *Journal of Clinical Child & Adolescent Psychology, 34*(1), 193–205. https://doi.org/10.1207/s15374424jccp3401_18

Kane, P., & Garber, J. (2004). The relations among depression in fathers, children's psychopathology, and father-child conflict: A meta-analysis. *Clinical Psychology Review, 24*(3), 339–360. https://doi.org/10.1016/j.cpr.2004.03.004

Keenan, K., Shaw, D. S., Walsh, B., Delliquadri, E., & Giovannelli, J. (1997). DSM-III-R disorders in preschool children from low-income families. *Journal of the American Academy of Child and Adolescent Psychiatry, 36*, 620–627.

Kiff, C. J., Lengua, L. J., & Zalewski, M. (2011). Nature and nurturing: Parenting in the context of child temperament. *Clinical Child & Family Psychology Review, 4*(3), 251–301. https://doi.org/10.1007/s10567-011-0093-4

Kuckertz, J. M., Michell, C., & Wiggns, J. L. (2018). Parenting mediates the impact of maternal depression n child internalizing symptoms. *Depression and Anxiety, 35*(1), 89–97. https://doi.org/10.1002/da.22688

Lavigne, J. V., Gibbons, R. D., Christoffel, K. K., Arend, R., Rosenbaum, D., Binns, H., Dawson, N., Sobel, H., & Isaacs, C. (1996). Prevalence rates and correlates of psychiatric disorders among preschool children. *Journal of the American Academy of Child and Adolescent Psychiatry, 35*(2), 204–214.

Lavigne, J. V., LeBailly, S. A., Hopkins, J., Gouze, K. R., & Binns, H. J. (2009). The prevalence of ADHD, ODD, depression and anxiety in a community sample of 4-year-olds. *Journal of Clinical Child and Adolescent Psychology, 38*, 315–328. https://doi.org/10.1080/15374410902851382

Lovejoy, M. C., Graczyk, P. A., O'Hare, E., & Neuman, G. (2000). Maternal depression and parenting behavior: A meta-analytic review. *Clinical Psychology Review, 20*(5), 561–592.

Maccoby, E. (2000). Parenting and its effects on chidlren: On reading and misreading behavior genetics. *Annual Review of Psychology, 51*, 1–27. https://doi.org/10.1146/annurev.psych.51.1.1

Madigan, S., Denault, A. A., Duschinsky, R., Bakermans-Kranenburg, M. J., Schuengel, C., Van IJzendoorn, M. H., Ly, A., Fearon, R. M. P., Eirich, R., & Vanhage, M. L. (2024). Maternal and paternal senstivity: Key determininants of child attachment security examined through a meta-analysis. *Psychological Bulletin., 150*, 839. https://doi.org/10.1037/bul0000433

Martins, C., & Gaffan, E. A. (2000). Effects of early maternal depression on patterns of infant-mother attachment: A meta-analytic investigation. *Journal of Child Psychology and Psychiatry, 4*(6), 737–746.

Masten, A. S. (2021). Resilience in developmental systems: Principles, pathways, and protecive processes in research and practice. In M. Ungar (Ed.), *Multisystemic resilience: Adpatation and transformation in contexts of change* (pp. 113–134). Oxford University Press. https://doi.org/10.1093/oso/9780190095888.003.0007

Maughan, A., Cicchetti, D., Toth, S. L., & Rogosch, F. A. (2007). Early-occurring maternal depression and maternal negativity in predicting young children's emotion regulation and socioemotional dificulties. *Journal of Abnormal Child Psychology, 35*(5), 685–703. https://doi.org/10.1007/s10802-007-9129-0

McCarty, C. A., McMahon, R. J., & Conduct Problems Prevention Research Group. (2003). Mediators of the relation between maternal depressive symptoms and child internalizing and disruptvie behavior disorders. *Journal of Family Psychology, 17*(4), 545–556. https://doi.org/10.1037/0893-3200.17.4.545

McClure, E. B., Brennan, P. A., Hammen, C., & LeBrocque, R. M. (2001). Parental anxiety disorders, child anxiety disorders, and the perceived parent-child relationship in an Australian high-risk sample. *Journal of Abnormal Child Psychology, 29*(1), 1–10. https://doi.org/10.1023/a1005260311313

McDaniel, M., & Lowenstein, C. (2013). Depression in low income mothers of young children. Are they getting the treatment they need? The Urban Institute. https://www.urban.org/sites/default/files/publication/23546/412804-Depression-in-Low-Income-Mothers-of-Young-Children-Are-They-Getting-the-Treatment-They-Need-

McKee, L., Colletti, C., Rakow, A., Jones, D. J., & Forehand, R. (2008). Parenting and child externalizing behaviors: Are the associations specific or diffuse? *Aggression and Violent Behavior, 13*, 201–215. https://doi.org/10.1016/j.avb.2008.03.005

McLeod, B. D., Weisz, J. R., & Wood, J. J. (2007a). Examining the association between parenting and childhood depression: A meta-analysis. *Clinical Psychology Review, 27*(8), 986–1003. https://doi.org/10.1016/j.cpr.2007.03.001

McLeod, B. D., Wood, J. J., & Weisz, J. R. (2007b). Examining the association between parenting and childhood anxiety: A meta-analysis. *Clinical Psychology Review, 27*(2), 155–172. https://doi.org/10.1016/j.cpr.2006.09/002

Moller, E. L., Nikolic, M., Majdandzic, M., & Bogels, S. M. (2016). Associations between maternal and paternal parenting behaviors, anxiety and its precursors in early childhood: A meta-analysis. *Clinical Psychology Review, 45*, 17–33. https://doi.org/10.1016/j.cpr.2016.03.002

Munson, J. A., MacMahon, R. J., & Spieker, S. J. (2001). Structure and variability in the developmental trajectory of children's externalizing problems: Impact of infant attachment, maternal depressive symptomatology, and child sex. *Development and Psychopathology, 13*(2), 277–296. https://doi.org/10.1017/s095457940100205x

Natsuaki, M. N., Shaw, D. S., Neiderhiser, J. M., Ganiban, J. M., Harold, G. T., Reiss, D., & Leve, L. D. (2014). Raised by depressed parents: Is it an environmental risk? *Clinical Child & Family Psychology Review, 17*(4), 357–367. https://doi.org/10.1007/s10567-014-0169-z

Negreiros, J., & Miller, L. D. (2014). The role of parenting in childhood anxiety: Etiological factors and treatment implications. *Clinical Psychology: Science and Practice, 21*, 3–17.

Panaccione, V. F., & Wahler, R. G. (1986). Child behavior, maternal depression, and social coeercion as factors in the quality of child care. *Journal of Abnormal Child Psychology, 14*(2), 263–278. https://doi.org/10.1007/BF00915445

Pinquart, M. (2017). Associations of parenting dimensions and styles with externalizing problems of children and adolescents: An updated meta-analysis. *Developmental Psychology, 53*(5), 873–932. https://doi.org/10.1037/dev0000295

Pinto, R., Soares, I., Carvalho-Correia, E., & Mesquita, A. (2015). Gene-environment interactions in psychopathology throughout early childhood. *Psychiatric Genetics, 25*(6), 223–233. https://doi.org/10.1097/YPG.0000000000000106

Reuben, J. D., Shaw, D. S., Neiderhiser, J. M., Natsuaki, M. N., Reiss, D., & Leve, L. D. (2016). Warm parenting and effortful control in toddlerhood: Independent and interactive predictors of school-age externalizing behavior. *Journal of Abnormal Child Psychology, 44*(6), 1083–1096. https://doi.org/10.1007/s10802-015-0096-6

Riley, A. W., Coiro, M. J., Broitman, M., Colantuoni, E., Hurley, K. M., Bandeen-Roche, K., & Miranda, J. (2009). Mental health of children of low-income depressed mothers: Influences of parenting, family environment, and raters. *Psychiatric Services, 60*, 329–336.

Rose, J. S., Roman, N., Mwaba, K., & Ismail, K. (2018). The relationship between parenting and internalizing behaviours of children: A systematic review. *Early Childhood Development and Care, 188*(10), 1468–1486. https://doi.org/10.1080/03004430.2016.1269762

Rothbart, M. K., & Ahadi, S. A. (1994). Temperament and the development of personality. *Journal of Abnormal Psychology, 103*(1), 55–66.

Rothbaum, F., & Weisz, J. R. (1994). Parental caregiving and child externalizing behavior in non-clinical samples: A meta-analysis. *Psychological Bulletin, 116*(1), 55–74. https://doi.org/10.1037/0033-2909-116.1.55

Sameroff, A. J. E. (2009). *The transactional model of development: How children and contexts shape each other*. https://doi.org/10.1037/11877-0000

Schreier, A., Wittchen, H. U., Hofler, M., & Lieb, R. (2008). Anxiety disorders in mothers and their children: Prospective longitudinal community study. *British Journal of Psychiatry, 192*(4), 308–309. https://doi.org/10.1192/bjp.bp.106.033589

Shaw, D. S., Gilliom, M., Ingoldsby, E. M., & Nagin, D. S. (2003). Trajectories leading to school-age conduct problems. *Developmental Psychology, 39*(2), 189.

Shaw, D. S., Connell, A., Dishion, T. J., Wilson, M. N., & Gardner, F. (2009). Improvements in maternal depression as a mediator of intervention effects on early childhood problem behavior. *Development and Psychopathology, 21*(2), 417–439. https://doi.org/10.1017/S0954579409000236

Sliwerski, A., Kossakowska, K., Jarecka, K., Switalska, J., & Bielawska-Batorowicz, E. (2020). The effect of maternal depression on infanct attachment: A systematic review. *International Journal of Environmental Research and Public Health, 17*(8), 2675. https://doi.org/10.3390/ijerph17082675

Sroufe, L. A. (2005). Attachment and development: A prospective, longitudinal study from birth to adulthood. *Attachment & Human Development, 7*(4), 349–367. https://doi.org/10.1080/14616730500365928

Sutherland, S., Brunwasser, S. M., Nestor, B. A., McCauley, E., Diamond, G., Schloredt, K., & Garber, J. (2019). Prospective relations between parents; depressive symptoms and children's attributional style. *Journal of Clinical Child and Adolescent Psychology, 50*(1), 77–87. https://doi.org/10.1080/15374416.2019.1567346

Thomas, A., Chess, S., & Birch, H. G. (1968). *Temperament and behavior disorders in children*. New York University Press.

van der Sluis, C., & van Steensel, F. J. A. (2015). Parenting and children's internalizing symptoms: How important are parents? *Journal of Child and Family Studies, 24*, 3652–3661. https://doi.org/10.1007/s10826-015-0174-y

Verissimo, M., Santos, A., Fernandes, C., Shin, N., & Vaughn, B. (2014). Associations between attachment security and social competence in preschool children. *Merrill-Palmer Quarterly, 60*(1), 80–79.

Waller, R., Gardner, F., Hyde, L. W., Shaw, D. S., Dishion, T. J., & Wilson, M. N. (2012). Do harsh and positive parenting predict parent reports of deceitful-callous behavior in early childhood? *Journal of Child Psychology and Psychiatry, 53*(9), 946–953. https://doi.org/10.1111/j.1469-7610.2012.02550.x

Weissman, M. M., Berry, O. O., Warner, V., Gameroff, M. J., Skipper, J., Talati, A., Pilowsky, D. J., & Wickramaratne, P. (2016). A 30-year study of 3 generations at high risk and low risk for depression. *JAMA Psychiatry, 73*(9), 970–977. https://doi.org/10.10001/jamapsychiatry.2016.1586

Whittenburg, P. N., Stern, J. A., Brett, B. E., Straske, M. D., & Cassidy, J. (2023). Maternal depressive symptoms and child behavior problems: Attachment security as a protective factor. *Development and Psychopathology, 35*(2), 678–688. https://doi.org/10.1017/S0954579421001802

Wiggins, J. L., Mitchell, C., Hyde, L. W., & Monk, C. S. (2015). Identifying early pathways of risk and resilience: The codevelopment of internalizing and externalizing symptoms and the role of harsh parenting. *Development and Psychopathology, 27*(4 Pt 1), 1295–1312. https://doi.org/10.1017/S0954579414001412

Wolkind, S. N., Zajicek, E., & Ghodsian, M. (1980). Continuities in maternal depression. *International Journal of Family Psychiatry, 1*, 167–181.

Yap, M. B. H., Pilkington, P. D., Ryan, S. M., & Jorm, A. F. (2014). Parental factors associated with depression and anxiety in young people: A systematic review and meta-analysis. *Journal of Affective Disorders, 156*, 8–23. https://doi.org/10.1016/jad.2013.11.007

Chapter 5
Child Risk Factors: Impact on Early Childhood Mental Health

In the previous two chapters, we discussed the influence of distal, contextual factors, specifically SES, family conflict, and stress (Chap. 3), and those factors operating at a more proximal level to the child, specifically parental depression and parenting (Chap. 4), on child outcome. In addition, children themselves have specific strengths and vulnerabilities that may lead to adaptive or maladaptive outcomes. Temperament, which is biologically based but influenced by environmental factors, and attachment security are among the most frequently studied of these child variables. Both temperament and attachment are associated with a range of child outcomes, including internalizing and externalizing disorders. Of course, there are genetic and biological vulnerabilities in addition to temperament that may also affect a child's development. A review of those factors is beyond the scope of this book, which focuses on psychosocial factors.

Temperament

History and Definition

The study of temperament as a risk factor for psychopathology originates with the Greek philosophers, going as far back as 460 B.C. Hippocrates (Bos, 2009), in a view counter to the prevailing notion that mental illness was caused by evil spirits, was the first to posit the "humoral theory" which held that an excess of one of the four humors (black bile, yellow bile, phlegm, and blood), led to mental illness. Later, Galen (Irwin, 1947) extended this theory, positing that an imbalance among the four humors resulted in specific temperaments that affected the individual's feelings and behavior. Although Galen's theory had no scientific basis, it did introduce the concept of temperament as an explanation for human behavior.

K. R. Gouze et al., *Early Childhood Psychopathology*,
https://doi.org/10.1007/978-3-031-68877-5_5

The modern era of child temperament research originated with the seminal New York Longitudinal Study of Thomas and colleagues (Thomas & Chess, 1977; Thomas et al., 1968) in the 1960s. These researchers defined temperament as differences in "behavioral style" and described nine categories of behavioral style, including activity level, persistence and attention span, threshold of responsiveness, mood, rhythmicity, approach vs. withdrawal, intensity of reaction, adaptability, and distractibility. Based on their observations of the children in the New York Longitudinal Study, Thomas and Chess (1977) further asserted that the "fit" between the child's temperament and various characteristics of their environment determined whether the child experienced an optimal or less than optimal developmental outcome. This notion of "goodness of fit" between what the child brought with them into the world and the world in which they found themselves was the first iteration of later developmental psychopathology theories regarding bidirectional and transactional effects.

Following the work of Thomas & Chess, Rothbart and colleagues made major advancements in the refinement of the concept of temperament and the role it played in child development (Rothbart & Ahadi, 1994; Rothbart et al., 2001; Rothbart & Derryberry, 1981; Rothbart & Rueda, 2005). These researchers developed a definition of temperament that included two major components: reactivity and regulation. Specifically, according to Rothbart and Derryberry, temperament refers to biologically based dispositions modulating the expressions of reactivity and regulation. Furthermore, they posited that, although biologically based, these tendencies develop and change transactionally over time in the context of the individual's interactions with the environment. This is consistent with the systems principle in developmental psychopathology described in Chapter One, which maintains that the child's characteristics (i.e., temperament) interact with multiple other systems, such as parenting and parent psychopathology, in determining outcomes.

To provide a means for studying temperament systematically, Rothbart and colleagues (Rothbart et al., 2001) used an empirically based approach to develop a questionnaire, the Child Behavior Questionnaire, to assess temperament in 3- to 7-year-old children. A factor analysis of this questionnaire led to a 3-factor solution that included three broad dimensions of temperament: Negative Affectivity (NA), Effortful Control (EC), and Extraversion/ Surgency (ES).

NA and EC are complementary, with NA referring to the reactive component and EC to the regulatory component of temperament. According to Rothbart and Rueda (Rothbart & Rueda, 2005), NA refers to individual differences in the tendency to respond to environmental stimuli with negative affect (including sadness, fear, anger, and frustration). EC is defined as the ability to modify a dominant response to perform a subdominant one according to situational demands using attentional, emotional, and behavioral regulation. NA and EC have consistently been identified as risk factors in the developmental psychopathology literature (see below), but research on the role of ES is relatively limited. Therefore, we included only NA and EC as the temperamental risk factors in developing the PACT multi-domain models.

NA and EC are interlinked since a highly reactive child will have more difficulty regulating themselves than one who is less reactive. Moreover, EC develops rapidly during the toddler and preschool years (Rothbart, 2012; Rothbart & Bates, 1998), which makes it likely that factors from other domains, such as parenting (see Chap. 4) will impact the child's development of EC. A considerable body of research has examined the role of these two aspects of temperament in increasing or decreasing the risk of psychopathology in young children.

NA: Direct Effects

Intuitively, it seems that highly reactive children would be more prone to develop symptoms of both internalizing and externalizing disorders. That is, it makes sense that high levels of fear and sadness predispose a child to symptoms of internalizing disorders, such as anxiety or depression, and that the concomitant anger and frustration would predispose them to symptoms of externalizing disorders, such as disruptive behavior and defiance.

The research literature on the role of NA in child psychopathology confirms these intuitive ideas by providing evidence that infants with higher levels of NA are, indeed, more likely to develop internalizing and externalizing problems over time (Eisenberg et al., 2009; Morales et al., 2015; Stifter et al., 2008). There also is evidence that clinic-referred children with internalizing and externalizing symptoms have higher levels of NA compared to an age- and gender-matched general population sample (Scheper et al., 2017). A recent study (Raines et al., 2023) revealed that NA contributes to the development of specific internalizing disorders such as anxiety and depression, as well as to a specific externalizing disorder, Oppositional Defiant Disorder in young children (Susa-Erdogan et al., 2017).

Effortful Control: Direct Effects

The EC component of temperament is subsumed under the broader construct of self-regulation and overlaps with two other aspects of self-regulation, specifically, emotion regulation (ER) and inhibitory control (IC). Thus, it is important to clarify the distinction between these three constructs before reviewing the role of EC as a risk factor. According to Eisenberg and colleagues (Eisenberg et al., 2004, 2007), ER refers to the processes used by the child to modify both their emotional feelings and their expression of emotions. EC involves a broader array of regulatory experiences than ER, with EC involved in the regulation of attention and behavior, as well as emotions.

Similarly, although IC and EC are sometimes used interchangeably, distinctions are also made between them. Inhibitory control, like EC, involves the inhibition of dominant responses to control behavior. While this is a core component of the temperamental factor of EC based on Rothbart and Ahadi's (Rothbart & Ahadi, 1994) conceptualization (e.g., inhibiting a first impulse to hit a peer and "use your words" instead), other researchers consider IC to be a specific skill within the broader construct of executive functioning (Nigg, 2017; Spinrad et al., 2007; Welsh & Peterson, 2014).

A wealth of evidence shows that poor EC is a risk factor for externalizing problems in young children. Eisenberg and her colleagues conducted a series of studies examining the relationship between EC in toddlers, preschoolers, and school-age children and externalizing disorders. These studies revealed that EC is a risk factor for the development of externalizing problems at each of these developmental periods (Eisenberg et al., 2009, 2010; Gartstein et al., 2012; Lengua, 2008; Olson et al., 2005).

There is also evidence that EC is a risk factor for internalizing problems, although the findings are inconsistent. Several studies show that poor effortful control is a risk factor for internalizing symptoms (Delgado et al., 2018; Nigg, 2006), but others do not (Dodd et al., 2017; Eisenberg et al., 2005, 2009).

NA and EC: Interactions and Child Psychopathology

To reiterate, NA and EC are clearly interrelated, and a highly reactive child will have more difficulty regulating themselves than one who is less reactive. Thus, a great deal of research attention has examined how these two aspects of temperament interact to increase or decrease the risk of psychopathology in young children. This research is notable for several findings. First, a combination of high NA and low EC increases the risk (Eisenberg et al., 2005, 2009; Lengua & Long, 2002), particularly for externalizing problems (Delgado et al., 2018; Raines et al., 2023).

Conversely, research also reveals that effortful control can serve a protective function in young children with high levels of reactivity. Specifically, Moran and colleagues (Moran et al., 2013) found that children with high levels of reactivity were less likely to develop externalizing symptoms if they also had high levels of EC. This led these investigators to conclude that greater NA may not be a risk factor for externalizing problems if the child also has well-developed regulatory abilities.

The impact of the interaction between these variables on the development of internalizing problems manifests differently than it does for externalizing disorders. Delgado and colleagues (Delgado et al., 2018) found that high levels of EC, combined with high levels of NA increased the risk of internalizing symptoms. Although, at first, this finding seems counter-intuitive, it is possible that some children who are highly reactive but also able to regulate their behavior internalize their negative feelings rather than acting them out in temper tantrums or other externalizing behavior. Over time, this internalization of negative feelings, perhaps in combination with other factors related to depression or anxiety, leads to internalizing problems.

The research examining interaction effects for EC and NA has yielded fruitful information about how they moderate each other to either increase (e.g., high NA and low EC increases risk) or decrease risk (e.g., high NA and high EC decreases risk) for different types of child psychopathology. However, less is known about the pathways whereby factors from other systems (e.g., caregiver depression, parenting) have an impact on child NA and EC, which, in turn, affect child outcome. Thus, in the PACT study we constructed the models of child psychopathology to shed light on these pathways.

NA and EC: Indirect Effects

As discussed in Chap. 4, NA and EC are also studied in research examining the mechanisms or mediators that help explain the associations between risk factors from other domains and child outcomes. This is particularly true for work in the areas of parent psychopathology and parenting. To briefly review these findings described in Chap. 4, there is evidence that parent depression and various aspects of parenting have indirect effects, via temperament, on both internalizing and externalizing symptoms in young children.

In addition to serving as a mediator in the relation between caregiver depression and parenting and child psychopathology, a study by Carrasco and colleagues (Carrasco et al., 2016) revealed that EC is a mechanism accounting for the relation between NA and externalizing problems in young (3- to 6-year-old) children.

Summary of Roles of NA and EC

A wealth of evidence attests to the fact that the reactive (NA) and regulatory (EC) aspects of temperament are risk factors for both internalizing and externalizing symptoms and disorders. Also, as described in Chap. 4, EC serves as a mechanism whereby effects of risk factors from other domains, such as caregiver psychopathology (i.e., depression) and parenting, influence child outcomes via their effects on temperament. Furthermore, there is evidence that the effects of NA on child outcomes are mediated by EC. However, there are still gaps in our knowledge about the complex ways in which these aspects of temperament lead to different outcomes because these studies examine only a limited number of domains and their effects on temperament. Thus, in general, these studies are not consistent with the basic developmental psychopathology principle described in Chap. 1, specifically that multiple systems at different levels work together to create hierarchically integrated and interactive processes leading to developmental outcomes.

In addition to parent depression and parenting, it is likely that contextual risk factors such as stress and conflict might influence child reactivity and regulation. For example, a child's initial high level of reactivity may decrease over time if the family environment becomes less stressful. Similarly, a child's ability to self-regulate is likely to increase in response to less family conflict, especially since young children learn self-regulation partially through co-regulation with adults. To overcome this limitation, in the PACT study we examined pathways from contextual risk factors, as well as from caregiver depression and parenting to NA and EC. This enabled us to shed light on how risk factors from multiple levels affect the reactive and regulatory aspects of child temperament, which, in turn, influence child outcome. We also included pathways from NA to EC to examine if EC served as a mediator in the relationship between NA and child outcome. Finally, in addition to examining the direct and indirect effects of NA and EC, we included another aspect of temperament, sensory regulation, as a risk factor.

Sensory Regulation

Sensory regulation (SR), also referred to as sensory sensitivity (Zeng et al., 2022), refers to the child's ability to detect, modulate, interpret, and organize reactions to sensory input. SR is an aspect of child functioning that has received very little attention in the developmental psychopathology literature. Indeed, to date, we have identified fewer than ten papers on SR and child psychopathology, except for the literature on its role in autism spectrum disorders. Historically, occupational therapy researchers, rather than mental health professionals, focused on the role of SR in a wide range of child problems. Indeed, an occupational therapist, Jean Ayres (1979), was the first to recognize the role of SR, which she referred to as sensory integration, in child functioning. Ayres theorized that deficits in sensory integration led to child difficulties in both socioemotional and cognitive functioning.

Today, there is no widespread agreement on the definition of SR or even which term to use when referring to this construct. Some researchers use the term sensory regulation, others use sensory processing, and still others use sensory sensitivity. There is also a question about whether SR should be conceptualized as a component of other aspects of temperament or instead functions as an important, distinct aspect of temperament. Thomas and Chess (1977) viewed sensory threshold as an important aspect of a reactive temperament. Rothbart and her colleagues (Rothbart et al., 2001) included two sensory scales in constructing the Child Behavior Questionnaire (CBQ), Perceptual Sensitivity and Discomfort, both of which were subsumed under other scales. Perceptual sensitivity was included as a subscale in the NA scale, and discomfort was included in the EC scale. To address the question of whether SR is an independent temperament factor we factor analyzed the PACT data to see whether the original factor structure of the CBQ held up in our sample or whether there was evidence that SR was actually a distinct temperamental factor. We found that the evidence did not support including SR within the NA and EC factors, but, instead, that it merits attention as a distinct component of temperament (Gouze et al., 2012). Thus, we examined SR as a distinct risk factor in constructing the PACT multi-domain models.

Sensory Regulation: Direct Effects

Although the evidence is sparse, there are a few studies showing that SR is, indeed, a risk factor for child psychopathology. Ben-Sasson and his colleagues (Ben-Sasson et al., 2010) conducted one of the first of these studies in 2010. This study revealed that poor SR was associated with both internalizing and externalizing symptoms in school-age children; however, this research still does not illuminate whether it is a risk factor in younger children.

Two recent studies shed light on the role of SR in internalizing problems in young children. Zeng and colleagues (Zeng et al., 2022) examined if parenting moderates the risk of preschool children with high sensory sensitivity and a specific gene associated with internalizing symptoms (the CRHBP gene) of developing internalizing disorders. This study yielded interesting findings illuminating the complex interactions between two child factors, genetic vulnerability and child sensory sensitivity, and a factor from another domain more distal to the child, parenting. Results revealed that preschoolers with the candidate gene and high sensory sensitivity developed fewer internalizing problems if they received more positive parenting. Furthermore, negative parenting increased the risk of internalizing problems in preschoolers with the candidate gene and high sensory sensitivity. There also is evidence (Carpenter et al., 2019) that sensory over-responsivity in preschoolers is a risk factor for anxiety in young school-age children. Although these studies suffer from the omitted variables problem, they highlight the importance of examining sensory regulation as a child characteristic that is likely to influence and be influenced by other child characteristics and factors from other systems more distal to the child.

Knowledge about the role of sensory over-responsivity in externalizing disorders in young children is lacking in the developmental psychopathology literature. Still, there is evidence from occupational therapy research that it is associated with these types of problems as well. Specifically, occupational therapy researchers have found a relationship between sensory sensitivity and Attention Deficit Hyperactivity Disorder (Dunn & Bennett, 2002; Mangeot et al., 2001; Parush et al., 2007).

Sensory Regulation: Indirect Effects

Because sensory threshold and the intensity of the child's response to sensory stimuli are usually considered aspects of temperamental EC or NA and are not studied as a distinct component of temperament, there are no studies that have examined whether it might serve as a mediator of contextual, parent, or parenting domains and either internalizing or externalizing symptoms. Now that there is evidence that SR is, indeed, a distinct aspect of temperament that serves as a risk factor for both internalizing and externalizing disorders, the next step is to examine the role of this variable in a multi-domain model, as we did in the PACT study. Including SR as a child risk factor in our multi-domain, longitudinal model enabled us to address gaps in the literature in two ways. First, it allowed us to determine if SR has direct effects on internalizing and externalizing disorders in young children. Second, it enabled us to examine if it serves as a mechanism whereby factors from other domains more distal to the child exert their influence, thus elucidating the complex effects among systems and various factors within different systems that lead to more negative outcomes.

Other Temperament Factors

Two aspects of temperament that have received considerable attention in the literature that we did not include in the PACT multi-domain models are behavioral inhibition and irritability.

Behavioral Inhibition (BI)

BI refers to the tendency to react to unfamiliar stimuli with heightened levels of arousal and withdrawal (Kagan, 1989). Across studies, higher levels of BI are associated with anxiety, particularly social anxiety, in preschoolers and young children (Biederman et al., 1995; Clauss & Blackford, 2012; Niditch & Varela, 2018). Studies examining whether BI is associated with a general internalizing symptoms factor, which includes symptoms of depression as well as anxiety, show mixed results, with Williams et al. (2009) reporting a significant association between BI and internalizing symptoms but Paulus et al. (2022) reporting a nonsignificant association of BI with emotional symptoms. In addition, Biederman et al. (1990) report that the association of BI with depression was not significant.

Evidence for the association of BI with symptoms of externalizing disorders is not supported, with Paulus et al. (2022) finding a nonsignificant relation between BI and conduct problems. Biederman et al. (1995) reported that BI was not significantly associated with ADHD. A recent meta-analysis (Kostyrka-Allchorne et al., 2020) found a small but significant association of BI with overall psychopathology. The relation of negative emotionality with overall psychopathology was stronger than that for BI. Kostyrka-Allchorne and colleagues concluded that negative emotionality has the potential to be a transdiagnostic risk factor for psychopathology, while BI may be a useful predictor for specific types of problems rather than a transdiagnostic risk factor. We elected not to include BI in the PACT multi-domain models because its effects seemed likely to be specific to anxiety, whereas our interest was in more generalizable risk factors that potentially impacted multiple outcomes in different ways.

Irritability

There is recent evidence that irritability, a sub-component of the broader temperamental component of NA is a risk factor for both internalizing and externalizing psychopathology in young children (Ali et al., 2023; Doughery et al., 2015). A problem in studying irritability as a risk factor for child psychopathology is that there is no universally accepted definition of this construct. For example, Zentner & Bates (2008) consider this dimension to be a low threshold to react with irritability/frustration. Rothbart and Posner (2006) define it as a tendency to react with irritability/anger to mild provocation. Another issue is that, in addition to being considered a sub-component of NA, DSM-5 includes irritability as a symptom of several psychiatric disorders in children (e.g., Major Depression, Oppositional Defiant Disorder), making it difficult to distinguish its role as a risk factor from that of its role as a symptom. Given these conceptual and definitional issues and the fact that irritability is a component of the broader construct of NA, we did not include temperamental irritability as a separate risk factor in the PACT multi-domain models.

Attachment Security

In addition to temperamental factors, attachment security is another child characteristic that has been examined in relation to both child adaptation and maladaptation. According to Bowlby (1969), who first developed attachment theory, infants are predisposed to develop a selective attachment to a primary caregiver, typically a parent, through repeated interactions with that caregiver. Bowlby initially defined infant attachment as an ethological motivational construct that regulates the balance of infant proximity seeking to a primary caregiver during danger and infant exploration during times of safety. A student of Bowlby, Mary Ainsworth and her colleagues (Ainsworth, 1969; Ainsworth et al., 1978) made a major contribution to attachment theory by developing a standardized procedure, the Strange Situation Paradigm, which consists of a series of separations and reunions with a primary caregiver, to study attachment. She then identified different patterns of attachment, a secure pattern, and two insecure patterns, based on the infant's pattern of behavior during reunions. This led to a program of research, the "Minnesota study" conducted by Alan Sroufe and his colleagues (Sroufe, 1988, 2005; Sroufe et al., 1999) at the University of Minnesota on the antecedents and consequences of different attachment patterns. This groundbreaking work confirmed that infant attachment organization was based on the infant's history of repeated interactions with the caregiver over the course of the first year of life and also revealed that insecure infant attachment was a risk factor for negative outcomes ranging from poorer cognitive skills to emotional and behavior disorders. Following this initial work, researchers focused on the role of attachment beyond infancy (i.e., in preschoolers). This research revealed that insecure attachment in preschoolers is also a risk factor for later psychopathology, including both externalizing (Denault et al., 2022; DeVito & Hopkins, 2001) and internalizing disorders (Madigan et al., 2013).

Remarkably, the Strange Situation Paradigm developed by Ainsworth is still considered the "gold standard" for assessing attachment in infants and toddlers. However, it has been modified slightly to be developmentally appropriate for preschool-age children. There is also consensus that another observational system, The Attachment Q-Sort, developed by Waters and Deane (Waters & Dean, 1985) is a valid measure of attachment security. In the PACT study, we decided to use the Attachment Q-Sort (Waters, 1987) to assess attachment because we conducted the research in the families' homes, which meant it was not feasible to use the Strange Situation paradigm, which has to be done in the lab.

Attachment Security: Direct Effects

Research in the 1990s and early 2000s focusing largely on mother-child attachment examined attachment as a risk factor for psychopathology. These studies revealed that insecure mother-child attachment greatly increases vulnerability for developing later internalizing and externalizing problems (Moss et al., 1996, 2006; Shamir-Essakow et al., 2005; Speltz et al., 1990, 1995). A more recent study examined these effects for both fathers and mothers (Dagan et al., 2021). Findings from this study reveal that secure attachment to both parents predicts the lowest risk for internalizing problems, and insecure attachment to either mothers or fathers increases risk. Insecure or disorganized attachment to one or both parents also increases the risk of externalizing problems. Disorganized attachment, a category first identified by Main & Solomon (1986), refers to infants who do not show an organized pattern of behavior in response to the separations and reunions during the Strange Situation Paradigm.

Unfortunately, a majority of previous attachment studies examined attachment as a single risk factor, or in combination with only a few other child variables, and, thus, probably overestimated its effects (i.e., due to the omitted variables problem). Perhaps the best estimate of the effects of attachment security comes from two meta-analyses. Fearon and colleagues (Fearon et al., 2010) conducted a meta-analysis of 69 longitudinal studies examining the relationship between attachment and later externalizing problems. This meta-analysis showed that insecure and disorganized attachment patterns significantly predicted externalizing problems, but the effects were modest. Another meta-analysis (Madigan et al., 2013) examining the role of attachment on internalizing problems also showed significant but modest effects. Again, this highlights the developmental psychopathology principle that child psychopathology arises from a complex interplay between multiple risk factors from different systems, not a single risk factor or a single system. Although a few studies examined the role of attachment security in combination with other factors, these studies typically included only a few other variables. Nevertheless, they add to knowledge about variables that increase risk in combination with attachment. Specifically, they reveal that, together, caregiver depression and insecure attachment increase risk (Keyser et al., 2017), as does less secure attachment with less sensitive (Sirois & Bernier, 2018) and more permissive parenting (DeVito & Hopkins, 2001).

Attachment Security: Indirect Effects

Studies designed to elucidate the mechanisms whereby attachment affects the development of internalizing and externalizing symptoms are less common than those examining the direct effects of attachment on outcomes. Stefan & Avram (2017) posited that since attachment and self-regulation are associated, child self-regulation is a likely mediator in this association. Results from their study showed that insecure attachment at age 6 led to poorer self-regulation, which, in turn, led to higher levels of internalizing problems at age 8. However, they did not find evidence that self-regulation serves as the mediator whereby insecure attachment leads to externalizing problems. Clearly, further research is needed to elucidate the processes that underlie the relationship between insecure attachment and psychopathology in early childhood. We included the direct and indirect effects of attachment security in the PACT multi-domain models of externalizing and internalizing symptoms to increase our understanding of how attachment influences child outcomes.

Clearly, insecure attachment is a risk factor for psychopathology in young children; it has both direct and indirect effects mediated, perhaps, by self-regulation. It is also indisputable that attachment alone does not lead to psychopathology, but, similar to child temperament, it operates within a complex set of influences among factors from different systems.

Summary

Among the child risk factors, there is a wealth of evidence that temperament, particularly NA and EC, and attachment security are risk factors for internalizing and externalizing symptoms in young children. It is also clear that the reactive and regulatory components of temperament interact with each other to either increase or decrease the risk for both types of symptoms. However, there are gaps in our knowledge about the processes whereby these variables impact child maladaptation. First, there is limited information about how factors from other systems such as SES, stress, family conflict, parent depression, and parenting affect NA and EC, which, in turn, have an impact on child outcomes. Second, the role of a particular aspect of temperament, sensory regulation, is largely unknown. Finally, little attention has been paid to how attachment security influences child outcomes.

Thus, it is difficult to derive conclusions from the different studies on these child risk factors to develop a comprehensive understanding of the various pathways whereby risk factors from other domains, specifically contextual, parent psychopathology, and parenting, influence these child risk factors, which, in turn, have an effect on an outcome. Most studies include only a few risk factors from one or two domains; for example, studies on the effects of temperament often include the roles of temperament and parenting but do not include the roles of stress and parental depression. Examining a limited range of domains and risk factors is not in keeping with the developmental psychopathology principle that child psychopathology arises from a complex interplay between multiple risk factors from different systems. Another issue, as previously noted, is that including only a few risk factors leads to the "omitted variables" problem, whereby the effects of a particular variable may be overestimated. To overcome these issues, in the PACT multi-domain models of risk factors for symptoms of internalizing (i.e., depression and anxiety) and externalizing (Oppositional Defiant Disorder and Attention Deficit Hyperactivity Disorder) disorders, we included the following risk factors: distal, contextual factors (SES, stress and family conflict); more proximal factors (parent depression and parenting); and factors inherent to the child (temperament and attachment). Moreover, we examined the pathways whereby factors from more distal domains affected more proximal ones, which, in turn, impacted child outcomes. The following chapter, Chap. 6, describes the methodology we used to construct the PACT multi-domain models of symptoms for two externalizing disorders (Oppositional Defiant Disorder and Attention Deficit Hyperactivity Disorder) and two internalizing disorders (depression and anxiety) and how we made decisions regarding the choice of measures to assess the risk variables in each domain.

References

Ainsworth, M. D. (1969). Object relations, dependency, and attachment: A theoretical review of the infant-mother relationship. *Child Development, 40*(4), 969–1025. https://doi.org/10.2307/1127008

Ainsworth, M. D. S., Blehar, M. C., Waters, E., & Wall, S. (1978). *Patterns of attachment: A psychological study of the strange situation*. Lawrence Erlbaum Associates.

Ali, O. M., Gabel, L. N., Stanton, K., Kaufman, E. A., Klein, D. N., & Hayden, E. P. (2023). Observational measures of early irritability predict children's psychopathology risk. *Development and Psychopathology, 334*, 1531–1543. https://doi.org/10.1017/S0954579421000183

Ayres, J. (1979). *Sensory integration and the child*. Western Psychological Services.

Ben-Sasson, A., Carter, A. S., & Briggs-Gowan, M. J. (2010). The development of sensory over-responsitivity from infancy to elementary school. *Journal of Abnormal Child Psychology, 38*(8), 1193–1202. https://doi.org/10.1007/s10802-010-9435-9

Biederman, J., Rosenbaum, J. F., Hirshfield, D. R., Faraone, S. V., Boldue, E. A., Gersten, M., Meminger, S. R., Kagan, J., Snidman, N., & Reznick, J. S. (1990). Psychiatric correlates of behavioral inhibition in young children of parents with and without psychiatric disorders. *Archives of General Psychiatry, 47*, 21–26. https://doi.org/10.1001/archpsyc.1990.01810130023004

Biederman, J., Rosenbaum, J. F., Chaloff, J., & Kagan, J. (1995). Behavioral inhibition as a risk factor for anxiety disorders. In J. S. March (Ed.), *Anxiety disorders in children and adolescents* (pp. 61–81). Guilford Press.

Bos, J. (2009). The rise and decline of character: Humoral psychology in ancient and early modern medical theory. *History of the Human Sciences, 22*(3), 29–50. https://doi.org/10.1177/0952695109104422

Bowlby, J. (1969). *Attachment and loss: Vol. 1. Attachment.* Basic Books.

Carpenter, K. L. H., Baranek, G. T., Copeland, W. E., Compton, S. N., Zucker, N., Dawson, G., & Egger, H. E. (2019). Sensory over-responsitivity: An early risk factor for anxiety and behavioral challenges in young children. *Journal of Abnormal Child Psychology, 47*(6), 1075–1088. https://doi.org/10.1007/s10802-018-0502-y

Carrasco, M. A., Holgado-Tello, F. P., Francisco, P., Delgado, B., & Gonzalez-Pena, P. (2016). Reactive temperament traits and behavioural problems in children: The mediating role of effortful control across sex and age. *European Journal of Developmental Psychology, 13*(2), 197–212. https://doi.org/10.1080/17405629.2015.1083852

Clauss, J., & Blackford, J. U. (2012). Behavioral inhibition and risk for developing social anxiety disorder: A meta-analytic study. *Journal of the American Academy of Child and Adolescent Psychiatry, 51*(10), 1066–1075. https://doi.org/10.1016/j.jaac.2012.08.002

Dagan, O., Schuengel, C., Verhage, M. L., van IJzendoorn, M. H., Sagi-Schwartz, A., Madigan, S., Duschinsky, R., Roisman, G. I., Bernard, K., Bakermans-Kranenburg, M., Bureau, J. F., Volling, B. L., Wong, M. S., Colonnesi, C., Brown, G. L., Eiden, R. D., Fearon, R. M. P., Oosterman, M., Aviezer, O., & Cummings, E. M. (2021). Configurations of mother-child and father-child attachment as predictors of internalizing and externalizing behavioral problems: An individual participant data (IPD) meta-analysis. *New Directions for Child and Adolescent Development, 2021*(180), 67–94. https://doi.org/10.1002/cad.20450

Delgado, B., Carrasco, M. A., Gonzelez-Pena, P., & Holgado-Tello, F. P. (2018). Temperament and behavioral problems in young children: The protective role of extraversion and effortful control. *Journal of Child and Family Studies, 27*(10), 3232–3240. https://doi.org/10.1007/s10826-018-1163-8

Denault, A. A., Bureau, J. F., & Yurkowski, K. (2022). Do child-father and child-mother preschool insecure attachment types predict the development of externalizing behaviors in boys and girls during middle childhood? *Development and Psychopathology, 13*(2), 215–231. https://doi.org/10.1017/S0954579401002024

DeVito, C., & Hopkins, J. (2001). Attachment, parenting, and marital dissatisfaction as predictors of disruptive behavior in preschoolers. *Developmental Psychopathology, 13*, 215–231.

Dodd, H. F., Hudson, J. L., & Rapee, R. M. (2017). Temperament in youth internalizing disorders. In D. McKay, J. S. Abramowitz, & E. A. Storch (Eds.), *Treatments for psychological problems and syndromes* (pp. 504–524). Wiley. https://doi.org/10.1002/9781118877142

Doughery, L. R., Smith, V. C., Bufferd, S. J., Kessel, E., Carlson, G. A., & Klein, D. N. (2015). Preschool irritability predicts child psychopathology, functional impairment, and service use at age nine. *Journal of Child Psychology and Psychiatry, 56*(9), 999–1007. https://doi.org/10.1111/jcpp.12403

Dunn, W., & Bennett, D. (2002). Patterns of sensory processing in children with attention deficit hyperactivity disorder. *Occupational Therapy Journal of Research, 22*, 4–15.

Eisenberg, N., Smith, C. L., Sadovsky, A., & Spinrad, T. L. (2004). Effortful control: Relations with emotion regulation, adjustment, and socialization in childhood. In R. F. Baumeister & K. D. Vohs (Eds.), *Handbook of self-regulation: Research, theory, and applications* (pp. 259–282). Guilford Press.

Eisenberg, N., Zhou, Q., Spinrad, T. L., Valiente, C., Fabes, R. A., & Liew, J. (2005). Relations among positive parenting, children's effortful control, and externalizing problems: A three-wave longitudinal study. *Child Development, 76*(5), 1055–1071. https://doi.org/10.1111/j.1467-8624.2005.00879.x

Eisenberg, N., Hofer, C., & Vaughan, J. (2007). Effortful control and its socioemotional consequences. In J. J. Gross (Ed.), *Handbook of emotion regulation* (pp. 287–306). Guilfor Press.

Eisenberg, N., Valiente, C., Spinrad, T. L., Cumberland, A., Liew, J., Reiser, M., Zhou, Q., & Losoya, S. H. (2009). Longitudinal relations of children's effortful control, impulsivity, and negative emotionality to their externalizing, internalizing, and co-occurring behavior problems. *Developmental Psychology, 45*, 988–1008. https://doi.org/10.1037/a0016213

Eisenberg, N., Spinrad, T. L., Eggum, N. D., Silva, K. M., Reiser, M., Hofer, C., Smith, C. L., Gaertner, B. M., Kupfer, A., Popp, T., & Michalik, N. (2010). Relations among maternal socialization, effortful control, and maladjustment in early childhood. *Development and Psychopathology, 22*(3), 507–525. https://doi.org/10.1017/S0954579410000246

Fearon, R. P., Bakermans-Kranenburg, M. J., van IJzendoorn, M. H., Lapsley, A. M., & Roisman, G. I. (2010). The significance of insecure attachment and disorganization in the development of children's externalizing behavior: A meta-analysis. *Child Development, 81*(2), 435–456. https://doi.org/10.1111/j.1467-8624.2009.01405.x

Gartstein, M. A., Putnam, S. P., & Rothbart, M. K. (2012). Etiology of preschool behavior problems: Contributions of temperament attributes in early childhood. *Infant Mental Health Journal, 33*(2), 197–211. https://doi.org/10.1002/imhj.21312

Gouze, K. R., Lavigne, J. V., Hopkins, J., Bryant, F. B., & LeBailly, S. A. (2012). The relationship between temperamental negative affect, effortful control, and sensory regulation: A new look. *Infant Mental Health Journal, 33*(6), 620–632. https://doi.org/10.1002/imhj.21363

Irwin, J. R. (1947). Galen on the temperaments. *Journal of General Psychology, 36*, 45–64.

Kagan, J. (1989). The concept of behavioral inhibition to the unfamiliar. In J. S. Reznick (Ed.), *Perspectives on behavioral inhibition* (pp. 1–23). University of Chicago Press.

Keyser, D., Ahn, H., & Unick, J. (2017). Predictors of behavioral problems in young children 3 to 9 yers old: The role of maternal and child factors. *Child and Youth Services Revew, 82*, 149–155. https://doi.org/10.1016/j.childyouth.2017.90.018

Kostyrka-Allchorne, K., Wass, S. V., & Sonuga-Barke, E. J. S. (2020). Research review: Do parent ratings of infant negative emotionality and self-regulation predict psychopathology in child and adolescence? A systematic review and meta-analysis of prospective longitudinal studies. *Journal of Child Psychology and Psychiatry, 61*(4), 401–416. https://doi.org/10.1111/jcpp.13144

Lengua, L. J. (2008). Anxiousness, frustration, and effortful control as moderators of the relation between parenting and adjustment in middle-childhood. *Social Development, 17*(3), 554–577. https://doi.org/10.1111/j.1467-9507.2007.438.x

Lengua, L. J., & Long, A. C. (2002). The role of emotionality and self-regulation in the appraisal-coping process: Tests of direct and moderating effects. *Applied Developmental Psychology, 23*, 471–493.

Madigan, S., Atkinson, L., Laurin, L., & Benoit, D. (2013). Attachment and internalizing behavior in early childhood: A meta-analysis. *Development and Psychopathology, 49*, 672. https://doi.org/10.1037/a0028793

Main, M., & Solomon, J. (1986). Discovery of an insecure-disorganized/disoriented attachment pattern. In T. B. Brazelton (Ed.), *Affective development in infancy* (pp. 95–124). Ablex Publishing Corporation.

Mangeot, S. D., Miller, I. J., McIntosh, D. N., McGrath-Clarke, J., Simon, J., Hagerman, R. J., & Goldson, E. (2001). Sensory modulation dysfunction in children with attention-deficit-hyperactivity disorder. *Development Medicine and Child Neurology, 43*(6), 399–406. https://doi.org/10.1017/S001262201000743

Morales, S., Beekman, C., Blandon, A. Y., Stifter, C. A., & Buss, K. A. (2015). Temperament and the development of personality. *Developmental Psychology, 57*(1), 105–119. https://doi.org/10.1002/dev.21267

Moran, L. R., Lengua, L. J., & Zaleswski, M. (2013). The interaction between negative emotionality and effortful control in early social-emotional development. *Social Development, 22*(2), 340–362. https://doi.org/10.1111/sode.12025

Moss, E., Parent, S., Gosselin, C., Rousseau, D., & St-Laurent, D. (1996). Attachment and teacher-reported behavior problems during the preschool and early school-age period. *Development and Psychopathology, 8*(3), 511–525. https://doi.org/10.1017/S0954579400007240

Moss, E., Smolla, N., Cyr, D., Dubois-Comtois, K., Mazzarello, T., & Berthiaume, C. (2006). Attachment and behavior problems in middle childhood as reported by adult and child informants. *Development and Psychopathology, 8*(2), 425–444. https://doi.org/10.1017/S0954579406060238S

Niditch, L. A., & Varela, R. E. (2018). A longitudinal study of inhibited temperament, effortful control, gender, and anxiety in early chidlhood. *Child & Youth Care Forum, 47*(4), 463–479. https://doi.org/10.1007/s10566-018-9447-0

Nigg, J. T. (2006). Temperament and developmental psychopathology. *Journal of Child Psychology and Psychiatry, 47*, 395–422. https://doi.org/10.1111/j.1469-7610.2006.01612.x

Nigg, J. T. (2017). Annual research review: On the relations among self-regulation, self-control, executive functioning, efforful control, cognitive control, impulsivity, risk-taking, and inhibition for developmental psychopathology. *Journal of Child Psychology and Psychiatry, 58*(4), 361–383. https://doi.org/10.1111/jcpp12675

Olson, S. L., Sameroff, A. J., Kerr, D. C. R., Lopez, N. L., & Wellman, H. M. (2005). Developmental foundations of externalizing problems in young children: The role of effortful control. *Development and Psychopathology, 17*, 25–45.

Parush, S., Sohmer, H., Steinberg, A., & Kaitz, M. (2007). Somatosensory function in boys with ADHD and tactile defensiveness. *Physiology and Behavior, 90*(4), 553–558.

Paulus, F. W., Mohler, E., Festag, L., & Joas, J. (2022). Preschool temperament as a factor of risk and protection for later childhood psychopathology. *Frontiers in Psychiatry, 13*(1–12), 803959. https://doi.org/10.3389/fpsyt2022.803969

Raines, E. M., Viana, A. G., Trent, E. S., Conroy, H. E., Silva, K. M., Avolensky, M. J., & Storch, E. A. (2023). Effortful control moderates the relation between negative emotionality and child anxiety and depressive symptom severity in children with anxiety disorders. *Child Psychiatry and Human Development, 54*(1), 17–25. https://doi.org/10.1007/s10578-021-01218-2

Rothbart, M. K. (2012). Advances in temperament: History, concepts, and measures. In M. Zentner & R. L. Shiner (Eds.), *Handbook of temperament* (pp. 3–20). Guilford Press.

Rothbart, M. K., & Ahadi, S. A. (1994). Temperament and the development of personality. *Journal of Abnormal Psychology, 103*(1), 55–66.

Rothbart, M. K., & Bates, J. E. (1998). Temperament. In W. Damon & N. Eisenberg (Eds.), *Handbook of child psychology: Social, emotional, and personality development* (Vol. 3, pp. 105–176). Wiley.

Rothbart, M. K., & Derryberry, D. (1981). Development of individual differences in temperament. In M. E. Lamb & A. L. Brown (Eds.), *Advances in developmental psychology* (Vol. 1, pp. 37–86). Erlbaum.

Rothbart, M. K., & Posner, M. I. (2006). Temperament, attention, and developmental psychopathology. In D. Cicchetti & D. J. Cohen (Eds.), *Developmental psychopathology: Developmental neuroscience* (Vol. 2, 2nd ed., pp. 465–501).

Rothbart, M. K., & Rueda, M. R. (2005). The development of effortful control. In U. Mayr (Ed.), *Developing individuality in the human brain: A tribute to Michael I. Posner* (pp. 167–188). American Psychological Association. https://doi.org/10.1037/11108-009

Rothbart, M. K., Ahadi, S. A., Hershey, K. L., & Fisher, P. (2001). Investigations of temperament at three to seven years: The Children's behavior questionnaire. *Child Development, 72*(5), 1394–1408.

Scheper, F. Y., Majdanezic, M., van de Ven, P. M., Jansen, L. M. C., Doreleijers, T. A. H., Schuengel, C., & de Vries, A. L. D. (2017). Temperament traits and psychopathology in young clinically referred children compared to a general population sample. *Child Psychiatry and Human Development, 48*(6), 841–850. https://doi.org/10.1007/s10578-016-0708-6

Shamir-Essakow, G., Ungerer, J. A., & Rapee, R. M. (2005). Attachment, behavioral inhibition, and anxiety in preschool children. *Journal of Abnormal Child Psychology, 33*(2), 131–143. https://doi.org/10.1007/s10802-005-1822-2

Sirois, M. S., & Bernier, A. (2018). Mother-child relationships and children's psychosocial functioning: The specific roles of attachment security and maternal behavior. *Parenting: Science and Practice, 18*(3), 172–189. https://doi.org/10.1080/15295192.2018.1465305
Speltz, M. L., Greenberg, M. T., & DeKlyen, X. (1990). Attachment in preschoolers with disruptive behavior: A comparison of clinic-referred and nonproblem children. *Development and Psychopathology, 2*, 31–46.
Speltz, M. L., DeKlyen, M., Greenberg, M. T., & Dryden, M. (1995). Clinic referral for oppositional defiant disorder: Relative significance of attachment and behavioral variables. *Journal of Abnormal Child Psychology, 23*(4), 487–507. https://doi.org/10.1007/BF01447210
Spinrad, T. L., Eisenberg, N., Gaertner, B., Popp, T., Smith, C. L., Kupfer, A., Greving, K., Liew, J., & Hofer, C. (2007). Relations of maternal socialization and toddlers' effortful control to children's adjustment and social competence. *Developmental Psychology, 43*, 1170. https://doi.org/10.1037/0012-1649.43.5.1170
Sroufe, L. A. (1988). The role of infant-caregive attachment i development. In J. Belsky & T. Nezworski (Eds.), *Clinical implications of attachment* (pp. 18–38). Lawrence Erlbaum Associates.
Sroufe, L. A. (2005). Attachment and development: A prospective, longitudinal study from birth to adulthood. *Attachment & Human Development, 7*(4), 349–367. https://doi.org/10.1080/14616730500365928
Sroufe, L. A., Carlson, E. A., Levy, A. K., & Egeland, B. (1999). Implications of attachment theory for developmental psychopathology. *Development and Psychopathology, 11*(1), 1–13. https://doi.org/10.1017/S0954579499001923
Stefan, C. A., & Avram, J. (2017). Investigating direct and indirect effects of attachment on internalizing and externalizing problems through emotion regulation in a cross-sectional study. *Journal of Child and Family Studies, 26*(8), 2311–2323. https://doi.org/10.1007/s10826-017-0723-7
Stifter, C. A., Putnam, S., & Jahromi, L. (2008). Exuberant and inhbited toddlers: Stability of temperament and risk for problem behavior. *Development and Psychopathology, 20*(2), 401–421. https://doi.org/10.1017/S0954579408000199
Susa-Erdogan, G., Benga, O., & Marina, C. (2017). Attentional orientation patterns toward emotional faces and temperamental correlates of preschool oppositional defiant problems: The moderating role of callous-unemotional traits and anxiety symptoms. *Frontiers in Psychiatry, 8*(7), 1–15. https://doi.org/10.3389/fpsyg2017.01928
Thomas, A., & Chess, S. (1977). *Temperament and development*. Brunner/Mazel.
Thomas, A., Chess, S., & Birch, H. G. (1968). *Temperament and behavior disorders in children*. New York University Press.
Waters, E. (1987). *Attachment Q-set (version 3.0)*. State University of New York at Stony Brook.
Waters, E., & Dean, K. E. (1985). Defining and assessing individual differences in attachment relationships: Q-methodology and the organization of behavior in infancy and early childhood. *Monographs of the Society for Research in Child Development, 50*(1–2), 41–65. https://doi.org/10.2307/3333826
Welsh, M., & Peterson, E. (2014). Issues in the conceptualization and assessment of hot executive functions in childhood. *Journal of the International Neuropsychological Society, 20*(2), 152–156. https://doi.org/10.1017/S1355617713001379
Williams, L. R., Degnan, K. A., Perez-Edgar, K. E., Henderson, H. A., Rubin, K. H., Pine, D. S., Steinberg, L., & Fox, N. A. (2009). Impact of behavioral inhibition and parenting style on internalizing and externalizing problems from early childhood through adolescence. *Journal of Abnormal Child Psychology, 37*(8), 1063–1075. https://doi.org/10.2307/1127008
Zeng, S., Liu, C., & Wang, Z. (2022). The effect of crhbp rs10062367 polymorphism and parenting styles on internalizing problems in preschoolers: The moderating effect of sensory processing sensitivity. *Child Psychiatry and Human Development, 55*, 644. https://doi.org/10.1007/s10578-022-01418-4
Zentner, M., & Bates, J. E. (2008). Child temperament: An integrative review of concepts. *European Journal of Developmental Science, 2*, 7–37. https://doi.org/10.3233/DEV-2008-21203

Chapter 6
The Challenges of Study Design: Considerations in Developing the PACT Research Program

Designing a theoretically and empirically grounded study to examine the risk factors contributing to the development of early childhood psychopathology required that we address several fundamental issues. Two key design choices were obvious. First, given our interest in studying the development of psychopathology in young children, a longitudinal design was essential. Second, examining the mechanisms by which risk factors were intertwined and associated with different symptom types required that we develop a complex, multi-domain model that enabled us to explore the links between a number of distal and proximal risk factors and the pathways whereby they influenced child outcome. Other decisions, however, were less obvious. As in all research, the final decisions on conducting the study involved a blend of decisions based on science and practical issues, not the least of which was money.

In responding to the National Institute of Mental Health (NIMH) request for proposals to address the development of Oppositional Defiant Disorder and comorbid depression in young children, we were committed to designing a study that was theoretically robust, adhered to the tenets of developmental psychopathology, and focused on a longitudinal understanding of the preschool and early childhood period. The advantages of conducting research from within a theoretical framework are well-known. Scientific fields with well-developed theories, like physics, tend to advance more rapidly than fields lacking such theories. Further, theories may point toward phenomena that need to be understood but have not yet been recognized in research. In addition, theory-driven research is less likely to result in chance findings. The decision of our research group to focus on risk factors during the preschool period emerged from a strong belief in the importance of these early foundational experiences and a commitment to designing a study with clinical utility. Choices regarding distal and proximal risk factors and child outcomes were guided by the theoretical underpinnings and empirical findings reviewed in Chaps. 3, 4, and 5 of this book. Furthermore, in addition to understanding developmental risk factors, we aimed to gather information that could be useful in guiding the development of early prevention and intervention programs.

K. R. Gouze et al., *Early Childhood Psychopathology*,
https://doi.org/10.1007/978-3-031-68877-5_6

Choosing a Target Sample

Race/Ethnicity (What's the Optimal Diversity Mix?)

An early decision involved choosing the target population of children from whom to draw the sample. Readers are likely aware that a substantial number of studies in the fields of developmental psychology and developmental psychopathology have included samples primarily consisting of White, middle-class children. There also have been some valuable studies focusing on children from historically marginalized and under-resourced communities (Shaw et al., 1997, 2003). Furthermore, many studies of psychopathology are drawn from clinical rather than community samples. Our goal was to obtain a reasonably diverse, community-based sample of children and their parents. Lacking a gold standard on what is "reasonable," we decided to target recruiting a sample approximating that of the population of the county where this study would be conducted, Cook County, Illinois.

At the time the study began, the racial/ethnic distribution of Cook County was 45.4% White non-Latino; 22.2% Latino; 26.4% Black, and 5.9% "other"(United States Census Bureau, 2007). This is substantially the same as it is for Cook County in the most recent (2020) United States census: 42.5% White non-Latino; 25.2% Latino; 23.2% African American, 7.1% Asian American, 0.1% Native American, and 1.9% "other"(Bestneighborhood.org/race-in-cook-county-il. In 2020, Cook County was slightly more diverse than the United States as a whole (census.gov/library/stories/2021/2020-united-states-population-more-racially-ethnically-diverse-than-2010.html), with Cook County including a somewhat larger White (57.8% for the US versus 42.5% for Cook County), a slightly larger Black/African American (12.1% for the US versus 23.2% for Cook County) and a slightly smaller Latino (18.7% for the US versus 25.2% for Cook County) population.

Age at Entry and Longitudinal Scope (How Old to Start? How Long to Study?)

We also needed to make decisions about the age at which participating children would be enrolled and for how long we would follow them. Obviously, given the focus on early childhood, we wanted to begin with the earliest age possible, allowing us to collect the type of information we were interested in. Although starting in infancy or as early in the toddler years as possible made sense from a developmental perspective, practical considerations regarding data collection due to our desire to follow children until school entry limited our choice of beginning age given the number of years we had to complete the study based on our funding.

The ceiling on the length of the interval during which the children could be followed was set by the maximum length of 5 years that NIMH will fund a project. Given the need to recruit staff, start data collection, and have a wind-down period in the end to wrap up data entry and begin data analyses, we estimated that there would be a maximum of about 4 years in which recruitment and data collection could occur.

A four-year data collection window raises the possibility that four waves of data could be collected annually if the entire sample could be recruited and evaluated in a single year. Given the size of the staff needed to collect these data and the sample size needed, however, the recruitment window needed to be extended for approximately 18–20 months. This limited the number of waves of data collection to three.

With three annual waves of data collection possible, if the age at study entry was age 3 years, annual data collection would occur at ages 3, 4, and 5 years. As a result, virtually all children would be in kindergarten at the end of the study period, and most would not have entered the elementary school grades at all. That transition from preschool to elementary school is an important developmental transition point, with children having made important advances in cognition and language and taking on increasing academic challenges as they enter grade one. Starting study enrollment with children at age 4 years, followed by an annual assessment at ages 5 and 6, allowed us to examine longitudinal changes in the impact of the multi-domain risk factors throughout that transition process across three key developmental periods: preschool, kindergarten, and elementary school entry. Thus, we settled on age 4 as the age of study eligibility.

Why annual assessments? Although we refer to annual assessments above, there would have been advantages to shorter intervals between assessments, possibly semi-annually, or even quarterly. This would have allowed for a more fine-grained analysis of developmental changes. We settled on annual evaluations rather than more frequent ones for two reasons. First, the costs involved in adding assessments were prohibitive. Second, assessing the multi-domain risk factors through a combination of questionnaires, observations of family interactions and child behavior, and child tasks was very time-consuming. Each assessment required between 2 and 2.5 h of time from each parent/child combination. Although parents and children often found the visits interesting and enjoyable, it did not seem reasonable to increase the participant burden and request more time from each family.

From Where to Recruit?

There were significant challenges in finding a way to access 4-year-old children with the degree of racial/ethnic diversity we wanted to include. Since a census-style canvassing process would have been too expensive, we decided that the optimal way to access a large number of preschool children would be through preschools. In terms of the number of enrolled children in Chicago and Cook County, the largest single group of children in preschool are those preschoolers enrolled in the Chicago Public School (CPS) system. Furthermore, CPS preschools provide access to many children whose parents self-identify as people of color. The racial-ethnic composition of CPS schools when the study was conducted was 51% African American,

36% Latino, and 3% parent-identified as Other. (www.cps.edu/school/data). The limitation to enrolling exclusively through the CPS system is that it was not possible to recruit a representative sample of White children: only 10% of the children in CPS were parent-identified as White, non-Latino. We needed to recruit in a broader range of settings to meet the targets.

The challenges of recruiting through the preschools of other school systems placed that option beyond our reach. Cook County is home to over five million people, and it includes approximately 135 cities, towns, and villages, most of which include preschools in their public school systems and often multiple private preschools. It simply was not possible to devise a sampling strategy that we would need to develop relationships with school personnel to enroll children from across preschools in the county to achieve the racial/ethnic diversity targets we sought.

Fortunately, there is another place where parents bring their preschool children-pediatric practices. Because our research team had a track record of almost 20 years of research on psychological aspects of delivering pediatric care, we had developed good working relations with city and suburban pediatric practices enrolled in our hospital's Pediatric Practice Research Group (PPRG) (Christoffel et al., 1988), a consortium of local practices interested in primary care research. The PPRG practices were recruited from across the county and gave us access to children not attending preschools. Thus, we decided to select the PPRG as our second recruitment site. The combination of CPS preschools and pediatric practices enabled us to closely approximate our targeted racial/ethnic sample composition.

Parent Participation (Mothers Only Versus Both Parents?)

As noted above, using convenience samples too often leads to obtaining predominantly White samples, thus limiting the generalizability of findings. Similarly, developmental studies in which data collection is limited to mothers prevent us from gathering information on fathers' important influence on their child's development. Unfortunately, there is no easy solution to this problem, with each possible choice either limiting the generalizability of results or leading to other issues. First, requiring the participation of both parents limits generalizability: in the United States, almost a quarter (23%) of children live in a single-parent home (www.pewresearch.org/fact-tank/2019/12/12/u-s-children-more-liekly-than-children-in-other-countries-to-live-with-just-one-parent/) and gaining access to non-resident parents is extremely difficult. Further, in families where mothers worked at home, and fathers worked in places of employment, scheduling visits when both parents were available was a challenge, especially given that early evening visits were not possible due to the early bedtimes of preschoolers. We elected to try an approach in which we collected data from the at-home daytime parent, either mothers or fathers, and supplemented this with obtaining questionnaire-based measures from the working parent who was not at home during the day whenever possible. Soon, however, we learned that it was impossible to collect enough data from the parent working outside of the home, of any gender, to gather a sample of the size needed to properly analyze their data. As a result, we settled on a sample in which we included only the work-at-home parent of any gender, resulting in a mix of participants, mainly mothers and a small number of fathers.

Participants: The Final Longitudinal Sample

In the final sample of children recruited at age 4 there were 796 children and their parents (the need for this sample size is discussed below) who were recruited from 23 primary care pediatric clinics in Cook County and 13 Chicago Public School preschool programs. To contain recruitment costs, we worked with staff in the CPS early childhood education program to identify schools with large enrollments located in various racial/ethnic communities.

In addition to requiring that children be age 4 years at enrollment, there were a few additional inclusion criteria. Because of limitations in our ability to translate measures, all eligible children needed to be English- or Spanish-speaking. To guarantee that the participating parent knew the child's behavior well, the child was required to have lived with that parent for at least 6 months. In addition, the tasks the child was required to do necessitated age-appropriate receptive language skills, so we required that the child obtain a standard score on the Peabody Picture Vocabulary Test greater than 70 (PPVT) (Dunn & Dunn, 1997). Finally, due to the task demands for verbal, intellectual, and certain social interaction skills, the child could not meet criteria for Autism Spectrum Disorder.

When approached at the schools and offices at the initial contact with the Parents and Children Together (PACT) study's research assistants, 1738 families expressed an interest in learning more about the study. Subsequently, they were contacted by telephone and the details of study participation were described to them. From that group, 827 (47.5%) families agreed to participate and completed the age 4 assessment at their home. There were 31families who were ineligible based on the other study inclusion rules, mostly because of scores below the needed PPVT cutoff. This resulted in a final sample of 796.

Of the 796 4-year-olds, there was a near-equal distribution of boys and girls (391 boys, 49.1%). The mean age of the sample was 4.44 years. Our efforts to obtain a racially/ethnically diverse sample were successful, with the final sample consisting of approximately 54% White and 46% children of color. Our efforts to match the racial/ethnic diversity of Cook County were also reasonably successful. The final age 4 sample was 433 (54.4%) White, non-Latino; 133 (16.7%) Black; 162 (20.4%) Latino; 19 (2.4%) Asian; 35 (4.4%) and multi-racial or "Other." Race/ethnicity was not reported by 14 (1.8%) parents. Compared to Cook County census data (United States Census Bureau, 2007), the study sample had slightly more White non-Hispanic children than the county (Cook County, 45.4% White), and was similar to that of the county for Hispanic/Latino children (Cook County, 22.2%) and Asian children (Cook County 5.5%). There were, however, somewhat fewer African

American children (Cook County, 26.4%) in the final sample. With "other"included in the non-White category, the overall percentage of children of color in the sample (45.6%) was slightly lower than in the county (54.1%).

In addition, all social classes were included in the final sample, with 303 (38.1%) children in the highest class (Class I), 290 (36.4%) in Class II, 79 (9.9%) in Class III, 63 (7.9%) in Class IV, and 61 (7.7%) in Class V (Hollingshead, 1975). As happens frequently, the study skews toward having more parents from higher social classes agreeing to participate.

The second evaluation was conducted when the children were age 5, and the third time when they were age 6, with a few having recently turned 7 (referred to as the age 6 wave in our reports). Overall, a total of 626 children and families (78.6%) participated in all three waves of data collection. We examined demographic differences in the age 4 and age 6 samples. The families who completed all three waves differed from those who did not with respect to (a) race, with a greater proportion of dropouts among non-White participants χ^2 (5, N (796) = 77.7, p = 0.001; (b) lower SES groups χ^2 (4, N = (796) = 69.61, p = 0.001; and (c) younger children, 25 days younger at study entry, t(773) = 2.41, p = 0.02. As discussed in the data analysis section below, missing data were imputed, so the final sample analyzed at all 3 waves was 796.

Measures

We also had to make decisions about the approach to take to measure the risk factors and symptom types. These decisions involved two fundamental issues: (a) who should serve as raters if we used raters to assess the child's, temperament, behavior, and symptoms of psychopathology; and (b) should we use observer ratings, laboratory measures, or both to examine the child's temperament, behavior, and symptoms?

Raters: Who Should Rate the Child's Characteristics?

Researchers in developmental psychopathology have long been aware that there can be considerable differences in the way children's behavior is viewed by different observers. A review of that literature was published by Achenbach et al. (1987) over 35 years ago. That review showed there were only low to moderate correlations across different types of raters, including parents, teachers, and independent observer ratings, as well as differences within categories of raters, e.g., between two parents or two observers. In recent years, increased attention has been devoted to understanding what is involved in rater differences (De Los Reyes & Kazdin, 2005), but there is still no clear way to resolve discrepancies between raters.

Parent Ratings of At-Home Behavior Versus Laboratory Tasks

Along with rater differences, there can be differences in results when different methods are used for evaluating a child's temperament, behavior, or symptoms. In developmental psychopathology, the most common method differences are found between ratings from someone familiar with the child, such as a parent or teacher, and independent observer ratings of the child obtained when they are engaged in a specific, structured, "laboratory"task or set of tasks. The core problem mirrors what occurs when choosing which type of rater to employ. The correlations between ratings obtained from raters familiar with the child in their day-to-day environment, such as parents or teachers, and those obtained by independent observers in laboratory-based situations are relatively low, signaling little agreement between the two (Lo et al., 2015). There are proponents of both approaches, as well as counterarguments for each strategy.

Parent Ratings: Pros and Cons

There is a practical argument supporting the use of parent ratings. Parent ratings are more economical, making it easier to collect information in large-scale studies (Lo et al., 2015). A second argument is of greater importance from a scientific perspective. Because the parent sees the child in multiple, naturally occurring settings, and the parent ratings are likely to involve the parent's generalization about the child's behavior across those settings, their ratings will be more likely to represent the child's "real-world" behavior, whereas the child's behavior in a controlled measurement situation (the "laboratory") may be less typical and subject to specific circumstances (e.g., the child did not sleep well the night before) or is anxious in this new setting.

Critics of the parent report approach argue that parent ratings may be influenced or biased by parent characteristics. This is due to the fact that studies have shown a statistically significant association between maternal depression and anxiety and parental or family stress and ratings of child temperamental characteristics (Lo et al., 2015).

The role that a parent's depression might play in their perception of a child's characteristics (temperament, cognition, symptoms, etc.) has attracted the most attention and is often discussed under the rubric of the "depression-distortion hypothesis" (Chi & Hinshaw, 2002). Presently, it is perhaps most accurate to say that the evidence for this hypothesis is mixed; there are a number of studies showing that parental depression promotes a negative bias on the part of the mothers (fathers are studied much less often) (Liskola et al., 2021), and this is associated with the parent's perception of the child's emotional problems. There are, however, a number of other studies that do not fully support this finding; critics have noted that parent ratings are correlated with those of other raters and that methodological problems have affected the results of a number of the depression-distortion studies, thereby weakening any conclusions that can be drawn (Richters, 1992).

Laboratory Measures: Pros and Cons

Arguments supporting laboratory tasks (Lo et al., 2015) include the ability to standardize those tasks in a way that is impossible with parent reports and the possibility that laboratory tasks can be structured in such a way as to elicit low-frequency behaviors that are not readily seen in the home environment. Typically, standardizing these tasks involves administering the tasks uniformly to all study participants and training raters to be as reliable in their ratings of the child's behavior as possible. Critics of laboratory tasks emphasize that novel settings of laboratory tasks may reduce their ecological validity (Barkley, 1991) and not be representative of the child's behavior. Counterarguments note that parents who observe their child's behavior on laboratory tasks report that their behaviors are typical of their child's behavior at home (Lo et al., 2015) and they can predict important, "real world" outcomes such as child behavior problems (Lo et al., 2015).

Laboratory Tasks Versus Parent Ratings: Weighing the Arguments, Seeking Resolution

In seeking a way to navigate the laboratory versus parent rating issue, perhaps a reframed perspective would be more useful than trying to demonstrate the superiority of either approach. To start, we need to recognize that there is an error associated with all measurements. Sometimes the error is random and sometimes specific, non-random factors contribute to measurement error, but the source of that error is not known. In other instances, the source of the error, as with the possibility of parental mood affecting their ratings of the child's behavior and temperament, is known.

Error in Measurement for Both Approaches Proponents of "objective" laboratory approaches to measurement emphasize the error associated with parent ratings, but in criticizing the parent questionnaire approach, they often seem to overlook sources of error that may occur in the assessment of the child's behavior on those laboratory tasks. For example, in laboratory tasks, trained research assistants often code videotapes and may undergo rigorous training to become reliable coders. In one application of the well-regarded Lab-Tab tasks (Faisca et al., 2021), for example, trained coders showed agreement on various tasks as measured by the intraclass correlation coefficient (ICC) that is reported as moderate to excellent, ranging from 0.66 to 0.94. In another report (Durbin et al., 2005), the ICCs were 0.66 and 0.64 for the two Lab-Tab tasks used. In other reports, a mean inter-rater agreement may be reported that is quite high, but the range of ICCs on all the tasks used is not reported, so the variability regarding agreement cannot be assessed (Gagne et al., 2011). While good, the level of disagreement between raters in these well-done studies for at least some measures cannot simply be dismissed because the raters have achieved a statistically significant level of agreement. In reality, the level of agreement between raters may not be that much better than between the child's two parents.

As discussed above, critics argue that bias of some kind may enter into ratings of child characteristics by parents and teachers, and they have identified possible contributing factors such as maternal depression. Differences among raters in laboratory tasks may also involve bias ("laboratory rater depression distortion"). Still, the personality difference in raters is not investigated in any studies we are aware of, and we are left not knowing what that source of laboratory "bias," if any, might be. Since there is evidence that we can learn about the relations of risk factors of various kinds and their association with child psychopathology from both parent reports and laboratory tasks, it seems there is a place for both types of approaches in the study of developmental psychopathology. There are certainly advocates for using both approaches (Lo et al., 2015). Thus, to "make the "best of both worlds," we used a multi-informant approach that included both parent reports and reliable laboratory measures.

Measures of Risk Factors and Child Psychopathology

Our multi-informant approach included parent reports and interviews to assess outcomes and several risk factors, observer (research assistants) ratings gathered in a 2–2 ½ h home visit to assess risk factors of child attachment and parent scaffolding, and a laboratory-style measure of inhibitory control (IC) (This measure was typically not included in the longitudinal models because its overlap with measures of effortful control led to problems with the structural equations converging). We could not use child self-reports because the children were too young, nor could we include teacher ratings because of the problems coordinating data collection across the hundreds of different preschools attended by the children.

We used multiple indicators of a construct to estimate latent factors and reduce measurement error associated with single measures whenever possible. When multiple indicators could not be used, either a single measure or a composite measure was used to assess the particular construct (see the data analyses section below for details). The measures we used are listed in Table 6.1; Appendix A provides more detail on these measures and their psychometric properties.

Table 6.1 Measures

Category	Variable	Measure(s)
Demography	Demographics	Family Background Questionnaire (study created)
Screening	Language	Peabody Picture Vocabulary Test (Dunn & Dunn, 1997)
Risk factors	Socioeconomic status (SES)	Hollingshead-Redlich Four-Factor Index of Social Status (Hollingshead, 1975)
	Stress	Parenting Stress Inventory (Abidin, 1995) Cohen Life Stress Scale (Cohen et al., 1983) McCubbin Stress scale (Family Strains and Changes) (McCubbin & Patterson, 1996)
	Conflict	Family Environment Scale (Moos & Moos, 1986) McCubbin Family Distress (McCubbin et al., 1996b) McCubbin Family Problem Solving/ Communication (McCubbin et al., 1996a)
	Parent depression	Beck Depression Inventory (Beck et al., 1996) Center for Epidemiologic Studies-Depression Scale (CES-D) (Radloff, 1977)
	Parental support-engagement	Parent Behavior Inventory: support-engagement scale (Lovejoy et al., 1999)
	Parental hostility	Parent Behavior Inventory: hostility/coercion scale (Lovejoy et al., 1999)
	Parental scaffolding skills	Three Boxes Task (NICHD Early Childhood Research Network, 1999)
	Temperament: negative affect	Child Behavior Questionnaire (CBQ): Negative Affectivity Scale (Rothbart et al., 2001)
	Temperament: effortful control	Child Behavior Questionnaire: Effortful Control Scale (Rothbart et al., 2001)
	Temperament: sensory regulation	Short Sensory Profile (McIntosh et al., 1999)
	Attachment security	Attachment Q-Sort (Waters, 1987)
Outcomes	Opposition defiant disorder symptoms (ODD)	DISC-YC ODD (Fisher & Lucas, 2006) Eyberg Scale (Eyberg & Pincus, 1999) CSI-ODD (Gadow & Sprafkin, 2000)
	Attention deficit/hyperactivity disorder symptoms	CSI ADHD inattention scale (Gadow & Sprafkin, 2000) CSI ADHD hyperactive- impulsive scale (Gadow & Sprafkin, 2000) DuPaul ADHD Scales (inattentive and hyperactive-impulsive scales) (DuPaul et al., 1998) DISC-YC ADHD scales (Fisher & Lucas, 2006)
	Anxiety symptoms	DISC-YC GAD (Fisher & Lucas, 2006) CSI-GAD (Gadow & Sprafkin, 2000) CSI-SAD (Gadow & Sprafkin, 2000)
	Depression symptoms	DISC-YC dysthymia (Fisher & Lucas, 2006) DISC-YC MDD (Fisher & Lucas, 2006) CSI-Dysthymia (Gadow & Sprafkin, 2000) CSI-MDD (Gadow & Sprafkin, 2000)

Procedure

When parents dropped off or picked up their child, parents were approached by research assistants in the waiting rooms of pediatric offices and at the classroom entrances in the preschools. Parents expressing interest were subsequently contacted by telephone, and a home visit was arranged for them, at which time study measures were completed, including a diagnostic interview with the Diagnostic Interview Schedule-Young Child Version (DISC-YC) (Fisher & Lucas, 2006); parent-report questionnaires; and behavioral observation measures including inhibitory control tasks, parent scaffolding, and attachment security.

Parents were re-contacted one and 2 years after the initial visit for another home visit during which the diagnostic interview, study questionnaires, and observational tasks were re-administered. This study was approved by the authors' Institutional Review Boards; written consent to participate was obtained each year.

Data Analysis

Initially, missing data and item frequencies were examined within each age group. From the forms completed in each age group, less than 5% of data were missing within each group. However, not all participants completed questionnaires at all three ages (4, 5, and 6). Because imputation is generally less biased than listwise deletion (Graham, 2009), we chose to manage missing data by imputation using SPSS V15.0 Expectation Maximization methodology using maximum likelihood procedures for multiple imputations.

In most statistical analyses, such as regression analyses and t-tests, there is only one measure (the manifest indicator) for each underlying ("latent") construct that is measured. Although there will inevitably be measurement error, there is no way to measure or reduce that error, so the measured score is assumed to be the true estimate of the latent construct. One way to avoid this pitfall is to use structural equation modeling, a statistical approach in which multiple measures, when available, can be used to measure the latent construct. The use of multiple indicators serves to control for measurement error in latent factors. This led to our decision to seek multiple measures of each construct whenever possible; for most latent constructs, we were able to identify multiple reliable and valid measures to use as manifest indicators, but not for all. When the only developmentally-appropriate manifest indicator that we could find involved a questionnaire with multiple items, we followed a procedure often used in structural equation modeling (Brown, 2006) in which individual items were combined into subsets called parcels to create three manifest indicators for each latent factor. A single manifest indicator was used when the measure of the construct involved a single item, e.g., the Hollingshead-Redlich (Hollingshead, 1975) measure of socioeconomic status. If a good fit for a latent construct could not be achieved using multiple indicators, a composite indicator was created by summing the standardized scores from multiple scales (Nunnally & Bernstein, 1994).

Another measurement concern that we had involved the possibility that the content of an item on a measure of one of the risk factors was highly similar to an item on one of the outcome measures. For example, if an item on a temperament measure and an item on the symptom scale for anxiety or depression were highly similar, the resulting item contamination (Lengua et al., 1998) could inflate the estimates of the strength of the relations between these latent factors, which would lead to spurious findings.

We addressed this problem using a procedure developed by Lengua, West, and Sandler (1998) to identify items and measure each construct while reducing item contamination across constructs. Two expert panels comprised of either 7 or 8 doctoral-level psychologists and advanced clinical child psychology graduate students each rated half of the items of the measures used to assess effortful control (EC), negative affect (NA), and sensory regulation (SR), and the behavioral symptoms associated with anxiety, depression, Attention Deficit Disorder (ADHD), and Oppositional Defiant Disorder (ODD). For each item, the quality of the item as a sensory, temperament, or behavior problem indicator was rated on a 5-point Likert scale. For the sensory regulation measure, we retained sensory items rated as significantly better indicators of sensory problems than temperament or behavioral symptoms; similarly, we retained EC and NA items rated as significantly better indicators of temperament than sensory or behavior problems.

Structural Equation Modeling (SEM)

SEM with LISREL 8.8 (Joreskog & Sorbom, 2006) was used to evaluate hypothesized models. We followed a two-step analytic approach (Anderson & Gerbing, 1988) in which CFA was used first to test the goodness-of-fit of the measurement models before examining the structural models. Specifics related to decisions regarding model fit are described in Appendix B.

Experts differ in the standards that apply for deciding if a model shows good fit. For this study, we followed Brown's recommendation that multiple fits of different types be used (Brown, 2006), so we used the following guidelines, describing models with RMSEA < approximately 0.06, NNFI >0.95, CFI > 0.95, and SRMR of <0.08 as good fitting models. If RMSEA is >0.06 but <0.08, NNFI >. 90 but <0.95, CFI >0.90 but <0.95, and SRMR <0.08, the model fit is described as moderately good. We described models whose fit indices do not reach these thresholds are described as poor fitting. The significance of specific indirect effects was typically determined using joint significance testing (JST) (Taylor & MacKinnon, 2012; Taylor et al., 2008). While bootstrapping procedures, as described by Mallinckrodt, Abraham, Wei, and Russell (2006), are often preferred, JST often performs better with regard to Type 1 error (Mallinckrodt et al., 2006; Taylor & MacKinnon, 2012).

Building the Longitudinal Models

An Initial Cross-Sectional Model

As discussed in Chap. 2, the process of developing a multi-domain model began with identifying the outcomes of interest followed by an exploration of the current literature to determine potential risk factors linked to those outcomes. Risk factors in multiple domains, both more distal and more proximal to the child, were identified, as were the paths between risk factors within and across domains. The statistically significant phenomena that were identified were found in studies using different designs, some cross-sectional and some longitudinal. Almost all were identified in studies that examined the relations between just a few risk factors (often just one) and symptom type. Because of the omitted variable problem described in the previous chapters, the strength of the associations between those risk factors and symptom types that were specific to that risk factor was likely to be overestimated. Although the long-term goal was to build a longitudinal model that examined direct and indirect paths between risk factors and symptom types in a mediational model, we felt it would be useful to begin with a cross-sectional model of one of the symptom types and use the information derived from that model along with theoretical and empirical information from the extant literature to build the longitudinal models of interest. Starting with a cross-sectional model allowed us to explore the possibility that some risk-risk or risk-symptom types found to be significant in earlier single-variable studies would not be significant in a multi-factor model. This information could be useful in developing the overall longitudinal models that were our primary interest.

Mediational Processes in Cross-Sectional Designs

The process of studying mediational processes in cross-sectional designs has important critics. In a series of reports (Cole & Maxwell, 2003; Maxwell & Cole, 2007; Maxwell et al., 2011), Maxwell and colleagues note that cross-sectional models may be biased when compared to the study of mediation in longitudinal models. Therefore, they argue that a cross-sectional model should not be considered a substitute for a longitudinal model.

We agree but with an important caveat. Their criticism, however, applies primarily to situations in which investigators simply expect that the cross-sectional model is unbiased and conducting a longitudinal study and testing a longitudinal model is not necessary. As the reader knows, our intention was to test a longitudinal model while using a cross-sectional model as a bridge in the process of moving from specific phenomena (linking risk factor to risk factor or risk factor to symptom types) to a longitudinal model for one of the symptom types and then modifying that model based on its results and other theoretical considerations to apply to other symptom types. In following this process, we were engaging in the iterative process recommended by Borsboom et al. (2021) and described in Chap. 2 in which models are tested repeatedly followed by further refinement. We thought that using a cross-sectional model as a bridge to develop a longitudinal model was preferable to relying on the phenomena identified in the literature in studies using different design approaches. We felt that examining the results for an array of variables studied simultaneously in a cross-sectional model was likely to yield a more conservative estimate of the unique variance associated with each pathway from X to Y than can occur in the studies of the associations between individual variables studied in separate studies. The specific cross-sectional and longitudinal models identified and tested, the rationale for their development and the findings regarding risk for early childhood psychopathology are discussed in Chap. 7 for externalizing symptoms, Chap. 8 for internalizing symptoms and Chap. 9 for broadband externalizing and externalizing symptoms and a transdiagnostic approach.

References

Abidin, R. R. (1995). *Manual for the parenting stress index*. Psychological Assessment Resources.

Achenbach, T. M., McConaughy, S. H., & Howell, C. T. (1987). Child/adolescent behavioral and emotional problems: Implications of cross-informant correlation for situational specificity. *Psychological Bulletin, 101*(2), 213–232.

Anderson, J. C., & Gerbing, D. W. (1988). Structural equation modeling in practice: A review and recommended two-step approach. *Psychological Bulletin, 103*, 411–423.

Barkley, R. A. (1991). The ecological validity of laboratory and analogue assessment methods of ADHD symptoms. *Journal of Abnormal Child Psychology, 19*(2), 149–175.

Beck, A., Steer, R. A., & Brown, G. K. (1996). *Manual for the Beck Depression Inventory-2*. Psychological Corporaton.

Borsboom, D., van der Maas, H. L. J., Dalege, J., Kievit, R. A., & Haig, B. D. (2021). Theory construction methodology: A practical framework for building theories in psychology. *Perspectives on Psychological Science, 16*(4), 756–766. https://doi.org/10.1077/1745691620969647

Brown, T. A. (2006). Confirmatory factor analysis for applied research. .

Chi, T. C., & Hinshaw, S. P. (2002). Mother-child relationships of children with ADHD: The role of maternal depressive symptoms and depression-related distortions. *Journal of Abnormal Child Psychology, 30*(4), 387–400.

Christoffel, K. K., Binns, H. J., Stockman, J. A., McGuire, P., Poncher, J., Unti, S., Typlin, B., Lasin, G., & Seigel, W. (1988). Practice-based research: Opportunities and obstacles. *Pediatrics, 82*, 399–406.

Cohen, S., Kamarck, T., & Mermelstein, R. (1983). A global measure of perceived stress. *Journal of Health and Social Behavior, 24*, 385–396.

Cole, D. A., & Maxwell, S. E. (2003). Testing mediational models with longitudinal data: Questions and tips in the use of structural equation modeling. *Journal of Abnormal Psychology, 112*(4), 558–577. https://doi.org/10.1037/0021-843X.112.4.558

De Los Reyes, A., & Kazdin, A. E. (2005). Informant discrepancies in the assessment of childhood psychopathology: A critical review, theoretical framework, and recommendations for further study. *Psychological Bulletin, 131*(4), 483–509.

Dunn, L., & Dunn, L. (1997). *The Peabody picture vocabulary test* (3rd ed.). American Guidance Service.

DuPaul, G. J., Anastopoulos, A. D., Power, T. J., Reid, R., Ikeda, M. J., & McGoey, K. E. (1998). Parent ratings of attention-deficit/hyperactivity disorder symptoms: Factor structure and normative data. *Psychopathology and Behavioral Assessment, 20*, 83–102.

Durbin, E. C., Klein, D. N., Hayden, E. P., Buckley, M. E., & Moerk, K. C. (2005). Temperamental emotionality in preschoolers and parental mood disorders. *Journal of Abnormal Psychology, 114*(1), 28–37.

Eyberg, S., & Pincus, D. (1999). *Eyberg child behavior inventory manual*. Psychological Assessment Resources.

Faisca, L., Ferreira, L. I., Fernande, C. C., Gagne, J. R., & Martins, A. T. (2021). Behavioral inhibition in childhood: European Portuguese adaptation of an observational measure (Lab-TAB). *Children, 8*(on-line version). https://doi.org/10.3390/children8020162

Fisher, P., & Lucas, C. (2006). *Diagnostic interview schedule for children (DISC-IV)-young child*. Columbia University.

Gadow, K. D., & Sprafkin, J. (2000). *Early childhood symptom inventory-4* (Screening manual). Checkmate Plus.

Gagne, J. R., Van Hulle, C. A., Aksan, N., Essex, M. J., & Goldsmith, H. H. (2011). Deriving temperament measures from emotion-eliciting episodes: Scale construction and initial validation. *Psychological Assessment, 23*(2), 337–353. https://doi.org/10.1037/a0021746

Graham, J. W. (2009). Missing data analysis: Making it work in the real world. *Annual Review of Psychology, 60*, 549–576. https://doi.org/10.1146/annurev.psych.58.110405.085530

Hollingshead, A. B. (1975). *Four-factor index of social position*. Yale University Department of Sociology.

Joreskog, K. G., & Sorbom, D. (2006). *LISREL for windows*. Scientific Software International.

Lengua, L. J., West, S. G., & Sandler, I. N. (1998). Temperament as a predictor of symptomatology in children: Addressing contamination of measures. *Child Development, 69*(1), 164–181.

Liskola, K., Raaska, H., Lapinleimu, H., Lipsanen, J., Sinkkonen, J., & Elovainio, M. (2021). The effects of maternal depression on their perception of emotional and behavioral problems of ther internationally adopted children. *Child and Adolescent Psychiatry and Mental Health, 15*(41), 1–9. https://doi.org/10.1186/s13034-021-00396-0

Lo, S. L., Vroman, L. N., & Durbin, C. E. (2015). Ecological validity of laboratory assessments of child temperament: Evidence from parent perspectives. *Psychological Assessment, 27*(1), 280–290. https://doi.org/10.1037/pas0000033

Lovejoy, M. C., Weis, R., O'Hare, E., & Rubin, E. C. (1999). Development and initial validation of the parent behavior inventory. *Psychological Assessment, 11*(4), 1–12. https://doi.org/10.1037/1040-3590.11.4.534

Mallinckrodt, B., Abraham, W. T., Wei, M., & Russell, D. W. (2006). Advances in testing the statistical significance of mediation effects. *Journal of Counseling Psychology, 53*, 372–378. https://doi.org/10.1037/0022-0167.53.3.372

Maxwell, S. E., & Cole, D. A. (2007). Bias in cross-sectional analyses of longitudinal mediation. *Psychological Methods, 1*, 23–44. https://doi.org/10.1037/1082-989X.12.23

Maxwell, S. E., Cole, D. A., & Mitchell, M. A. (2011). Bias in cross-sectional analyses of longitudinal mediation: Partial and complete mediation under an autoregressive model. *Multivariate Behavioral Research, 46*(5), 816–841. https://doi.org/10.1037/1082-989X.12.1.23

McCubbin, H. I., & Patterson, J. (1996). Family member well-being. In *Family assessment: Resiliency, coping and adaptation* (pp. 735–782).

McCubbin, M. A., McCubbin, H. I., & Thompson, A. (1996a). Family problem solving and communication. In H. I. McCubbin, A. Thompson, & M. A. McCubbin (Eds.), *Family assessment: Resiliency, coping,and adaptation-inventories for research and practice* (pp. 639–686). University of Wisconsin.

McCubbin, H. I., Thompson, A., & Elver, K. M. (1996b). Family distress index. In H. I. McCubbin, A. Thompson, & M. A. McCubbin (Eds.), *Family assessment: Resiliency, coping, and adaptation-inventories for research and practice* (pp. 783–788). University of Wisconsin.

McIntosh, D., Miller, L., Shyu, V., & Dunn, W. (1999). Overview of the short sensory profile (SSP). In W. Dunn (Ed.), *The sensory profile: Examiner's manual* (pp. 59–73).
Moos, R. H., & Moos, B. S. (1986). *Family environment scale manual.* Consulting Psychologists Press.
NICHD Early Childhood Research Network. (1999). Child care and mother-child interaction in the first three years of life. *Developmental Psychology, 35*, 1399–1413.
Nunnally, J., & Bernstein, I. (1994). *Psychometric theory* (3rd ed.). McGraw-Hill.
Radloff, L. A. (1977). The CES-D scale: A self-report depression scale for research in the general population. *Applied Psychological Measurement, 1*, 385–401.
Richters, J. E. (1992). Depressed mothers as informants about their children: A critical review of the evidence for distortion. *Psychological Bulletin, 112*(3), 485–499.
Rothbart, M. K., Ahadi, S. A., Hershey, K. L., & Fisher, P. (2001). Investigations of temperament at three to seven years: The children's behavior questionnaire. *Child Development, 72*(5), 1394–1408.
Shaw, D. S., Keenan, K., Vondra, J. I., Delliquadri, E., & Giovannelli, J. (1997). Antecedents of preschool children's internalizing problems: A longitudinal study of low-income families. *Journal of the American Academy of Child and Adolescent Psychiatry, 36*(12), 1760–1767.
Shaw, D. S., Gilliom, M., Ingoldsby, E. M., & Nagin, D. S. (2003). Trajectories leading to school-age conduct problems. *Developmental Psychology, 39*(2), 189.
Taylor, A. B., & MacKinnon, D. P. (2012). Four applications of permutation methods to testing a single-mediator model. *Behavior Research Methods, 44*, 806–844.
Taylor, A. B., MacKinnon, D. P., & Tein, J. Y. (2008). Tests of the three-path mediated effect. *Organizational Research Methods, 11*, 241–269. https://doi.org/10.1177/1094428107300344
United States Census Bureau. (2007). *State and county quick facts.* http://quickfacts.census.gov/qfd/states/17/17031.html
Waters, E. (1987). *Attachment Q-set (version 3.0).* State University of New York at Stony Brook.

Chapter 7
Multi-domain Models of Externalizing Disorders: Risk Factors and Complex Pathways

Externalizing disorders are generally characterized by problematic behaviors that exceed the boundaries of the child's environment and, consequently, have a strong impact on others (caretakers, peers, teachers, etc.). As a result, particularly in young children, these behaviors are often identified more quickly than disorders characterized by problematic emotions the child experiences internally (e.g., anxiety and depression). Epidemiological studies indicate that the prevalence of externalizing behaviors in preschool children is considerably higher than that for internalizing disorders, with prevalence rates of 6.6–13.4% for Oppositional Defiant Disorder (ODD) and 3.3–12.8% for Attention Deficit/Hyperactive Disorder (ADHD) (Egger & Angold, 2006; Lavigne et al., 2009). For children, the primary DSM-5 diagnoses that are considered externalizing disorders are ODD and ADHD. In developing a multi-domain model for externalizing disorders, we focused on the symptoms associated with ODD and ADHD as described in DSM 4/5, but with the symptom types for those two disorders measured as continuous variables.

Consistent with the Theory Construction Methodology approach to theory building (Borsboom et al., 2021) described in Chap. 2, we began by identifying the relevant phenomena (i.e., previously identified associations of specific risk factors with specific symptom types) associated with symptoms of ODD and ADHD. This involved reviewing the existing research literature to identify studies examining the associations of contextual, parent, parenting, and child risk factors with either ODD or ADHD symptoms or with externalizing symptoms in general (see Chaps. 3, 4 and 5 for an extended review).

K. R. Gouze et al., *Early Childhood Psychopathology*,
https://doi.org/10.1007/978-3-031-68877-5_7

Developing a Cross-Sectional Model

We then developed a prototypical cross-sectional model for ODD symptoms by identifying both direct and indirect pathways previously identified in the literature as risk factors for symptoms of this disorder in young children. That model is displayed in Fig. 7.1. By testing that model, we identified the significant paths, both direct and indirect, across domains that were associated with ODD symptoms at age 4 in our large community sample. That cross-sectional modeling process allowed us to examine the significance of each pathway in the context of multiple other pathways and served as an intermediate step in identifying specific risk factors relevant to the development of the longitudinal model. The significant pathways identified in that manner were then incorporated into the longitudinal model for ODD and, subsequently, the model for ADHD. While we could have built that longitudinal model by relying exclusively on theory and previous empirical findings that approach was likely to overestimate the magnitude of the associations given the frequent occurrence of the omitted variable problem that was prevalent in so much of the earlier ODD research (see Chaps. 1 and 2). Developing the longitudinal model based on the cross-sectional model, which itself was built on a theoretical understanding of ODD symptoms and previous findings, seemed preferable because it allowed us to build from better estimates of the magnitude of the path coefficients and their statistical significance as decisions were made about the pathways to explore in the longitudinal model. As discussed in Chap. 2, a cross-sectional model is not a substitute for a longitudinal model. Still, it can be a useful intermediate step toward developing and testing a longitudinal model when earlier research has relied primarily on individual

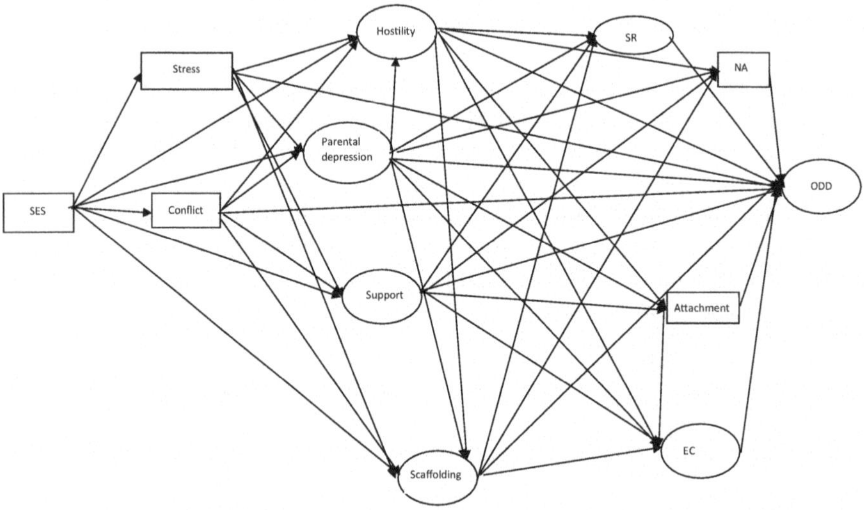

Fig. 7.1 Cross-sectional multi-domain model of risk factors associated with ODD, used as a basis for developing a longitudinal model. *SES* socioeconomic status. *EC* effortful control. *NA* negative affect. *SR* sensory regulation. *ADHD* attention deficit/hyperactivity disorder symptoms

association studies that are compromised by the omitted variables problem. Findings from the resulting cross-sectional model are provided by Lavigne et al. (2012).

The Longitudinal Model for Symptoms of ODD

Figure 7.2 illustrates the resulting longitudinal model (Lavigne et al., 2016). Appendix B describes the components of the structural model in detail. That model measured contextual factors of SES, family conflict, and family stress; parent depression; parenting factors of hostility, support, and scaffolding skills; and child attachment at age 4. At age 5, conflict, the three parenting factors, and child temperament factors of effortful control (EC), negative affect (NA), and sensory regulation (SR) were measured. At age 6, ODD symptoms were measured as a continuous variable that reflected the number and severity of ODD symptoms for each child. That model showed good model fit.[1]

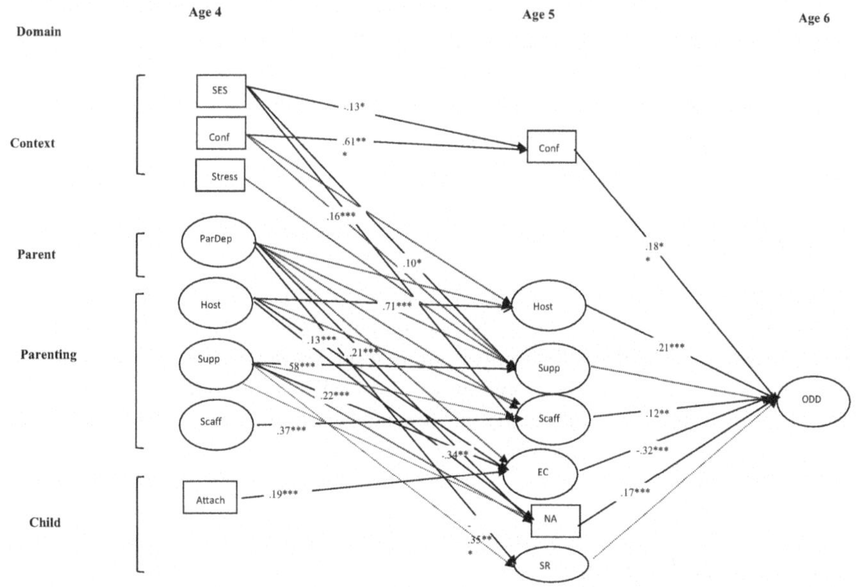

Fig. 7.2 ODD. Multi-domain (multiple level) cascade model of factors at age 4 and 5 associated with levels of symptoms of ODD at age 6 regardless of ODD symptom levels at age 4 and 5. Solid lines illustrate significant paths; dotted lines, nonsignificant paths. *SES* socioeconomic status. *EC* effortful control. *NA* negative affect. *SR* sensory regulation. *ODD* oppositional defiant disorder symptoms. *$p < 0.05$. **$p < 0.01$. ***$p < 0.001$

[1] SB χ^2 (475, $N = 796$) = 1415.41, RMSEA = 0.05, NNFI = 0.94, CFI = 0.95, SRMR = 0.07.

In this longitudinal model, seven direct pathways from age 5 risk factors to age 6 ODD symptom severity were assessed. These included pathways to ODD symptoms from family conflict at the contextual level, hostility, support, and scaffolding at the parenting level, and effortful control, negative temperament, and sensory regulation at the child level. Because these seven variables were measured in the same model, the magnitude of each path coefficient reflects the strength of the association with ODD symptoms that is specific to that factor and does not share any variance with the other age 5 risk factors.

There were also numerous indirect effects that were assessed, measuring the indirect paths of age 4 contextual, parent, parenting, and child attachment to ODD symptoms with age 5 contextual, parenting, and child factors as mediators. It is important to note that family conflict and the three parenting factors were measured at both age 4 and age 5. In doing so the variable at age 5 reflects the change in that factor from age 4 to 5 and not the scores on that factor at age 5, i.e., the path from SES to conflict represents the path from age 4 SES to an increase or decrease in conflict between ages 4 and 5. Finally, we also examined this longitudinal model with ODD symptoms at ages 4 and 5 and at age 6, which allowed us to determine the change in ODD symptoms over time in relation to the other risk factors (see Fig. 7.3). Further information on model fit indices and other methodological and statistical considerations can be found in Appendix B. Also, in each figure, an oval depicts a latent factor for which there were two or more observable measures (i.e., manifest indicators) of the underlying "latent" factor. Variables depicted in rectangles were measured by a single indicator.

Overall Model Fit

As expected, based on the previous literature and the results from our cross-sectional model (Lavigne et al., 2012), the multi-domain model revealed a complex set of risk factors associated with the development of child ODD symptoms at age 6. These included both direct and indirect paths from the contextual, parenting, and child variables to ODD.

Contextual Risk Factors

SES We examined only the indirect effects of SES assessed at age 4 on ODD symptoms at age 6 since SES is not likely to change in a year. SES assessed at this age had several indirect effects on age 6 symptoms. Specifically, age 4 SES was linked to age 6 ODD symptoms via: (a) a statistically significant pathway[2] through

[2] Indirect effect path coefficient [PC] = −0.01, 95% CI = −0.002 – −0.02).

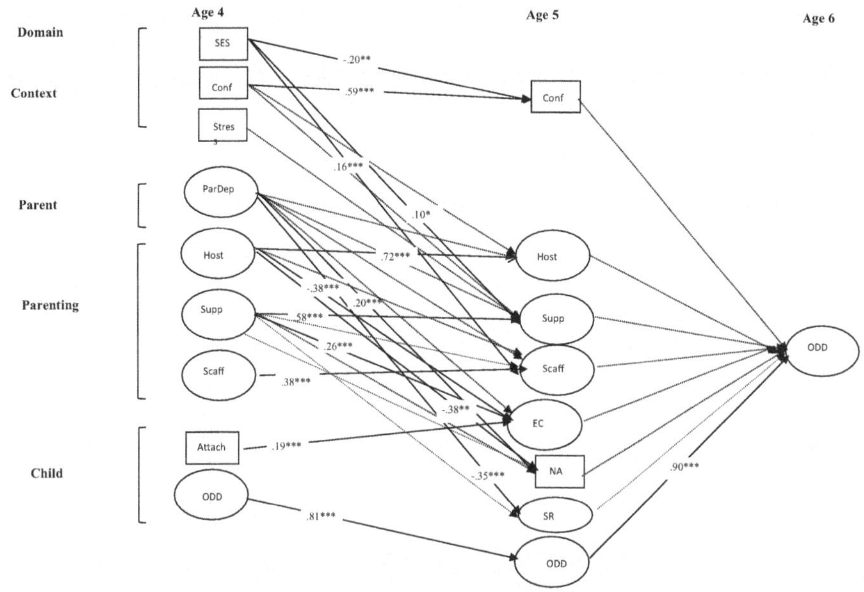

Fig. 7.3 Multi-domain (multiple level) cascade model of factors at age 4 and 5 associated changes in ODD symptom levels to age 6. .Solid lines illustrate significant paths; dotted lines, nonsignificant paths. *SES* socioeconomic status. *EC* effortful control. *NA* negative affect. *SR* sensory regulation. *ODD* oppositional defiant disorder symptoms. $^{*}p < 0.05$. $^{**}p < 0.01$. $^{***}p < 0.001$

age 5 family conflict, with lower age 4 SES levels linked to increases in family conflict from age 4 to 5 which, in turn, were linked to higher levels of ODD symptoms and (b) higher levels of age 4 SES were associated with increases in scaffolding skills from age 4 to age 5 which, because better scaffolding skills seemed to facilitate ODD symptoms, led to significantly higher levels of symptoms of ODD at age 6.[3] Although the finding of an association between higher SES parents and better scaffolding skills is consistent with prior literature that posits that higher SES parents have more resources available to them for spending time working with their children (see Chap. 3 for a discussion of models of SES effects), the relation between better scaffolding skills and greater ODD symptomatology is counterintuitive. One hypothesis is that parents with more difficult children recognize that they need more scaffolding to accomplish difficult tasks. Nevertheless, this result bears further exploration in additional research.

In Chap. 3, we noted that numerous studies found an association between SES and child psychopathology, but the mechanisms involved received relatively little attention. Paths linking SES and child psychopathology via increased family

[3] Indirect effect PC = 0.02, 95% CI = 0.01–0.03).

conflict have been suggested, and we also found evidence for that pathway. Previous researchers have not examined whether that association might also be mediated by positive parenting behavior such as scaffolding skills. Our results suggest that scaffolding might mediate the relationship between SES and child psychopathology in an unexpected way, with higher SES associated with better scaffolding skills which, in turn, are related to higher levels of ODD symptoms. As noted above, this finding is counterintuitive and bears further exploration.

Family Conflict Family conflict had both a direct and a small indirect effect on age 6 ODD symptoms. Higher levels of age 5 family conflict led to higher levels of ODD symptoms, and higher levels of age 4 family conflict led to an increase in family conflict at age 5, which, in turn, predicted higher levels of age 6 symptoms.

Stress Family stress did not show any direct or indirect effects on age 6 ODD symptoms.

Parent Risk Factors: Parent Depression

Parent depression assessed at child age 4 had an indirect effect on age 6 ODD symptom levels via the child temperament factor of NA. That is, higher levels of age 4 parent depression were associated with higher levels of age 5 child NA, which, in turn led to higher levels of ODD symptoms at age 6. It is interesting to hypothesize about the process whereby parental depression influences child NA and subsequently ODD symptoms. As noted in Chap. 4, the impact of parent depression on externalizing behaviors is well-established (Ivanova et al., 2022), but less is known about the pathways through which these associations might operate. The PACT study reveals that parent depression might impact ODD symptoms through its effect on child NA. Although one might hypothesize that this relation is biologically based (i.e., the tendency for high negative affect in parents, which manifests in depression, is associated with high negative affect in children), studies examining biological versus psychosocial relations between parental depression and child outcomes suggest that psychosocial factors might play a more prominent role (Natsuaki et al., 2014). Psychosocial explanations for this pathway might include modeling effects, i.e., depressed parents model the expression of negative affect for their children, or lack of availability of depressed parents, which, in turn, leads to increased NA in children who feel ignored or invalidated. Subsequent relations between child NA and ODD symptoms suggest, quite plausibly, that higher levels of child irritability and anger lead to increased tantrums and refusal to comply with parental directions which are the hallmarks of ODD at age 6.

Parenting Factors

Hostility As noted in Chap. 4, parental negativity in the form of hostility, excessive anger, and excessive harshness has long been associated with externalizing outcomes in children (Barrios et al., 2017; Campbell et al., 2000; Eiden et al., 2007; Maccoby, 2000; Rothbaum & Weisz, 1994; Shaw et al., 2003; Waller et al., 2012). Similarly, in the PACT study, we found a moderately strong association between age 5 parental hostility and age 6 ODD symptoms, with higher levels of age 5 hostility associated with higher levels of age 6 symptoms. Parental hostility at age 4 also had indirect effects on age 6 ODD symptoms via several pathways. First, parenting hostility was quite stable from age 4 to age 5; thus, higher levels of age 4 parental hostility were associated with increased age 5 parental hostility, which, in turn, led to higher levels of age 6 ODD symptoms.

Second, age 4 parental hostility was associated with higher levels of age 6 ODD symptoms via age 5 child EC. Specifically, higher levels of age 4 parental hostility predicted poorer child EC at age 5, and poorer age 5 EC was associated with higher levels of age 6 ODD symptoms. This pathway from parental hostility to ODD symptoms through child EC provides one possible explanation for the consistency and strength of previous findings linking parent hostility, anger, and harshness to child ODD symptoms. Parental hostility in and of itself is significant as noted in the direct paths from age 4 parent hostility through age 5 parent hostility to child ODD symptoms. However, the direct effects of child EC on ODD outcomes are stronger than the direct effects of hostility, suggesting that this pathway may be a particularly important one. Thus, it is likely that the effects of parent hostility on age 6 ODD symptom levels began at age 4, rather than at age 5. Overall, that indirect effect was small but significant.

Parental Support Parental support at age 5 did not have a direct effect on age 6 ODD symptoms, but, once again, child EC appears to play a significant role. This can be seen in the indirect effect that parental support had on age 6 ODD symptoms via child EC. Specifically, higher levels of age 4 parental support predicted higher levels of age 5 child EC, and higher levels of age 5 child EC were associated with lower levels of age 6 ODD symptoms.[4] It is interesting that the indirect effects of both parental hostility and support were mediated by the same child factor, EC. The parental factor, hostility, associated with a decrease in EC predicted higher levels of ODD symptoms at age 6, while the parent factor, support, associated with an increase in EC predicted lower symptom levels.

Scaffolding The third parenting variable examined was scaffolding. Parent scaffolding at child age 5 was related to age 6 ODD symptoms, but the direction of this effect was contrary to our expectations. We predicted that better parent scaffolding at age 5 would be associated with lower levels of ODD symptoms at age 6.

---

[4] Indirect effect PC = −0.08, 95% CI = −0.14 – −0.04).

Specifically, we hypothesized that stronger scaffolding skills would lead to better parental structuring of potentially frustrating tasks, making the child experience the challenge more manageable. This, in turn, might reduce the tendency for the child to refuse to comply with the task or to throw a tantrum in response to their experience of frustration. The results, however, showed that the opposite was occurring; parents with better age 5 scaffolding skills were more likely to rate their child as exhibiting higher levels of age 6 ODD symptoms.[5] This counterintuitive finding could be due to statistical suppression (please refer to Appendix C for a discussion of suppression effects). Further exploration of the PACT data revealed that, in this case, there were no suppression effects, leading us to the conclusion that there indeed was a relation between better parental scaffolding and a greater number or frequency of child ODD symptoms. One possible explanation for this finding is that sensitive parents who have experienced a history of oppositional child behavior and recognize that their children have difficulty with frustration proactively attempt to avoid refusals or tantrums by spending more time structuring tasks before requesting that their children attempt to complete them. This hypothesis requires further investigation in future research.

Child Factors

The child temperament variables of NA, EC, and SR were only included in the model at age 5 because of the examination of an earlier cross-sectional model in which the child temperament variables were modeled at age 4 to explore their influence on parenting attitudes and behaviors at age 5 demonstrated poor fit statistics.

NA Age 5 NA had a small direct effect on age 6 ODD symptoms such that higher levels of age 5 NA led to higher levels of ODD symptoms. This finding is consistent with prior literature (see Chap. 5) and makes conceptual sense. It seems apparent that children who are more easily prone to negative affect in the form of anger, frustration, and irritability would be more reactive and resistant to requests for compliance and more likely to tantrum in response to such requests. The PACT data support this hypothesis.

EC Age 5 EC had a medium direct effect on age 6 ODD symptoms. Specifically higher levels of EC predicted lower levels of age 6 symptoms. Again, this finding is consistent with a robust literature which indicates that low levels of EC constitute a risk factor for externalizing behaviors at all developmental levels (Eisenberg et al., 2009; Gartstein et al., 2012; Lengua, 2008; Olson et al., 2005). Given that EC is conceptualized as the regulatory function that allows children to control their emotions and to perform more socially desirable behaviors while inhibiting fewer

[5] PC = 0.12, $p < 0.01$).

desirable responses, it makes perfect sense that lower EC would be associated with more behaviors that parents perceive as unacceptable or oppositional.

SR Contrary to expectation, age 5 SR did not have a direct effect on age 6 ODD symptoms. Given that there are no prior studies demonstrating an association between SR and ODD symptoms in children this age, it may be that this relation does not, in fact, exist and that the associations only hold for older children (Ben-Sasson et al., 2009) and for symptoms of ADHD (Dunn & Bennett, 2002; Mangeot et al., 2001; Parush et al., 2007) .

Attachment Attachment was included in the model at age 4, but not at age 5, so we could only examine its indirect effects. We did find that age 4 attachment had indirect effects on levels of ODD symptoms via its effect on child age 5 EC. That is, higher levels of age 4 attachment security predicted better age 5 EC and as previously stated, better age 5 EC led to fewer symptoms of age 6 ODD.

It is particularly interesting that several risk factors from different domains exerted their effects on age 6 ODD symptom levels via the same child variable, EC. That is, parent depression, parent support, parent hostility, and attachment all had indirect effects on age 6 ODD symptoms through their effect on child EC. This makes it clear that the child's self-regulatory skills at age 5 are an extremely important determinant of ODD symptom outcome. Poorer EC is a risk factor for this externalizing disorder, and better EC appears to be protective.

Testing Change in ODD Symptom Levels from Age 5 to 6

The model described above provides information about the pathways, direct and indirect, from risk factors to the level of ODD symptoms observed at age 6. We also tested a second model (Lavigne et al., 2016) that examined how the multi-domain factors were associated with *changes* in ODD symptoms between ages 4 and 6 (see Fig. 7.3). It differs from the model depicted in Fig. 7.2 by adding a latent ODD factor at ages 4 and 5 and including paths for the autoregressions of ODD between ages 4, 5, and 6. By "controlling for" the baseline level of ODD at ages 4 and 5, we could examine the risk factors for changes in ODD (i.e., increases or decreases in symptoms) between ages 5 and 6. This change model also showed good model fit.[6]

In the change model (Fig. 7.3), the magnitude of the contributions of the multi-domain risk factors to changes in ODD between ages 5 and 6 depends upon the stability of ODD over time. If the symptom levels of ODD a child exhibits over time are very stable, then the contribution of contextual, parent, parenting, and child factors to increases in ODD symptom levels at age 6 will be small. If ODD symptom

[6] SB χ^2 (678, $N = 796$) = 33500.12, RMSEA = 0.06, NNFI = 0.92, CFI = 0.93, SRMR = 0.08.

levels are not very stable over time, however, then other factors may contribute to changes in levels of ODD symptoms.

When we tested this model, we found that ODD was, in fact, quite stable from age 4 to age 5 and from age 5 to age 6. Interestingly, none of the other age 5 contextual, parenting, or child temperament variables contributed to changes in ODD symptom levels between ages 5 and 6. This suggests that early levels of ODD symptoms account far more for the continuity of these symptoms during this period of development than do other factors, although other factors may be contributing to absolute levels of ODD symptoms. This revised model showed moderately good fit,[6] and the results for the revised model were the same as those for the initial model described in Lavigne et al. (Lavigne et al., 2016). As expected, the stability of ODD symptoms from ages 4 to 6 was very high (the autoregressive PC for age 4 ODD to age 5 ODD was 0.81; from age 5 ODD to age 6 ODD, PC = 0.90). As a result, none of the direct effects for risk factors other than age 5 ODD made a significant contribution to changes in ODD between age 5 and 6. There were also no indirect, cascading effects from age 4 variables on changes in ODD symptom levels from ages 5 to 6. It is thus likely that the risk factors were having an ongoing effect on the expression of ODD rather than only occurring from age 5 to age 6.

ADHD Symptoms and Psychosocial Factors

It is widely recognized that there is a strong genetic component to Attention-Deficit/Hyperactivity Disorder (ADHD). Although heritability estimates approximate 0.76 (Faraone et al., 2005), it is also the case that concordance rates do not approach 100%. For that reason, experts argue that it is important to understand more about the psychosocial factors that play an important role in the onset, course, and sequelae of ADHD in children. Johnston and Chronis-Tuscano (2014, 2017) argue that a developmental-transactional model best describes the complex interplay between parental and family factors and the development, maintenance, and exacerbation of ADHD symptoms. Although the role of parenting is emphasized in such models, other researchers note the importance of examining the role of other factors, including contextual ones. In 2010, Deault (2010) commented on the lack of research examining the relation of family contextual variables to the development of ADHD in children. Coghill et al. (2005) argued that causal models need to examine multiple pathways to the symptoms of the disorder because multiple pathways may represent alternative routes to ADHD that contribute to children's symptoms. Nigg et al. (2004) focus on the relation of temperament to ADHD symptoms, suggesting that there may be multiple pathways involving temperamental reactivity (e.g., negative affect) and effortful control.

Overall, research devoted to ADHD in preschoolers has been limited, with some increased attention in recent years. There has been little emphasis on examining multiple levels of factors associated with preschool-onset ADHD, particularly during the important developmental period of the transition from preschool to kindergarten and elementary school. The relatively few advances made in exploring the multi-domain psychosocial factors impacting the development of symptoms of ADHD across those developmental periods suggested that this was an area ripe for further research.

A Longitudinal Model for ADHD Symptoms

The model we developed to explore multi-domain psychosocial influences on the development and maintenance of ADHD symptoms included the same age 4 contextual (SES, family stress and conflict), parent (parent depression), parenting (hostility, support and scaffolding) and child (temperament and attachment) risk variables as did the ODD model. It also included the same age 5 variables as did the ODD model, specifically conflict, the three parenting factors, and child temperament (NA, EC, and SR). ADHD symptoms at age 6 included the total number of symptoms of ADHD combined type (ADHD-C) (see Fig. 7.4).

Our multi-domain model focused on the symptoms for the combined type of ADHD-C (including both attentional problems and hyperactivity/impulsivity). Furthermore, while much research is done on clinical samples with children who meet DSM 4/5 criteria for one of the types of ADHD, it is likely that ADHD symptoms are dimensional and not categorical, and that subclinical levels of ADHD symptoms may impact the child's functioning. For those reasons, it was important to examine the multi-domain risk factors associated with ADHD symptoms viewed across a continuum and not just among children meeting the criteria for an ADHD disorder.

Overall Model Fit

With ADHD showing a strong genetic component, we were aware that overall model fit for a multi-domain psychosocial model might be difficult to achieve. Surprisingly, the longitudinal multi-domain model for ADHD showed good fit.[7] Further information on model fit and other methodological and statistical considerations can be found in Appendix B.

[7] RMSEA = 0.05 (SB χ^2 (475, N = 796) = 666.20, NNFI = 0.95, CFI = 0.96, and SRMR = 0.06.

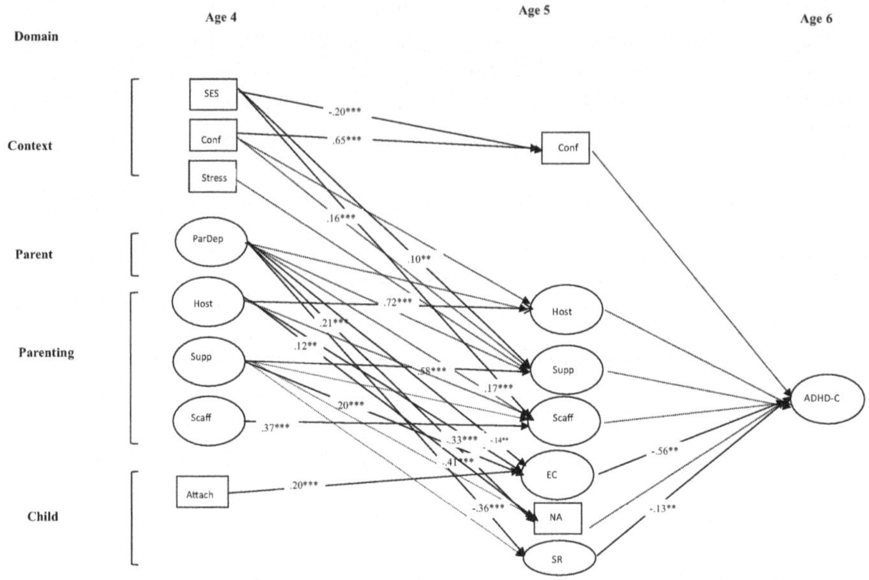

Fig. 7.4 Multi-domain (multiple level) cascade model of factors at age 4 and 5 associated with levels of symptoms of ADHD at age 6 regardless of ADHD symptom levels at age 4 and 5.Solid lines illustrate significant paths; dotted lines, nonsignificant paths. *SES* socioeconomic status. *EC* effortful control. *NA* negative affect. *SR* sensory regulation. *ADHD* attention deficit/hyperactivity disorder symptoms. *$p < 0.05$. **$p < 0.01$. ***$p < 0.001$

Contextual Risk Factors

SES, Family Conflict and Stress In contrast to the model for ODD, there were no direct or indirect effects of SES or family conflict on age 6 ADHD symptoms. Also, as in the ODD model, there were no indirect effects of stress.

Parent Risk Factor: Parental Depression

Age 4 parent depression was associated with age 6 ADHD-C symptom levels via two age 5 child temperament factors. Specifically, higher levels of age 4 parent depression were associated with (a) lower levels of age 5 child EC, which, in turn, were associated with higher levels of age 6 ADHD-C symptoms; and (b) poorer age 5 child sensory regulation which then led to higher levels of age 6 ADHD-C symptoms. As described in Chap. 4, several researchers have identified relations between parental depression and ADHD (Chronis et al., 2007; Cunningham & Boyle, 2002), with some finding specific effects that operate through temperament variables such as effortful control. In a bi-directional study spanning 7 years, Choe and colleagues

(Choe et al., 2014) found that boys with low levels of effortful control are particularly vulnerable to the impact of early maternal depression on later externalizing behaviors. Given that even the most skilled parents can find themselves challenged in the context of parenting a "hard-to-manage" child (Campbell et al., 1991), it is not surprising to find relations between parental depression and child ADHD-C. The PACT study illuminates some complex pathways through which these associations might operate. The finding that there also was a pathway from parent depression at age 4 via sensory regulation at age 5 to ADHD symptoms makes a novel contribution to the literature since this variable has not been examined in previous research. ADHD is, in some ways, a problem in self-regulation, so finding that SR may be one aspect of self-regulation related to this disorder has implications for treatment that are described in Chap. 11.

Parenting Factors: Hostility, Support, Scaffolding

Surprisingly, no direct effects were found between age 5 parenting and age 6 ADHD-C symptoms. These findings differ from those for ODD in which parenting was directly associated with age 6 ODD symptoms. There were indirect effects of age 4 parenting on age 6 ADHD-C symptom levels via the child temperament variable of EC. Specifically, higher levels of age 4 parental hostility and lower levels of age 4 parental support were associated with poorer age 5 child EC, which then led to higher levels of age 6 ADHD-C symptoms. Again, the role of EC as a mediating variable was apparent. Strong associations between child EC and child externalizing outcomes are well-documented in the literature (see Chap. 5). This study demonstrates the role that EC also plays as a mediator and offers some explanation for the associations found between other variables, including parenting and ADHD-C, in the literature. The PACT study indicated quite clearly that these parenting effects do not operate directly (i.e., there was no direct relation between age 5 parenting and age 6 ADHD), but rather through the impact of parenting on the regulatory aspect of child temperament and its impact on ADHD-C. Interestingly, SR which has not been well studied previously also played a significant role as a mediator between parenting and ADHD-C symptom outcomes at age 6.

Child Factors

NA No direct effects were found between age 5 NA and age 6 ADHD-C symptoms. This contrasted with the findings for ODD symptoms in which NA played a significant direct role. The finding that age 5 NA was not associated with age 6 ADHD-C symptoms indicated that it did not contribute independently to age 6 ADHD-C symptoms in a model in which the variance it shares with other aspects of temperament was reduced.

EC Strong direct effects were found between age 5 EC and age 6 ADHD-C symptoms, with higher levels of EC predicting lower levels of ADHD-C; that is, children with better effortful control seemed to better manage their ADHD-C symptoms. This is consistent with literature documenting strong relations between good child EC and fewer externalizing problems (Eisenberg et al., 2009, 2010; Gartstein et al., 2012; Lengua, 2008; Olson et al., 2005), as well as with the PACT findings for ODD symptoms. As with ODD, it makes sense that children who are better able to suppress an undesirable response would be better able to control their ADHD-C symptoms of distractibility and hyperactivity.

SR A direct effect was found between age 5 SR and age 6 ADHD-C symptoms with better sensory regulation associated with lower levels of ADHD-C symptoms. This suggests that there is a relation between the child's ability to regulate their sensory input and their ability to manage their ADHD-C symptoms. This is, in fact, consistent with prior literature documenting an association between SR and ADHD (Dunn & Bennett, 2002; Mangeot et al., 2001; Parush et al., 2007).

Attachment Finally, we found an indirect relation between age 4 child attachment and age 6 ADHD-C symptoms, which operated through child EC at age 5. Specifically, more secure attachment at age 4 was related to better EC at age 5, which, in turn, was related to children's lower levels of ADHD-C symptoms. This pattern was identical to that found for ODD symptoms. Taken together, these findings suggest that secure early attachment is a good buffer for later externalizing symptoms and that it operates through its role in supporting the child's ability to self-regulate emotionally and behaviorally (better child EC).

Testing Change in ADHD Symptom Levels From Age 5 to 6

We then tested a second model that examined how the multi-domain factors were associated with *changes* in ADHD-C symptoms between ages 5 and 6 (Fig. 7.5). As with ODD symptoms, the magnitudes of those effects depend upon the longitudinal stability of the ADHD symptoms. The change model for ADHD-C showed good model fit.[8] As expected, the stability of ADHD-C symptoms from ages 4 to 6 was very high (the autoregressive path coefficient from age 4 ADHD-C to age 5 ADHD-C was 0.71; from age 5 ADHD-C to age 6 ADHD-C, PC = 0.60). Only one of the age 5 multi-domain factors, age 5 EC, was significantly associated with changes in ADHD-C from age 5 to 6, with lower levels of age 5 EC associated with increases in ADHD-C symptoms from ages 5 to 6. Because age 5 EC was significant, however, there were also several significant indirect effects, with higher levels of age 4

[8] SB χ^2 (678, $N = 796$) = 2167.98, RMSEA = 0.05, NNFI = 0.95, CFI = 0.96, SRMR = 0.08.

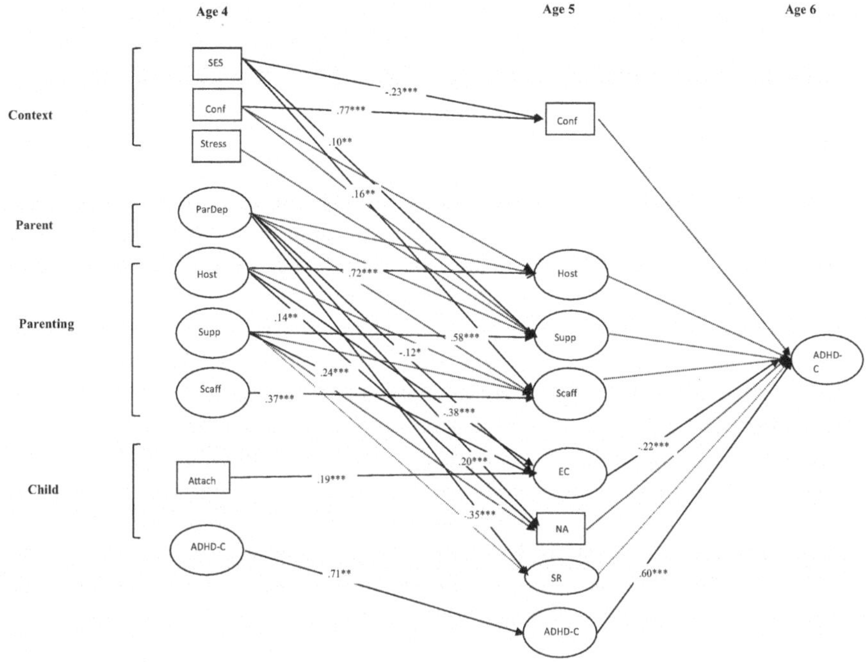

Fig. 7.5 ADHD change to include path from w1Host to w1EC and w1Mdep to w2EC. Multi-domain (multiple level) cascade model of factors at age 4 and 5 associated with levels of symptoms of ADHD at age 6 regardless of ODD symptom levels at age 4 and 5. *SES* socioeconomic status. *EC* effortful control. *NA* negative affect. *SR* sensory regulation. *ODD* oppositional defiant disorder symptoms. $*p < 0.05$. $**p < 0.01$. $***p < 0.001$

parent depression and parent hostility and lower levels of age 4 parental support and child attachment associated with lower levels of age 5 EC and, subsequently greater increases in ADHD-C symptoms between ages 5 and 6.

Risk Factors for Externalizing Disorders: Comparison to Prior Literature

As noted in Chap. 3 on contextual risk factors, relatively little is known about the mechanisms whereby contextual risk factors influence the development of externalizing symptoms in young children. We identified a pathway from age 4 SES to age 6 ODD symptoms via family conflict. Prior studies suggest there is a relation between stress and externalizing symptoms, but those studies tended not to look at the independent contributions of family stress when their shared variance with SES and family conflict were reduced. In that context, our findings support a relation between age 4 SES and conflict with age 6 ODD symptoms but not an independent contribution to age 4 stress. In contrast to the findings for ODD, we found these contextual factors did not have any direct or indirect effects on age 6 ADHD-C symptoms.

As Chap. 4 illustrates, there is considerable evidence for an association between parental depression and parenting and both externalizing and internalizing symptoms. Several studies show that negative or hostile parenting mediates the effects of maternal depression on child symptoms. In contrast, our findings did not indicate that the effects of hostility or any other aspect of parenting mediated the relation between age 4 parent depression and age 6 ODD or ADHD-C symptoms. Instead, the pathway between age 4 parent depression and both ODD and ADHD symptoms at age 6 were mediated by age 5 child temperament variables, NA in the case of ODD and EC and SR in the case of ADHD-C. The difference between our results and prior work is likely related to the present model assessing multiple risk factors at once, thereby estimating the specific, independent contributions of each factor to age 6 ODD, while prior work examined models in which the omitted variable effects inflated estimates of association. This finding has implications for treatment that are discussed in Chap. 11 since parent management training is considered the most effective treatment for externalizing disorders, specifically ODD symptoms.

How Do These Pathways Differ for ODD and ADHD-C?

Discussion of the structure of psychopathology in Chap. 2 makes it clear that symptoms of ODD and ADHD-C are correlated and that there is an underlying externalizing dimension to both symptom types. If they are both connected to a common factor, it seems likely that the risk factors associated with both would be similar. Furthermore, it seems likely that there would be substantial similarities in the indirect effects (mechanisms) leading from contextual risk factors, parent depression, and parenting via child effects to both ODD and ADHD-C symptoms. Of course, differences in the direct and indirect effects for the two symptom types could also inform us about the differences in the way psychosocial factors are related to these different symptom pictures. While we have some prior literature to guide our understanding of possible risk factors directly related to ODD and ADHD-C symptoms, we have little prior multi-domain research to guide us in identifying which pathways may be related to both types of symptoms or how they might differ from one another. To address this question of similarities and differences in pathways to these two disorders, this next section provides a summary of the direct and indirect effects of the age 4 and 5 risk factors on both types of symptoms.

Summary of Risk Factor Comparisons Between ADHD-C and ODD

The statistically significant age 5 direct effects that were related to age 6 ODD and ADHD-C symptom levels were strikingly different from one another. Age 5 factors of family conflict and parental hostility significantly predicted age 6 ODD symptom levels but did not predict age 6 ADHD-C levels. Age 5 EC predicted both age 6 ODD and ADHD-C symptoms, but age 5 NA only predicted age 6 ODD symptoms. Sensory regulation predicted age 6 ADHD-C symptom levels, but not age 6 ODD levels. Thus, of all the age 5 to age 6 direct effects on externalizing outcomes, there was only one transdiagnostic risk factor from the seven factors included in the model, specifically EC. Clearly, there are risk factors that operate differently for ODD and ADHD-C, but EC emerges as an important risk factor for both.

Given the difference in significant direct effects, it is not surprising that the significant indirect effects leading to age 6 ODD and ADHD-C symptoms also differed considerably (Table 7.1). Of the 22 indirect paths examined across domains and ages, only one was the same for both ODD and ADHD-C symptoms. This was the indirect path in which higher levels of age 4 parental support predicted an increase in age 5 EC which, in turn, predicted lower levels of both age 6 ODD and ADHD-C symptoms. There were several indirect effects involving contextual, parent, and parenting factors for ODD that were not significant for ADHD-C. Once again, evidence for a common transdiagnostic effect for multi-domain risk factors was limited, with EC being the most significant transdiagnostic factor.

Examining a Parenting Bidirectional Model for ADHD-C and ODD

The multi-domain model provides a way to examine pathways linking direct associations across risk factors and domains. It does not, however, allow for examining reciprocal relations, or bidirectional effects, between variables (e.g., how ADHD-C symptoms at each age may have affected parenting at a subsequent age and vice versa). This second level of analysis, that of the reciprocal effects, can also be informative as we examine the relations between risk factors. Because existing research (Breaux & Harvey, 2019) found consistent, albeit sometimes small, associations between parenting and both ADHD and ODD, we conducted additional analyses of possible bidirectional effects of ADHD-C symptoms, ODD symptoms, and the three types of parenting behavior we studied. Examining bi-directional effects between parenting and externalizing symptoms was also consistent with our commitment to the tenets of developmental psychopathology which posit that children's developmental outcomes are a result of reciprocal transactional processes between children and their environments that occur over time.

Table 7.1 Indirect effects for ODD and ADHD-C

Pathway to age 6 symptoms	ODD	ADHD-C	
	Significant effect?	Significant effect?	Same direction for ODD and ADHD?
Context			
Age 4 SES → Age 5 conflict → Age 6 symptoms	Yes	No	Different
Age 4 SES → Age 5 parent support → Age 6 symptoms	No	No	n/a
Age 4 SES → Age 5 parent scaffolding → Age 6 symptoms	Yes*	No	Different
Age 4 Conflict → Age 5 conflict → Age 6 symptoms	Yes	No	Different
Age 4 Conflict → Age 5 parent hostility → Age 6 symptoms	No	No	n/a
Age 4 Conflict → Age 5 parent support → Age 6 symptoms	No	No	n/a
Age 4 Stress → Age 5 parent support → Age 6 symptoms	No	No	n/a
Parent			
Age 4 parent depression → Age 5 parent hostility → Age 6 symptoms	No	No	n/a
Age 4 parent depression → Age 5 parent support → Age 6 symptoms	No	No	n/a
Age 4 parent depression → Age 5 parent scaffolding → Age 6 symptoms	No	No	n/a
Age 4 parent depression → Age 5 Child EC → Age 6 symptoms	No	Yes	Different
Age 4 parent depression → Age 5 child NA → Age 6 symptoms	Yes	No	Different
Age 4 parent depression → Age 5 child SR → Age 6 symptoms	No	Yes	Different
Parenting			
Age 4 parent hostility → Age 5 parent hostility → Age 6 symptoms	Yes	No	Different
Age 4 parent hostility → Age 5 child EC → Age 6 symptoms	Yes	No	Different
Age 4 parent support → Age 5 parent support → Age 6 symptoms	No	No	n/a
Age 4 parent support → Age 5 parent scaffolding → Age 6 symptoms	No	No	n/a
Age 4 parent support → Age 5 child EC → Age 6 symptoms	Yes	Yes	Same
Age 4 parent support → Age 5 child NA → Age 6 symptoms	No	No	n/a
Age 4 parent support → Age 5 child SR → Age 6 symptoms	No	Yes	Different

(continued)

Table 7.1 (continued)

Pathway to age 6 symptoms	ODD	ADHD-C	
	Significant effect?	Significant effect?	Same direction for ODD and ADHD?
Age 4 parent scaffolding → Age 5 parent scaffolding → Age 6 symptoms	Yes*	No	Different
Child			
Age 4 attachment security → Age 5 child EC → Age 6 symptoms	Yes	No	Different

Note: * indicates significant effects in opposite direction from that expected; n/a indicates effects were not significant and, therefore, examining patterns of similarity is not appropriate; *EC* effortful control, *NA* negative affect, *SR* sensory regulation

Chronis-Tuscano and Johnston (Chronis-Tuscano et al., 2017; Johnston and Chronis-Tuscano, 2014) suggested specifically that a developmental-transactional model may best describe the complex interplay between parental and family factors and the development and maintenance of ADHD-C symptoms specifically. That model suggests that parenting influences the development of ADHD symptoms while the presence of ADHD-C symptoms affects subsequent parenting behavior. Furthermore, Breaux and Harvey (2019) note that the association between parenting and child ADHD-C symptoms may be affected by comorbidities associated with ADHD. Among those comorbidities, symptoms of ODD are particularly important since oppositional behavior and frequent tantrums are likely to have an impact on parenting attitudes and behaviors. In the models in which we examined bidirectional effects with parenting, we included both ADHD-C and ODD symptoms, allowing us to determine the *specific* effects of parenting on both of those types of symptoms rather than the more general effect of parenting on ODD and ADHD-C when their shared variance would make it difficult to determine if, say, a parenting factor was significantly associated with ADHD-C because it also was related to the comorbid ODD behavior rather than to ADHD symptoms per se.

Bi-directional Effects: Parenting and Subsequent Changes in Child Symptoms Figures 7.6, 7.7, and 7.8 show the bi-directional effects between parenting and ODD and ADHD-C symptoms. The bi-directional ADHD-C, ODD, and parenting models revealed a larger number of statistically significant associations between parental hostility and increases in child symptoms than between parental support or scaffolding skills and child symptoms. Both age 4 and age 5 parental hostility were associated with increases in child ADHD-C symptoms at the subsequent age level. Age 4 parental hostility was associated with increases in ODD symptoms at age 5, but age 5 parental hostility was not associated with increases in ODD symptoms between ages 5 and 6.

The associations of higher levels of parental support with subsequent decreases in symptoms were limited to a decrease in ADHD-C symptoms from age 5 to age 6. Parental scaffolding skills were not associated with changes in ODD or ADHD-C.

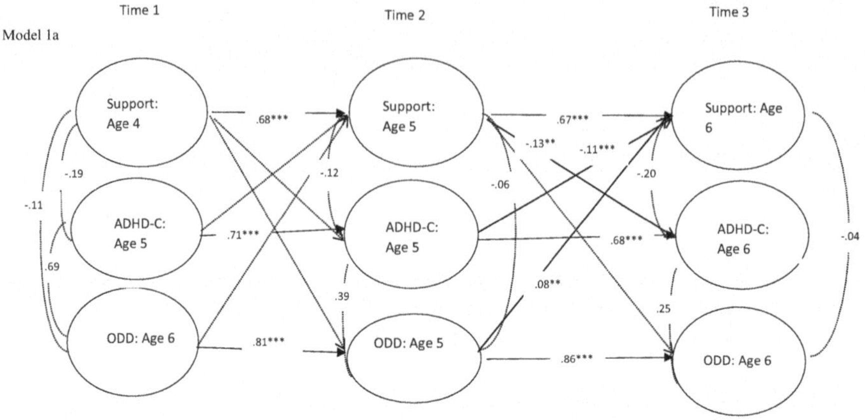

Fig. 7.6 Independent influences of parental support, with child ADHD-Combined type. Structural model for autoregressions and cross-lagged paths, showing the relationships between latent factors included in each model. Each latent factor included 3 measured indicators not indicated. Correlations between latent factors are represented by italicized curved lines. *$p < 0.05$, ** $p < 0.01$, *** $p < 0.001$

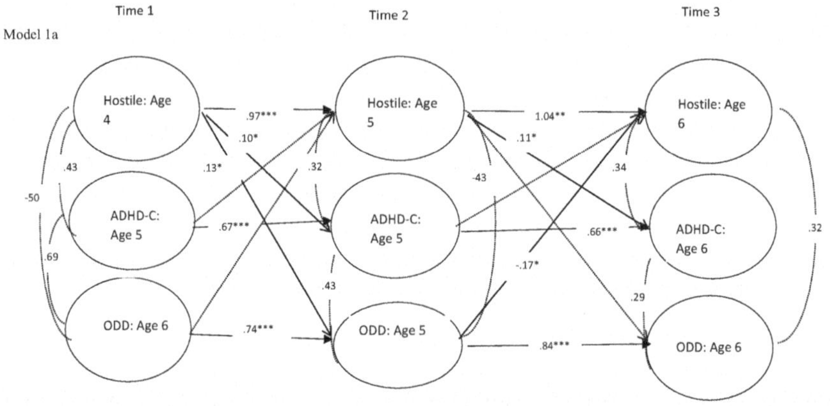

Fig. 7.7 Independent influences of parental hostility, with child ADHD-Combined type. Structural model for autoregressions and cross-lagged paths, showing the relationships between latent factors included in each model. Each latent factor included 3 measured indicators not indicated. Correlations between latent factors are represented by italicized curved lines. *$p < 0.05$, ** $p < 0.01$, *** $p < 0.001$

Bi-directional Effects: Child Symptoms and Subsequent Changes in Parenting The impact of symptom levels on changes in parenting was more widespread. These findings are particularly interesting because there is extensive literature on parenting effects on child behavior, reviewed earlier, but there is much less research on child effects on parenting. First, higher levels of age 5 ADHD-C symptoms led to a decrease in parent support at age 6. Higher levels of these symptoms

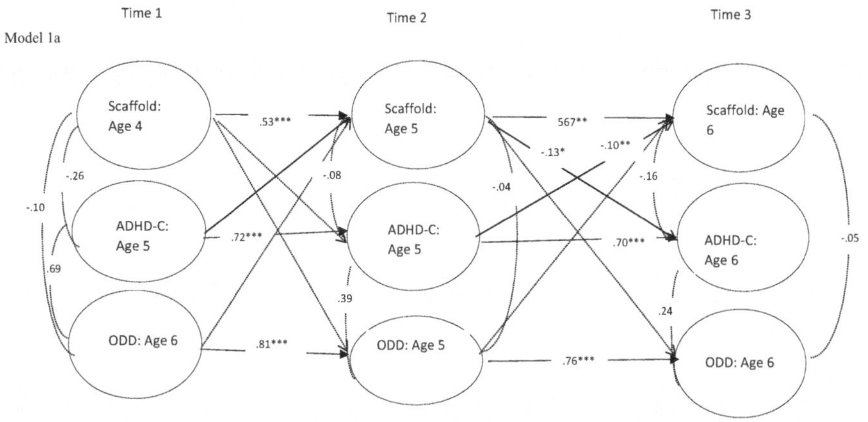

Fig. 7.8 Independent influences of parental scaffolding skills, with child ADHD-Combined type. Structural model for autoregressions and cross-lagged paths, showing the relationships between latent factors included in each model. Each latent factor included 3 measured indicators not indicated. Correlations between latent factors are represented by italicized curved lines. $*p < 0.05$, $** p < 0.01$, $*** p < 0.001$

at age 5 also led to a decrease in parental scaffolding skills at age 6. Thus, although higher levels of age 5 parental support led to a decrease in ADHD-C symptoms, for many parents, it was hard to maintain this level of support in light of their child's continuing ADHD-C symptoms. Rather, it appeared that as time went on, their child's symptoms wore parents out, so they became both less supportive and less skilled at or less willing to scaffold their children's behavior. Interestingly, ODD seemed to have the opposite effect: higher levels of age 5 ODD symptoms led to increases in both parental support and parental scaffolding between ages 5 and 6! It raises the question of parents' perceptions of the causes of their child's behaviors; perhaps in the case of ODD, they felt like they could have more impact than in the case of ADHD-C, which is often presented as a biologically based disorder. This hypothesis is consistent with findings that psychoeducation alone is much less effective in addressing ADHD symptoms in preschoolers than teaching parents specific behavioral techniques, such as administering appropriate consequences (Hornstra et al., 2023).

Comparison to Prior Research on Parenting, ADHD, and ODD

How does this compare with prior studies? Several prior studies that did not control for comorbidities found an association between parenting and subsequent levels/changes in ADHD. When controlling for ODD symptoms, Burke et al. (2008) found no evidence that parental behaviors (timid discipline, poor communication) were associated with subsequent changes in ADHD symptoms in school-age children. Our findings for ADHD differed from those of Burke et al., with two of three parenting factors (less support, greater hostility) associated with increases in ADHD-C from ages 5 to 6.

Summary

In this chapter, we reviewed a large body of research related to two different externalizing disorders, ODD and ADHD-C. First, we examined multi-dimensional risk models for both symptom types and identified the similarities and differences in the risk factors and risk-related pathways that contribute to these externalizing symptom types. We also examined risk factors and pathways associated with changes in both types of symptoms. The similarities and differences between ODD and ADHD-C identified in the multi-domain models were discussed in detail earlier. Second, we described two different approaches to examining the relation of parenting and symptom types, using both multi-domain models and bidirectional models of parenting and symptom types. At first glance, some of the findings related to parenting may seem contradictory across these two types of models. It is time to try to pull this information together and integrate these findings to whatever degree possible.

With no significant direct effects of parenting on ADHD-C identified in the multi-domain model, how is it that two types of parenting are associated with increases in ADHD-C symptoms during a critical developmental transition period, from age 5 to age 6?

As discussed in Chap. 6, in designs in which a single (or very limited) number of predictors of an outcome are included, the magnitude of that predictor on the outcome includes the effects of all variables correlated with the predictor that are not being measured. In models in which there are multiple predictors, the shared variance is reduced and the effect of the included variable on the predictor can be measured more precisely. We believe this "omitted variable problem" sheds some light on the differences in the multi-domain and bidirectional models of parenting and ADHD-C. Specifically, in the multi-domain model, none of the parenting variables are associated with ADHD-C because they do not have specific effects on ADHD-C symptom levels, but two of the three are associated with changes in ADHD-C when each is measured by itself, thereby including the shared effects of all three. Thus, parenting may have an overall, non-specific effect on ADHD-C symptom levels that cannot readily be attributed specifically to supportive, hostile parenting, or parental scaffolding skills. For ODD the results are more consistent across the multi-domain and bidirectional models, showing that hostility is associated with ODD in both models and support is not associated with ODD in either model. The ODD models diverge only for scaffolding, in that the bidirectional model showed no association of scaffolding with subsequent changes in ODD, while a suppression effect was noted for scaffolding and ODD at the multi-domain level. The difference in the findings for scaffolding across the two models is revealing. The bidirectional model suggests that scaffolding has little relation to ODD symptoms overall, but there may be a component of scaffolding that is highly specific to the scaffolding process that leads to higher levels of ODD symptoms. For scaffolding and ODD, it appears that the relation of higher scaffolding skills associated with higher levels of ODD is related to that aspect of parental scaffolding that is not shared with other elements of parenting because there is no association of scaffolding to ODD in the reciprocal models when the shared variance is included in the model. Similarly, the association between higher levels of parental support and ADHD-C seems related to specific aspects of parental support not associated with other aspects of parenting.

The next chapter provides the multi-domain models for risk factors for internalizing disorders in young children, specifically symptoms of depression and anxiety. In that chapter, we describe findings from the multi-domain models of each of those types of symptoms. The risk factors examined in those internalizing models differed from those in the models examined for ODD and ADHD (the reason for this is explained in that chapter). In Chap. 9 on transdiagnostic approaches to the structure of psychopathology, we then examine identical versions of these models across symptom types, as well as transdiagnostic factors.

References

Barrios, C., Bufferd, S. J., Klein, D. N., & Dougherty, L. (2017). The interaction between parenting and children's cortisol reactivity at age 3 predicts increases in children's internalizing and externalizing symptoms at age 6. *Development and Psychopathology, 29*(1–13), 1319. https://doi.org/10.1017/S0954579417000293

Ben-Sasson, A., Carter, A. S., & Briggs-Gowan, M. J. (2009). Sensory over-responsivity in elementary school: Prevalence and social-emotional correlates. *Journal of Abnormal Child Psychology, 37*, 705–716. https://doi.org/10.1007/s10802-008-9295-9

Borsboom, D., van der Maas, H. L. J., Dalege, J., Kievit, R. A., & Haig, B. D. (2021). Theory construction methodology: A practical framework for building theories in psychology. *Perspectives on Psychological Science, 16*(4), 756–766. https://doi.org/10.1077/1745691620969647

Breaux, R. P., & Harvey, E. A. (2019). A longitudinal study of the relation between family functioning and preschool ADHD symptoms. *Journal of Clinical Child & Adolescent Psychology, 48*(5), 749–764. https://doi.org/10.1080/15374416.2018.1437737

Burke, J. D., Pardini, D. A., & Loeber, R. (2008). Reciprocal relationships between parenting behavior and disruptive psychopathology from childhood through adolescence. *Journal of Abnormal Child Psychology, 36*, 679–692. https://doi.org/10.1007/s10802-008-9219-7

Campbell, S. B., March, C. L., Pierce, E. W., Ewing, L. J., & Szumowski, E. K. (1991). Hard-to-manage preschool boys: Family context and the stability of externalizing behavior. *Journal of Abnormal Child Psychology, 19*, 301–318.

Campbell, S. B., Shaw, D. S., & Gilliom, M. (2000). Early externalizing behavior problems: Toddlers and preschoolers at risk for later maladjustment. *Development and Psychopathology, 12*(03), 467–488.

Choe, A. M., Shaw, D. S., Brennan, L., Dishion, T. J., & Wilson, M. (2014). Inhibitory control as a mediator of bidirectional effects between early oppositional behavior and maternal depression. *Development and Psychopathology, 24*(4 Pt 1), 1129–1147. https://doi.org/10.1017/S0954579414000613

Chronis, A. M., Lahey, B. B., & Pelham, W. E. (2007). Maternal depression and early positive parenting predict future conduct problems in young children wiht attention-deficit/hyperactivity disorder. *Developmental Psychology, 43*, 70–82. https://doi.org/10.1037/0012-1649.43.1.70

Chronis-Tuscano, A., Wang, C. H., Woods, K. E., Strickland, J., & Stein, M. A. (2017). Parent ADHD and evidence-based treatment for their children: Review and directions for future research. *Journal of Abnormal Child Psychology, 45*, 501–517. https://doi.org/10.1007/s10802-016-0238-5

Coghill, D., Nigg, J. T., Rothenberger, A., Sonuga-Barke, E., & Tannock, R. (2005). Whither causal models in the neuroscience of ADHD? *Developmental Science, 8*, 105–114.

Cunningham, C. E., & Boyle, M. H. (2002). Preschoolers at risk for attention-deficit hyperactivity disorder and oppositional defiant disorder: Family, parenting, and behavioral correlates. *Journal of Abnormal Child Psychology, 30*(6), 555–569. https://doi.org/10.1023/a.1020855429085

Deault, L. C. (2010). A systematic review of parenting in relation to the development of comorbidities and functional impairments in children with attention-deficit/hyperactivitiy disorder (ADHD). *Child Psychiatry and Human Development, 41*, 168–192. https://doi.org/10.1007/s10578-009-0159-4

Dunn, W., & Bennett, D. (2002). Patterns of sensory processing in children with attention deficit hyperactivity disorder. *Occupational Therapy Journal of Research, 22*, 4–15.

Egger, H. E., & Angold, A. (2006). Common emotional and behavioral disorders in preschool children: Presentation, nosology, and epidemiology. *Journal of Child Psychology and Psychiatry, 47*, 313–337.

Eiden, R., Mink, E., & Leonard, K. (2007). A conceptual model for the development of externalizing behavior problems among kndergarten children of alcoholic families: Role of parenting and children's self-regulation. *Development and Psychopathology, 43*, 1187–1201. https://doi.org/10.1037/0012-1649.43.5.1187

Eisenberg, N., Valiente, C., Spinrad, T. L., Cumberland, A., Liew, J., Reiser, M., Zhou, Q., & Losoya, S. H. (2009). Longitudinal relations of children's effortful control, impulsivity, and negative emotionality to their externalizing, internalizing, and co-occurring behavior problems. *Developmental Psychology, 45*, 988–1008. https://doi.org/10.1037/a0016213

Eisenberg, N., Spinrad, T. L., Eggum, N. D., Silva, K. M., Reiser, M., Hofer, C., Smith, C. L., Gaertner, B. M., Kupfer, A., Popp, T., & Michalik, N. (2010). Relations among maternal socialization, effortful control, and maladjustment in early childhood. *Development and Psychopathology, 22*(3), 507–525. https://doi.org/10.1017/S0954579410000246

Faraone, S. V., Perlis, R. H., Doyle, A. E., Smoller, J. W., Goralnick, J. J., Holmgren, M. A., & Sklar, P. (2005). Molecular genetics of attention-deficit/hyperactivity disorder. *Biological Psychiatry, 57*, 1313–1326. https://doi.org/10.1016/j.biopsych.2004.11.024

Gartstein, M. A., Putnam, S. P., & Rothbart, M. K. (2012). Etiology of preschool behavior problems: Contributions of temperament attributes in early childhood. *Infant Mental Health Journal, 33*(2), 197–211. https://doi.org/10.1002/imhj.21312

Hornstra, R., Groenman, A. P., van der Oord, S., Luman, M., Dekkers, T. J., van der Veen-Mulders, J., Hoekstra, P. J., & van den Hoofdakker, B. J. (2023). Review: Which components of behavioral parent and teacher training work for children with ADHD? – A metaregression analysis on child behavioral outcomes. *Journal of Child and Family Studies, 28*(2), 258–268. https://doi.org/10.1111/camh.12561

Ivanova, M. Y., Achenbach, T. M., & Turner, L. V. (2022). Associations of parental depression with children's internalizing and externalizing problems: Meta-analyses of cross-sectional and longitudinal effects. *Journal of Clinical Child & Adolescent Psychology, 51*(6), 827–849. https://doi.org/10.1080/15374416.2022.2127104

Johnston, C., & Chronis-Tuscano, A. (2014). Families and ADHD. In R. A. Barkley (Ed.), *Attention-deficit hyperactvity disorder: A handbook for diagnosis and treatment* (4th ed., pp. 191–209). Guilford.

Johnston, C., & Chronis-Tuscano, A. (2017). Parental ADHD: Relations to parenting, child behavior, and treatment outcomes. *Journal of Abnormal Child Psychology, 45*, 411–413. https://doi.org/10.1017/s10802-017-0274-9

Lavigne, J. V., LeBailly, S. A., Hopkins, J., Gouze, K. R., & Binns, H. J. (2009). The prevalence of ADHD, ODD, depression and anxiety in a community sample of 4-year-olds. *Journal of Clinical Child and Adolescent Psychology, 38*, 315–328. https://doi.org/10.1080/15374410902851382

Lavigne, J. V., Gouze, K. R., Hopkins, J., Bryant, F. B., & LeBailly, S. A. (2012). A multi-domain model of risk factors for ODD symptoms in a community sample of 4-year-olds. *Journal of Abnormal Child Psychology, 40*(5), 741–757. https://doi.org/10.1007/s10802-011-9603-6

Lavigne, J. V., Gouze, K. R., Hopkins, J., & Bryant, F. (2016). A multi-domain cascade model of early childhood risk factors associated with ODD symptoms in a community sample of 6-year-olds. *Development and Psychopathology, 28*, 1547–1562. https://doi.org/10.1017/S0954579415001194

Lengua, L. J. (2008). Anxiousness, frustration, and effortful control as moderators of the relation between parenting and adjustment in middle-childhood. *Social Development, 17*(3), 554–577. https://doi.org/10.1111/j.1467-9507.2007.438.x

Maccoby, E. (2000). Parenting and its effects on children: On reading and misreading behavior genetics. *Annual Review of Psychology, 51*, 1–27. https://doi.org/10.1146/annurev.psych.51.1.1

Mangeot, S. D., Miller, I. J., McIntosh, D. N., McGrath-Clarke, J., Simon, J., Hagerman, R. J., & Goldson, E. (2001). Sensory modulation dysfunction in children with attention-deficit-hyperactivity disorder. *Development Medicine and Child Neurology, 43*(6), 399–406. https://doi.org/10.1017/S0012162201000743

Natsuaki, M. N., Shaw, D. S., Neiderhiser, J. M., Ganiban, J. M., Harold, G. T., Reiss, D., & Leve, L. D. (2014). Raised by depressed parents: Is it an environmental risk? *Clinical Child & Family Psychology Review, 17*(4), 357–367. https://doi.org/10.1007/s10567-014-0169-z

Nigg, J. T., Goldsmith, H. H., & Sachek, J. (2004). Temperament and attention deficit hyperactivity disorder: The development of a multiple pathway model. *Journal of Clinical Child and Adolescent Psychology, 33*, 42–53.

Olson, S. L., Sameroff, A. J., Kerr, D. C. R., Lopez, N. L., & Wellman, H. M. (2005). Developmental foundations of externalizing problems in young children: The role of effortful control. *Development and Psychopathology, 17*, 25–45.

Parush, S., Sohmer, H., Steinberg, A., & Kaitz, M. (2007). Somatosensory function in boys with ADHD and tactile defensiveness. *Physiology and Behavior, 90*(4), 553–558.

Rothbaum, F., & Weisz, J. R. (1994). Parental caregiving and child externalizing behavior in nonclinical samples: A meta-analysis. *Psychological Bulletin, 116*(1), 55–74. https://doi.org/10.1037/0033-2909-116.1.55

Shaw, D. S., Gilliom, M., Ingoldsby, E. M., & Nagin, D. S. (2003). Trajectories leading to school-age conduct problems. *Developmental Psychology, 39*(2), 189.

Waller, R., Gardner, F., Hyde, L. W., Shaw, D. S., Dishion, T. J., & Wilson, M. N. (2012). Do harsh and positive parenting predict parent reports of deceitful-callous behavior in early childhood? *Journal of Child Psychology and Psychiatry, 53*(9), 946–953. https://doi.org/10.1111/j.1469-7610.2012.02550.x

Chapter 8
Multi-domain Models of Internalizing Disorders: Risk Factors and Complex Pathways

Externalizing disorders primarily involve observable problematic behaviors in young children; in contrast, internalizing disorders are characterized by negative emotions experienced by the child internally. These negative feelings, specifically sadness and anxiety, may be accompanied by other more noticeable symptoms, such as a lack of energy, although the child's experience of these symptoms is frequently not obvious to others. Compared to externalizing symptoms, internalizing symptoms may be less bothersome to caregivers and preschool teachers. Therefore, they may go unrecognized, particularly when they occur at less severe levels. Depression and anxiety are the two internalizing disorders diagnosed in children, although, until relatively recently, there was a belief that children younger than school age did not suffer from depression.

Epidemiological studies reveal that internalizing disorders are much less common in young children than externalizing ones. Community prevalence estimates for depression in preschool children range between 0.3% (Lavigne et al., 2009) and 2.1% (Egger & Angold, 2006), for generalized anxiety between 0.6% (Lavigne et al., 2009) and 6.5% (Egger & Angold, 2006), and for separation anxiety between 2.4% (Egger & Angold, 2006) and 3.9% (Lavigne et al., 2009). A recent meta-analysis (Vasileva et al., 2021) of pooled prevalence rates of psychiatric disorders in children younger than age 7 from eight different countries (including the United States) indicated that depression was rare, with a pooled prevalence of 1.1%. The pooled prevalence of 6% for generalized anxiety was the same as that found by Lavigne et al. and Egger & Angold. For separation anxiety, the pooled prevalence of 1.6% was lower than that reported by these researchers. However, it is also the case that a direct comparison of these figures is complicated by the fact that the meta-analysis included children who were 6 years old, which is not considered part of the preschool period (ages 3–5).

In fact, the actual prevalence of these disorders may be even higher since preschool children may not be able to verbalize their sad or anxious feelings. Thus, parents or preschool teachers do not report them, or erroneously attribute them to

K. R. Gouze et al., *Early Childhood Psychopathology*,
https://doi.org/10.1007/978-3-031-68877-5_8

other factors such as fatigue or shyness, rather than to symptoms of depression or anxiety. For example, a preschool teacher or daycare provider is much less likely to notice a child sitting quietly and not engaged in play than one running around the classroom and having frequent temper tantrums.

Developmental Issues in Diagnosing Depression and Anxiety in Early Childhood

The symptoms of depression and anxiety identified in the DSM-5 are the same across the entire age range from early childhood to adulthood, with a couple of exceptions. The mood symptom for child depression may be irritability rather than sadness, and the duration for the diagnosis of Persistent Depressive Disorder requires only one year of persistent symptoms for children rather than two. As noted in Chap. 2, the DSM is not always sensitive to developmental issues, and although there are aspects of anxiety and depression that do not change over time (e.g., the physiological components of anxiety), there are also clear developmental differences in how these disorders manifest in young children compared to older children and adults. For example, it is unlikely that a preschool child will have suicidal ideation. This contrasts with the DSM symptoms of the two externalizing disorders, ODD and ADHD, which are based on their manifestations during childhood.

Although symptoms of ODD and ADHD were included in the 1980 version of the DSM, the recognition that children can suffer from symptoms of depression is more recent. It was not until 1989, almost a full decade after the publication of DSM III, that clinicians and researchers came to a consensus regarding the existence and manifestation of depression in school-age children (Weiss & Garber, 2003). As late as 2002, there was still some question as to whether children younger than age five could be depressed. This idea was partly based on a naïve belief that early childhood was a period characterized by general happiness as well as the unfounded assumption that preschool children did not yet have the cognitive ability to experience some of the features of depression, such as hopelessness. Fortunately, this notion was dispelled in the early 2000s, as a series of studies were published validating the existence of depression in children as young as three years of age and documenting its features. Joan Luby and her colleagues (Luby et al., 2002, 2003) conducted a series of studies on the symptom patterns of depression in preschoolers as young as three years of age using developmentally modified DSM criteria. The modifications consisted of using sadness or irritability for the mood symptom and a loss of interest in play for the symptom of anhedonia. Using these developmentally modified criteria, Luby and colleagues reported that depressed preschoolers showed symptoms typical of depression as specified in the DSM and that anhedonia was a specific marker of preschool depression. In a later study designed to replicate these findings in a larger, more diverse community sample, this group of researchers (Luby et al., 2009) found that symptoms of guilt and extreme fatigue were particular markers of preschool depression since these symptoms differentiated between the children who met criteria for depression and those with anxiety disorders, externalizing disorders, or no disorder. In this study results also indicated that anhedonia was a marker of a particular subtype of preschool depression. The work of Luby et al. is notable for showing that preschool children do, indeed, suffer from depression and that developmental modifications of the DSM-5 criteria are necessary to accurately determine if they meet criteria for a diagnosis of major depression.

Regarding developmental issues in diagnosing anxiety in young children, The DSM-5-TR (American Psychiatric Association, 2022) specifies only one difference in the criteria for a diagnosis of Generalized Anxiety Disorder (GAD) in children compared to the adult criteria. Specifically, in children, only one symptom associated with excessive worry is required to make this diagnosis, whereas in adults, three symptoms are required. However, there is no recognition that young children may not be able to verbalize that they are worried or anxious about a number of events or activities, which is the primary criterion for diagnosing GAD. Instead, young children may "act out" their worry behaviorally by refusing to engage in activities that make them anxious, and these behaviors are easily misinterpreted as oppositionality instead of anxiety. There are also developmental issues in diagnosing Separation Anxiety Disorder (SAD) in young children. First, the key criterion for SAD is "developmentally inappropriate and excessive fear at separation from an attachment figure," but most preschoolers show distress at separation, particularly in an unfamiliar situation (e.g., the first day of preschool), which makes it difficult to determine what is excessive and developmentally inappropriate distress. Also, the DSM specifies that the excessive fear of separation must be displayed in specific ways, two of which include the child worrying about experiencing an "untoward" event or about harm befalling an attachment figure. However, young children may have difficulty verbalizing that they are worried about a possible future event or harm befalling an attachment figure.

Given the developmental differences in cognition and socioemotional development in young children compared to adults, it makes sense that DSM symptoms based on adult criteria may not be directly applied to children younger than middle school age. Thus, it behooves the clinician working with young children to have a thorough understanding of what is developmentally "normal" to determine if a particular behavior is the manifestation of a developmental adjustment (e.g., separation anxiety) or a symptom warranting concern. For example, understanding and recognizing that play is foundational for normal preschool development is essential for the clinician to recognize that a preschooler who shows little interest in play activities may be experiencing symptoms of depression.

Developing a Longitudinal Model

The longitudinal multidomain models we developed for anxiety and depression (Gouze et al., 2022; Hopkins et al., 2020) were derived from cross-sectional models of each of these symptom types (Hopkins et al., 2013) and findings of previous studies of risk factors related to internalizing disorders in general, and to anxiety and depression, specifically. This research suggested that we needed to include the pathways from the age 4 risk factors to the same risk factors at age 5; in contrast, we did not include the same age 4 risk factors at age 5 in the models for the externalizing symptom types. Thus, the models examined for the internalizing disorders differed from the models for the externalizing disorders in two ways: (a) the model for the internalizing symptoms included autoregressions for age 4 and 5 parent, parenting, and child variables (e.g., in the internalizing models, maternal depression was included at both ages 4 and 5, while only its cascading effects via parenting and child temperament were included in the models for externalizing disorders); (b) conflict was only included in the internalizing models at age 4, whereas in the externalizing models it was included at both ages 4 and 5. Consistent with the externalizing models, depression and anxiety symptoms at age 6 were measured as continuous variables.

As with the externalizing disorders, we examined two models for symptoms of each type of disorder at school entry (age 6), identifying both direct and indirect pathways reported in the literature linking those risk factors with both disorders. The first model included risk factors from each domain during preschool and kindergarten. The second model included the same risk factors as the first model while adding the age 4 and 5 symptom levels of that disorder. The first model provides information about multidomain risk factors and pathways that predict levels of depression or anxiety symptoms at school entry regardless of their time of onset. That is, this model answers the question "What are the pathways by which multidomain factors during preschool (age 4) and kindergarten (age 5) contribute to levels of depression or anxiety symptoms at school entry (age 6), regardless of the age when those symptoms started." The second model examines the risk factors and pathways that contribute to *changes* in depression and anxiety symptoms between preschool and formal school entry, thus addressing the question "What multidomain factors and pathways between preschool and kindergarten are associated with changes in depression or anxiety symptoms between ages 4 and age 6.

Model One for Depression

The first longitudinal model (see Fig. 8.1 for a schematic representation of the general model) examined contextual factors of SES, conflict, and stress, the parent factor of parent depression, parenting factors of hostility, support, and scaffolding skills, and child factors of temperament (NA, EC, SR) and attachment at age 4. The same parent, parenting, and child factors were examined at age 5; the contextual

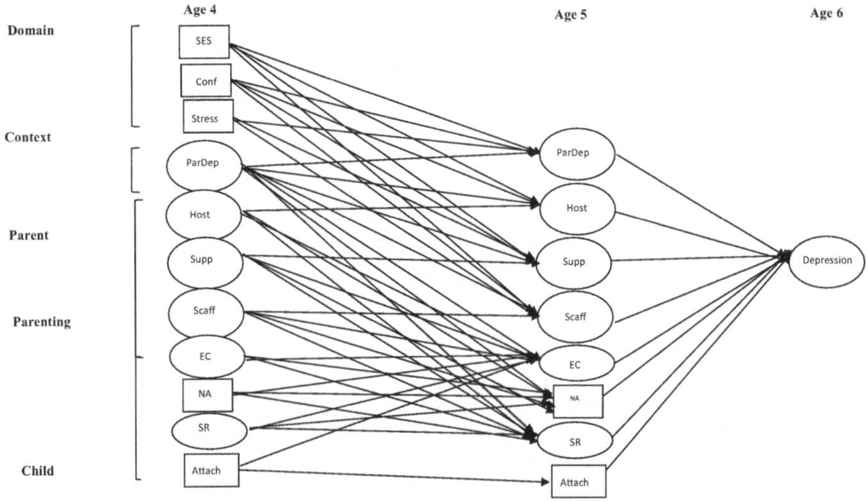

Fig. 8.1 Schematic representation of all paths examined in Model 1 of factors at age 4 and 5 associated with levels of symptoms of depression at age 6 without autoregressive effects for depression at ages 4 and 5. *SES* socioeconomic status. *EC* effortful control. *NA* negative affect. *SR* sensory regulation

variables were not measured at that age. The depression variable assessed at age 6 reflected the number and severity of depression symptoms for each child. Direct effects refer to paths from risk factors at age 5 to child depression symptoms at age 6, and indirect effects refer to paths from risk factors at age 4 to child outcome via their effects on risk factors at age 5. We had three hypotheses. First, we hypothesized that contextual risk factors at age 4 would have indirect effects on age 6 depression symptoms through their effects on risk factors more proximal to the child, including parental depression, parenting (support, hostility, and scaffolding) and child temperament (NA, EC, and SR) and attachment at age 5. Second, we expected that age 4 parent, parenting, and child risk factors would have indirect effects on age 6 symptoms via their effects on age 5 risk factors. Finally, we predicted that age 5 parent, parenting, and child risk factors would have direct effects on age 6 symptoms.

Model One for Depression: Model Fit

When the longitudinal model depicted in Fig. 8.1 was tested, the overall model fit was moderately good.[1] Figure 8.2 depicts the significant paths in the structural model.

[1] The fit statistics for Model 1 for depression (moderately good fit) SB $\chi^2(721, N = 796) = 2359.76$, RMSEA = 0.053, NNFI = 0.94, CFI = 0.95, SRMR = 0.06.

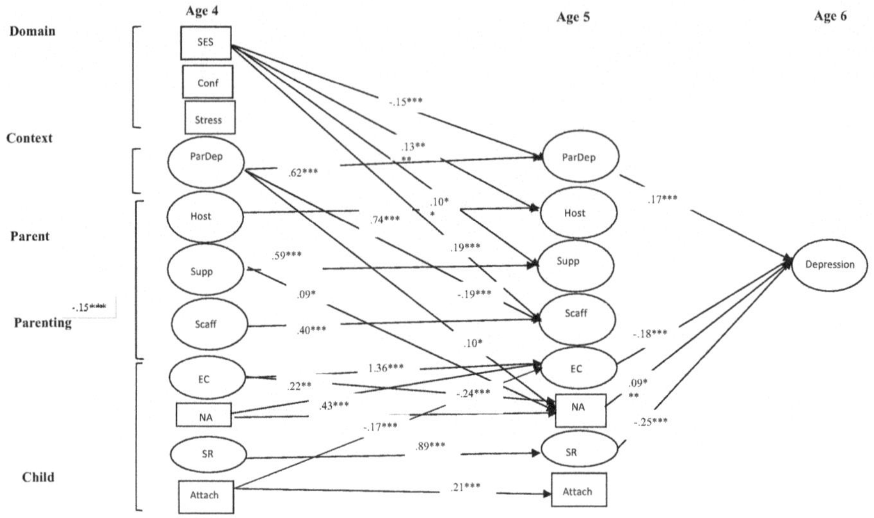

Fig. 8.2 Significant pathways in multidomain Model 1 of factors at age 4 and 5 associated with levels of symptoms of depression at age 6 without autoregressive effects for depression at ages 4 and 5. *SES* socioeconomic status. *EC* effortful control. *NA* negative affect. *SR* sensory regulation. $*p < 0.05$; $**p < 0.01$; $***p < 0.001$

Contextual Risk Factors

The only contextual factor measured that emerged as a significant risk factor for depression symptoms was socioeconomic status. Socioeconomic status had indirect effects on child depression symptoms via its effects on age 5 parent depression. Lower SES at age 4 led to higher levels of parental depression when the children were 5 years old, and higher levels of age 5 parental depression led to more depression symptoms when the children entered formal schooling. This finding is interesting because it highlights the impact of social determinants of health, such as financial stability, on parental depression and subsequent downstream effects on child mental health in the form of depression symptoms.

Parental Risk Factors

Parent depression at age 5 had direct effects on child depression at age 6, and age 4 parent depression had indirect effects via its association with two age 5 risk factors, specifically, age 5 parental depression and age 5 child NA. Higher levels of age 4 parental depression were associated with greater increases in age 5 parent depression and higher levels of age 5 child NA which, in turn, predicted higher levels of child depression symptoms at age 6. Given that child NA captures the child's irritability and negative emotions, it is not surprising to find this association. It may be that parental propensity for depression is transmitted to the child biologically in the form of higher levels of negative emotionality. Still, it is equally possible that the factors related to parental depression discussed in Chap. 4, such as parental withdrawal, lack of validation, and focus on negative behavior place the child at risk for both higher negative affect and later depressive symptoms.

It is worth noting that the effects of parental depression were not channeled through the parenting variables examined in this model. Although parental depression was associated with one parenting variable, age 5 scaffolding skills, these scaffolding skills were not related to later child depression. Rather, the indirect path of parental depression to age 6 child depression was routed through age 5 parental depression and the age 5 child temperament variable of negative affect.

Parenting

Surprisingly, none of the age 5 parenting factors had direct effects on child depression symptoms at age 6. There was only one indirect effect of parenting on these symptoms. Parent support at age 4 had an indirect effect on age 6 symptoms via its effect on age 5 child NA. In examining Fig. 8.1, the reader will notice that the sign of the path coefficient from age 4 parent support to age 5 child NA is positive, which indicates that higher levels of parent support led to higher levels of age 5 child NA. Since this is theoretically implausible (see Chap. 4), we examined the relations between these variables to determine if negative suppression was the reason for this unexpected finding (see Appendix C for an explanation of negative suppression). This, indeed, was the case, and the relations were in the expected direction. Thus, higher levels of age 4 parent support predicted lower levels of child NA at age 5, which, in turn, were associated with lower levels of age 6 depression symptoms. The fact that parental hostility did not appear to be a significant risk factor for later child depression symptoms was surprising given previous empirical research on the impact of hostility on child internalizing symptoms. It is possible that when the other variables included in this model, such as parental depression, are considered they account for much of the variance previously attributed to parenting in models that did not include this variable (the omitted variables problem discussed earlier, in Chaps. 1 and 2). It is also possible that the parenting variables measured in this study did not capture those aspects of parenting that are most impacted by parental depression and that lead to subsequent child affective disturbance.

Child Factors

The reactive (NA) and regulatory aspects of temperament (EC and SR) in kindergarten each had significant, small direct effects on child depression at school entry. Specifically, higher levels of NA, and lower levels of SR and EC at age 5 predicted higher levels of child depression symptoms at age 6.

Additionally, age 4 temperament had indirect effects on age 6 depression symptoms through its effects on age 5 risk factors. Specifically, age 4 NA had indirect effects via its effects on age 5 NA and EC. Higher levels of age 4 NA were associated with greater increases in age 5 NA, which then predicted higher levels of age 6 symptoms. Higher levels of age 4 NA also were related to higher levels of age 5 EC, which, as expected, were associated with lower levels of age 6 symptoms. It is unexpected that higher levels of NA in preschool would lead to greater increases in EC in kindergarten. Perhaps parents of children who are highly reactive as preschoolers spend a great deal of time teaching their children self-regulation skills, which, over time, leads to better EC.

Age 4 EC also had indirect effects via its effects on age 5 EC and NA. Higher levels of age 4 EC were associated with a greater increase in age 5 EC, which then predicted lower levels age 6 child depression symptoms. Higher levels of age 4 EC were also related to lower levels of age 5 NA, which, in turn, predicted lower levels of symptoms at age 6. Age 4 SR had indirect effects via its effects on age 5 SR, such that higher levels of age 4 SR predicted a greater increase in age 5 SR, which subsequently predicted lower levels of age 6 child depression symptoms. The strength of the child temperament variables as risk factors for child depression are not surprising. Because temperament captures both affective states and the ability to modulate or regulate those affective states, it stands to reason that these factors would impact the affective symptoms captured in child depression symptoms.

Surprisingly, attachment security in kindergarten (age 5) did not have a direct effect on child symptoms in first grade. However, it had an indirect effect, with higher levels of age 4 attachment security associated with higher levels of age 5 EC, which, in turn, predicted lower levels of age 6 symptoms.

Model Two for Depression

As previously mentioned, we developed model two to examine the multidomain risk factors that were related to changes in depression symptoms between preschool and school entry. This model included the same risk factors as the first model at ages 4 and 5, with the addition of depression symptoms at both ages. When this longitudinal model was tested, the overall model fit was good.[2] Figure 8.3 depicts the path coefficients of the significant paths in this model.

[2]The fit statistics for Model 2 for depression (good fit) SB $\chi^2(969, N = 796) = 3217.52$, RMSEA = 0.054, NNFI = 0.95, CFI = 0.96, SRMR = 0.07.

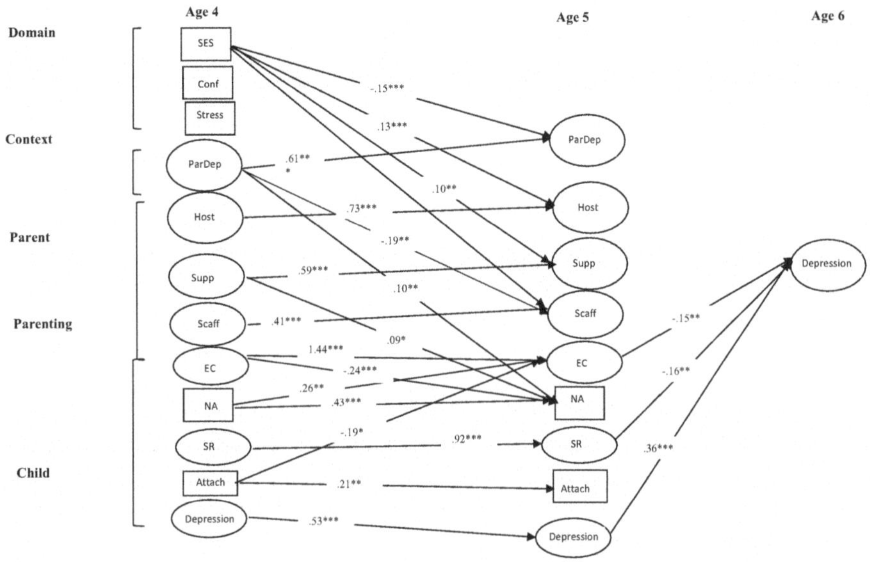

Fig. 8.3 Significant pathways in multidomain Model 2 of factors at age 4 and 5 associated with levels of symptoms of depression at age 6 including autroregressive effects for depression at ages 4 & 5. *SES* socioeconomic status. *EC* effortful control. *NA* negative affect. *SR* sensory regulation. $*p < 0.05$; $**p < 0.01$; $***p < 0.001$

Direct Effects

In this second model (see Fig. 8.3), symptoms of child depression in preschool were associated with a greater increase in child symptoms in kindergarten, which, in turn, were associated with a greater increase in child depression symptoms at school age. The paths from symptoms at age 4 to 5 and from age 5 to 6 were moderate in size, showing that depression in preschoolers is stable. This is consistent with the findings of Luby and colleagues (Luby et al., 2014) and suggests that it is critical to intervene early to prevent the long-term effects of chronic child depression.

After accounting for initial levels of depression in preschool, the model revealed that only two age 5 risk factors, both in the child domain, specifically EC and SR, led to increases in depression symptoms across the three developmental periods. Lower levels of EC and SR in kindergarten led to an increase in depression symptoms at school entry, even after accounting for initial levels of depression at the two previous time periods. There was only one indirect effect from an age 4 risk factor, also in the child domain, attachment security. Lower levels of age 4 attachment security led to lower levels of age 5 child EC, which, in turn, predicted greater increases in child depression symptoms between preschool and formal school entry.

Model One for Anxiety

The multidomain models for anxiety paralleled those for depression. The first longitudinal model for anxiety symptoms (see Fig. 8.4) was identical to the one for depression symptoms (with one exception) since the literature indicated they shared many of the same risk factors (see Chaps. 3, 4, and 5). This model examined contextual factors of SES, conflict, and stress, the parent factor of parent depression, parenting factors of hostility, support, and respect for autonomy (instead of parent scaffolding), and child factors of temperament (NA, EC, SR) and attachment at age 4. The same parent, parenting, and child factors were examined at age 5. We included respect for child autonomy as one of the parenting risk factors instead of scaffolding since previous research indicates that this aspect of parenting is related specifically to child anxiety (Fox et al., 2023; Negreiros & Miller, 2014; Rose et al., 2018). The anxiety variable assessed at age 6 reflected the number and severity of generalized and separation anxiety symptoms for each child. When this longitudinal model was tested, the overall model fit was good.[3] Fig. 8.4 depicts the path coefficents of the significant paths in this model.

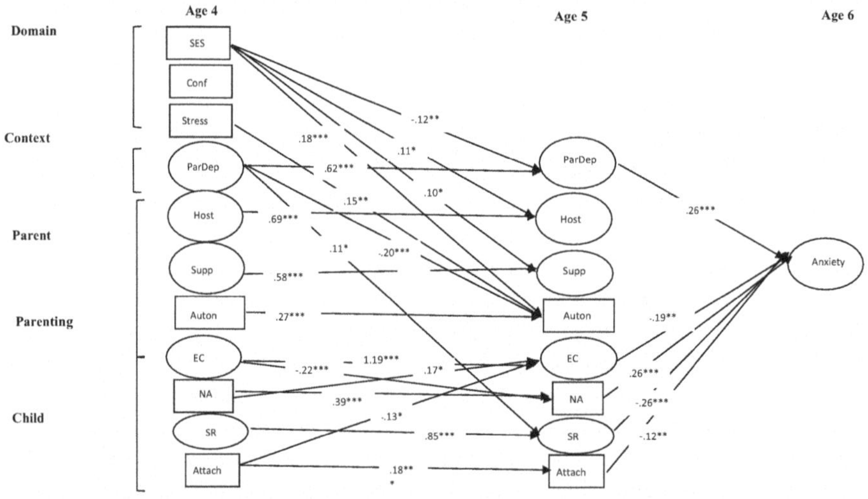

Fig. 8.4 Multidomain (multiple level) model of significant pathways across ages 4 and 5 associated with levels of symptoms of anxiety at age 6 without autroregressive effects for anxiety at ages 4 and 5. *SES* socioeconomic status. *EC* effortful control. *NA* negative affect. *SR* sensory regulation. $*p < 0.05$. $**p < 0.01$. $***p < 0.001$

[3] The fit statistics for Model 1 for anxiety (good fit) SB $\chi^2(569, N = 796) = 1987.30$, RMSEA = 0.056, NNFI = 0.92, CFI = 0.94, SRMR = 0.06.

Contextual Risk Factors

As with depression, SES during preschool was the only contextual risk factor that had an indirect effect on anxiety symptoms at school entry. Lower SES at age 4 was associated with higher levels of parent depression at age 5, which, in turn, were associated with higher levels of age 6 anxiety symptoms.

Parent Depression

Parental depression at age 5 had a small, direct effect on child anxiety symptoms at age 6, with higher levels of parental depression associated with higher levels of age 6 child anxiety. Age 4 parental depression had indirect effects via its effects on age 5 parental depression and age 5 child NA. Age 4 parental depression predicted greater increases in age 5 parental depression and higher levels of child NA, which in turn led to higher symptom levels at age 6. These results mirror the results for child depression symptoms, suggesting that parental depression exerts a strong influence on the development of child internalizing symptoms.

Parenting

Consistent with our findings for depression and contrary to expectations, none of the age 5 parenting factors had a direct effect on age 6 anxiety symptoms, nor were there any significant indirect effects from age 4 parenting to age 6 anxiety symptoms. It is particularly surprising that parental respect for child autonomy was not associated either directly or indirectly with age 6 anxiety symptoms, since this association has been fairly robust in the previous literature on child anxiety (see Chap. 4). This may reflect the impact of the omitted variable problem, discussed earlier. If respect for autonomy had been measured in previous research without considering other aspects of parenting's effects on child anxiety, the magnitude of its association with child anxiety might have appeared stronger. The present finding indicated that it did not have an independent effect after the variance it shared with other age 5 risk factors, particularly parental depression, was removed. It is possible that parenting has an earlier effect, specifically during toddlerhood when the child is beginning to explore more freely on their own. The parents' lack of encouragement for exploration could lead to a sense that the world is a dangerous place.

Child Risk Factors

The reactive and regulatory aspects of temperament (NA, EC, and SR) had small, direct effects on anxiety symptoms at age 6. Higher levels of NA and lower levels of EC and SR at age 5 led to higher levels of anxiety symptoms at age 6.

Age 4 NA, EC, and SR also had indirect effects on anxiety symptoms through their effects on age 5 temperament risk factors. Higher levels of each of the age 4 temperament factors led to a greater increase in its counterpart at age 5, which, in turn, had the expected effect on anxiety symptoms. Specifically, higher levels of age 4 NA led to greater increases in age 5 NA, which, in turn, led to higher levels of age 6 anxiety symptoms. Lower levels of age 4 EC and SR led to decreases in these variables at age 5, which, in turn, led to higher levels of age 6 anxiety symptoms. As expected, higher levels of age 4 EC led to lower levels of age 5 NA, which predicted lower levels of age 6 symptoms. However, unexpectedly, higher levels of age 4 NA were significantly associated with higher levels of age 5 EC. This relation was found in the depression model as well and is hard to explain. As noted in that instance, it is possible that parents of preschoolers with higher levels of NA focus more effort than parents of less reactive children on helping their children develop self-regulation skills and this, in turn, leads to the improvement in EC seen a year later.

Additionally, previous research has documented that high levels of NA and EC that co-occur are associated with the presence of internalizing disorders (Delgado et al., 2018), suggesting that there is something about this combination that leads to the development of internalizing symptoms. Perhaps high negative affect paired with a tendency towards over-control results in an internalization of negative feelings, which ultimately manifests in symptoms of depression or anxiety. Further research is needed to explore the complex interplay between these temperament variables and their ultimate role as risk factors for early childhood internalizing disorders.

Attachment security at age 5 had a direct protective effect, such that higher levels of age 5 attachment security predicted lower levels of age 6 anxiety symptoms. Also, preschool attachment security had two indirect effects, one via age 5 attachment security and the other via age 5 EC. The indirect effect of age 4 attachment security on age 5 attachment security was as expected: lower levels of age 4 attachment security led to a decrease in age 5 attachment security, which in turn led to higher levels of age 6 anxiety symptoms. However, the sign of the path between age 4 attachment security and age 5 EC was negative, which was contrary to expectation (see Chap. 5) and raised the question of a possible suppression effect. To determine if this was the case, we tested for suppression. We found that there was, indeed, a suppression effect and that the actual association between attachment security and EC was in the expected direction; specifically, greater attachment security predicted stronger EC, which, in turn, led to fewer anxiety symptoms at age 6.

Model Two for Anxiety

As previously mentioned, we developed model two to examine the multidomain risk factors that were related to *changes* in anxiety symptoms between preschool and school entry. This model included the same risk factors as the first model at ages 4 and 5, with the addition of anxiety symptoms at both ages. When this longitudinal model was tested, the overall model fit was good.[4] Fig. 8.5 depicts the path coefficients of the significant paths in this model.

The associations between anxiety symptoms at each age were significant and moderate, revealing that anxiety levels between preschool and kindergarten, and between kindergarten and school entry are quite stable. This is like the stability we found in preschool depression, and, again, suggests that early intervention for anxious preschoolers is critically important since the avoidant behavior associated with their anxiety will lead them to miss many developmentally enhancing experiences and activities.

After accounting for earlier levels of anxiety, only one age 5 risk factor in the child domain, attachment security, had a direct effect on an increase in age 6 anxiety

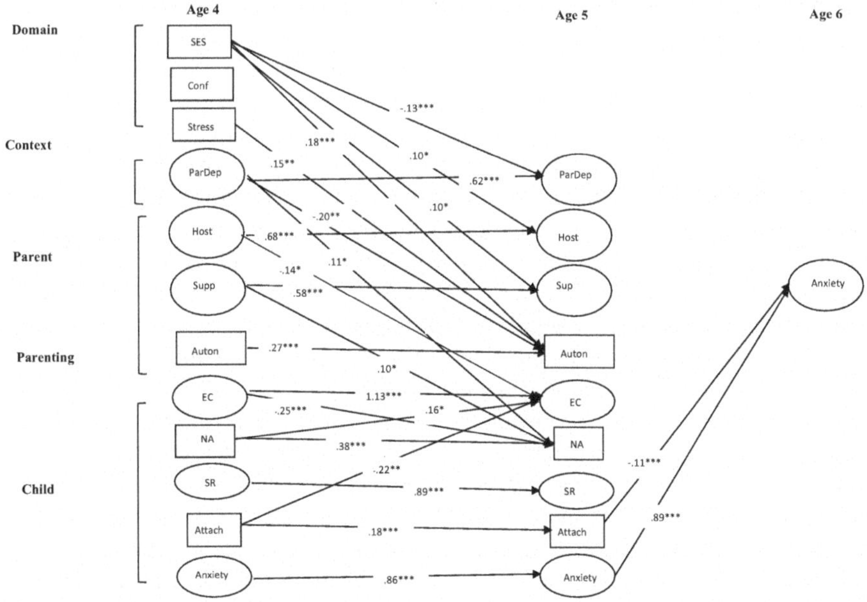

Fig. 8.5 Multidomain (multiple level) model of significant pathways associated with significant levels of symptoms of anxiety at age 6 including autroregressive effects for anxiety at ages 4 and 5. *SES* socioeconomic status. *EC* effortful control. *NA* negative affect. *SR* sensory regulation. $*p < 0.05$. $**p < 0.01$. $***p < 0.001$

[4] The fit statistics for Model 2 for anxiety (good fit) SB χ^2 (784, $N = 796$) = 2961.62, RMSEA = 0.059, NNFI = 0.92, CFI = 0.94, SRMR = 0.06.

symptoms. Specifically, less secure attachment at age 5 predicted an increase in anxiety symptoms at age 6.

Comparison of Longitudinal Models for Depression and Anxiety

The longitudinal models for depression and anxiety symptoms at age 6 revealed many similarities in risk factors and pathways leading to these two types of symptoms, as well as several differences. For both types of symptoms, SES was the only contextual risk factor that had an indirect effect on child outcome, and these effects were via the effects of SES on parental depression at age 5. This helps to explain the relation between a distal risk factor, such as SES, and child internalizing disorder outcomes—that is, SES exerts its effects on child depression via parental depression, a factor that has a more direct impact on the child. In addition to the theoretical significance of this finding, it has encouraging implications for intervention. Specifically, while it may not be feasible for a treatment program to increase families' SES, there are effective treatments for adult depression that could ameliorate the impact of this contextual factor on child depression and anxiety. Furthermore, the relations between SES, parental depression, and child outcomes support the need for public policy that raises children and families out of poverty and more directly addresses SES as a social determinant of health.

In the parent domain, age 5 parent depression had direct effects on both depression and anxiety symptoms. Parental depression at age 4 also played an indirect role in the development of both types of symptoms via its effect on leading to increases in child NA at age 5. The fact that depression had both direct and indirect effects seems to highlight the importance of early treatment of depressive symptoms in parents of young children. However, the process by which this might improve child internalizing disorders is not at all clear. It might be the case that the pathway by which an improvement in parent depression improves the child's internalizing symptoms is through an improvement in parenting attitudes or practices for less depressed parents, but those pathways (from age 4 parent depression to age 6 child internalizing symptoms via parenting) in our internalizing models are all nonsignificant. These surprising findings might be due to the omitted variables problem in other parenting research, as discussed earlier, or to the selection or measurement of parenting variables in the PACT study that did not capture the relevant aspects of parenting. It does, however, raise a question regarding the mechanisms through which intervening in a parent's disorder might alter a child's outcome trajectory. Further discussion of this issue will occur in Chap. 11 on treatment implications.

Contrary to expectation, parenting practices and behaviors in kindergarten did not have direct effects on either depression or anxiety. Regarding indirect effects, there was one difference in the pathways to each symptom type. Specifically, age 4 parent support had an indirect effect on age 6 depression symptoms via age 5 child

NA, but there were no indirect effects from age 4 parenting risk factors to age 6 anxiety symptoms. We expected that parenting during preschool and kindergarten would have both direct and indirect effects on child symptoms due to the large body of literature that points to the importance of parenting on child behavior and development (see Chap. 4 for a complete review). It is possible that these parenting behaviors and practices may have earlier effects on child characteristics (i.e., prior to age 4) that, in turn, lead to the development of depression and anxiety at age 6, which means that we need to begin studying the effects of parenting at an earlier age. This explanation is bolstered by the fact that secure attachment played a role in both types of symptoms, and secure attachment is based on earlier sensitive parenting. The importance of attachment security further suggests that other aspects of parenting, such as synchrony or "mirroring" are more important in their effects on child outcomes than the specific variables we studied. The difference between our findings and those of previous findings may be related, as well, to the omitted variable problem described earlier: we examined the effects of parenting and parent depression together and thus identified the specific contribution of each parenting behavior (e.g., the specific aspect of parent hostility not sharing variance with parent depression, scaffolding, support, or child temperament), and this was not done in most prior studies.

In the child domain, age 5 child temperament, including negative affect, effortful control, and sensory regulation, played a significant, direct role in both types of symptoms. The direction of the effects of NA and EC was consistent with previous research (i.e., higher levels of age 5 NA and lower levels of age 5 EC led to higher levels of both types of symptoms at age 6) (Eisenberg et al., 2009; Moran et al., 2013). Notably, age 5 EC had one of the strongest effects on both types of symptoms. This makes it clear that self-regulation is a critically important factor associated with age 6 child depression and anxiety symptoms. It also suggests that interventions targeted directly at improving child EC may be important components of both primary prevention and early intervention. The treatment implications of this finding are further discussed in Chap. 11.

The finding that SR, another aspect of child temperament, has direct effects on age 6 child depression and anxiety symptoms makes a novel contribution to the literature since this aspect of self-regulation has not been studied extensively. It is also noteworthy that the magnitude of the direct association of age 4 SR with age 5 child depression and anxiety was greater than that for any other variable. This provides further support to the argument of Gouze et al. (2012) that sensory regulation is a conceptually distinct aspect of temperament that warrants further examination as a risk factor for early child psychopathology.

In addition to the recognition that increasing attention should be focused on SR as a risk factor, the present findings also suggest that effective interventions to promote better SR might be an important adjunct in the treatment of depression and anxiety symptoms in young children. To date, no empirically supported psychological interventions are targeted at improving sensory regulation. The present findings indicate that developing such interventions would be an innovative, potentially effective, approach to treating both types of internalizing symptoms.

Along with the direct effects of age 5 temperament, age 4 child temperament had several indirect effects on both depression and anxiety. Each of these aspects of temperament were relatively stable between age 4 and 5, leading to increases in their counterparts at age 5 (e.g., higher levels of age 4 NA led to an increase in age 5 NA). The relations between the reactive (NA) and regulatory aspects (EC) of temperament between these two ages and the subsequent indirect effects of these relations on child outcome also were the same for depression and anxiety. In both models, higher levels of age 4 EC led to lower levels of age 5 NA, which, in turn, led to lower levels of each symptom type, again highlighting the importance of child self-regulation. In both models, higher levels of age 4 NA led to higher levels of age 5 EC, which, in turn, were related to lower levels of symptoms. The complex interplay between these reactive and regulatory aspects of temperament and how they impact child mental health outcomes at different ages warrants further study. Some researchers have shown that high levels of EC moderate the impact of high levels of NA on child outcomes (Delgado et al., 2018; Raines et al., 2023), but our findings suggest that high levels of NA in young children might lead to higher levels of EC over time. As stated earlier, it is possible that parents of more reactive preschoolers work with their child to develop better self-regulation during these early years because they are aware that this will be important for their child's success in kindergarten. However, this hypothesis requires further study.

Attachment security in kindergarten did not have a direct effect on depression symptoms, whereas, for anxiety, it did. For both types of symptoms, preschool attachment security had an indirect effect via its effects on EC in kindergarten. That is, more secure age 4 attachment led to higher levels of age 5 EC, which, in turn, predicted lower levels of age 6 depression and anxiety symptoms. Attachment theory (Bowlby, 1989) posits that earlier levels of secure attachment predict better self-regulation at later ages, and this supposition is supported by empirical evidence (Sroufe, 2005). Thus, the finding that attachment security exerted its effect via EC is consistent with theory and previous research. For anxiety symptoms, age 4 attachment security had an additional indirect effect via its effect on age 5 attachment. The finding that attachment security had significant effects on both types of symptoms at age 6 reveals that attachment plays an important role in child outcome, not only in infancy, but throughout the course of early childhood (albeit less important than the role of child temperament or the ongoing effects of parent depression). Also, it provides a possible explanation for the fact that parenting did not have much of an impact on either depression or anxiety symptoms. That is, there is extensive evidence that secure attachment is based on sensitive, supportive parenting (DeWolff & van Ijzendoorn, 1997), which means that the children who were more securely attached as preschoolers likely had experienced these positive aspects of parenting earlier in their development, that is, prior to age 4. Thus, parenting may have earlier effects on the child by leading to more secure attachment.

Comparing the change models for depression and anxiety (i.e., the models that included symptoms at each age) also revealed similarities and differences in the factors that led to changes in symptom levels after accounting for previous levels. Both change models showed that symptoms of depression and anxiety in preschool are relatively stable. They also showed that, after accounting for previous symptoms, only a few risk factors at age 5 had significant direct effects on changes in age 6 symptoms. In both change models, only child risk factors at age 5 had significant, direct effects on age 6 symptoms after accounting for prior levels of the respective symptom type at ages 4 and 5. There was, however, a difference in the specific age 5 child factors that predicted changes in levels of each type of symptom. For depression, higher levels of child EC and SR at age 5 predicted greater decreases in age 6 depression symptoms. In contrast, for anxiety, only higher levels of age 5 attachment security predicted greater decreases in age 6 symptoms.

In summary, comparing the models for the two disorders reveals that there are more similarities than differences in the risk factors and pathways leading to each one. To be exact, both models revealed that four of the same age 5 risk factors, specifically parental depression, child EC, NA, and SR had direct effects on age 6 symptoms. The only difference in direct effects between the two models was that attachment security had a direct effect on age 6 anxiety symptoms, but not on age 6 depression symptoms. Furthermore, nine indirect pathways to child outcomes from age 4 risk factors via age 5 risk factors were the same in the two models. The model for depression revealed an additional indirect pathway than the one for anxiety, specifically a pathway from age 4 parent support via age 5 child NA to depression symptoms. For anxiety symptoms, but not for depression symptoms, there was an indirect pathway from age 4 attachment security to age 6 symptoms via age 5 attachment security. These numerous similarities in risk factors and pathways are an excellent illustration of the developmental psychopathology principle of multifinality (i.e., that the same risk factors predict different disorders).

Examining a Parenting Bidirectional Model for Depression and Anxiety Symptoms

The multidomain model provides a way to examine the effects of risk factors from different domains and pathways during preschool and kindergarten on child symptoms at age 6. It does not, however, allow for examining reciprocal relations, or bidirectional effects, between child symptoms and specific risk variables such as parenting. A core principle of developmental psychopathology is that there are transactional, reciprocal influences between different systems; for example, parenting affects child behavior, and child behavior affects parenting.

Thus, we conducted additional analyses of possible bidirectional effects between different aspects of parenting and child symptoms. First, we examined the bidirectional effects between parenting and child anxiety symptoms (Gouze et al., 2017) and found several reciprocal effects between parenting and child anxiety. Specifically, results of those analyses revealed that: (a) higher levels of parent hostility at age 4 predicted increased levels of age 5 child anxiety; (b) higher levels of age 4 anxiety led to decreased levels of age 5 parental respect for child autonomy;

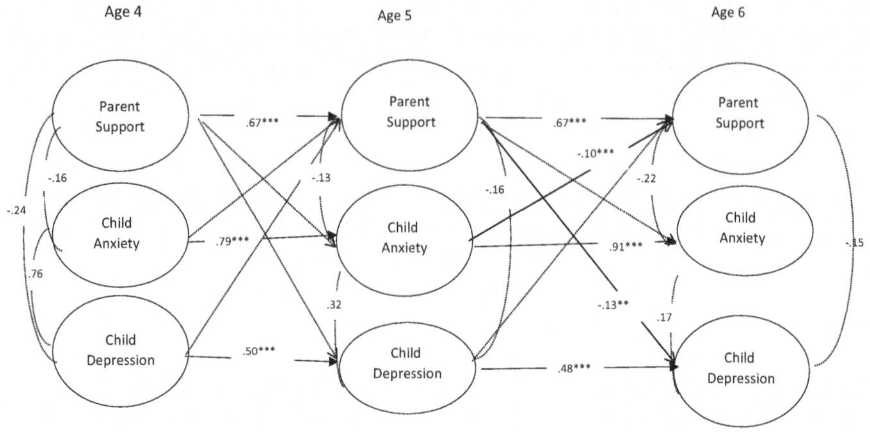

Fig. 8.6 Bidirectional effects of parenting support with child anxiety and depression symptoms. Structural model for autoregressions and cross-lagged paths, showing the relationships between latent factors included in each model. Each latent factor included 3 measured indicators not indicated. Correlations between latent factors are represented by italicized curved lines. *$p < 0.05$, ** $p < 0.01$, *** $p < 0.001$

(c) higher levels of parental support at age 5 led to decreased levels of age 6 anxiety; and (d) higher levels of age 5 anxiety predicted reductions in age 6 parental support and increases in parent hostility.

We then examined bidirectional associations between parenting and both types of internalizing symptoms, depression, and anxiety, at ages 4, 5, and 6. It is clear that symptoms of these two internalizing disorders are correlated. Thus, we wanted to examine whether parenting was associated with specific aspects of symptoms of depression and anxiety when their shared variance was reduced in a bidirectional model that included both types of symptoms. Figures 8.6, 8.7, and 8.8 show the bidirectional relations, including both the significant and non-significant paths between parental support (Fig. 8.6), hostility (Fig. 8.7) and scaffolding (Fig. 8.8) and symptoms of depression and anxiety at ages 4, 5, and 6.

Parenting and Subsequent Changes in Child Symptoms

Overall, parenting at age 4 had little effect on changes in levels of child anxiety and depression from ages 4 to 5, with the exception of parental hostility. Specifically, higher levels of age 4 parental hostility led to an increase in child depression symptoms between ages 4 and 5, but there were no effects of age 4 parenting on age 5 anxiety when the shared variance between depression symptoms and anxiety was removed by including symptoms of both disorders in the model. Parenting at age 5 had more of an impact on changes in depression and anxiety symptoms between ages 5 and 6, particularly for child depression. At age 5, all three aspects of

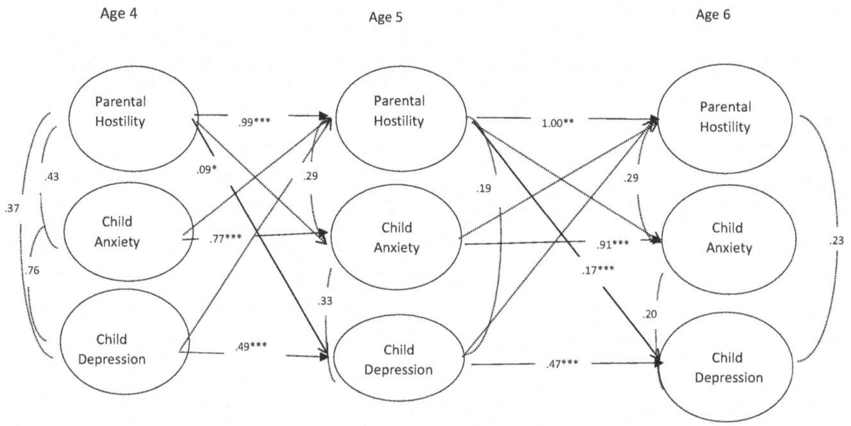

Fig. 8.7 Bidirectional effects of parental hostility with child anxiety and depression symptoms. Structural model for autoregressions and cross-lagged paths, showing the relationships between latent factors included in each model. Each latent factor included 3 measured indicators not indicated. Correlations between latent factors are represented by italicized curved lines. *$p < 0.05$, ** $p < 0.01$, *** $p < 0.001$

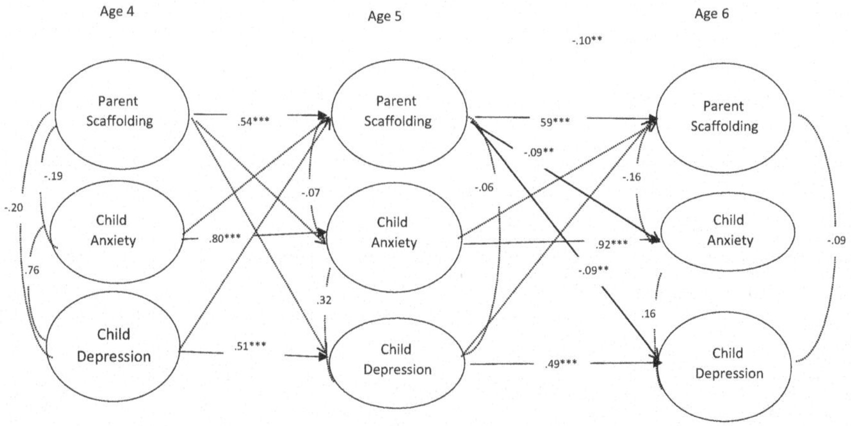

Fig. 8.8 Bidirectional effects of parental scaffolding with child anxiety and depression symptoms. Structural model for autoregressions and cross-lagged paths, showing the relationships between latent factors included in each model. Each latent factor included 3 measured indicators not indicated. Correlations between latent factors are represented by italicized curved lines. *$p < 0.05$, ** $p < 0.01$, *** $p < 0.001$

parenting, hostility, support, and scaffolding had an impact on changes in child depression from age 5 to 6. Specifically, higher levels of age 5 support and scaffolding led to decreases in depression symptoms between ages 5 and 6, and higher levels of hostility led to an increase. Only one aspect of parenting at age 5, scaffolding, had an impact on age 6 anxiety, such that higher levels of age 5 scaffolding predicted decreased levels of anxiety between ages 5 and 6.

Child Symptoms and Subsequent Changes in Parenting

Surprisingly, child symptoms had little impact on parenting. At age 4, neither child anxiety nor depression symptoms had an effect on changes in any of the parenting factors between ages 4 and 5. Anxiety at age 5 led to a decrease in parental support between ages 5 and 6. Child depression at age 5 had no impact on any subsequent changes in parenting. It is interesting that anxiety symptoms, but not depression symptoms, when the child was in kindergarten (age 5), led to a decrease in parental support once their children started first grade (age 6). This may be because the child's anxiety symptoms have more of an impact on family activities than depression symptoms. It is possible that as their children become older and demand for their participation in activities outside the home increases, parents become less tolerant of avoiding particular activities or events due to their children's fearfulness.

There may appear to be an inconsistency between the findings regarding parenting in the multidomain model as compared to those in the bidirectional model. Specifically, parenting did not have any significant direct effects on either anxiety or depression at age 6, and only parent support had an indirect effect on age 6 depression in the multidomain model, but parenting did emerge as an important factor in the maintenance of child internalizing symptoms in the bidirectional model. However, these two different sets of findings are not actually inconsistent. The differences in results can be attributed to the fact that the multidomain model examined all three parenting components simultaneously. Since the three aspects of parenting are correlated, they share some variance with each other. By including all of them in the multidomain model, the shared variance is reduced or eliminated. This means that, in the multidomain model, we were examining, for example, the relation of that portion of support specific to support and how that support-specific factor is related to anxiety or depression at age 6. In the analyses on the bidirectional effects between parenting and child symptoms, we entered one parenting factor separately in each model, which means we were examining, for example, the relation between "general" support (i.e., support that includes the variance it shares with hostility and scaffolding) and subsequent anxiety and depression. Thus, the effect will be greater for "general" support (in the bidirectional model) than for "specific" support (in the multidomain model).

To summarize, the results of the bidirectional analyses when both anxiety and depression symptoms were included in the model revealed interesting transactional effects between parenting and child depression and anxiety, although fewer than we expected. Interestingly, parenting had more effects on depression than on anxiety, such that parental hostility led to increases in subsequent child depression, and higher levels of age 5 support and scaffolding led to a decrease in child depression symptoms between ages 5 and 6. Scaffolding was the only component of parenting that led to a change in anxiety, and it had an effect only at age 5, leading to a decrease in anxiety between ages 5 and 6. Only child anxiety symptoms at age 5 had an effect on subsequent parenting, leading to a decrease in parental support at age 6.

Temporal Sequencing of Depression and Anxiety Symptoms

In addition to studying risk factors for symptoms of depression and anxiety at age 6, we (Lavigne et al., 2015) also examined the temporal sequencing of these two disorders across the developmental periods we studied: preschool (age 4), kindergarten (age 5), and elementary school entry (age 6). Determining the temporal order of these two types of internalizing symptoms is important since knowing which type of symptom typically develops first could lead to the development of preventive strategies to reduce the risk of later developing the other type of symptom. In older children previous research examining this question (Cole et al., 1998; Keenan et al., 2009; Snyder et al., 2009) revealed that anxiety predicted subsequent depression. In two of these studies, specifically Cole et al. and Snyder et al., results showed that depression had a subsequent inhibitory effect on anxiety (i.e., depression at an earlier age predicted decreased anxiety at a later age). In contrast, Keenan et al. (2009) reported that depression did not have a significant association with later anxiety.

Thus, to extend the findings on the temporal sequencing of anxiety and depression to younger ages than previously studied and to resolve these discrepant findings, we examined the bidirectional relations between these two types of symptoms at ages 4, 5, and 6. At first, our findings appeared similar to those shown in older children—that is, anxiety at an earlier age predicted depression at the subsequent age (e.g., higher levels of anxiety at age 4 predicted increased depression at age 5), and depression at an earlier age had a negative relation to anxiety at a later age. However, we determined that this apparent negative association was due to negative suppression and that actually it was the case that the relation between depression at one age and anxiety at the subsequent age was positive. Since Snyder et al. (2009) and Cole et al. (1998) did not examine if negative suppression could account for the negative association they found between depression and anxiety in their studies, it is possible that this also was the case in the older children, such that depression actually predicts later anxiety, rather than having an inhibitory effect on anxiety. This supposition awaits further research. Nevertheless, our findings indicate that in younger children, high levels of both anxiety and depression predict increased levels of the other type of symptom at a later age. This has implications for the assessment and treatment of each of these types of symptoms in young children, which are discussed in Chap. 11.

Summary

This chapter focuses on findings from the multidomain longitudinal risk models we examined to study risk factors and pathways related to the emergence of and changes in depression and anxiety symptoms across three developmental periods: preschool, kindergarten, and entry to first grade. It also includes findings from two other studies on these internalizing symptoms, specifically (a) bidirectional relations between parenting and child depression and anxiety symptoms and (b) the temporal sequencing of anxiety and depression symptoms between ages 4 and 6. Taken together, what did all of these studies reveal about internalizing disorders in young children?

The multidomain, longitudinal risk models of depression and anxiety symptoms at age 6 revealed a wealth of findings that were consistent with previous studies and also contributed new knowledge about risk factors for both symptom types. Consistent with previous results, the models for both symptom types showed that risk factors from different domains, including contextual (see Chap. 3), parental (see Chap. 4), parenting (see Chap. 4), child temperament (see Chap. 5), and attachment security (see Chap. 5) are related to anxiety and depression symptoms at age 6. A distal factor, SES, exerted its effects on both types of symptoms via several factors in other domains that were more proximal to the child. The finding that poorer sensory regulation also leads to increased levels of both types of symptoms contributes new knowledge about this component of child temperament, showing that it serves as a risk factor for both types of internalizing symptoms. Another novel finding is that each of the risk factors in both models only had small effects, whereas previous studies had reported stronger effect sizes, possibly due to the omitted variables problem. These results highlight the importance of distal effects of contextual factors such as socioeconomic status on child outcomes over time. The models also illuminated the multiple pathways whereby risk factors from one domain at one age were related to variables in another domain at a later age that, in turn, predicted levels of symptoms at age 6.

The models examining risk factors for changes in levels of depression and anxiety after accounting for earlier symptoms of each of these types of symptoms revealed that both depression and anxiety are stable between preschool, kindergarten, and first grade. They also showed that only age 5 child risk factors (EC, SR, and attachment) predicted changes in levels of symptoms at age 6.

Models of bidirectional effects of parental support, hostility and scaffolding on depression and anxiety revealed that specific aspects of parenting have an impact on child symptoms. Parental hostility at both ages 4 and 5 led to an increase in children's subsequent depression symptoms at age 6. Also, in keeping with the developmental psychopathology principle that there are reciprocal transactional effects between children and their environment, child symptoms of anxiety at age 5 had an effect on parental support, leading to a decrease in this aspect of parenting at age 6.

The PACT findings on the bidirectional relations between anxiety and depression at ages 4, 5, and 6 contributed new knowledge about the temporal sequencing of these two symptom types in a younger age group than had been studied previously. We found that higher levels of anxiety at ages 4 and 5 predicted subsequent depression. Perhaps more importantly, the PACT study on the temporal sequencing of anxiety and depression revealed a novel finding that, rather than inhibiting subsequent anxiety, depression at ages 4 and 5 also predicted later anxiety. In addition to the theoretical importance of this finding, it has critical implications for assessment and intervention in young children. Clinicians working with this age group need to assess routinely for symptoms of both disorders, particularly since, as previously mentioned, symptoms of depression may not be as obvious as those of other disorders.

This chapter and the previous one (Chap. 7) focus on multidomain models of risk factors for symptoms of externalizing disorders (ODD and ADHD) and internalizing ones (depression and anxiety). In the next chapter, we take a different transdiagnostic approach and examine the same multidomain model of risk factors to transdiagnostic measures of psychopathology.

References

American Psychiatric Association. (2022). *Diagnostic and statistical manual of mental disorders* (5th ed, text ref). American Psychiatric Association. https://doi.org/10.1176/appi.books.9780890425787

Bowlby, J. (1989). The role of attachment in personality development and psychopathology. In S. I. Greenspan & G. H. Pollock (Eds.), *The course of life* (Infancy) (Vol. 1, pp. 229–270). International Universities Press.

Cole, D. A., Peeke, L. G., Martin, J. M., Truglio, R., & Serczynski, A. D. (1998). A longitudinal look at the relation between depression and anxiety in children and adolescents. *Journal of Consulting and Clinical Psychology, 66*, 451–460.

Delgado, B., Carrasco, M. A., Gonzelez-Pena, P., & Holgado-Tello, F. P. (2018). Temperament and behavioral problems in young children: The protective role of extraversion and effortful control. *Journal of Child and Family Studies, 27*(10), 3232–3240. https://doi.org/10.1007/s10826-018-1163-8

DeWolff, M., & van Ijzendoorn, M. H. (1997). Sensitivity and attachment: A meta-analysis on parental antecedents of infant attachment. *Child Development, 68*(4), 571–591.

Egger, H. E., & Angold, A. (2006). Common emotional and behavioral disorders in preschool children: Presentation, nosology, and epidemiology. *Journal of Child Psychology and Psychiatry, 47*, 313–337.

Eisenberg, N., Valiente, C., Spinrad, T. L., Cumberland, A., Liew, J., Reiser, M., Zhou, Q., & Losoya, S. H. (2009). Longitudinal relations of children's effortful control, impulsivity, and negative emotionality to their externalizing, internalizing, and co-occurring behavior problems. *Developmental Psychology, 45*, 988–1008. https://doi.org/10.1037/a0016213

Fox, J. K., Sital, M., Halpern, L. F., & Ryan, J. L. (2023). Elucidating the roles of maternal overcontrol and warmth in the development of childhood anxiety and depression: A moderated mediation framework. *Child Psychiatry and Human Development, 54*(2), 609–622. https://doi.org/10.1007/s10578-021-01274-8

Gouze, K. R., Lavigne, J. V., Hopkins, J., Bryant, F. B., & LeBailly, S. A. (2012). The relationship between temperamental negative affect, effortful control, and sensory regulation: A new look. *Infant Mental Health Journal, 33*(6), 620–632. https://doi.org/10.1002/imhj.21363

Gouze, K. R., Hopkins, J., Bryant, F. B., & Lavigne, J. V. (2017). Parenting and anxiety: Bi-directional relations in young children. *Journal of Abnormal Child Psychology, 45*(6), 1169–1180. https://doi.org/10.1007/s10802-016-0223

Gouze, K. R., Lavigne, J. V., & Bryant, F. B. (2022). A multi-level longitudinal model of risk factors for generalized and separation anxiety symptoms in a community sample of 6-year-olds. *Child Psychiatry and Human Development, 53*(3), 405–417. https://doi.org/10.1007/s-10578-021-01132-7

Hopkins, J., Lavigne, J. V., Gouze, K. R., LeBailly, S. A., & Bryant, F. B. (2013). Multidomain models of risk factors for depression and anxiety symptoms in preschoolers: Evidence for common and specific factors. *Journal of Abnormal Child Psychology, 41*(5), 705–722. https://doi.org/10.1007/s10802-013-9723-2

Hopkins, J., Gouze, K. R., Lavigne, J. V., & Bryant, F. B. (2020). Multidomain risk factors in early childhood and depression symptoms in 6-year-year-olds: A longitudinal pathway model. *Development and Psychopathology, 32*(1), 57–71. https://doi.org/10.1017/S0954579418001426

Keenan, K., Feng, X., Hipwell, A. E., & Klosterman, S. (2009). Depression begets depression: Comparing the predictive utility of depression and anxiety symptoms to later depression. *Journal of Child Psychology and Psychiatry, 50*, 1167–1175. https://doi.org/10.1111/j.1469-7610.2009.02080.x

Lavigne, J. V., LeBailly, S. A., Hopkins, J., Gouze, K. R., & Binns, H. J. (2009). The prevalence of ADHD, ODD, depression and anxiety in a community sample of 4-year-olds. *Journal of Clinical Child and Adolescent Psychology, 38*, 315–328. https://doi.org/10.1080/15374410902851382

Lavigne, J. V., Bryant, F. B., Hopkins, J., & Gouze, K. R. (2015). Dimensions of oppositional defiant disorder in young children: Model comparisons, gender and longitudinal invariance. *Journal of Abnormal Child Psychology, 43*, 423–439. https://doi.org/10.1007/s10802-014-9919-0

Luby, J. L., Heffelfinger, A. K., Mrakotsky, C., Hessler, M. J., & K, B., & Hildebrand, T. (2002). Preschool major depressive disorder: Preliminary validation for developmentally modified DSM-IV criteria. *Journal of the American Academy of Child and Adolescent Psychiatry, 41*(8), 928–937.

Luby, J. L., Mrakotsky, C., Heffelfinger, A., Brown, K., Hessler, M. J., & Spitznagel, E. (2003). Modifications of DSM-IV criteria for depressed preschool children. *American Journal of Psychiatry, 160*(6), 1169–1172. https://doi.org/10.1176/appi.ajp.160.6.1169

Luby, J. L., Si, X., Belden, A. C., Tandon, M., & Spitznagel, E. (2009). Preschool depression: Homotypic continuity and course over 24 months. *Archives of General Psychiatry, 66*(8), 897–2005.

Luby, J., Gaffrey, M. S., Tillman, R., April, L. M., & Belden, A. C. (2014). Trajectories of preschool disorders to full DSM depression at school age and early adolescence: Continuity of preschool depression. *American Journal of Psychiatry, 171*, 768–776.

Moran, L. R., Lengua, L. J., & Zaleswski, M. (2013). The interaction between negative emotionality and effortful control in early social-emotional development. *Social Development, 22*(2), 340–362. https://doi.org/10.1111/sode.12025

Negreiros, J., & Miller, L. D. (2014). The role of parenting in childhood anxiety: Etiological factors and treatment implications. *Clinical Psychology: Science and Practice, 21*, 3–17.

Raines, E. M., Viana, A. G., Trent, E. S., Conroy, H. E., Silva, K. M., Avolensky, M. J., & Storch, E. A. (2023). Effortful control moderates the relation between negative emotionality and child anxiety and depressive symptom severity in children with anxiety disorders. *Child Psychiatry and Human Development, 54*(1), 17–25. https://doi.org/10.1007/s10578-021-01218-2

Rose, J. S., Roman, N., Mwaba, K., & Ismail, K. (2018). The relationship between parenting and internalizing behaviours of children: A systematic review. *Early Childhood Development and Care, 188*(10), 1468–1486. https://doi.org/10.1080/03004430.2016.1269762

Snyder, J., Bullard, L., Wagener, A., Leong, P. K., Snyder, J., & Jenkins, M. (2009). Childhood anxiety and depressive symptoms: Trajectories, relationship, and association with subsequent depression. *Journal of Clinical Child and Adolescent Psychology, 38*, 837–849. https://doi.org/10.1080/15374410903258959

Sroufe, L. A. (2005). Attachment and development: A prospective, longitudinal study from birth to adulthood. *Attachment & Human Development, 7*(4), 349–367. https://doi.org/10.1080/14616730500365928

Vasileva, M., Graf, R. K., Reinelt, T., Petermann, U., & Petermann, F. (2021). Research review: A meta-analysis of the international prevalence and comorbidity of mental disorders in children between 1 and 7 years. *Journal of Child Psychology and Psychiatry, 62*(4), 372–381. https://doi.org/10.1111/jcpp.13261

Weiss, B., & Garber, J. (2003). Developmental differences in the phenomenology of depression. *Development and Psychopathology, 15*(2), 403–430.

Chapter 9
Unraveling the Structure of Psychopathology: Transdiagnostic Approaches, Risk Factors, and Complex Pathways

In Chaps. 7 and 8, we presented multidomain models of risk factors contributing to externalizing (ODD and ADHD) and internalizing (anxiety and depression) symptoms in young children. In the present chapter, we begin by discussing a different conceptualization of the structure of psychopathology, one in which symptoms are viewed from a transdiagnostic perspective. Consistent with the models developed in Chaps. 7 and 8, the approach used in developing a transdiagnostic model was dimensional rather than taxonomic. As noted in Chap. 2, proponents of the dimensional approach to psychopathology argue that it can resolve the diagnostic problems associated with comorbidity in a taxonomic system (e.g., that anxiety and depression, for instance, frequently co-occur). They argue that, ultimately, the dimensional approach will prove to be more logical and useful than the taxonomic approach in helping us understand the factors associated with the development of psychopathology and in promoting effective clinical applications related to diagnosis, treatment decisions, and predicting outcomes.

In the present chapter, we begin by discussing current thinking about transdiagnostic approaches to the structure of psychopathology, starting with an overview of the primary types of models used to do so, specifically hierarchical and bifactor models, and whether they apply to young children. We then examine whether hierarchical and bifactor models that are stable across the preschool, kindergarten, and entry to elementary school years can be identified. Subsequently, we examine which risk factors are transdiagnostic and which are specific to different symptom types.

K. R. Gouze et al., *Early Childhood Psychopathology*,
https://doi.org/10.1007/978-3-031-68877-5_9

Dimensional Models of the Structure of Psychopathology in Children

As previously stated, there are two primary ways of examining the structure of psychopathology when symptom types are measured dimensionally: a hierarchical (or correlated) approach and a bifactor approach. Both approaches recognize that elements of the structure of psychopathology exist that cut across symptom types and, thus, are transdiagnostic. These transdiagnostic factors may arise from general risk factors that are not specific to different types of symptoms.

Hierarchical Models

Hierarchical models are constructed based on the patterns of correlations between the factors at each level. Consider, for example, the classic correlated factor model developed by Achenbach (Achenbach, 1966, 2020), which has been applied in numerous studies. In that model, the second-order internalizing factor loads on the symptom types for anxiety and depression, which tend to correlate highly with one another. The externalizing factor loads on symptom types, including oppositional/disruptive behavior and ADHD symptoms, which also tend to be correlated. The first-order symptom types in the internalizing (anxiety, depression) and externalizing (ODD, ADHD) factors may also be correlated with one another, but typically less strongly than are symptom types within the internalizing and externalizing factors. In addition, the internalizing and externalizing factors also correlate, and it is often assumed they can be grouped under a third-order, general psychopathology (general p) factor. Figure 9.1 provides an example of such a two-level model. Other, more complex hierarchical models also have been developed. These models may differ on the number and types of levels in the symptom structure and on the number and types of factors at each level in the hierarchy.

One of the strengths of this hierarchical approach to the structure of psychopathology is that the dimensions and factors are empirically derived and are relatively easy to understand. Each higher level merely subsumes the lower levels of symptom types. Those in each group correlate with each other more strongly than with the factors subsumed under a different category. It is an empirically supported grouping process.

The p factor (also called general p) in hierarchical models reflects the positive correlations between symptoms and higher-order factors (e.g., internalizing, externalizing). In these models, the higher-order and lower-order factors are correlated and not statistically independent. Therefore, it is impossible to determine their unique correlates (Lahey et al., 2021).

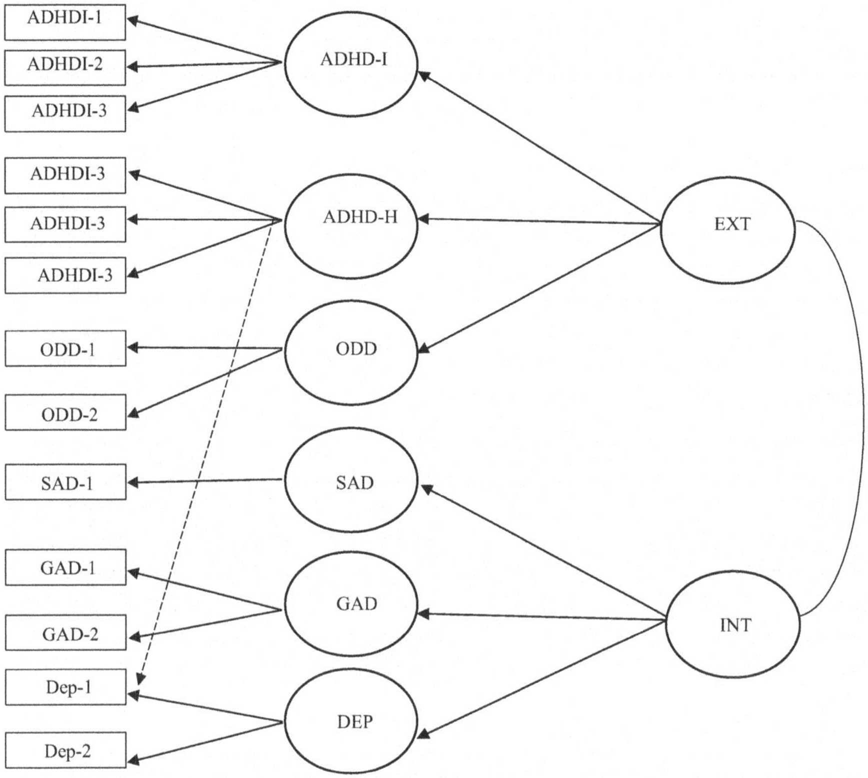

Fig. 9.1 Two-factor hierarchical model with correlated factors. At age 4, the model included two depression indicators and a cross-load from ADHDH to one of two depression indicators. Model fit was not as good if the third depression indicator was included in the model. At ages 5 and 6, model fit was better if all three depression indicators were included and the cross-load was to the second depression indicator. Abbreviations: *ADHD-I* ADHD inattentive type, *ADHD-H* ADHD hyperactive type, *ODD* oppositional defiant disorder, *SAD* separation anxiety disorder, *GAD* generalized anxiety disorder, *Dep* depressive disorder, *INT* internalizing, *EXT* externalizing

Bifactor Models

Bifactor and hierarchical models are similar in that they include a general p factor, more specific latent factors, and symptom-related first-order factors. Although both hierarchical and bifactor approaches may use the same "general p" term to describe the broadest general factor in the model, there are fundamental differences in how general p factors are associated with other latent factors in hierarchical and bifactor models. In the hierarchical model, the overarching general p factor merely subsumes more specific latent factors (e.g., internalizing, externalizing) without modifying them in any way, and the latent specific factors are allowed to correlate with one another. In contrast, in the bifactor model, including a second-order general p factor alters the other second-order latent factors (internalizing, externalizing) in important ways. In the bifactor model, two higher-order factors load on each symptom type (i.e., manifest indicator), and the specific factors are not allowed to correlate. For example, if generalized anxiety is one of the symptom types included in the bifactor model, the general p and internalizing factor will both load on generalized anxiety, and the general p, internalizing, and externalizing factors are set to be orthogonal (i.e., have a zero correlation with one another). As a result, any variance shared between those second-order factors is eliminated. For that reason, the factor loadings in the bifactor model reflect the association of that portion of the factor that is unique to that factor and the shared variance between the internalizing and externalizing factors is attributed to the general p factor. Because of the ways these factors are constructed, the general p, internalizing, and externalizing factors that potentially might be seen in a hierarchical model may be quite different than the factor loadings bearing the same names in a bifactor model.

Problems Associated with Bifactor Models There are, however, problems associated with bifactor models that do not appear in hierarchical models. The bifactor approach reduces the shared variance between the second-order factors, resulting in substantially reduced factor loadings compared to standard hierarchical models. They may even produce negative factor loadings. Critics of the bifactor approach (Burns et al., 2020; Eid et al., 2017) refer to such findings as "anomalous," and they argue that (a) zero factor loadings and small magnitude factor loadings mean the factor does not exist; (b) factors with negative loadings are problematic because the latent factors cannot represent the lower-order symptom (or symptom type)—only factors with positive loadings can do so.

These critics argue for abandoning the standard approach to modeling bifactors developed by Gibbons and Hedeker (1992), preferring a theory-driven approach, the bifactor S-1 model (Burns et al., 2020; Eid et al., 2017). There are important limitations to the interpretation of S-1 models; however, they are less useful in studies of the structure of psychopathology. See Appendix D for a fuller discussion of these issues.

One additional concern that has been raised about bifactor models pertains to the low reliability of some of the factors derived from such models. Lahey et al. (2021) raise the possibility that the reliability coefficients, measured by a reliability statistic known as coefficient H, may be low. Still, in some studies such factors appear stable at different ages or developmental periods. As noted earlier, although there are problems associated with the bifactor model, there are also proponents of this approach; thus, we examined the stability of both hierarchical and bifactor models.

Studies of the Structure of Psychopathology in Young Children

Hierarchical Models in Young Children Interest in hierarchical models began with the work of Thomas Achenbach in the 1960s and 1970s (Achenbach, 1966, 2020). These studies used a variety of statistical approaches to develop hierarchical models. Studies by Achenbach used exploratory factor analyses to identify first-order, correlated clusters of symptom types and second-order factors (internalizing and externalizing) that correlated with one another. In this approach, the first-order factors did not necessarily correspond to the recognizable symptom types associated with DSM diagnoses of disorders (e.g., first-order factors include "rule-breaking" behavior). A higher level of total symptoms was assumed to supersede the second order of internalizing and externalizing factors, but this three-factor model was not typically examined using a confirmatory factor analytic approach. Other studies (Sterba et al., 2007; Strickland et al., 2011) with young children used confirmatory factor analyses to demonstrate that the symptom groups identified as DSM disorders (e.g., clusters of anxiety symptoms, depression symptoms) show good model fit for the DSM approach, but these studies did not examine whether there was good model fit for clusters of those first-order factors.

Studies that did examine model fit for the structure of psychopathology that included more than two levels of factors used a "bass-ackward" approach (Goldberg, 2006), the only approach that allows for the creation of more than two levels of factors (Michelini et al., 2023). Rather than a "bottom-up" approach that begins with symptom clusters associated with DSM disorders followed by a determination of the structure of the higher-level factors, this is a "top-down" approach. This process begins with a factor analysis that extracts a single, higher-level factor (general p), followed by a factor analysis allowing two uncorrelated (orthogonal) factors, then a factor analysis with three factors, etc., until the extraction process is no longer useful. While this allows for developing multi-level hierarchical factor structures, it tends to yield novel first-order symptom groupings. This makes sense if the goal is to derive an empirically supported structure but has the disadvantage of identifying symptom groups that are not typically recognized by clinicians.

Bifactor Models in Young Children While interest in bifactor models as the basis for understanding the structure of psychopathology increased over the last 10–15 years, relatively little attention has focused on the applicability of a bifactor model to the structure of psychopathology in young children. Because there are indications of possible developmental differences in what an optimal model might look like (Caspi et al., 2014; Kotov et al., 2017; Mann et al., 2020), it is important to determine whether such a model helps elucidate the structure of psychopathology in young children.

A few studies examined bifactor models in young children. Each such study has its strength and weaknesses. McElroy et al. (2018) report good model fit in a preschool sample for a model including internalizing and externalizing factors, an attentional factor, and general p. The attention factor, however, accounted for little of the overall variance. Michelini et al. (2023) found a good model fit for a bifactor model including a general p factor and six specific factors (i.e., distress, separation anxiety, social anxiety, inattention-hyperactivity, fear, and oppositionality). Unfortunately, Michelini et al. did not report factor loadings. Given that bifactor models can sometimes yield "anomalous" findings (Eid et al., 2017), as noted above, it is a drawback that factor loadings were not presented. Finally, Olino et al. (2014) did not find a good model fit for a standard bifactor model that included internalizing and externalizing factors loading on their respective symptom types and a general p factor that loaded on all first-order symptom types and the internalizing and externalizing factors. They were able to obtain a good model fit, however, by modifying the standard bifactor model so that the general p factor did not load on the first-order phobic symptom type. An additional limitation to the existing studies of bifactor models with young children is that the racial composition of the samples in two of the studies was limited primarily to White children (Olino et al., 2014, 2018) or not reported (Michelini et al.). Given the limited number of prior studies and the limitations in the racial composition of the samples, an examination of different models of the structure of psychopathology in young children is still needed. Furthermore, few studies examined both hierarchical and bifactor models in their samples to allow for a comparison of the models. Given these limitations, we chose to examine both hierarchical and bifactor versions of the structure of psychopathology using data from the more diverse PACT sample.

The Structure and Stability of Hierarchical and Bifactor Models in Young Children

Using data from the PACT study, we examined both hierarchical and bifactor models in young children. Initially, we sought to determine whether we could identify a single hierarchical model and a single bifactor model, each of which consistently showed good model fit across ages 4, 5, and 6 as the children transitioned from preschool into kindergarten and elementary school.

Both the hierarchical and bifactor models we examined included 6 first-order factors. Five of the first-order factors were latent factors with either two or three manifest indicators (i.e., measures) each. One factor, separation anxiety, was measured by a single symptom and thus was not a latent factor. All measures used to construct these factors are described elsewhere (see Chap. 6 and Appendix A). Both models also included second-order factors with (a) an internalizing factor loading on first-order symptom types, including generalized anxiety, separation anxiety and depression/dysthymia; and (b) an externalizing factor loading on ADHD-I, ADHD-H and ODD.

There were general p factors that were included in both models but with different structures. As described in a prior section, in the hierarchical model, the general p factor is a higher-order factor that loads on internalizing and externalizing factors, which are likely to be correlated with one another to some degree; their correlation may arise because they share a common, higher-order general p factor. The second-order internalizing or externalizing factors, in turn, then load onto the first-order symptom types. In the bifactor model, the general p factor is a second-order factor, just as are the internalizing and externalizing factors, with the general p factor loading on all six symptom types. In contrast, the internalizing and externalizing factors load only on their respective symptom groups.

Structure and Stability: Hierarchical Models

Establishing a Stable, Two-Level Hierarchical Model Initially, we sought to identify a model that showed good model fit at all three ages with correlations allowed between manifest indicators but without cross-loads between externalizing and internalizing symptoms. Such a model would maintain a very clear distinction between those two types of symptoms. We were not able to identify such a model, suggesting that there is some overlap between internalizing and externalizing symptom types. Rather, we identified a hierarchical, two-level model showing good model fit[1] in which the second-order factors included (a) an internalizing factor that loaded on generalized anxiety, separation anxiety and depression/dysthymia; (b) an externalizing factor that loaded on ADHD-I, ADHD-H and ODD (Fig. 9.1). There also were cross-loads from ADHD-H to one of the two depression manifest indicators (see Fig. 9.1 for a schematic diagram of this model).

Two-Level Model with General p Although it is not possible to create a three-level model in which general p is the highest level factor, as discussed above, subsuming internalizing and externalizing second-order factors, it was possible that an alternative two-level model, in which the internalizing and externalizing factors were removed and replaced at the second level by a general p factor loading on the six first-order symptom types, would show better model fit than the standard model with internalizing and externalizing second-order factors. That two-level model showed poor model fit at ages 4 and 5, with general p as the second-order factor rather than second-order internalizing and externalizing factors.[2] At age 6, however, model fit for this two-level model with general p did show good fit.[2] While this may reflect a developmental trend, overall, the two-level model that included internalizing and externalizing second-order factors and general p was more stable across these three age groups.

Structure and Stability: Bifactor Models

The bifactor model we examined included the same six first-order factors and second-order internalizing and externalizing factors as the hierarchical model. Factor loadings for those factors were also the same as in the hierarchical model. In addition, the bifactor model included a general p factor that loaded on all six first-order symptom types. Following standard procedures for bifactor models, the second-order factors (general p, internalizing, and externalizing) were not allowed to correlate. This process eliminates the shared variance between the three second-order effects so that each factor measures the variance specific to that particular factor. Because the hierarchical models included certain cross-loadings, we also examined the bifactor models with cross-loadings to see if a good model fit could not be achieved without them.

At ages 4, 5, and 6, the model with no cross-loads yielded an inadmissible solution. In addition, if cross-loads from ADHD to depression indicators, such as those that had been included in the hierarchical models, were added to the bifactor model, the analyses yielded inadmissible solutions at each age.

Our examination of the preliminary results of these analyses suggested the inadmissible solutions may have resulted from having both a specific second-order factor (e.g., internalizing or externalizing factors) and general p loading on each of the internalizing symptom types and not allowing cross-loadings. Therefore, we examined models that included the second-order internalizing factor, but the general p did not load on GAD, and cross-loads between internalizing and externalizing factors and symptom types were allowed.

While we were able to identify a model (see Fig. 9.2) that showed good model fit[3] with a minor variation in cross-loadings at age 4 compared to ages 5 and 6, there were important variations in specific factor loadings across the ages. At all three ages, the factor loadings for the second-order general p and internalizing factors to first-order factors were statistically significant and positive. This was not the case for the externalizing factor. While the factor loadings of the externalizing factor on the first-order symptom types were all significant in the hierarchical model at all three ages, that was not the case in the bifactor model, in which all were nonsignificant at age 4 and one was not significant at age 5 (see Table 9.1). In addition, while the factor loadings of the first-order factors on their manifest indicators were all positive in the hierarchical model at all three ages, in the bifactor model, several were nonsignificant.

Comparing Hierarchical and Bifactor Models

For the hierarchical model, it was possible to obtain a two-level model that included the six first-order symptom type factors (ADHD-I, ADHD-H, ADHD-C, ODD, depression and anxiety) and second-order internalizing and externalizing factors, but not in the manner originally described by Achenbach (Achenbach, 1966, 2020) in which there were no specified cross-loads between internalizing and externalizing factors or symptoms but internalizing and externalizing symptoms were likely to be correlated with one another. Clearly, the best-fitting model showed that the internalizing and externalizing factors are closely intertwined: in addition to the second-order factors correlating highly with one another, cross-loads across the internalizing and externalizing factors were needed. Developmentally, this structure was stable from preschool to entry into elementary school, with minor variations in the manifest indicators used to measure depression.

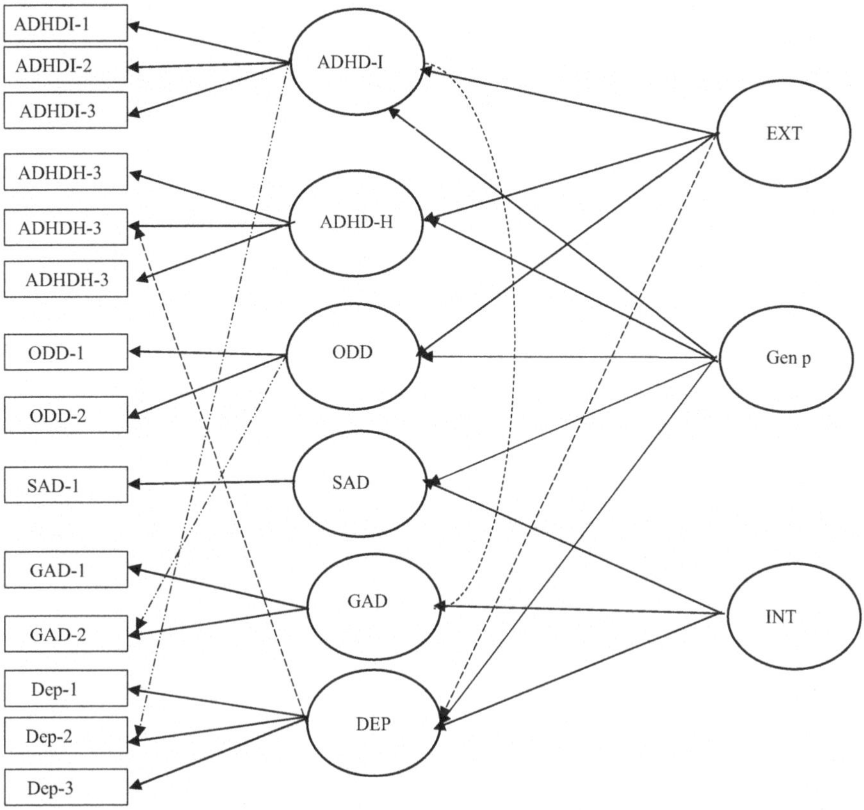

Fig. 9.2 Schematic representation of the bifactor model across all ages. Cross factor indicated with dashed line. One loading (ADHDI to Dep-2) occurs only at age 4. All factor loadings are indicated in Table 9.1. Abbreviations: *ADHD-I* ADHD inattentive type, *ADHD-H* ADHD hyperactive type, *ODD* oppositional defiant disorder, *SAD* separation anxiety disorder, *GAD* generalized anxiety disorder, *Dep* depressive disorder, *INT* internalizing, *EXT* externalizing, *Gen p* general p factor

In contrast, for the bifactor model, model fit could be achieved at each developmental level, but it was not stable from age 4 through 6. In particular, the pattern of negative factor loadings varied across developmental periods, with a decrease in the number of negative factor loadings by elementary school entry.

With the same factor loadings being positive in the hierarchical model but negative in the bifactor model when shared variance is reduced, those specific factors (with no shared variances) are measuring something different than they do in the hierarchical model. Understanding exactly what they measure remains to be determined, most likely by examining correlates of those specific factors in future research. Overall, the hierarchical model seems to better characterize the structure of psychopathology in young children between preschool and formal school entry into grade 1 than the bifactor model does. However, the ultimate test in comparing

Table 9.1 Factor loadings: Hierarchical and Bifactor models

			Hierarchical models			Bifactor models		
			Age 4	Age 5	Age 6	Age 4	Age 5	Age 6
Second-order factor loadings								
Internalizing	GAD		1.04***	1.04***	1.19***	0.92***	0.90***	0.56***
	SAD		0.67***	0.94***	0.60***	0.25***	0.86***	0.63***
	Dep		1.05***	0.67***	1.03***	0.74***	0.45***	0.92***
Externalizing	ADHD-I		0.97***	0.85***	0.79***	−0.42 (ns)	0.01	0.53***
	ADHD-H		0.97***	0.92***	1.00***	−0.16 (ns)	0.24***	0.45***
	ODD		0.70***	0.65***	0.56***	0.11 (ns)	0.65***	0.46***
	Dep					0.04 (ns)	0.4***	1.04***
General p	GAD							
	SAD					0.75***	0.41***	0.48***
	Dep					0.68***	0.60***	0.10***
	ADHD-I					0.99***	1.00***	0.78***
	ADHD-H					1.03***	0.79***	0.77***
	ODD					0.69***	0.52***	0.32***
ADHD-I > GAD						0.69***	0.46***	0.89***
First-order								
ADHD-I	ADHD-I-1	DUPin[a]	0.55***	0.67***	0.5***	0.55***	0.67***	0.50***
	ADHD-I-2	patsy	0.67***	0.77***	0.74***	0.72***	0.64***	0.66***
	ADHD-I-3	adhdi	0.63***	0.69***	0.7***	0.62***	0.70***	0.64***
	Dep-3	pmdsy				0.70***		
ADHD-H	ADHD-H-1	DUPhy	0.45***	0.68***.	0.63***	0.57***	0.63***	0.58***
	ADHD-H-2	patsy	0.7***	0.80***	0.72***	0.69***	0.84***	0.82***
	ADHD-H-3	adhdh	0.71***	0.64***	0.64***	0.66***	0.70***	0.72***
	GAD-2	dep	−0.22***	0.37***	0.47***			

			Hierarchical models			Bifactor models		
			Age 4	Age 5	Age 6	Age 4	Age 5	Age 6
ODD	ODD-1	podsy	1	0.90***	1	1	0.88***	1
	ODD-2	eytot	0.67***	0.56***	0.60***	0.64***	0.56***	0.55***
		gad				0.06	0.27***	−0.02
GAD	GAD-1	pgasy	0.9***	1.0***	0.47***	0.88***	0.95***	0.73***
	GAD-2	gad	0.52	0.34	0.69	0.49	0.29	0.44
SAD	SAD-1	sepan	1	1.06***	1	1	1	1
Dep	Dep-1	dysth	0.63***	0.55***	0.60***	0.6***	0.53***	0.62***
	Dep-2	dep	1.1***	0.66**	0.48***	0.94***	0.87***	0.49***
	Dep-3	pmdsy		0.63***		−0.11	0.57***	0.79***
	ADHDH-3	DUPhy				−0.15**	0.07	0.09

[a]Abbreviations of measures. Measures for ADHDI-1, ADHDH-1 are the DuPaul scales. Measures for ADHDI, ADHDH are from the DISC. Measures for ADHDI-1 and ADHDH-2 are from the Child Symptom Inventory. Measures for Dep-1 and Dep- 2 are from the Child Symptom Inventory. The measure for ADHDH-3 is from the DISC. See Appendix A

the two types of models resides in their clinical utility and, perhaps, in their utility for identifying risk factors for disorders. For this reason, we examined risk factors in both models.

Risk Factors

After examining the structure of both hierarchical and bifactor models in young children, we turned our attention to determining which risk factors in different domains described in the multidomain models discussed in Chaps. 7 and 8 might be transdiagnostic and which were symptom specific.

Identifying Shared Transdiagnostic Risk Factors

In recent years, the emphasis on comorbidity and on correlations among measures of specific symptom types has contributed to an emphasis on identifying transdiagnostic risk factors that cut across a range of specific symptoms such as a general p factor, internalizing, or externalizing factors. The goal in doing this is to identify the shared, transdiagnostic mechanisms that can account for similarities in syndromes and symptom types (Clark et al., 2017; Lahey et al., 2017).

Does "Unimorbidity" Exist?

With the emphasis on the need to reexamine the approach to taxonomic psychiatric classification such as that in the DSM system because of the high rates of comorbidity and multimorbidity that are generated when using such systems, it is also important to keep in mind that there will be children who meet diagnostic criteria for a single disorder or, cast in a dimensional framework, individuals who score high on a dimensional scale for anxiety, but not for any other symptom type. As we turn our attention to efforts to identify transdiagnostic risk factors, we need to recognize that it is important also to examine risk factors, or patterns of risk factors, that might favor the development of one symptom type rather than another. Thus, identifying both transdiagnostic and diagnosis-specific risk factors or interactions between risk factors is important.

Research on Transdiagnostic Risk Factors in Children and Adolescents: Existing Literature

Presently, the range of potential transdiagnostic risk factors that have been identified is rather limited. Attention has been focused on genetic, temperamental, and executive-functioning factors, all of which appear to have an impact transdiagnostically. For example, Brikell et al. (2020), Jones et al. (2018), Riglin et al. (2020), and Lahey et al. (2011) all found that genetic factors were associated with general p, internalizing, and externalizing factors. In this section we provide a review of the evidence regarding psychosocial risk factors.

Contextual Factors

To date, few studies have examined whether contextual factors, including SES, stress, and family conflict, serve as transdiagnostic risk factors. This is rather surprising. As discussed in Chapter Three, the association of each of these risk factors and child psychopathology has been examined for several specific disorders. More attention is needed, therefore, to examine their transdiagnostic qualities.

Parent and Parenting Factors

While many studies examined whether parent depression and parenting are associated with specific child psychiatric disorders, relatively few studies explored whether these factors exhibit transdiagnostic properties. One of the few such studies was conducted by Deutz et al. (2020). In a sample of children ages 8 and 14, these researchers found that maternal depression was associated with general p, but not internalizing and externalizing factors. Further, they found that positive parenting was associated with general p, but not with internalizing and externalizing factors. Harsh parenting was not associated significantly with any of these three transdiagnostic factors. The risk variables we assessed in PACT provided the opportunity to systematically determine if these variables serve as transdiagnostic risk factors in young children across a wide range of variables.

Child Factors: Temperamental Negative Affect (NA), Effortful Control (EC), and Inhibitory Control (IC)

Negative Affect Although there is extensive evidence that NA is linked to both externalizing and internalizing disorders (see Chap. 5), the role of NA as a risk variable in transdiagnostic studies is not as consistent. Several studies (Deutz et al., 2020; Hankin et al., 2017; Tackett et al., 2013) found an association between NA and general p. Olino and colleagues (Olino et al., 2014, 2018) reported that NA was positively associated with general p in young children. Other studies, however, report somewhat different findings. Deutz et al. found NA was associated with the internalizing but not the externalizing factor, while Hankin et al. found a consistent relation of NA with general p across age groups, but the relation of NA with internalizing and externalizing factors differed by age.

Inhibitory Control, Effortful Control Developmental psychologists have recognized that, as children become socialized, they need to develop the ability to suppress an initial, socially undesirable, behavioral (or emotional) response and replace it with a less automatic but more socially appropriate response. Researchers use different terms to describe this process, including inhibitory control (IC) and effortful control (EC), with IC tending to focus on the inhibition of unwanted thoughts and behavior and EC focusing on suppressing inappropriate emotions or behavior. Regardless of the term used, the crucial factor is the ability to suppress unwanted thoughts, feelings, and behaviors. In studying transdiagnostic risk factors, poorer IC was found to be associated with higher levels of general p (Deutz et al., 2020; Hankin et al., 2017; Harden et al., 2020; Hatoum et al., 2018; Olino et al., 2018; Shields et al., 2019; Snyder et al., 2019; Wang et al., 2020). EC has been associated with specific disorders, including symptoms of ODD (Lavigne et al., 2016), anxiety (Gouze et al., 2022), and depression (Hopkins et al., 2020) in young children. This suggests that it also may serve as a transdiagnostic risk factor.

To date, other factors such as family conflict, stress and child attachment, which have emerged as risk factors for specific types of symptoms, have been largely ignored in studies of transdiagnostic risk factors.

Improving Our Understanding of Transdiagnostic and Symptom-Type-Specific Risk Factors and the Structure of Psychopathology in Children

As this review has shown, the range of possible risk factors studied thus far to determine if they are transdiagnostic or symptom-specific is small. Given the limited exploration of the risk factors related to transdiagnostic dimensions of psychopathology, more research is clearly needed. That research should focus on identifying which psychosocial risk factors may be fully transdiagnostic (applicable across all symptom types studied) and which may be associated with a single disorder or specific group of disorders (e.g., internalizing disorders). Finally, as noted earlier, Clark et al. (2017) and Beauchaine and Cicchetti (2016) noted the importance of researching which pathways of direct and indirect effects in a multidomain risk model are transdiagnostic and disorder-specific. We addressed each of these issues in the transdiagnostic models we developed with the children who participated in the PACT study. In addition, for the reasons we described, we examined risk factors in both hierarchical and bifactor transdiagnostic models at each of three levels of analysis.

Level 1

We argue that examining whether particular risk factors are transdiagnostic or not can be done at three levels of analysis. At the first level, researchers examined whether risk factors are associated with transdiagnostic factors such as general p, internalizing and externalizing factors. Most of the published studies of transdiagnostic risk factors used that approach. Using the data from the PACT study, we examined psychosocial risk factors for such transdiagnostic factors identified in both hierarchical and bifactor models.

Level 2

At the second level, we examined the consistency with which risk factors are associated with different types of symptoms. We believed this approach to identifying transdiagnostic risk factors was an important complement to determining if a particular risk factor was associated with general p, etc. For example, using this approach we examined whether risk factors, such as maternal depression and child NA, were consistently associated with each symptom type examined in the PACT study, i.e., anxiety, depression, ODD, and ADHD. For a risk factor to truly be transdiagnostic, we expected that (a) it would be significantly associated with each of those symptom types and (b) also would be associated with the transdiagnostic risk factors measured at the level of general p, internalizing, and externalizing factors. Risk factors that are not associated with all symptom types at the symptom-type and general factor levels may be more symptom-specific than transdiagnostic.

Level 3

At the third level, we sought to determine whether the risk factor pathways in a multi-domain model are transdiagnostic or symptom-specific by examining similarities and differences in the multidomain models of risk factors studied in the PACT study and discussed in Chaps. 7 and 8. Beauchaine and Cicchetti (2016) argue that there needs to be a "new generation" of research examining the etiological and pathophysiological mechanisms (i.e., mediators, indirect effects) across multiple levels of analysis. Models examining such mechanisms need to specify how environmental adversities (i.e., risk factors) interact with one another to understand the development of concurrent comorbid and heterotypic continuity in child and adolescent psychopathology.

We agree and feel that this approach is an important complement to identifying which particular risk factors are transdiagnostic. The principle of multifinality suggests that children may exhibit high levels of the same set of risk factors but differ in the symptom patterns they develop, i.e., one child coming from a low SES environment whose mother is depressed may exhibit high levels of ODD symptoms, while a second child exposed to similar risk factors develops high levels of anxiety or depression. The differences in the symptoms they develop may be related to differences in the pathways by which the multi-domain risk factors have their effect. For that reason, examining similarities and differences in the multi-domain pathways for different symptom types may be important. To illustrate, in the previous example in which two children with the same risk factors (i.e., low SES and maternal depression) develop different disorders, one child may develop ODD because the mother's depression leads to increased hostility in her parenting, and hostile parenting is a risk factor for ODD. The other child may develop depression because the mother's depression leads to increased levels of child negative affect, which are directly associated with depression.

Before examining risk factors at each of those three levels, we need to mention two other issues about the approach we took. First, most existing studies of transdiagnostic issues were conducted in a cross-sectional manner and no attention was paid to the stability of the associations that were found between risk factors and psychopathology. In our approach we examined whether any transdiagnostic qualities of the risk factors at age 4 were stable across ages 4, 5, and 6.

Finally, because it was possible that bifactor models might be useful when seeking to identify potentially transdiagnostic risk factors, we chose to examine the association of risk factors with the factors in both hierarchical and bifactor models in spite of the limitations of the bifactor model described above.

Level 1: Transdiagnostic Risk Factors for General P, Internalizing, and Externalizing Factors

At this level, we examined whether the risk factors in the multi-domain model measured at age 4 were consistently associated with general p, internalizing and externalizing factors across ages 4, 5, and 6. We examined these associations for those factors as identified in hierarchical and bifactor models.

Transdiagnostic Risk Factors: General p, Internalizing, and Externalizing Factors in Hierarchical Models We examined the associations of the age 4 risk variables (i.e., SES, stress, family conflict, parent depression, parental support, parental hostility, parent scaffolding, child NA, EC, SR, and attachment security) and second-order internalizing and externalizing factors in hierarchical models for ages 4 to 6. In addition, because studies often look at total behavior problems rather than separate internalizing and externalizing second-order factors, we examined the association of those risk factors with a second-order hierarchical general p factor, even though model fit for such a factor was not as good as that for a model in which internalizing and externalizing factors are included without a hierarchical general p factor.

Of the 11 age 4 risk factors examined, all but SES (i.e., stress, stress, conflict, parent depression, parental support, parental hostility, parent scaffolding, child NA, EC, SR, and attachment security) were transdiagnostic and stable across all three ages in their associations with the second-order factors of internalizing, externalizing, or a hierarchical general p factor. At the second-order level, SES was consistently associated with a second-order general p factor and internalizing factors but not consistently associated across all age groups with the second-order externalizing factor.

Transdiagnostic Risk Factors: General p, Internalizing, and Externalizing Factors in Bifactor Models While attempting to examine the association of age 4 risk factors with the second-order factors in the bifactor model, we encountered problems that made it difficult to do so. First, to examine the association of the risk factors with the bifactors, it is necessary to calculate an actual score for each bifactor following the procedures described by Joreskog (2006). While it was possible to do that for each bifactor at ages 4 and 5, we encountered an inadmissible solution in trying to do so for age 6. This limited our ability to examine the stability of the associations of the age 4 risk factors with the bifactors at all three ages, from 4 to 6.

Second, earlier in the chapter, we noted that bifactor models of the structure of psychopathology often yield anomalous findings, in which factor loadings in the bifactor model may be negative while the equivalent factor loadings in hierarchical models are positive. We found these anomalous findings for the associations of each risk with the second-order bifactors.

To summarize, for each hierarchical risk factor, the direction of the association between the risk factor and a second-order hierarchical factor made psychological sense, i.e., higher scores on the hierarchical internalizing, externalizing, and general p factors were associated with lower levels of SES, parental support and scaffolding skills, poorer child effortful control and sensory regulation skills, and less secure attachment, as well as with higher levels of family stress and conflict, higher levels of parental depression and hostility, and higher levels of child negative affect. In contrast, for each of the bifactors (internalizing, externalizing, and general p), the direction of the association of risk factor and bifactor was usually in the opposite direction than it was for the hierarchical model and did not make psychological sense, i.e., higher levels of each of the bifactors was associated with higher levels of SES, parental support, parental scaffolding skills, child effortful control, and child sensory regulation skills, while higher levels of each bifactor were associated with lower levels of parent stress and conflict, parental depression, and child negative affect.

Since one measure of the utility of a model of the structure of psychopathology is its utility in helping us understand the relation of risk factors to dimensions of disorder and these findings are theoretically inexplicable, these results raise concerns about the utility of a bifactor model as the basis for studying the structure of psychopathology, at least in young children.

Level 2: Consistency with Which Risk Factors Are Associated with Different Types of Symptoms

In the analyses at level 1, the association of each risk factor to a transdiagnostic factor, such as general p, was examined. For each of those transdiagnostic factors, there were factor loadings for several different symptom types (the first-order factors). While each factor loading was statistically significant, they varied in magnitude. As a result, it is possible that a risk factor was significantly associated with a transdiagnostic measure of psychopathology, such as general p, because the risk factor was strongly associated with some of the symptom types loading on general p but not with others. For that reason, to complement the level one analyses, we also examined the association of each risk factor with each specific symptom type. A risk factor that was clearly transdiagnostic should be associated with, say, the general p factor but also with each of the symptom types loading on general p.

The first-order (symptom type) factors are the same in both the hierarchical and the bifactor models. For that reason, we did not need to conduct separate analyses for the two types of models of the structure of psychopathology.

In the analyses of the PACT data, seven risk factors were transdiagnostic and stable across all three ages in both types of models, specifically: contextual risk factors of stress and conflict; parent factor of parent depression; parenting factor of parent hostility; and child factors of NA, EC, SR, and attachment security. One parent risk factor, scaffolding, was transdiagnostic within the internalizing symptom group but not within the externalizing symptom group. One child risk factor, EC, was transdiagnostic in the externalizing but not the internalizing group. Two of the risk factors, SES and parental support, showed symptom-specific patterns only and were not transdiagnostic (SES was associated with depression, ADHD-I, and ADHD-H. Support was associated with depression and ADHD-I).

Thus, there are seven age 4 risk factors that appear to be transdiagnostic at both the first-order (symptom type) and hierarchical second-order levels: stress, conflict, maternal depression, parental hostility, NA, sensory regulation skills, and attachment security. Others, including SES, parental support, EC, and scaffolding-all appear to be transdiagnostic at the level of a hierarchical general p factor but not at the level of first-order symptom types and second-order internalizing and externalizing factor levels. Studying those factors only at the second-order level may miss subtle relations across symptom types that emerge when transdiagnostic characteristics of risk factors are studied at both the symptom-type and at higher levels.

Level 3: Transdiagnostic and Symptom-Type-Specific Pathways Across Multidomain Risk Factors at the Symptom-Type and Higher-Order Levels

At this level, we were less interested in specific risk factors than in determining which risk factor pathways in a multidomain model are transdiagnostic and which are symptom-specific. Leading researchers have argued that it is time to move to another level of analysis and focus on the multi-level or multidomain processes by which these risk factors may exert influence. As mentioned earlier, Beauchaine and Cicchetti (2016) stressed the need for studies examining the etiological and pathophysiological mechanisms (i.e., mediators, indirect effects) across multiple levels of analysis. Models examining such mechanisms need to specify how environmental adversities (i.e., risk factors) affect other risk factors to understand the development of concurrent comorbid and heterotypic continuity in child and adolescent psychopathology.

The research that Clark et al. (2017) and Beauchaine and Cicchetti (2016) call for involving the multidomain relations of risk factors to help us understand how they may be related to comorbidity can also be done at the symptom-type level and higher-order levels. In the following, we describe the results of the multidomain models that examine such relations. We begin by comparing pathways in multidomain models beginning at the symptom level for anxiety, depression, combined ADHD (ADHD-C) (to reduce the number of analyses, we examined the combined type of ADHD rather than the inattentive and hyperactive-impulsive types separately), and ODD, followed by examining multidomain models of higher-order factors (internalizing, externalizing, and general p).

Comparing Multidomain Models at the Symptom-Type Level In Chaps. 7 and 8 we presented multidomain models showing the risk factors and pathways whereby contextual, parent, parenting and child factors at ages 4 and 5 predict age 6 symptom levels for ODD and ADHD, depression and anxiety, respectively. In those chapters, there were slight differences in the multidomain models used for internalizing and externalizing disorders. Those differences arose because the longitudinal models for externalizing disorders (ODD and ADHD) were developed based on a cross-sectional analysis of risk factors for these disorders at age 4 (see Chap. 7). The models for the internalizing disorders were derived from findings from the cross-sectional examination of depression and anxiety and the extant longitudinal literature.

The differences in the models used for internalizing and externalizing disorders consisted of: (a) the model for the internalizing symptoms included autoregressions of child temperament and attachment variables at ages 4 and 5 (i.e., pathways from age 4 NA, EC, SR and attachment to the same risk factor at age 5) but these autoregressions were not included in the externalizing symptom models; (b) in the internalizing models, maternal depression was included at both ages 4 and 5, while only its cascading effects via parenting and child temperament were included in the models for externalizing disorders; (c) conflict was included at ages 4 and 5 in the externalizing models but only at age 4 in the internalizing models.

To allow for more direct comparisons of which pathways are fully transdiagnostic and which are specific to a disorder or subset of disorders, we re-analyzed the pathways for the internalizing disorders following the same model as that used for the externalizing ones. We chose this approach because it simplified the analyses and reduced the number of autoregressions from ages 4 to 5, which were less important than the cascading effects measured in both models. Overall, this approach simplified the analyses across all symptom types. Table 9.2 includes the path coefficients for the multidomain models leading to age 6 first-order (symptom type) and second-order (externalizing, internalizing, general p) factors.

First-Order (Symptom-Type Level): Pathway Results There were numerous findings of transdiagnostic risk effects at the level of main effects reported in Table 9.2 at the symptom type level. In contrast to the main effects of risk factors, multidomain pathways are likely to be more discriminating and differentiating than fully transdiagnostic, at least at the level of symptom-type analyses. Of the 21 multidomain paths assessed for 4 symptom types, only three were fully transdiagnostic (i.e., significant paths from age 4 and 5 risk factors to age 6 symptom levels were the same for all four symptom types). These were:

1. Age 4 parent hostility → age 5 EC → all age 6 symptom types.
2. Age 4 parent support → age 5 EC → all age 6 symptom types.
3. Age 4 attachment security → age 5 EC → all age 6 symptom types.

It is striking that all measured pathways fully transdiagnostic were funneled through age 5 EC and no other parenting or child factor. It is also striking that, when these models were examined, parenting appeared to be a more significant factor (at least as it impacted child EC, which in turn impacted all outcomes) than it was in the models examined in Chaps. 7 and 8.

Table 9.2 Multidomain pathways to age 6 first-order and hierarchical second-order factors

		Anxiety	Depression	ADHD	ODD	Internalizing	Externalizing	General p
From	To	Path coefficient	Path coefficient	Path coefficient	Path coefficient	Path coefficient	Path coefficient	Path coefficient
Age 4	**To Age 5**							
SES	Conflict	−0.19***	−0.20***	−0.20**	−0.13*	−0.12***	−0.12***	−0.12***
	Support	0.10**	0.10**	0.10*	0.1	−0.11**	−0.11**	−0.12**
	Scaffolding/ autonomy	0.16***	0.16***	0.16***	0.16***	0.14	0.14	0.14
Stress	Support	0.06	0.06	0.06	0.06	−0.05	−0.05	−0.05
Conflict	Conflict	0.63***	0.63***	0.65***	0.61***	0.36***	0.36***	0.36***
	Hostility	0.03	0.03	0.03	0.03	0.02	0.02	0.03
	Support	0.01	0.01	0.01	0.01	−0.01	−0.01	−0.01
Parent depression	Hostility	0.00	0	0.01	0.00	−0.12*	−0.12*	−0.12*
	Support	−0.09	−0.09	−0.09	−0.09	0.10	0.10	0.10
	Scaffolding/ autonomy	−0.08	−0.08	−0.08	−0.08	−0.13	−0.13	−0.13
	Negative affect	0.21***	0.21***	0.21***	0.21***	−0.08	−0.08	−0.08
	Effortful control	−0.13*	−0.12*	−0.14**	−0.09	−0.11	−0.13	−0.11
	Sensory regulation	−0.40***	−0.38***	−0.36***	−0.35***	−0.54***	−0.54″***	−0.49***
Hostility	Hostility	0.72***	0.72***	0.72***	0.71***	−0.77***	−0.77***	−0.78***
	Scaffolding/ autonomy	0.02	0.01	0.01	0.01	0.06	0.06	0.06
	Negative affect	0.13**	0.13**	0.12**	0.13**	−0.19***	−0.19***	−0.19***
	Effortful control	−0.34***	−0.35***	−0.33***	−0.34***	−0.37***	−0.42***	−0.40***
Support	Support	0.58***	0.58***	0.58***	0.58***	−0.57***	−0.57***	−0.57***

(continued)

Table 9.2 (continued)

		Anxiety	Depression	ADHD	ODD	Internalizing	Externalizing	General p
From	To	Path coefficient	Path coefficient	Path coefficient	Path coefficient	Path coefficient	Path coefficient	Path coefficient
	Scaffolding/ autonomy	0.04	0.04	0.04	0.04	0.05	0.05	0.04
	Negative affect	−0.04	−0.04	−0.04	−0.04	0.19***	0.19***	0.19***
	Effortful control	0.24***	0.23***	0.20***	0.22***	0.15*	0.18*	0.19*
	Sensory regulation	0.10	0.10	0.10	0.11	0.22*	0.23*	0.23**
Scaffolding	Scaffolding/ autonomy	0.38***	0.37***	0.37***	0.37***	0.38*	0.38*	0.38*
Attachment	Effortful control	0.17***	0.18***	0.20***	0.19***	0.17**	0.19**	0.20***
Age 5	**To Age 6**							
Conflict		0.26***	0.21***	0.10	0.18**	0.05	0.03	0.11**
Hostility		0	−0.01	0.02	0.21**	−0.03	0.04	0.02
Support		0.03	−0.03	0.00	0.01	−0.06	−0.05	−0.10*
Scaffolding/ autonomy		−0.04	−0.01	0.01	0.12**	0.07	0.07	0.02
Effortful control		−0.27***	−0.28***	−0.56***	−0.32***	−0.45***	−0.28**	−0.36***
Negative affect		0.25***	0.06	0.05	0.17**	−0.05	−0.01	−0.01
Sensory regulation		−0.36***	−0.30***	−0.13**	−0.07	−0.22**	−0.21**	−0.26***

At the symptom-type level, other pathways were related specifically to the two types of internalizing symptoms but were not consistently associated across both externalizing symptom types. These included:

1. Age 4 SES → age 5 conflict → both age 6 internalizing symptom types (anxiety, depression) and to the externalizing symptoms of ODD but not ADHD.
2. Age 4 parent depression → age 5 EC → both age 6 internalizing symptom types (anxiety, depression) and to the externalizing symptoms of ADHD but not ODD.
3. Age 4 parent depression → age 5 sensory regulation → both age 6 internalizing symptoms (anxiety and depression) and to externalizing symptoms associated with ADHD but not ODD.

One additional pathway, age 4 conflict → age 5 conflict → both age 6 internalizing symptom types, was significant for both internalizing symptoms and ODD but not ADHD-C; this pathway included the autoregression for age 4 to age 5 conflict rather than a cascading effect across different risk factors.

Another set of three symptom-level pathways was noteworthy. These three paths were significant for the age 6 ODD symptom type but not for any other symptom types. These include:

1. Age 4 SES → age 5 scaffolding → age 6 ODD symptom type.
2. Age 4 parent hostility → age 5 NA → age 6 ODD symptom type.
3. Age 4 parent hostility → age 5 parent hostility → age 6 ODD symptom type; this model included the autoregression of parent hostility from age 4 to 5 rather than cascading effects across risk factors.

None of the multidomain pathways were transdiagnostic across the two externalizing symptom types, not the internalizing symptom types.

Multidomain Models for Second-Order Factors The goodness of fit for the multidomain models to age 6 symptom-level factors for the cascade models were all good. Chapter 7 provides the fit statistics for cascading models for ODD and ADHD. For the cascading multidomain models for anxiety and depression presented in this chapter, the model fit was also good for both symptom types.[4] In contrast, model fit was not good[5] for each multidomain cascading model leading to the second order factors for either internalizing, externalizing, or general p.

We compared the direct effects and multidomain pathways for the first- and second-order factors to determine why the model fit was not ideal for the second-order factors. The significant multidomain pathways to age 6 second-order internalizing and externalizing factors differed from those of their corresponding first-order factors in some important respects (Table 9.2). If direct effects were significant for both first-order symptom types categorized as internalizing problems (i.e., anxiety, depression), the pathways were also significant for both the second-order internalizing factor and for general p for both EC and SR; similarly, if the direct effects were nonsignificant for both internalizing symptom types, they were also nonsignificant for the second order internalizing factors. If the direct effects were significant for only one of the internalizing symptom types, the second-order internalizing factor was not significant (e.g., for NA).

For externalizing, the pattern was similar. If both direct effects for ADHD and ODD were significant, then the direct effects of the second-order externalizing factor were also significant (e.g., for EC). However, the pattern was not consistent if only one of the first-order direct effects was significant; in that case, the direct effects of externalizing were significant when only one of the two first-order pathways was significant in some instances (e.g., for SR) but was not significant for the second order externalizing factor if the direct effects for only one of the first order factors was significant (as occurred for conflict, hostility, scaffolding, and NA).

For general p, the pattern for direct effects was also variable. The direct pathway to general p was significant if 3 or 4 pathways to specific symptoms were significant but not if only one or two pathways to specific disorders were significant.

At the symptom level, there were three multidomain pathways that were fully transdiagnostic (significant for all four symptom types). Those pathways were also fully transdiagnostic (statistically significant) for the internalizing, externalizing, and general p factors, all of which involved mediation at age 5 by EC. At the second-order factor level, there were two additional paths that were fully transdiagnostic (significant for internalizing, externalizing, and general p) at that level but were not at the symptom level. Both paths were mediated by SR at age 5 (maternal depression→sensory regulation→all three second-order factors, and parental support→sensory regulation→all three second-order factors).

These differences in pathways for first- and second-order factors argue for the importance of examining both transdiagnostic factors and the pathways to these factors at multiple levels, both to identify multidomain pathways to disorders at the transdiagnostic level and their important differences at the symptom level.

Conclusions

The transdiagnostic approach offers promise for developing an empirically supported structure of psychopathology based on a dimensional rather than a taxonomic approach to psychiatric problems. While interest in this approach began decades ago, the level of interest in this approach is rapidly increasing. Although progress has been made, important issues remain to be resolved, and, ultimately, whether this approach will be more useful than the taxonomic one remains to be determined. We note some findings and issues that remain to be addressed.

1. Within the hierarchical model of the structure of psychopathology in early childhood, a two-level model that includes a second-order internalizing and externalizing factor shows a better fit than a two-level model in which general p replaces the internalizing and externalizing factors. Unless a back-asswards approach is used, it is not possible to test hierarchical models with three or more levels, and that approach has the disadvantage of examining symptom clusters that are not

readily interpretable to clinicians. As a result, the utility of the bass-ackwards approach seems, at best, dubious.

2. In this developmental period, hierarchical models that clearly distinguish between internalizing and externalizing factors do not show optimal fit. The close connections between symptoms and symptom types in the internalizing and externalizing groups need to be included (via cross-loads) in such models.
3. While it is possible to identify bifactor models at ages 4, 5, and 6, there are important differences between them at each age, which seems to limit their utility.
4. When examined as main effects, numerous risk factors appear to be transdiagnostic at both level one, symptom-type and level two, higher-order factors. Subtle differences also emerge at the symptom-type level that are not apparent for the higher-order factors. Thus, in examining risk factors to see which may be transdiagnostic, a multi-level approach has advantages in confirming the strength of transdiagnostic status across levels of analyses.
5. It is striking that all measured pathways to first-order symptom types that were transdiagnostic were funneled through age 5 EC and no other parenting or child factor, while two additional pathways were significant when mediated by SR, another self-regulatory skill that develops in early childhood, for all three hierarchical second-order factors.
6. These differences in pathways for first- and second-order factors argue the importance of examining disorders transdiagnostically and the pathways at multiple levels to these disorders. This provides the opportunity to both identify multidomain pathways to these disorders but also their important differences at the symptom level.

We have now discussed risk factors for externalizing (Chap. 7) and internalizing disorders (Chap. 8) and a transdiagnostic approach (this chapter) to psychopathology in early childhood. Of course, the importance of understanding these risk factors lies in how this knowledge informs treatment, and so the next two chapters of this book focus on treatment. Chapter 10 describes current approaches to the treatment of ODD, ADHD, depression, and anxiety in young children. In Chap. 11, we provide our recommendations for a new treatment approach based on what we have learned from the various risk factors models.

References

Achenbach, T. M. (1966). The classification of children's psychiatric symptoms: A factor-analytic study. *Psychological Monographs, 80*(7), 1–37.

Achenbach, T. M. (2020). Bottom-up and top-down paradigms for psychopathology: A half-century odyssey. *Annual Review of Clinical Psychology, 16*, 1–24. https://doi.org/10.1146/annurev-clinpsy-0711119-115831

Beauchaine, T. P., & Cicchetti, D. (2016). A new generation of comorbidity research in the era of neuroscience and research domain criteria. *Development and Psychopathology, 28*, 891–894. https://doi.org/10.1017/S0954579416000602SW

Brikell, I., Larsson, H., Lu, Y., Pettersson, E., Chen, Q., Kuja-Kalkola, R., Karlsson, R., Lahey, B. B., Lichtenstein, P., & Martin, J. (2020). The contribution of common genetic risk variants for ADHD to a general factor of childhood psychopathology. *Molecular Psychiatry, 25*, 1809–1821. https://doi.org/10.1038/s41380-018-0109-2

Burns, G. L., Geiser, C., Servera, M., Becker, S. P., & Beauchaine, T. P. (2020). Application of the bifactor S-1 model to multisource ratnigs of ADHD/ODD symptoms: An appropriate bifactor model for symptom ratings. *Journal of Abnormal Child Psychology, 48*, 881–894. https://doi.org/10.10007/s10802-019-00608-4

Caspi, A., Houts, R. M., Belsky, D. W., Goldman-Mellor, S. J., Harrington, H., Israel, S., Meier, M. H., Ramrakha, S., Shalev, I., Poulton, R., & Moffitt, T. E. (2014). The p factor: One general psychopathology factor in the structure of psychiatric disorders? *Psychological Science, 2*(2), 119–137. https://doi.org/10.1177/2167702613497473

Clark, L. A., Cuthbert, B., Lewis-Fernandez, R., Narrow, W. E., & Reed, G. M. (2017). Three approaches to understanding and classifying mental disorder: *ICD-11*, *DSM-5*, and the national institute of mental health's research domain criteria (RDoC). *Psychological Science in the Public Interest, 18*(2), 72–145. https://doi.org/10.1177/1529100617727266

Deutz, M. H. F., Geeraerts, S. B., Belsky, J., Dekovic, M., van Baar, A. L., Prinzie, P., & Patalay, P. (2020). General psychopathology and dysregulation profile in a longitudinal community sample: Stability, antecedents and outcomes. *Child Psychiatry and Human Development, 51*, 114–126. https://doi.org/10.1007/s10578-019-00916-2

Eid, M., Geiser, C., Koch, T., & Heene, M. (2017). Anomalous results in G-factor models: Explanations and alternatives. *Psychological Methods, 22*(3), 541–562. https://doi.org/10.1037/me0000083

Gibbons, R. D., & Hedeker, D. R. (1992). Full-information item bi-factor analysis. *Psychometrika, 57*(3), 423–436.

Goldberg, L. R. (2006). Doing it all bass-ackwards: The development of hierarchical factors structures from the top down. *Journal of Research in Personality, 40*, 347–358. https://doi.org/10.1016/jrp.2006.01.001

Gouze, K. R., Lavigne, J. V., & Bryant, F. B. (2022). A multi-level longitudinal model of risk factors for generalized and separation anxiety symptoms in a community sample of 6-year-olds. *Child Psychiatry and Human Development, 53*(3), 405–417. https://doi.org/10.1007/s-10578-021-01132-7

Hankin, J., Poggi Davis, E., Snyder, H., Young, J. F., Glynn, L. M., & Sandman, C. A. (2017). Temperament factors and dimensional, latent bifactor models of child psychopathology: Transdiagnostic and specific associations in two youth samples. *Psychiatry Research, 252*, 139–146. https://doi.org/10.1016/j.psychres.2017.02.061

Harden, K. P., Engelhardt, L. E., Mann, F. D., Patterson, M. W., Grotzinger, A. D., Savicki, S. L., Thibodeaux, M. L., Freis, S. M., Tackett, J. L., Church, J. A., & Tucker-Drob, E. M. (2020). Genetic associations between executive functions and a general factor of psychopathology. *Journal of the Academy of Child and Adolescent Psychiatry, 59*(6), 749–758.

Hatoum, A. S., Rhee, S. H., Corley, R. P., Hewitt, J. K., & Friedman, N. P. (2018). Do executive functions explain the covariance between internalizing and externalizing behaviors? *Develoment and Psychopathology, 30*, 1371–1387. https://doi.org/10.1017/S0954579417001602

Hopkins, J., Gouze, K. R., Lavigne, J. V., & Bryant, F. B. (2020). Multidomain risk factors in early childhood and depression symptoms in 6-year-year-olds: A longitudinal pathway model. *Develoment and Psychopathology, 32*(1), 57–71. https://doi.org/10.1017/S0954579418001426

Jones, H. J., Heron, J., Hammerton, G., Stochl, J., Jones, P. B., Cannon, M., Smith, G. D., Holmans, P., Lewis, G., Linden, D. E. J., O'Donovan, M. C., Owen, M. J., Walters, J., & Zammit, S. (2018). Investigating the genetic architecture of general and specific psychopathology in adolescence. *Translational Psychiatry, 8*, 1–11. https://doi.org/10.1038/s41398-018-0204-9

Joreskog, K. G., Sorbom, D., & Wellentin, F. Y. (2006). *Latent variable scores and observational residuals* [Unpublished report, Uppsala University, February 2006]. https://citeseerx.ist.psu.edu

Kotov, R., Krueger, R. F., Watson, D., Achenbach, T. M., Althoff, R. R., Bagby, R. M., Brown, T. A., Carpenter, W. T., Caspi, A., Clark, L. A., Easton, N. R., Forbes, M. K., Forbush, K. T., Goldberg, D., Hasin, D., Hyman, S. E., Ivanova, M. Y., Lynam, D. R., Markon, K., et al. (2017). The hierarchical taxonomy of psychopathology (HiTOP): A dimensional alternative of traditional nosologies. *Journal of Abnormal Psychology, 126*(4), 454–477. https://doi.org/10.1037/abn0000258

Lahey, B. B., Van Hulle, C. A., Singh, A. L., Waldman, I. D., & Rathouz, P. J. (2011). Higher-order genetic and environmental structure of prevalent forms of child and adolescent psychopathology. *Archives of General Psychiatry, 68*(2), 181–189.

Lahey, B. B., Krueger, R. F., Rathouz, P. J., Waldman, I. D., & Zald, D. H. (2017). A hierarchical causal taxonomy of psychopathology across the life span. *Psychological Bulletin, 143*(2), 142–186. https://doi.org/10.1037/bul0000069

Lahey, B. B., Moore, T. M., Kaczkurkin, A. N., & Zaid, D. H. (2021). Hierarchical models of psychopathology: Empirical support, implications, and remaining issues. *World Psychiatry, 20*(1), 57–63.

Lavigne, J. V., Gouze, K. R., Hopkins, J., & Bryant, F. (2016). A multidomain cascade model of early childhood risk factors associated with ODD symptoms in a community sample of 6-year-olds. *Development and Psychopathology, 28*, 1547–1562. https://doi.org/10.1017/S0954579415001194

Mann, F. D., Atherton, O. E., DeYoung, C. G., Krueger, R. F., & Robins, R. W. (2020). Big five personality traits and common mental disorders within a hierarchical taxonomy of psychopathology: A longitudinal study of Mexican-origin youth. *Journal of Abnormal Psychology, 129*(8), 769–787. https://doi.org/10.1037/abn0000633

McElroy, E., Belsky, J., Carragher, N., Fearon, P., & Patalay, P. (2018). Developmental stability of general and specific factors of psychopathology from early childhood to adolescence: Dynamic mutualism or p-differentiation? *Journal of Child Psychology and Psychiatry, 59*(6), 667–675. https://doi.org/10.1111/jcpp.12849

Michelini, G., Gair, K., Tian, Y., Miao, J., Doughtery, L. R., Goldstein, B. L., MacNeill, L. A., Barch, D. M., Luby, J., Wakschlag, L. S., Klein, D. N., & Kotov, R. (2023). Do general and specific factors of preschool psychopathology predict preadolescent outcomes? A transdiagnostic hierarchical approach. *Psychological Medicine, 53*, 5405–5414. https://doi.org/10.1017/S0033291172200246X

Olino, T. M., Douglas-Palumberi, H., Bufferd, S. J., Carlson, G. A., & Klein, D. N. (2014). Testing models of psychopathology in preschool-aged children using a structured interview-based assessment. *Journal of Abnormal Child Psychology, 42*, 1201–1211. https://doi.org/10.1007/s10802-014-9865-x

Olino, T. M., Bufferd, S. J., Doughtery, L. R., Dyson, M. W., & Carlson, G. A. (2018). The development of latent dimensions of psychopathology across early childhood: Stability of dimensions and moderators of change. *Journal of Abnormal Child Psychology, 46*, 1373–1383. https://doi.org/10.1007/s10802-018-0398-6

Riglin, L., Thapar, A. K., Leppert, B., Martin, J., Richards, A., Anney, R., Smith, G. D., Tilling, K., Stergiakouli, E., Lahri, D. K., O'Donovan, M. C., Collishaw, S., & Thapar, A. (2020). Using genetics to examine a general liability to childhood psychopathology. *Behavior Genetics, 50*, 213–220. https://doi.org/10.1007/s10519-019-09985-4

Shields, A. N., Reardon, K. W., Brandes, C. M., & Tackett, J. L. (2019). The p factor in children: Relationships with executive funtions and effortful control. *Journal of Research in Personality, 82*, 1–8. https://doi.org/10.1016/j.jrp.2019.103853

Snyder, H. R., Friedman, N. P., & Hankin, B. L. (2019). Transdiagnostic mechanisms of psychopathology in youth: Executive functions, dependent stress, and rumination. *Cognitive Therapy and Research, 43*, 834–851. https://doi.org/10.1007/s10608-019-10016-z

Sterba, S. K., Egger, H. E., & Angold, A. (2007). Diagnostic specificity and nonspecificity in the dimensions of preschool psychopathology. *Journal of Child Psychology and Psychiatry, 48*(10), 1005–1013.

Strickland, J., Keller, J., Lavigne, J. V., Gouze, K. R., Hopkins, J., & LeBailly, S. A. (2011). The structure of psychopathology in a community sample of preschoolers. *Journal of Abnormal Child Psychology, 39*, 601–610. https://doi.org/10.1007/s10802-008-9236-6

Tackett, J. L., Lahri, D. K., van Hulle, C., Waldman, I., & Krueger, R. F. (2013). Common genetic influences on negative emotionality and a general psychopathology factor in childhood and adolescence. *Journal of Abnormal Psychology, 122*(4), 1142–1153. https://doi.org/10.1037/a0034151

Wang, F. L., Galan, C. A., Lemery-Chalfant, K., Wilson, M. N., & Shaw, D. S. (2020). Evidence for two genetically-distinct pathways to co-occurring internalizing and externalizing problems in adolescence characterized by negative affectivity or behavioral inhibition. *Journal of Abnormal Psychology, 129*(6), 633–645. https://doi.org/10.1037/abn0000525

Chapter 10
Current Treatments for Externalizing and Internalizing Disorders in Young Children: A Review

Young children are commonly referred for mental health services when they exceed the tolerance limits of the adults in their environment. Developmentally, preschoolers reach a point when they have clear ideas about what they want and begin to assert themselves more strongly, sometimes coming into conflict with the adults in their world. At the same time, they may have inadequate frustration tolerance and difficulty delaying gratification or lack the verbal skills to help them regulate their own emotions. Since children this age frequently have difficulty expressing internalized affective distress in a socially appropriate manner, they are most likely to be referred because of oppositional, disruptive (crying, tantrums), or hyperactive behaviors. As a result, preschool children are identified with externalizing disorders at 5–10 times the rate they are identified for internalizing ones (Lavigne et al., 2009). Consequently, many intervention studies have been developed to treat externalizing disorders in young children, with the greatest number focusing on the reduction of disruptive or oppositional behaviors.

Treatments for Oppostional Behavior

Young children are heavily reliant on their parents and spend more time at home than older children, so their externalizing behaviors most frequently manifest in interactions with their parents. As a result, a majority of early childhood treatments developed to address externalizing behaviors are parent focused and fall under the rubric of parent management training.

Parent-Focused Parent Management Training Parent management training (PMT), derived from principles of social learning and attachment theory (Bandura, 1977; Bowlby, 1969; Zisser & Eyberg, 2010), is a widely used, empirically based intervention for addressing externalizing symptoms in young children. A number of

K. R. Gouze et al., *Early Childhood Psychopathology*,
https://doi.org/10.1007/978-3-031-68877-5_10

systematic reviews and meta-analyses document the effectiveness of various types of PMT programs in reducing disruptive and oppositional behaviors in young children (Bayer et al., 2009; Comer et al., 2013; Everett et al., 2021; Helander et al., 2024; Hudson et al., 2023; Kaminski & Claussen, 2017; Leijten et al., 2018a, b, 2020; Nogueira et al., 2022; Riise et al., 2021; Thomas et al., 2017; Tully & Hunt, 2016). PMT focuses primarily on building positive parent-child relationships and teaching parents specific skills for managing their child's behavior. These skills generally include providing positive reinforcement (e.g., earning points for compliance on a good behavior chart), giving effective praise (e.g., "I like the way you picked up your clothes the first time I asked you"), and implementing natural (e.g., "if you do not get dressed you will be late for preschool"), and logical (e.g., "if you do not eat your dinner you cannot have dessert") consequences. Meta-analyses comparing PMT with or without a child treatment component have generally noted that a parent component alone is as effective as a parent component along with an individual child component (Epstein et al., 2015), although individual studies have sometimes found the most significant immediate post-treatment effects for combined treatment (Drugli & Larsson, 2006; Webster-Stratton & Hammond, 1997), particularly when the combined treatment is school-based e.g., Dinosaur School (Webster-Stratton et al., 2004). Parent management programs designed for parents of young children with the strongest empirical support include The Incredible Years Program (IY) (Webster-Stratton, 2005), the Positive Parenting Program (Triple P) (Sanders, 1999), and Parent-Child Interaction Training (PCIT) (Eyberg & Funderburk, 2011). All three of these programs emphasize building more positive parent-child relationships and teaching parents specific skills for managing child behavior.

The Incredible Years Program The parent management training component of the Incredible Years Program (IY) (Webster-Stratton, 2005) is comprised of three sets of materials, one for parents of children ages 1–3, one for preschoolers aged 3–5 years old and one for parents of children aged 6 to 8. The program is delivered in a group format with 8–15 parents meeting weekly in two-hour sessions for 12–20 weeks. The first weeks of the program focus on building positive parent-child relationships by teaching parents how to engage in child-directed play, deliver appropriate use of praise, and support children in their use of emotional skills. The second half of the program is directed towards building parent management skills that address difficult behaviors and includes topics such as effective limit setting, selective ignoring, use of time-out, natural and logical consequences, and use of techniques such as "when-then" statements. The core components of the program are presented through a series of videotapes that illustrate a range of child-parent interactions, including the skills being taught and are used by group leaders to facilitate discussion among the parents. This observational learning method is supplemented by weekly parent goal setting, skills to practice at home, and weekly phone calls between group members for support. Positive outcomes documented for the IY parenting program include less negative parenting by both mothers and fathers, more positive parenting by mothers, and fewer externalizing behaviors in children (Webster-Stratton et al., 2004). There also is evidence for behavioral improvements in children from under-resourced community settings (McGilloway et al., 2012) and other countries, including Sweden and Portugal (Axberg & Broberg, 2012; Homem et al., 2014; Seabra Santos et al., 2016). Effect sizes for behavior changes found in meta-analyses fall in the small to medium range (Leijten et al., 2018b; Menting et al., 2013), with larger effect sizes when the initial externalizing behaviors are more severe and when observations rather than parent report are used as the outcome measure (Menting et al., 2013). There is also evidence that treatment with the IY program materials can be effective when presented in alternative settings (i.e., primary care pediatric settings) or by alternative trainers (i.e., nurses) (Lavigne et al., 2008).

The Positive Parenting Program (Triple P) Triple P (Sanders, 1999, 2012) was originally developed in Australia and has evolved to have different formats for different ages and levels of intervention needed. Standard Triple P, which was developed for implementation with children from preschool through 12 years of age, is probably the most widely used form of the program. It can be administered individually in ten one-hour sessions or in a group of up to 12 parents who meet together with a trained therapist for 5 two-hour sessions and then individually via telephone consultation for three shorter sessions. Similar to IY, Triple P shows small-to-moderate effect sizes in reducing externalizing behavior in young children (Bayer et al., 2009; Leijten et al., 2019; Nogueira et al., 2022; Nowak & Heinrichs, 2008; Sanders et al., 2000; Thomas & Zimmer-Gembeck, 2007; Tully & Hunt, 2016).

Parent-Child Interaction Training (PCIT) PCIT differs from both the IY and Triple P programs; whereas those two programs only include parents, in PCIT the parent management training is embedded in parent-child interaction sessions that include both parent and child (Eyberg et al., 1995; Eyberg & Funderburk, 2011). The first phase of PCIT is referred to as child-directed interaction (CDI), while the second phase is referred to as parent-directed interaction (PDI). In contrast to the IY and Triple P programs, which have a set number of sessions, in PCIT, parents engage in the CDI portion of the program until they reach criteria based on using the skills taught a specified number of times. This is followed by the PDI portion of the program, which is administered only after the parents have mastered the CDI skills. As a result, this treatment frequently requires parents to remain engaged in therapy for much longer than either the IY program or the Triple P program, both of which have a finite number of sessions. During the CDI portion of PCIT, parents learn how to engage their children in activities using skills such as praise, verbal reflection, imitation, behavioral description, and enjoyment (referred to as the PRIDE skills). During PDI, parents learn how to increase child compliance, decrease disruptive behaviors, give appropriate commands, and follow through on commands. Unlike IY or Triple P, which can be administered either individually or in a group setting, PCIT is always conducted with individual parent-child dyads. The model is a coaching model in which the therapist is behind a one-way mirror, observing the parent engage in the skills and providing instructions through a "bug-in-the-ear." Support for the effectiveness of PCIT in reducing child disruptive behavior, from both individual studies and larger meta-analyses shows relatively large effect sizes immediately post-treatment but smaller effect sizes comparable to those of IY and Triple P in longer-term follow-up (Campbell et al., 2023; Cooley et al., 2014; Helander et al., 2024; Matos et al., 2009; Nixon et al., 2004; Nixon et al., 2003; Schuhmann et al., 1998; Thomas et al., 2017; Thomas & Zimmer-Gembeck, 2007; Valero-Aguayo et al., 2021; Ward et al., 2016). Additionally, PCIT has been shown to be effective with different populations, including children from different cultural and ethnic backgrounds and historically under-resourced areas (Cooley et al., 2014; Fernandez et al., 2011; Leung et al., 2003; Matos et al., 2009; McCabe & Yeh, 2009).

Summary: Comparison of Effectiveness Across PMT Programs As described above, there is evidence that all three PMT programs are at least somewhat effective in reducing child externalizing symptoms, particularly in younger children. Additional benefits include possible reductions in parenting stress, improved perceptions of parent-child relations, and reduced parental negativity. However, there are some important limitations to the effectiveness of existing PMT programs and the existing studies of their effectiveness.

First, studies that have calculated effect sizes for PMT treatments show that the effect sizes are typically small to moderate. Effect sizes of that magnitude show that PMT overall is more effective than no treatment. Nonetheless, they also indicate clearly that many parents seeking help for their young child with an externalizing disorder do not experience the desired improvement from PMT treatment.

Second, if a clinic or program is trying to decide which form of PMT they should implement in their setting, several factors need to be considered. One of the most important factors is the relative effectiveness of these programs compared to one another. Unfortunately, we have not identified any studies that directly compared the major forms of PMT. Another consideration is a more practical one. For example, PCIT requires reaching criterion on CDI skills before moving on to PDI or behavior management skills; it might thus be less helpful for families from under-resourced communities where higher attrition rates suggest that PCIT may not be as effective (Clark et al., 2017; Fernandez et al., 2011; Fernandez & Eyberg, 2009; Lyon & Budd, 2010). Parent management programs such as IY, which are designed to be completed in a set number of sessions, often fewer, might be preferable for these families. Additionally, some parents might prefer a group format such as that offered by IY or Triple P to the parent-child format offered by PCIT, or vice versa. However, such recommendations need to be made with care because of the lack of data on the comparative effectiveness of different types of PMT.

Parent-Focused Attachment-Based Interventions While PMT is based on the tenets of both attachment theory and social learning theory, other treatments for young children rely exclusively on attachment theory (Lieberman & Van Horn, 2008). Attachment-based interventions are theoretically based on the well-established association between secure attachment and healthy early development, including positive peer relations, effective self-regulation, and good cognitive development (Sroufe, 2005). Moreover, there is a robust association between early insecure attachment patterns and externalizing behaviors (DeVito & Hopkins, 2001; Fearon et al., 2010; Greenberg, 1999; Groh et al., 2016; Sroufe, 2005). Attachment-based treatments are designed to repair the attachment relationship by (a) teaching caretakers to be more sensitive and responsive to their child's emotional cues and (b) increasing their understanding of the ways in which their reactions to and mental representations of their children are shaped by their own past experiences and current internal states (Berlin et al., 2016). The two most thoroughly researched attachment-based interventions are Circle of Security (COS) (Powell et al., 2014) and Child-Parent Psychotherapy (CPP) (Lieberman et al., 2006a, b). In both cases, the research focus is on attachment-related outcomes, such as parental sensitivity and security of attachment; child outcomes, such as oppositional behavior, have been studied less frequently and reveal more equivocal findings (Barlow et al., 2016; Kohlhoff & Cibralic, 2022).

Circle of Security-Parenting (COS-P) The primary goal of COS-P (Powell et al., 2014) is to promote a parent's insight into their child's emotional needs and to enhance parental sensitivity towards those needs. The original COS-I (the "I" stands for Intensive) program was designed as a 20-week group intervention requiring a trained psychotherapist who utilized videotaped feedback of participating parents interacting with their children to teach them about child emotional cues and how to respond sensitively to those cues. Since the original roll-out, a shorter, manualized 8-week group intervention labeled COS-P (the "P" stands for Parenting), which can be implemented by a trained paraprofessional, was developed. In this more commonly implemented intervention, parents are taught about attachment and the importance of attachment security to advance children's sense of well-being and their ability to explore the world. Program materials also focus on teaching parents how to facilitate emotional co-regulation and build better relationships with their children. Pre-produced videotapes of challenging parent-child interactions are used to help parents reflect on their own emotions in challenging parent-child situations and understand the basis of their reactions to their children when they behave in these ways. Group discussion guides them toward recognizing more sensitive reactions and implementing relationship repair strategies following the inevitable relationship ruptures that occur during parenting. Based on results from a small number of well-designed, controlled trials (Bikic et al., 2022; Maxwell et al., 2021), the effectiveness of this intervention is questionable. Most extant studies report negligible (Cassidy et al., 2017; Zimmer-Gembeck et al., 2022) or small-to-moderate effects of the more extensive COS-I program on child behavior (Barlow et al., 2016; Huber et al., 2015). To some extent, the impact of COS-I and COS-P seems to vary depending on the outcome variables being examined. There is fairly robust evidence for improvements in parental sensitivity and reductions in parental hostility, two of the primary targets of both COS programs (Barlow et al., 2016; Cassidy et al., 2017; Yaholkoski et al., 2016), while reductions in child behavioral symptoms are more equivocal (Cassidy et al., 2017; Maxwell et al., 2021; Zimmer-Gembeck et al., 2022). To date, there do not appear to be any direct comparisons of outcomes from the two COS programs although COS-P is clearly more cost effective as it is shorter

(8 weeks as compared to 20) and it can be administered by trained paraprofessionals. Clearly, the impact of COS on modifying parental perceptions, sensitivity, and reactions suggests that it holds promise for positively impacting child behavior as well; however, more research is needed to establish its effectiveness.

Child-Parent Psychotherapy (CPP) In contrast to COS, there is somewhat greater support for the effectiveness of CPP in reducing oppositional behavior, but this support comes largely from research conducted by the original developers of the intervention (Ghosh Ippen et al., 2011; Lieberman et al., 2006a). This intervention was initially developed for use with children who experienced trauma or lived in homes where domestic violence or abuse led to fractured attachment relationships. Based on the premise that early attachment is fundamental to the development of good self-regulatory skills, Lieberman and colleagues hypothesized that improving parent-child attachment would lead to improvements in child self-control and emotion regulation that are critical to optimal behavioral functioning (DeKlyen & Greenberg, 2016). CPP (Lieberman et al., 2015) is a dyadic intervention in which the parent and child meet together for one to one-and-one half-hour sessions over approximately a year. Treatment can take place in any number of settings, including the child's home, but therapists are required to work extensively with certified trainers to learn how to deliver the intervention. The goal of treatment is to help the parent understand that their internal working model of their child, that is, their perceptions about their child and their explanations for their child's behavior, emanate from their own childhood experiences. Therapy is focused on helping parents identify the ways in which these negative childhood experiences make it hard for them to respond reflectively and sensitively to their child's needs and to help them and their child develop more sensitive synchrony around those needs. Outcome studies, primarily with populations of children who have been maltreated, experienced significant trauma, or live with domestic violence have demonstrated effectiveness in altering parental internal working models, improving parenting sensitivity and, in some cases, reducing oppositional or externalizing behaviors (Ghosh Ippen et al., 2011; Kohlhoff & Cibralic, 2022; Kohlhoff et al., 2022; Lieberman et al., 1991, 2005, 2006a; Toth et al., 2006).

Assessing the benefits of attachment-based interventions versus PMT is extremely difficult; to date, there are no direct comparisons of these treatments in preschool children. Among the many questions of interest (to mention just a few) are which treatments might be more effective for which sub-groups of children and parents, which treatments might be more effective at addressing some outcomes (e.g., child behavior) rather than others (e.g., parent feelings of efficacy), which treatments are more cost-effective, and are some treatments more acceptable than others to different ethnic or racial groups?

Child-Focused Play-Based Interventions Play therapy, based on the assumption that younger children frequently express themselves through play, is the primary child-focused treatment that does not involve parents. In this treatment, play is used as a means of communication between the child and therapist and is designed to provide an opportunity for the child to express feelings, thoughts, and experiences that they would not otherwise be able to communicate. The extent to which play therapy is effective in minimizing oppositional behavior is still open to question, with many clinical child psychologists calling for more rigorous research on the effectiveness of this approach. Some authors indicate that this therapy modality is largely ineffective (Kuhn et al., 2022), while others note that although somewhat efficacious, it does not compare favorably to PMT treatments (Kaminski & Claussen, 2017). Other meta-analyses reveal small to moderate effect sizes when comparing play therapy to no treatment or alternative treatment controls, particularly with younger children (Lin & Bratton, 2015; Parker et al., 2021). In general, concerns remain in the scientific community that play therapy studies are poorly designed and lack sufficient power or appropriate control/comparison groups (Bratton et al., 2005). Furthermore, like CBT and behavioral treatments with older children, results are better when parents are actively involved in treatment (Leblanc & Ritchie, 2001; Parker et al., 1999). Currently, there is little demonstrated additional benefit to exclusively child-focused therapeutic modalities for reducing externalizing symptoms in young children. That said, additional research is clearly needed to better understand which treatments are more effective for which children and families. Small-to-moderate effect sizes indicate that a substantial number of children seeking treatment are not benefitting from what clinicians currently have to offer.

Treatment for ADHD

Parent Management Training and ADHD The vast majority of studies examining the impact of PMT on ADHD indicate a small to moderate impact on ADHD symptoms (Coates et al., 2015; Daley et al., 2014; Groenman et al., 2022; Hornstra et al., 2023; Mulqueen et al., 2015; Murray et al., 2018; Wagner & McNeil, 2008). Several researchers (Tourjman et al., 2022), however, have questioned whether these outcomes truly apply to the core ADHD symptoms of hyperactivity and inattention or merely address the concomitant behavioral symptoms associated with ADHD (e.g., oppositionality and defiance). Consistent with this hypothesis, studies (Battagliese et al., 2015; Groenman et al., 2022) report that the effect sizes obtained for PMT for externalizing behaviors are larger than those found for PMT and the core ADHD symptoms of inattention and hyperactivity. Other factors affecting the impact of PMT on ADHD include whether the program is administered individually or in a group (Hornstra et al., 2023), whether the control is a waitlist or treatment-as-usual control (Groenman et al., 2022), and whether there is a long-term follow-up (Lee et al., 2012). The specific outcomes measured, symptoms or functional impairment, and who reports on those symptoms also appear to affect the findings on effectiveness (Groenman et al., 2022). Furthermore, it is well established that, particularly for young children, cross-informant differences in symptoms of ADHD are impacted by numerous other factors (Lavigne et al., 2016). Overall, with ADHD, as with other externalizing disorders, PMT appears to be the most helpful intervention in reducing symptoms in early childhood that potentially lead to cascading problems as children get older, including poor peer relations, fractured parent-child relationships, and difficulty with academic success. As noted above, however, the benefits of PMT for ameliorating oppositional symptoms, whether with or without accompanying ADHD symptoms, seem to be greater than the benefits of PMT for ameliorating the core ADHD symptoms of inattention and hyperactivity. For this reason, and because ADHD, unlike oppositional behavior, is considered to have a strong biological basis, school-age children are often treated for ADHD with a combination of medication and behavioral treatment. For preschoolers, however, the American Academy of Pediatrics (Wolraich et al., 2019) strongly recommends a trial of medication only after PMT/behavioral treatments have been unsuccessful.

Summary As noted earlier, externalizing symptoms are the most common symptoms for which young children are referred for treatment. At both clinical and subclinical levels, these are frequently the behaviors that come to the attention of adults first because they involve a mismatch between the child's behaviors and the demands of the environment during early childhood. As a result, early childhood interventions for externalizing symptoms are among the most extensively researched child treatments. This body of literature clearly identifies parent management training, which targets parents' relationships with their children and improved parent behavior management skills, as the most effective intervention. Nevertheless, interventions such as attachment-based dyadic interventions show promise as well, particularly when children's externalizing behaviors emanate from sources such as trauma exposure. Treatments for child internalizing symptoms in early childhood are less well-established and researched and are reviewed in the following sections of this chapter.

Current Treatments for Internalizing Disorders in Young Children

The extant literature on empirically-based treatments for internalizing disorders in young children is less extensive than that for externalizing ones. There may be several reasons for this. First, as stated in Chap. 8, depression is relatively uncommon in young children. Second, symptoms of depression and anxiety are often less bothersome to parents and preschool teachers than symptoms of oppositional behavior (ODD) and ADHD, so children displaying internalizing symptoms are less likely to be referred for treatment. Finally, it is difficult to adapt several of the cognitive-behavioral, empirically-based treatment strategies (e.g., cognitive restructuring) effective with older children and adolescents for young children due to their less developed cognitive abilities. Nevertheless, given the fact that these depression and anxiety symptoms are quite stable and cause significant distress and impairment, several treatment approaches have been developed, particularly for anxiety. The following sections provide a description and a review of the evidence base for the different approaches to the treatment of depression and anxiety in young children.

Depression Treatments

Similar to treatment approaches for ODD and ADHD, there are both PMT and attachment-based approaches to treating depression in young children.

Parent Management Training Interventions Parent-Child Interaction Therapy-Emotion Development (PCIT-ED), a dyadic parent-focused approach based on a modification of PCIT for the treatment of externalizing disorders, was designed specifically to treat the emotional deficits hypothesized to be central to preschool depression (Lenze et al., 2011). As in the manualized PCIT treatment for disruptive behavior disorders, PCIT-ED is comprised of two primary modules, one targeting child-directed play (CDI) and the other targeting parent-directed behavioral intervention (PDI). The major modification to standard PCIT for the treatment of preschool depression is the addition of a third module, emotion development (ED) that targets the emotional deficits central to preschool depression (Lenze et al., 2011). The ED module consists of eight sessions in which parents are trained to deal with their own difficulties in emotion regulation, teach their children how to identify their emotions and coach them in regulating their intense emotions. A pilot study (Luby et al., 2012) showed that PCIT-ED was significantly more effective than psychoeducation in increasing child executive functioning and emotion recognition skills. Still, the authors reported that this study did not have enough power to determine effect sizes for these outcome measures. A more recent randomized controlled trial, i.e. RCT (Luby et al., 2018) of this manualized intervention showed that, following treatment, children in the PCIT-ED group had significantly lower scores on depression measures than those in the waitlist control group, with large effect sizes. However, these findings did not elucidate whether it was the ED module, specifically, that contributed to treatment effectiveness. To address this question, Luby and colleagues (2020) conducted a component analysis of PCIT-ED, which showed that the ED module added to the efficacy of treatment for preschool depression after controlling for the effects of the PDI and CDI modules. However, it is possible that this effect was due to a longer time in treatment (as the authors themselves point out), rather than being attributable specifically to the ED strategies. Further research randomizing the order of the modules is needed to firmly determine if this module adds to the effectiveness of this manualized treatment for preschool depression.

Surprisingly, to date, PCIT-ED is the only evidence-based parent-focused approach designed specifically to treat preschool depression, although another approach, Tuning into Kids (TIK), seems promising. TIK is a group-based treatment developed to increase parents' ability to enhance preschoolers' emotional competence, and there is evidence that it is effective in decreasing behavior problems in young children (Havighurst et al., 2013). The effectiveness of TIK in treating internalizing problems, such as preschool depression, has not been studied yet. Still, the focus on fostering emotional competence (like the aims of PCIT-ED) suggests that it may well be effective as a treatment for this disorder. However, this supposition awaits further research with parents of depressed preschoolers.

Attachment-Based Interventions Child-Parent Psychotherapy (CPP), as described in the section on treatments for externalizing symptoms, is a parent-focused approach based on attachment theory that was originally developed to treat young children and their parents who have experienced trauma. To briefly reiterate, it is based on the central premise that emotional and behavioral problems in young children need to be addressed in the context of the primary attachment relationship. Converging evidence reveals that CPP is effective in enhancing the parent-child relationship, increasing attachment security (Kohlhoff & Cibralic, 2022), and reducing trauma symptoms in young children (Lieberman et al., 2006b). However, CPP has not been examined specifically as a treatment for depression in young children, although there is evidence that in addition to reducing trauma symptoms, CPP is also effective in decreasing child internalizing symptoms (Bernstein et al., 2019). This finding, combined with the commonsense idea that strengthening the parent-child relationship and improving parents' sensitivity to their child's emotional cues will enhance the child's emotional security, suggests that CPP is likely to be effective in decreasing children's excessive sadness and other symptoms of depression. Again, this supposition requires future research with young children who only have depression symptoms but have not been traumatized to determine if CPP is effective in treating preschool depression specifically.

Circle of Security (COS), also based on attachment theory, is an intervention designed specifically to target the parent-child attachment relationship, rather than specific child symptoms or disorders. As described in the section on treatments for externalizing disorders, COS is a group-based treatment focused on enhancing caregivers' ability to read their child's cues and respond to them appropriately and sensitively. A meta-analysis of this intervention that included 10 studies (Yaholkoski et al., 2016) revealed that COS was effective (with a medium effect size) in increasing child attachment security and parenting quality and decreasing maternal depression. Although encouraging, these findings do not necessarily indicate that COS is likely to be effective in decreasing depression symptoms in young children themselves. To date, no such research exists; there is clearly a need for further study of whether COS is effective for treating depressed preschoolers.

Child-Focused Interventions There is extensive evidence that cognitive behavioral interventions are effective for the treatment of depression in older children and adolescents (Oud et al., 2019). However, as previously mentioned, several of the cognitive-behavioral strategies fundamental to this approach, such as Socratic questioning and cognitive restructuring, cannot be used with young children since these strategies require a level of cognitive abstraction that is beyond their developmental capabilities On the other hand, there are several CBT strategies that could be modified quite easily for use with young children, for example, psychoeducation and coping skills training; but, to our knowledge, there are no studies on treating depressed preschoolers using CBT. However, there are several papers showing that CBT is an effective treatment for trauma-exposed young children (Scheeringa et al., 2011). In a RCT examining the feasibility and efficacy of trauma-focused cognitive behavior therapy (TF-CBT) in a sample of 3- to 6-year-old children, findings revealed that the intervention group had a significantly greater reduction in trauma symptoms compared to the waitlist control group, and the effect size was large. Moreover, the children in the intervention group also experienced a significant reduction in comorbid depression symptoms, and this effect size was moderate (Scheeringa et al., 2011). Importantly, in addition to the finding that TF-CBT significantly reduced depression symptoms, this study also demonstrated the feasibility of using specific CBT strategies in young children, which suggests that a modification designed to address the core symptoms of depression would be feasible, and, perhaps, effective.

Summary: Depression Treatments To date, PCIT-ED is the only treatment approach specifically designed to treat preschool depression with strong empirical support. It is surprising, given the evidence that other approaches, specifically Parent-Child Psychotherapy, Circle of Security, and cognitive behavioral treatment, have been shown to be efficacious in treating trauma, that little research has been conducted to determine if any (or all) of these approaches modified specifically for the treatment of depression in young children is effective. Although the reason for this is not clear, the most probable one is that this disorder is rare in young children, which would make it difficult to recruit enough participants to conduct a RCT. Thus, to recruit a large enough sample to determine the effectiveness of these treatments, it seems that a multi-site study is needed.

Anxiety Treatments

It is much easier to modify the CBT strategies effective in treating anxiety in older children to be developmentally appropriate for use with young children (i.e., graded exposure, coping skills training) than it is to modify the strategies effective for the treatment of depression in older children (i.e., cognitive restructuring). Thus, in contrast to the lack of empirically-based treatments developed specifically to treat depression in young children, there are a number of manualized behavioral (BT) and cognitive-behavioral (CBT) treatments for anxiety in young children, each of which has some empirical support for its effectiveness.

In addition to CBT approaches to anxiety treatment for young children, interventions derived from attachment theory have also been developed, in which the focus of treatment is on the parent-child relationship. To date, only a few studies have examined if an attachment-based approach is effective in reducing anxiety symptoms and disorders in young children.

Behavioral and Cognitive-Behavioral Treatments As previously mentioned, there are several behavioral (BT) and cognitive-behavioral (CBT) interventions designed to treat anxiety disorders in young children based on developmentally sensitive downward modifications of the treatments shown to be effective in older children. These interventions share many common strategies, such as parent psychoeducation about the development of anxiety, parent training to decrease practices that reinforce anxiety (i.e., overprotection, excessive reassurance), and increase practices that support "brave" behavior (i.e., reinforcing child approach behaviors, gradual exposure of the child to feared situations guided by the parent), and coping skills training for the child. They differ mainly in the format used (individual vs. group), number of sessions, and whether or not they include parents and children separately or in joint sessions or target only parents or only children. These programs include (a) Coaching Approach Behavior and Leading by Modeling CALM) (Puliafico et al., 2013); (b) Being Brave (Hirshfeld-Becker et al., 2010); (c) Tuning into Kids (Edrissi et al., 2019); (d) Cool Little Kids (Kennedy et al., 2009; Rapee et al., 2005, 2010); and (e) Fun FRIENDS (Barrett et al., 2015; Pahl & Barrett, 2007).

Coaching Approach Behavior and Leading by Modeling (CALM) (Puliafico et al., 2013) is a 12-session modification of PCIT designed specifically to treat a range of anxiety disorders in young children, including separation anxiety disorder, generalized anxiety disorder, and specific phobias. CALM incorporates the same bug-in-the-ear coaching sessions during parent-child interaction as does standard PCIT. Also, as in PCIT, the first phase of treatment consists of child-directed interaction (CDI) designed to improve the parent-child relationship. The major modification to standard PCIT is that CALM does not include a parent-directed (PDI) behavioral component. Instead, the second phase of treatment focuses on coaching parent behaviors designed to modify fearful child behaviors, including ignoring these behaviors and modeling and reinforcing "brave" (approach) child behaviors during exposure sessions. A feasibility and efficacy study of CALM with 9 young children (ages 4–8) with Separation Anxiety Disorder, Generalized Anxiety Disorder, Social Anxiety Disorder, or Specific Phobia (Comer et al., 2012) showed that 80% of them completed treatment. All but one of the treatment responders showed full remission of their anxiety disorder. However, to date, this program has not been tested in a large-scale RCT.

Being Brave (Hirshfeld-Becker et al., 2008, 2010), an amalgam of a parent-only and a parent-child approach, is based on a modification of Kendall's Coping Cat (Kendall et al., 2008), an empirically-based treatment for anxiety in older children. Hirshfeld-Becker and colleagues modified the strategies used in Coping Cat to be developmentally appropriate for young children and added a parent component. Being Brave consists of 20 sessions, the first six of which only include parents, followed by as many as 13 parent-child sessions, and a final parent-only session. The parent sessions focus on psychoeducation about anxiety and teaching effective strategies for parenting an anxious child. The parent-child sessions include graded exposure of the child to fearful situations that is reinforced by the parent and parent coaching of coping skills. One study of an RCT examining the effectiveness of

Being Brave (Hirshfeld-Becker et al., 2010) showed that this intervention led to significantly greater decreases in symptoms of anxiety disorders (including Generalized Anxiety Disorder, Separation Anxiety Disorder, and specific phobia) compared to a waitlist control group, with a moderate effect size, as well as increases in parent-rated coping, with a large effect size. However, this intervention has only been compared to a waitlist control condition and not to another active treatment.

Tuning Into Kids (TIK) (Edrissi et al., 2019) is a treatment targeted at parents only. It consists of six sessions focused on improving parent emotion socialization practices by teaching them how to improve their own emotion awareness and regulation and how to coach their children on emotion recognition and regulation. Edrissi and colleagues conducted an RCT of TIK in a sample of 3- to 6-year-old Iranian children with high levels of anxiety symptoms. This study revealed that anxiety scores of children of mothers in the intervention group decreased significantly more than those in the waitlist control group and the size of this effect was large. Furthermore, this effect was maintained at 6-month follow-up. These findings are promising, but this intervention has not been tested in a sample of children in the United States.

Fun FRIENDS, a child-only approach designed for 4- to 6-year-olds (Barrett, 2007) is based on a downward extension of the FRIENDS program (Barrett & Turner, 2001) for older children. A group-based program conducted with children (often in a school setting) consists of 12 sessions. It includes strategies such as teaching children to recognize and label feelings, relax, and regulate negative feelings. Interestingly, Fun FRIENDS is the only program for young children that directly teaches them cognitive strategies such as cognitive restructuring (i.e., how to identify helpful and unhelpful thoughts, and ways to modify these unhelpful thoughts). Although sessions include only children, parents attend information sessions and are provided with a workbook. A recent open trial study (van der Mheen et al., 2020) showed that Fun FRIENDS led to a significant decrease in anxiety disorders and anxiety problems pre- to post-treatment in 4- to 7-year-old children, and the effect sizes were large to very large. In addition to providing evidence of the effectiveness of Fun FRIENDS, this study is important in showing that children as young as 4 years old can use cognitive restructuring to modify their functionally impairing anxious thoughts.

In addition to these behavioral and cognitive-behavioral interventions to treat anxiety in young children, Rapee and colleagues (Rapee et al., 2005, 2010) developed a prevention program, Cool Little Kids, for preschoolers with high levels of behavioral inhibition, a known risk factor for the development of anxiety disorders (Kagan, 1989). Cool little Kids, a six-session intervention for parents, includes topics such as psychoeducation about anxiety, parent management strategies with an emphasis on the role of overprotection in maintaining anxiety and information on how to develop exposure hierarchies. Two RCT studies (Rapee et al., 2005, 2010) showed that children whose parents participated in Cool Little Kids developed significantly fewer anxiety disorders than children in the waitlist condition 12 months later. Surprisingly, however, there was no significant difference between the intervention and control groups in BI levels at the follow-up. A recent prevention study

(Doyle et al., 2021) using an adapted version of Cool Little Kids found that anxiety levels decreased in the children in both the intervention and waitlist control groups, with no significant differences between the two groups at follow-up. Given these mixed results, and the fact that the multi-domain models of anxiety described in Chap. 8 of this book reveal that factors from several domains place children at risk for the development of anxiety, it may be premature to develop prevention programs based on a single risk factor for anxiety such as behavioral inhibition.

Attachment-Based Treatments A specific type of play therapy, Theraplay (Jernberg & Booth, 1999), has been studied for its effectiveness in treating anxiety in young children. Based on attachment theory, Theraplay is a child-focused, dyadic treatment that aims to reduce the child's fears and anxious behaviors by strengthening the parent-child relationship. Therapists observe the parent and child during play and guide the parent in using strategies designed to enable the parent to co-regulate their child's negative emotions. Wettig and colleagues (Wettig et al., 2011) reported on two studies in which they examined the effects of Theraplay on children between 2 ½ and 6 years of age with language disorders and social anxiety. Both studies showed that scores on an anxiety measure decreased after treatment and were comparable to the scores of a normative group without any disorders. It is difficult to draw any firm conclusions from this study about the effectiveness of Theraplay for the treatment of anxiety, however, due to the dual diagnoses in the children studied and the lack of an appropriate, randomly assigned, control group. A more recent study (Smithee et al., 2021), using a quasi-single-case design, revealed that Theraplay led to a significant reduction in both maternal and child anxiety in a sample of children between 4 and 7 years of age. However, this study had a small sample size (only six mother-child dyads) and a questionable experimental design. Thus, to date, the evidence for the effectiveness of play therapy in the treatment of anxiety disorders is not very compelling (which mirrors results for play therapy in the treatment of externalizing disorders such as ODD).

Summary: Anxiety Treatments In summary, there are a number of empirically based BT and CBT treatments for anxiety in young children, but, to date, these different interventions have been compared only to a waitlist control condition or to a normative comparison group, and not to another active treatment in an RCT. This makes it difficult to determine which, if any of these treatments are more effective than another, and also, which specific components are critical. For example, is coping skills training essential in addition to exposure, or is exposure alone sufficient to ensure effectiveness? Another question about these treatments is whether it is critical to include parent-child interaction sessions or if programs targeting parents (or children) alone are sufficient. A recent systematic review of treatments for anxiety in young children (Comer et al., 2019), which classified treatments according to various levels of support, provides some clarity on this latter question. According to Comer and colleagues, the evidence base for treatments for anxiety in young children that include parents and children together is strong enough for them to be classified as well-established. In contrast, those that target parents alone or parents and children in separate sessions have only enough support to be classified as probably efficacious. Thus, similar to the research on the effectiveness of interventions for externalizing disorders, treatments for internalizing ones are more effective when parents are actively involved in treatment. Nevertheless, it is clear that RCTs comparing a specific intervention to another active treatment condition are needed, as well as studies using a dismantling design in which one group receives all of the intervention components and specific components are eliminated in the comparison group.

In addition to the various CBT treatments, there also is some evidence that attachment-based play therapies are effective in reducing children's fears. However, after reviewing the evidence base for these treatments, Comer et al. (Comer et al., 2019) concluded that the evidence is too weak for them to be considered efficacious and that they should be rated as experimental. Nevertheless, it is possible that adding attachment-based strategies to CBT-based parent-child interventions might amplify their effectiveness. This possibility awaits further research that incorporates strategies such as teaching parents how to co-regulate their child's negative emotions (i.e., fear) in response to the cognitive behavioral treatments for anxiety to determine if this increases their effectiveness.

Current Treatments: Issues

"All have won and all must have prizes" is, perhaps, an accurate summary of the relative effectiveness of the different PMT interventions developed to treat externalizing and internalizing symptoms in young children. There is evidence for the effectiveness of each of these programs, but, to date, they have not been compared to determine which is most effective for which population. Many attachment-based interventions have also been developed, but the quality of the evidence supporting the effectiveness of these programs is quite limited.

Furthermore, it is not yet clear which components of the different interventions are essential, which is important to determine cost-effectiveness and maximize completion rates, particularly in low-income families. If a component is not necessary for the intervention to be effective, then treatment can be shortened, which is less costly and is likely to result in more families completing the program. For example, the various treatments for anxiety disorders in young children range from as few as six (e.g., Cool Little Kids) to 20 sessions (e.g., Being Brave). Obviously, the longer the duration of a treatment, the more it costs, and the issue of cost-effectiveness is extremely important for widespread dissemination to enable families from lower income levels to successfully complete treatment. Moreover, the longer a treatment takes, the greater the attrition, particularly among low-income families (de Haan et al., 2013; Lyon & Budd, 2010). Additionally, length of treatment, in and of itself, appears to impact rates of dropout, with a majority of dropouts occurring within the first two sessions (Olfson et al., 2009), and early treatment gains may be a good predictor of overall outcomes (Cromley & Lavigne, 2008). Finally, the dose-effect size for an adequate treatment remains to be determined for each of these treatments. For example, in a study comparing therapist-led treatment of the Incredible Years program for young children who met the criteria for an ODD diagnosis, Lavigne et al. (2008) found that 7–9 sessions of PMT were needed before the reduction of ODD symptoms was significantly better than that achieved by having parents read the Incredible Years Book (Webster-Stratton, 1992). Thus, there is a significant need for RCTs that compare the relative effectiveness of different evidence-based treatments and studies to determine which components of the different interventions are essential.

Additionally, several other issues complicate the picture for clinicians who need to decide how to provide the most effective, practical treatment for a child who presents with symptoms of ODD, ADHD, depression, or anxiety, or a "mixed bag" of symptoms from more than one disorder. At the outset, before starting treatment, there is an issue related to assessment—what exactly should the clinician treat? The parent may refer a child for particular behaviors that they find upsetting or annoying, but, in many cases, the child's problems do not fit neatly into one diagnostic category. For example, children who suffer from severe anxiety may be referred for oppositional behavior due to their refusal to approach feared objects or situations. Still, the referring parent only complains about the oppositional behaviors. The clinician must determine if these are part of a constellation of externalizing symptoms or if the child is suffering from underlying anxiety symptoms that are not obvious to the parent. In addition to determining the source of a particular child's symptoms, that is, whether, as in the previous example, they are due to anxiety or are a symptom of a behavior problem, it is also possible (perhaps likely) that the child is suffering from more than one disorder. As noted in Chap. 9, there are many symptoms that are transdiagnostic, and it is well known that there is a high rate of diagnostic comorbidity in child psychopathology (Angold & Costello, 1999). Thus, the child might be struggling with symptoms of both anxiety and behavior problems. Additionally, most efficacy trials for treatments, especially manualized ones, are studied in a carefully selected population in which the children suffer from only one disorder. How then does the clinician decide which treatment to use? The answer does not lie in systematically using a specific treatment for each of the comorbid disorders that the child is suffering from since this would require too lengthy a course of treatment.

In response to this dilemma, researchers developed transdiagnostic treatments to address a range of emotional and behavioral issues (Ehrenreich-May et al., 2018; Weisz et al., 2017). However, these transdiagnostic treatments were developed mainly for use with older children and adolescents, and most do not include parents in treatment, which, as previously mentioned, is critically important in treating young children. Thus, the question remains: How can a comprehensive approach that addresses a range of symptoms in young children be developed? Based on what we have learned from the PACT research, we provide our recommendations for such an approach in Chap. 11.

The next hurdle for the clinician to overcome after determining what to treat is whether it is feasible to use any of the manualized interventions with a specific child and particular family, even if the child only has symptoms of one disorder. Many studies demonstrating the effectiveness of a particular treatment are conducted in academic medical centers with middle-class families with the resources to attend treatment, which is often provided free of charge. In the "real world" setting, the clinician has to decide if it is even feasible for the child and their family to attend sessions, especially if they lack financial resources or do not have easily available transportation to the treatment setting, whether in a clinic, a medical center, or a private practice office. Families also may experience a myriad of other difficulties in their daily lives, such as serious illness, job loss, or inadequate housing which make it difficult, if not impossible, to regularly attend sessions.

One possible solution to overcome these real-life issues is to adapt some of the current treatments so that they can be administered via Telehealth. Thus, it is surprising that, despite the increase in delivering services via telehealth to older children and adolescents (Riley et al., 2023), there are only a few studies on telehealth applications of treatments for disorders in young children even though developing telehealth applications for parent management training seems eminently feasible. For example, the different versions of PCIT (e.g., PCIT, PCIT-ED) already consist of a therapist in a different room providing feedback to the parent through a one-way mirror and a "bug-in the ear." There is evidence from a RCT conducted pre-pandemic (Morgan et al., 2017) that Cool Little Kids, delivered online, is effective (compared to a waitlist control group) in decreasing anxiety in 3- to 6-year-old children. A recent case-series study (Clemmons et al., 2024) provides support for the feasibility and acceptability of delivering CPP online, but this does not mean that this method of delivery is as effective as in-person CPP. Play therapy is not adaptable to a telehealth application, but this is not a major problem since the evidence for the effectiveness of this type of treatment is, at best, equivocal. Telehealth does provide the opportunity to overcome practical barriers to treatment such as lack of transportation, but it remains to be seen if this mode of delivery is as effective as in-person treatment.

Another issue in manualized treatments is that their effectiveness lies in strict adherence to the treatment protocol, which may be impractical in community settings. Indeed, there is evidence (Curtis et al., 2004) that treatment integrity suffers in these settings where therapists may lack the training and supervision required to conduct these treatments. Furthermore, particular family circumstances may warrant deviating from the manualized treatment.

A family's willingness to participate in treatment is another issue that arises in the "real" world (i.e., not in a research trial). It is not uncommon for parents to want the clinician only to treat their child, despite the fact that there is strong evidence that parental involvement is important and, in many cases, an essential component of treatment (i.e., parent management training, Circle of Security, and Child-Parent Psychotherapy). An ethical dilemma arises for the clinician who may have difficulty establishing a mutually agreeable treatment plan with the family.

The interventions developed to treat disorders in young children focus on the child's problems, which leads to another ethical and practical issue. As described in Chaps. 3 and 4, it is well known that more distal factors such as poverty, family stress and conflict and parental depression are risk factors for both internalizing and externalizing symptoms in young children. The PACT research, described in Chaps. 7 and 8, further supports the importance of indirect effects from other factors in the child's environment that impact the child over time in ways that create risk for the development of many types of symptoms. This has important implications for the development of effective treatments. Take, for example, parental depression—both the literature and our research reveal that this factor has significant direct and indirect associations with child mental health outcomes. Treating the child's disorder may lead to a decrease in the parent's depression since, in accordance with the developmental psychopathology principle of reciprocity, there is a bidirectional relation between the child's symptoms and parental depression. This does not mean, however, that the parent's depression completely remits just because their child's symptoms have improved. Thus, the clinician is left with the dilemma of deciding whether they should attempt to directly treat the parent's depression or refer them to an adult therapist or a psychiatrist for medication. Although the best option may be to refer the parent, it may not be feasible for them to see another therapist for practical reasons (e.g., cost and time). Being aware of this conundrum, the clinician is left with the ethical issue, as well as the practical one, as to how best to serve the needs of not only this particular child but also of the depressed (or anxious) family member. In Chap. 11, we recommend several strategies that may be effective in decreasing parental depression when working with the parent-child dyad.

As noted in Chap. 1, the tenets of developmental psychopathology make it clear that we cannot understand and, hence, effectively treat child mental health symptoms without first attending to principles of normal development, risk and protective factors at multiple levels, reciprocal influences, child agency, longitudinal patterns, and issues of equifinality and multifinality. Most single disorders and manualized treatments adhere only to the specific symptoms that the child manifests—for example, excessive sadness, avoidance of new places, or excessive temper tantrums. To develop more effective treatments that are efficient, cost-effective, and applicable in community settings where most children receive services, it will be critical to adhere more closely to these tenets of developmental psychopathology and particularly to address the processes through which both healthy and unhealthy developmental outcomes emerge.

Perhaps the most critical issue in this regard is that little is known about the mechanisms whereby the different interventions lead to significant decreases in child symptoms and disorders. Is it, to name a few possibilities, a more secure parent-child relationship, more effective parenting practices, or the child developing better emotional regulation or coping skills? Determining the mechanism(s) of change is necessary to develop the optimal combination of cost-effective treatments before the widespread dissemination of any particular treatment. We believe that the time has come for researchers to focus on these important issues. Thus, the next chapter provides our recommendations for a comprehensive approach to treatment based on developmental psychopathology principles and an understanding of the multi-domain risk factors and pathways (i.e., mechanisms) elucidated in Chaps. 7, 8, and 9 in this book.

References

Angold, A., & Costello, A. J. (1999). Comorbidity. *Journal of Child Psychology and Psychiatry, 40*(1), 57. https://doi.org/10.1111/1469-7610.00424

Axberg, U., & Broberg, A. G. (2012). Evaluation of "the incredible years" in Sweden: The transferability of an American parent-training program to Sweden. *Scandinavian Journal of Psychology, 53*(3), 224–232. https://doi.org/10.1111/j.1467-9450.2012.00955.x

Bandura, A. (1977). *Social learning theory*. Prentice Hall.

Barlow, J., Schrader-McMillan, A., Axford, N., Wrigley, Z., Sonthaliz, S., Wilkinson, T., Rawsthorn, M., Toft, A., & Coad, J. (2016). Attachment and attachment-related outcomes in preschool children-a review of recent evidence. *Child and Adolescent Mental Health, 21*(1), 11–20. https://doi.org/10.1111/camh.12138

Barrett, P. M. (2007). *Fun FRIENDS: The teaching and training manual for group leaders*. Fun Friends Publishing.

Barrett, P., & Turner, C. (2001). Prevention of anxiety symptoms in primary school children: Preliminary results from a universal school-based trial. *British Journal of Clinical Psychology, 40*(4), 399. https://doi.org/10.1348/014466501163887

Barrett, P., Fisak, B., & Cooper, M. (2015). The treatment of anxiety in young children: Results of an open trial of the fun FRIENDS program. *Behaviour Change, 32*, 231–242.

Battagliese, G., Caccetta, M., Luppino, O. I., Baglioni, C., Cardi, V., Mancini, F., & Buonanno, C. (2015). Cognitive-behavioral therapy for externalizing disorders: A meta-analysis of treatment effectiveness. *Behavior Research and Therapy, 75*, 60–71. https://doi.org/10.1016/j.brat.2015.10.008

Bayer, J., Hiscock, H., Scalzo, K., Mathers, M., McDonald, M., Morris, A., Birdseye, J., & Wake, M. (2009). Systematic review of preventive interventions for children's mental health. *Australian and New Zealand Journal of Psychiatry, 43*(8), 695–710. https://doi.org/10.1080/00048670903001893

Berlin, L. J., Zeanah, C. H., & Lieberman, A. F. (2016). Prevention and intervention programs to support early attachment security: A move to the level of the community. In J. Cassidy & P. R. Shaver (Eds.), *Handbook of attachment* (3rd ed.).

Bernstein, R. E., Timmons, A. C., & Lieberman, A. F. (2019). Interpersonal violence, maternal perception of infant emotion, and child-parent psychotherapy. *Journal of Family Violence, 34*(4), 309–320. https://doi.org/10.1007/s10896-019-00041-7

Bikic, A., Smith-Nielsen, J., Dalsgaard, S., Swain, J., Fonagy, P., & Leckman, J. F. (2022). Protocol for a randomized controlled trial comparing the circle of security-parenting (COS-P) with treatment as usual in child mental health services. *PLoS ONE, 17*, e0265676. https://doi.org/10.1371/journal.pone.0265676

Bowlby, J. (1969). *Attachment and loss: Vol. 1. Attachment*. Basic Books.

Bratton, S. C., Ray, D., Rhine, T., & Jones, L. (2005). The efficacy of play therapy with children: A meta-analytic review of treatment outcomes. *Professional Psychology: Research and Practice, 36*(4), 376–390. https://doi.org/10.1037/0735-77028.36.4.376

Campbell, S. M., Hawes, T., Swan, K., & Zimmer-Gembeck, M. J. (2023). Evidence-based treatment in practice: PCIT research on addressing individual differences and diversity through the lens of 20 years of service. *Psychology Research and Behavior Management, 16*, 2599–2617. https://doi.org/10.2147/PRBM.S360302

Cassidy, J., Brett, B. E., Gross, J. T., Stern, J. A., Martin, D. R., Mohr, J. J., & Woodhouse, S. S. (2017). Circle of security-parenting: A randomized controlled trial in head start. *Development and Psychopathology, 29*(2), 651–673. https://doi.org/10.1017/S0954579417000244

Clark, L. A., Cuthbert, B., Lewis-Fernandez, R., Narrow, W. E., & Reed, G. M. (2017). Three approaches to understanding and classifying mental disorder: *ICD-11, DSM-5,* and the National Institute of Mental Health's research domain criteria (RDoC). *Psychological Science in the Public Interest, 18*(2), 72–145. https://doi.org/10.1177/1529100617727266

Clemmons, N. G., Coates, E., & McLeod, A. (2024). Understanding the benefits of child-parent psychotherapy delivered via telehealth during the COVID-19 pandemic. *Children's Health Care, 53*(1), 41–59. https://doi.org/10.1080/02739615.2023.2179489

Coates, J., Taylor, J. A., & Sayal, K. (2015). Parenting interventions for ADHD: A systematic literature review and meta-analysis. *Journal of Attention Disorders, 19*, 831–843. https://doi.org/10.1177/1087054714535952

Comer, J. S., Puliafico, A. C., Aschenbrand, S. G., McKnight, K., Robin, J. A., Goldfine, M. E., & Albano, A. M. (2012). A pilot feasibility evaluation of the CALM program for anxiety disorders in early childhood. *Journal of Anxiety Disorders, 26*(1), 40–49. https://doi.org/10.1016/j.janxdis.2011.08.011

Comer, J. S., Chow, C., Chan, P. T., Cooper-Vince, C., & Wilson, L. A. (2013). Psychosocial treatment efficacy for disruptive behavior problems in very young childen: A meta-analytic examination. *Journal of Affective Disorders, 52*(1), 26–36. https://doi.org/10.1016/j.jaac.2012.10.001

Comer, J. S., Hong, N., Poznanski, B., Silva, K., & Wilson, M. (2019). Evidence base update on the treatment of early childhood anxiety and related problems. *Journal of Clinical Child & Adolescent Psychology, 48*(1), 1–15. https://doi.org/10.1080/15374416.2018.1534208

Cooley, M. E., Veldorale-Griffin, A., Petren, R. E., & Mullis, A. K. (2014). Parent-child interaction therapy: A meta-analysis of child behavior outcomes and parent stress. *Journal of Family Social Work, 17*, 191–208.

Cromley, T., & Lavigne, J. V. (2008). Predictors and consequences of early gains in child psychotherapy. *Psychotherapy, 45*(1), 42–60.

Curtis, N. M., Ronan, K. R., & Borduin, C. M. (2004). Multisystemic treatment: A meta-analysis of outcome studies. *Journal of Family Psychology, 18*(3), 411–419. https://doi.org/10.1037/0893-3200.18.3.411

Daley, D., van der Oord, S., Ferrin, M., Danckaerts, M., Doepfner, M., Cortese, S., Sonuga-Barke, E. J. S., & on behalf of the European ADHD Guidelines Group. (2014). Behavioral interventions in attention-deficit/hyperactivity disorder: A meta-analysis of randomized controlled trials across multiple outcome domains. *Journal of the Academy of Child and Adolescent Psychiatry, 53*(8), 835–847.

de Haan, A. M., Boon, A. E., de Jong, J. T., Hoeve, M., & Vermeiren, R. R. (2013). A meta-analytic review on treatment dropout in child and adolescent outpatient mental health care. *Clinical Psychology Review, 33*(5), 698–711. https://doi.org/10.1016/j.cpr.2013.04.005

DeKlyen, M., & Greenberg, M. T. (2016). Attachment and psychopathology in childhood. In J. Cassidy & P. R. Shaver (Eds.), *Handbook of attachment: Theory, research, and clinical applications* (pp. 639–666). Guilford.

DeVito, C., & Hopkins, J. (2001). Attachment, parenting, and marital dissatisfaction as predictors of disruptive behavior in preschoolers. *Developmental Psychopathology, 13*, 215–231.

Doyle, F. L., Dodd, H. F., Morris, T. M., Lazarus, R. S., Byrow, Y., & Hudson, J. L. (2021). Targeting risk factors for inhibited preschool children: An anxiety prevention program. *Behaviour Research and Therapy, 147*. https://doi.org/10.1016/j.brat.2021.103982

Drugli, M. B., & Larsson, B. (2006). Children aged 4–8 years treated with parent training and child therapy because of condct problems: Generalisation effects to day-care and school settings. *European Child and Adolescent Psychiatry, 15*(7), 392–399. https://doi.org/10.1007/s00787-006-0546-3

Edrissi, F., Havighurst, S. S., Aghebati, A., Habibi, M., & Arani, A. M. (2019). A pilot study of the tuning in to kids parenting program in Iran for reducing preschool children's anxiety. *Journal of Child and Family Studies, 28*(6), 1695–1702. https://doi.org/10.1007/s10826-019-01400-0

Ehrenreich-May, J., Kennedy, S. M., Sherman, J. A., Bilek, E. L., Buzzela, B. A., Bennett, S. M., & Barlow, D. H. (2018). *Unified protocols for transdiagnostic treatment of emotional disorders in children and adolescents: Therapist guide*. Oxford University Press.

Epstein, R. A., Fonnesbeck, D., Potter, S., Rizzone, K. H., & McPheeters, M. (2015). Psychosocial interventions for child disruptive behaviors: A meta-analysis. *Pediatrics, 136*(5), 947–960. https://doi.org/10.1542/peds.2015-2577

Everett, Y., Martin, C. G., & Zalewski, M. (2021). A systematic review focusing on psychotherapeutic interventions that impact parental psychopathology. *Clinical Child & Family Psychology Review, 24*(3), 579–598. https://doi.org/10.1007/s10567-021-00355-3

Eyberg, S. M., & Funderburk, B. W. (2011). *Parent-child interaction therapy protocol*. PCIT International.

Eyberg, S., Boggs, S. R., & Algina, J. (1995). Parent-child interaction therapy: A psychosocial model for the treatment of young children with conduct problem behavior and their families. *Psychopharmacology Bulletin, 31*, 83–91.

Fearon, R. P., Bakermans-Kranenburg, M. J., van IJzendoorn, M. H., Lapsley, A. M., & Roisman, G. I. (2010). *The significance of insecure attachment and disorganization in the development of children's externalizing behavior: A meta-analysis., 81*(2), 435–456. https://doi.org/10.1111/j.1467-8624.2009.01405.x

Fernandez, M. A., & Eyberg, S. M. (2009). Predicting treatment and follow-up attrition in parent-child interaction therapy. *Journal of Abnormal Child Psychology, 37*, 431–441. https://doi.org/10.1007/s10802-008-9281-1

Fernandez, M. A., Butler, A. M., & Eyberg, S. M. (2011). Treatment outcome for low socioeconomic status African American families in parent-child interaction therapy: A pilot study. *Child & Family Behavior Therapy, 33*, 32–48. https://doi.org/10.1080/07317107.2011.545011

Ghosh Ippen, C., Harris, W. W., Van Horn, P., & Lieberman, A. F. (2011). Traumatic and tressful events in early childhood: Can treatment help those at highest risk? *Child Abuse and Neglect, 35*, 504–513.

Greenberg, M. T. (1999). Attachment and psychopathology in childhood. In J. Cassidy & P. R. Shaver (Eds.), *Handbook of attachment: Theory, research, and clinical applications* (pp. 469–496). Guilford.

Groenman, A. P., Hornstra, R., Hoekstra, P. J., Steenhius, L., Aghebati, A., Boyer, B. E., Buitelaar, J. K., Chronis-Tuscano, A., Daley, D., Dehkordian, P., Dvorsky, M., Franke, N., DuPaul, G. J., Gershy, N., Harvey, E., Hennig, T., Herbert, S., Langberg, J., Mautone, J. A., . . . van der Oord, S. (2022). An individual participant data meta-analysis: Behavioral treatments for children and adolescents with attention-deficiti/hyperactivity disorder. Journal of the American Academy of Child and Adolescent Psychiatry, 61(2), 144–158.

Groh, A. M., Fearon, R. M. P., Van IJzendoorn, M., Bakermans-Kranenburg, M. J., & Roisman, G. I. (2016). Attachment in the early life course: Meta-analytic evidence for its role in socioemotional development. *Child Development Perspectives, 11*(1), 70–76. https://doi.org/10.1111/cdep.12213

Havighurst, S. S., Wilson, K. R., Harley, A. E., Kehoe, C., Efron, D., & Prior, M. R. (2013). "Tuning into kids:" Reducing young children's behavior problems using an emotion coaching parenting program. *Child Psychiatry and Human Development, 44*(2), 247–264. https://doi.org/10.1007/s10578-012-0322-1

Helander, M., Asperholm, M., Wetterborg, D., Ost, L. G., Hellner, C., Herlitz, A., & Enebrink, P. (2024). The efficacy of parent management training with or without involving the child in the treatment among children with clinical levels of disruptive behavior: A meta-analysis. *Child Psychiatry and Human Development, 55*(1), 164–181. https://doi.org/10.1007/s10578-022-01-1367-y

Hirshfeld-Becker, D. R., Masek, B., Henin, A., Blakely, L. R., Rettew, D. C., Dufton, L., Segool, N., & Biederman, J. (2008). Cognitive-behavioral intervention with young anxious children. *Harvard Review of Psychiatry, 16*(2), 113–126. https://doi.org/10.1080/10673220802073956

Hirshfeld-Becker, D. R., Masek, B., Henin, A., Blakely, L. R., Pollock-Wurman, R. A., McQuade, J., De Petrilllo, L., Briesch, J., Ollendick, T. H., Rosenbaum, J. F., & Biederman, J. (2010). Cognitive behavioral therapy for 4- to 7-year-old children with anxiety disorders: A randomized clinical trial. *Journal of Consulting and Clinical Psychology, 78*(4), 498–510. https://doi.org/10.1037/a0019055

Homem, T., Gaspar, M., Seabra Santos, M., Azevedo, A., & Canavarro, M. (2014). Incredible years parent training: Does it improve positive relationships in Portuguese families of preschoolers with oppositional/defint symptoms? *Journal of Child and Family Studies, 24*. https://doi.org/10.1007/s100826-014-9988-2

Hornstra, R., Groenman, A. P., van der Oord, S., Luman, M., Dekkers, T. J., van der Veen-Mulders, J., Hoekstra, P. J., & van den Hoofdakker, B. J. (2023). Review: Which components of behavioral parent and teacher training work for children with ADHD? – A metaregression analysis on child behavioral outcomes. *Journal of Child and Family Studies, 28*(2), 258–268. https://doi.org/10.1111/camh.12561

Huber, A., McMahon, C., & Sweller, N. (2015). Improved child behavioural and emotional functioning after circle of security 20-week intervention. *Attachment & Human Development, 17*, 547–569. https://doi.org/10.1080/14616734.2015.1086395

Hudson, J. L., Minihan, S., Chen, W., Carl, T., Fu, M., Tully, L., Kangas, M., Rosewell, L., McDermott, M. P., Wang, Y., Stubbs, T., & Martiniuk, A. (2023). Interventions for young children's mental health: A review of reviews. *Clinical Child & Family Psychology Review, 26*(3), 593–641. https://doi.org/10.1007/s10567-023-00443-6

Jernberg, A. M., & Booth, P. D. (1999). *Theraplay: Helping parents and children build better relationships through attachment-based play* (2nd ed.). Jossey-Bass.

Kagan, J. (1989). The concept of behavioral inhibition to the unfamiliar. In J. S. Reznick (Ed.), *Perspectives on behavioral inhibition* (pp. 1–23). University of Chicago Press.

Kaminski, J., & Claussen, A. H. (2017). Evidence base update for psychosocial treatments for disruptive behaviors in children. *Journal of Clinical Chidl, 46*(4), 477–499. https://doi.org/10.1080/15374416.2017.1310044

Kendall, P. C., Hudson, J. L., Gosch, E., Flannery-Schroeder, E., & Suveg, C. (2008). Cognitive-behavioral therapy for anxiety disordered youth: A randomized clinical trial evaluating child and family modalities. *Journal of Consulting and Clinical Psychology, 76*, 282–297. https://doi.org/10.1037/0022-006X.2.282

Kennedy, S. J., Rapee, R. M., & Edwards, S. L. (2009). A selective intervention program for inhibited preschool-aged children of parents with an anxiety disorder: Effects on current anxiety disorders and temperament. *British Journal of Clinical Psychology, 40*(4), 602–609. https://doi.org/10.1097/CHI.0b013e31819f6fa9

Kohlhoff, J., & Cibralic, S. (2022). The impact of attachment-based parenting interventions on externalizing behaviors in toddlers and preschoolers: A systematic narrative review. *Child and Youth Care Forum, 51*, 1005–1029. https://doi.org/10.1007/s10566-021-09667-5

Kohlhoff, J., Lieneman, C., Cibralic, S., Traynor, N., & McNeil, C. B. (2022). Attachment-based parenting interventions and evidence of changes in toddler attachment patterns: An overview. *Clinical Child & Family Psychology Review, 25*(4), 737–753. https://doi.org/10.1007/s10567-022-00405-4

Kuhn, J., Gonzalez, E., Weil, L., Izguttinov, A., & Walker, S. (2022). Effectiveness of child-focused interventions for externalizing behavior: A rapid evidence review. *Research on Child and Adolescent Psychopathology, 50*(8), 987–1009. https://doi.org/10.1007/s10802-022-00904-6

Lavigne, J. V., LeBailly, S. A., Gouze, K. R., Cicchetti, C., Pochyly, J., Arend, R., Jessup, B. W., & Binns, H. J. (2008). Treating oppositional defiant Disorder in primary care: A comparison of three models. *Journal of Pediatric Psychology, 33*(5), 449–461.

Lavigne, J. V., LeBailly, S. A., Hopkins, J., Gouze, K. R., & Binns, H. J. (2009). The prevalence of ADHD, ODD, depression and anxiety in a community sample of 4-year-olds. *Journal of Clinical Child and Adolescent Psychology, 38*, 315–328. https://doi.org/10.1080/15374410902851382

Lavigne, J. V., Gouze, K. R., Hopkins, J., & Bryant, F. B. (2016). Multi-domain predictors of attention deficit/hyperactivity disorder symptoms in preschool children: Cross-informant differences. *Child Psychiatry and Human Development, 47*(6), 841–856. https://doi.org/10.1007/s10578-015-0616-1

Leblanc, M., & Ritchie, M. (2001). A meta-analysis of play therapy coutcomes. *Counseling Psychology Quarterly, 14*(2), 149–163. https://doi.org/10.1080/09515070110059142

Lee, P. C., Niew, W. I., Yang, H. J., Chen, V. C., & Lin, K. C. (2012). Meta-analyses: Key parenting program components for disruptive child behavior. *Research in Developmental Disabilities, 33*(6), 2040–2049. https://doi.org/10.1016/j.ridd.2012.05.011

Leijten, P., Melendez-Torres, G. J., Gardner, F., van Aar, J., Schulz, S., & Overbeek, G. (2018a). Are relationship enhancement and behavior management "the golden couple" for disruptive child behavior? *Two meta-analyses. Child Development, 89*(6), 197–1982. https://doi.org/10.1111/cdev.13051

Leijten, P., Raaijmakers, M., Matthys, W., Menting, A., Hemink-van Putten, M., & Orobio de Castro, B. (2018b). Understanding who benefits from parenting interventions for children's conduct problems: An integrative data analysis. *Prevention Science, 19*(4), 579–588. https://doi.org/10.1007/s11121-018-0864-y

Leijten, P., Gardner, F., Melendez-Torres, G. J., van Aar, J., Hutchings, J., Schulz, S., Knerr, W., & Overbeek, G. (2019). Meta-analyses: Key parenting program components for disruptive child behavior. *Journal of the American Academy of Child and Adolescent Psychiatry, 58*(2), 180–190. https://doi.org/10.1016/j.jaac.2018.07.900

Leijten, P., Scott, S., Landau, S., Harris, V., Mann, J., Hutchings, J., Beecham, J., & Gardner, F. (2020). Individual participant data meta-analysis: Impact of conduct problem severity, comorbid attention-deficit/hyperactivity disorder and emotional problems, and maternal depression on parenting program effects. *Journal of the American Academy of Child and Adolescent Psychiatry, 59*(8), 933–943. https://doi.org/10.1016/j.jaac.2020.01.023

Lenze, S. N., Pautsch, J., & Luby, J. (2011). Parent-child interaction therapy emotion development: A novel treatment for depression in preschool children. *Depression and Anxiety, 28*(2), 153–159. https://doi.org/10.10002/da.20770

Leung, C., Sanders, M. R., Leung, S., Make, R., & Lau, J. (2003). An outcome evaluation of the implementation of the triple P-positive parenting program in Hong Kong. *Family Process, 42*, 531–544.

Lieberman, A. F., & Van Horn, P. (2008). *Psychotherapy with infants and young children: Repairing the effects of stress and trauma on early attahment*. Guilford Press.

Lieberman, A. F., Weston, D. R., & Pawl, J. H. (1991). Preventive intervention and outcome with anxiously attached dyads. *Child Development, 62*(1), 199–209.

Lieberman, A. F., Van Horn, P., & Ghosh Ippen, C. (2005). Toward evidence-based treatment: Child-parent psychotherapy with preschoolers exposed to marital violence. *Journal of the American Academy of Child and Adolescent Psychiatry, 44*, 1241–1248.

Lieberman, A. F., Ghosh Ippen, C., & Van Horn, P. (2006a). Child-parent psychotherapy: Six month follow-up of a randomized control trial. *Journal of the American Academy of Child and Adolescent Psychiatry, 45*(8), 913–918. https://doi.org/10.1097/0l.chi.0000222784.03735.92

Lieberman, A. F., Ippen, C. G., & Van Horn, P. (2006b). Child-parent psychotherapy: 6-month follow-up of a randomized controlled trial. *Journal of the American Academy of Child and Adolescent Psychiatry, 48*(8), 913–918. https://doi.org/10.1097/01.chi.0000222784.03735.92

Lieberman, A. F., Ghosh Ippen, C., & Van Horn, P. (2015). *Don't hit my mommy: A manual for child-parent psychotherapy with young children exposed to violence and other trauma* (2nd ed.). Zero to Three.

Lin, Y. W., & Bratton, S. C. (2015). A meta-analytic review of child-centered play therapy approaches. *Journal of Counseling and Development, 93*(1), 45–58. https://doi.org/10.1002/j.1556-6676.2015.00180.x

Luby, J., Lenze, S. N., & Tillman, R. (2012). A novel early intervention for preschool depression: Findings from a pilot randomized controlled trial. *Journal of Child Psychology and Psychiatry, 53*(3), 313–322. https://doi.org/10.1111/j.1469-7610.2011.02483

Luby, J. L., Barch, D. M., Whalen, D., Tillman, R., & Freedland, K. E. (2018). A randomized controlled trial of parent-child psychotherapy targeting emotion development for early childhood depression. *The American Journal of Psychiatry, 175*(11), 1102–1110. https://doi.org/10.1176/appi.ajp.2018.18030321

Luby, J. L., Gilbert, K., Whalen, D., Tillman, R., & Barch, D. M. (2020). The differential contribution of the components of parent-child interaction therapy emotion development for treatment of preschool depression. *Journal of the Academy of Child and Adolescent Psychiatry, 59*(7), 868–879. https://doi.org/10.1016/j.jaac.2019.07.937

Lyon, A. R., & Budd, K. S. (2010). A community mental health implementation of Parent-Child Interaction Therapy (PCIT). *Journal of Child and Family Studies, 19*(5), 654–668. https://doi.org/10.1007/s10826-010-9353-z

Matos, M., Bauermeister, J. J., & Bernal, G. (2009). Parent-child interaction therapy for Puerto Rican preschool children with ADHD and behavior problems: A pilot efficacy study. *Family Process, 48*(2), 232–252. https://doi.org/10.1111/j.1545-5300.2009.01279.x

Maxwell, A. M., Reay, R. E., Huber, A., Hawkins, E., Woolnough, E., & McMahon, C. (2021). Parent and practitioner perspectives on Circle of Security Parenting (COS-p): A qualitative study. *Infant Mental Health Journal, 42*(3), 452–468. https://doi.org/10.1002/imhj.21916

McCabe, K., & Yeh, M. (2009). Parent-child interaction therapy for Mexican Americans: A randomized clinical trial. *Journal of Clinical Child & Adolescent Psychology, 38*, 753–759. https://doi.org/10.1080/15374410903103544

McGilloway, S., Mhaille, G. N., Bywater, T., Furlong, M., Leckey, Y., Kelly, P., Comiskey, C., & Donnelly, M. (2012). A parenting intervention for childhood behavioral problems: A randomized controlled trial in disadvantaged community-based settings. *Journal of Consulting and Clinical Psychology, 80*(1), 116–127. https://doi.org/10.1037/a0026304

Menting, T. A., de Castro, B. O., & Matthys, W. (2013). Effectiveness of the incredible years parent training to modify disruptive and prosocial child behavior: A meta-analytic review. *Clinical Psychology Review, 33*, 901–913. https://doi.org/10.1016/j.cpr.2103.07.006

Morgan, A. J., Rapee, R. M., Salim, A., Goharpey, N., Tamir, E., McLellan, L. F., & Bayer, J. K. (2017). Internet-delivered parenting program for prevention and early intervention of anxiety problems in young children: Randomized controlled trial. *Journal of the American Academy of Child and Adolescent Psychiatry, 56*(5), 417–426. https://doi.org/10.1016/j.jaac.2017.02.010

Mulqueen, J. M., Bartley, C. A., & Bloch, M. H. (2015). Meta-analysis: Parental interventions for preschool ADHD. *Journal of Attention Disorders, 19*, 118–124. https://doi.org/10.1177/1087054713504135

Murray, D. W., Lawrence, J. R., & LaForett, D. R. (2018). The incredible years programs for ADHD in young children: A critical review of the evidence. *Journal of Emotional & Behavioral Disorders, 26*(4), 195–208.

Nixon, R. D. V., Sweeney, L., Erickson, D. B., & Touyz, S. W. (2003). Parent-child interaction therapy: A comparison of standard and abbreviated treatments for oppositional defiant preschoolers. *Journal of Consulting and Clinical Psychology, 71*, 251–260.

Nixon, R. D., Sweeney, L., Erickson, D. B., & Touyz, S. W. (2004). Parent-child interaction therapy: One- and two-year follow-up of standard and abbreviated treatments for oppositional preschoolers. *Journal of Abnormal Child Psychology, 32*(3), 263–271. https://doi.org/10.1023/b:jacp.0000026140.60558.05

Nogueira, S., Canario, A. C., Abreu-Lima, I., Teixeira, P., & Cruz, O. (2022). Group triple P intervention effects on children and parents: A systematic revew and meta-analysis. *International*

Journal of Environmental Research and Public Health, 19(4), 2113. https://doi.org/10.3390/ijerph19042113
Nowak, C., & Heinrichs, N. (2008). A comprehensive meta-analysis of triple P-positive parenting program using hierarchical linear modeling: Effectiveness and moderating variables. *Journal of Abnormal Child Psychology, 11*, 114–144.
Olfson, M., Mojtabai, R., Sampson, N. A., Hwang, I., Druss, B., Wang, P. S., Wells, K. B., Pincus, H. A., & Kessler, R. C. (2009). Dropout from outpatient mental health care in the United States. *Psychiatric Services, 60*(7), 898–907. https://doi.org/10.1176/ps.2009.60.7.898
Oud, M., de Winter, L., Vermeulen-Smit, E., Bodden, D., Nauta, M., Stone, L., van den Heuval, M., Taher, R. A., de Graaf, I., Kendall, T., Engels, R., & Stikkelbroek, Y. (2019). Effectiveness of CBT for children and adolescents with depression: A systematic review and meta-regression. *European Psychiatry, 57*, 33–45. https://doi.org/10.1016/j.eurpsy.2018.12.008
Pahl, K. M., & Barrett, P. M. (2007). The development of social-emotional competence in preschool-age children: An introduction to the fun FRIENDS program. *Australian Journal of Guidance and Counselling, 17*(1), 81–90. https://doi.org/10.1375/ajge.17.1.81
Parker, F. L., Boak, A. Y., Griffin, K. W., Ripple, C., & Peay, L. (1999). Parent-child relationship, home learning environments, and school readiness. *School Psychology Review, 28*(3), 413–425.
Parker, M. M., Hunnicutt Hollenbaugh, K. M., & Kelly, C. T. (2021). Exploring the impact of child-centered play therapy for children exhibiting behavioral problems: A meta-analysis. *International Journal of Play Therapy, 30*(4), 259–271. https://doi.org/10.1037/pla0000128
Powell, B., Cooper, G., Hoffman, K., & Marvin, B. (2014). *The circle of security intervention: Enhancing attachment in early parent child relationship*. Guilford Press.
Puliafico, A. C., Comer, J. S., & Albano, A. M. (2013). Coaching approach behavior and leading by modeling: Rationale. Principles, and a session-by-session description of the CALM program for early childhood anxiety. *Cognitive and Behavioral Practice, 20*(4), 517–528. https://doi.org/10.1016/j.cbpra.2012.05.002
Rapee, R. M., Kennedy, S., Ingram, M., Edwards, S. L., & Sweeney, L. (2005). Prevention and early intervention of anxiety disorders in inhibited preschool children. *Journal of Consulting and Clinical Psychology, 73*(3), 488–497. https://doi.org/10.1037/0022-006X.73.3.488
Rapee, R. M., Kennedy, S., Ingram, M., Edwards, S. L., & Sweeney, L. (2010). Altering the trajectory of anxiety in at risk young children. *American Journal of Psychiatry, 167*, 1518–1525. https://doi.org/10.1176/appi.ajp.2010.09111619
Riise, E. N., Wergeland, G. J. H., Njardvik, U., & Ost, L. G. (2021). Cognitive behavior therapy for externalizing disorders in children and adolescents in routine clinical care: A systematic review and meta-analysis. *Clinical Psychology Review, 83*, 101954. https://doi.org/10.1016/j.cpr.2020.101954
Riley, E. N., Cordell, K. D., Shimshock, S. M., Figueroa, R. E. P., Lyons, J. S., & Vsevolozhskaya, O. A. (2023). Evaluation of telehealth in child behavioral health services delivery during the COVID-19 pandemic. *Psychiatric Services, 74*(3), 237–243. https://doi.org/10.1176/appi.ps.20220141
Sanders, M. R. (1999). Triple-P-positive parenting program: Towards an empirically validated multilevel parenting and family support strategy for the prevention of behavior and emotional problems in children. *Clinical Child & Family Psychology Review, 2*, 71–90. https://doi.org/10.1023/A:1021843613840
Sanders, M. R. (2012). Development, evaluation, and multinational dissemination of the triple P-positive parenting program. *Annual Review of Clinical Psychology, 8*, 347-379. 10.1146-032511-143104.
Sanders, M. R., Markie-Dadds, C., Tully, L. A., & Bor, W. (2000). The triple P-positive parenting program: A comparison of enhanced, standard, and self-directed behavioral family interention for parents of children with early onset conduct problems. *Journal of Consulting and Clinical Psychology, 68*(4), 624–640.

Scheeringa, M. S., Weems, C. F., Cohen, J. A., Amaya, J. L., & Guthrie, D. (2011). Trauma-focused cognitive-behavioral therapy for posttraumatic stress disorder in three- through six-year-old children: A randomized clinical trial. *Journal of Child Psychology and Psychiatry, 52*, 8. https://doi.org/10.1111/j.1469-7610.2010.02354.x

Schuhmann, E. M., Foote, R. C., Eyberg, S., Boggs, S. R., & Algina, J. (1998). Efficacy of parent-child interaction therapy: Interim report of a randomized trial with short-term maintenance. *Journal of Clinical Child Psychology, 27*(1), 34–45.

Seabra-Santos, M. J., Gaspar, M. F., Azevedo, A. F., Homem, T. C., Guerra, J., Martins, V., Leitão, S., Pimentel, M., Almeida, M., & Moura-Ramos, M. (2016). Incredible years parent training: What changes, for whom, how, for how long? *Journal of Applied Developmental Psychology, 44*, 93–104. https://doi.org/10.1016/j.appdev.2016.04.004

Smithee, L. C., Krizova, K., Guest, J. D., & Case Pease, J. (2021). Theraplay as a family treatment for mother anxiety and child anxiety. *International Journal of Play Therapy, 30*(3), 206–218. https://doi.org/10.1037/pla0000153

Sroufe, L. A. (2005). Attachment and development: A prospective, longitudinal study from birth to adulthood. *Attachment & Human Development, 7*(4), 349–367. https://doi.org/10.1080/14616730500365928

Thomas, R., & Zimmer-Gembeck, M. J. (2007). Behavioral outcomes of parent-child interaction therapy and triple P -positive parenting program: A review and meta-analysis. *Journal of Abnormal Child Psychology, 35*(3), 475–495. https://doi.org/10.1007/s10802-007-9104-9

Thomas, R., Abell, B., Webb, H. J., Avdagic, E., & Zimmer-Gembeck, M. J. (2017). Parent-child interaction therapy: A meta-analysis. *Pediatrics, 140*, e20170352. https://doi.org/10.1542/peds.2017-0352

Toth, S. L., Rogosch, F. A., Manly, J. T., & Cicchetti, D. (2006). The efficacy of toddler-parent psychotherapy to reorganize attachment in the young offspring of mothers with major depressive disorder: A randomized preventive trial. *Journal of Consulting and Clinical Psychology, 74*(6), 1006.

Tourjman, V., Louis-Nascan, G., Ahmed, G., DuBow, A., Cote, H., Daly, N., Daoud, G., Sespinet, S., Flood, J., Gagnier-Marandola, E., Gignac, M., Graziosi, G., Mansuri, Z., & Sadek, J. (2022). Psychosocial interventions for attention deficit/hyperactivity Disorder: A systematic review and meta-analysis by the CADDRA guidelines work GROUP. *Brain Sciences, 12*, 1–29. https://doi.org/10.3390/brainsci12081023

Tully, L. A., & Hunt, C. (2016). Brief parenting interventions for children at risk of externalizng behavior problems: A systematic review. *Journal of Child and Family Studies, 25*(3), 705–719. https://doi.org/10.1007/s10826-015-0284-6

Valero-Aguayo, L., Rodriguez-Bocanegra, M., Ferro-Garcia, R., & Ascanio-Velasco, L. (2021). Meta-analysis of the efficacy and effectiveness of parent child interaction therapy (PCIT) for child behaviour problems. *Psichothema, 33*(4), 544–555. https://doi.org/10.7334/psicotherma2021.70

van der Mheen, M., Legersteen, J. S., Dieleman, G. C., Hillegers, M. H. J., & Utens, E. M. W. J. (2020). Cognitive behavioural therapy for anxiety disorders in young children: A Dutch open trial of the fun FRIENDS program. *Behaviour Change, 37*(1), 1–12. https://doi.org/10.1017/bec.2019.16

Wagner, S. M., & McNeil, C. B. (2008). Parent-child interaction therapy for ADHD: A conceptual overview and critical literature review. *Child & Family Behavior Therapy, 30*(3), 231–256. https://doi.org/10.1080/07317100802275546

Ward, M. A., Theule, J., & Cheung, J. (2016). Parent-child interaction therapy for child disruptive behaviour disorders: A meta-analysis. *Child and Youth Care Forum, 45*(5), 675–690. https://doi.org/10.1007/s10566-016-9350-5

Webster-Stratton, C. S. (1992). *The incredible years*. Umbrella Press.

Webster-Stratton, C. (2005). The incredible years: A training series for the prevention and treatment of conduct problems in young children. In E. D. Hibbs & P. S. Jensen (Eds.), *Psychosocial treatments for child and adolescent disorders: Empirically based strategies for clinical practice* (2nd ed., pp. 507–555). American Psychological Association.

Webster-Stratton, C. S., & Hammond, J. (1997). Treating children with early onset conduct problems: A comparison of child and parent training interventions. *Journal of Consulting and Clinical Psychology, 65*, 93–109. https://doi.org/10.1037/0022-006x.65.1.93

Webster-Stratton, C. S., Reid, M. J., & Hammond, M. (2004). Treating children with early-onset conduct problems: Intervention outcomes for parent, child, and teacher training. *Journal of Clinical Child & Adolescent Psychology, 33*, 105–124.

Weisz, J. R., Kuppens, S., Ng, M. Y., Eckshtain, D., Ugueto, A. M., Vaughn-Coaxum, R., Jensen-Doss, A., Hawley, K. M., Krumholz Marchette, L. S., Chu, B. C., Weersing, V. R., & Fordwood, S. R. (2017). What five decades of research tells us about the effects of youth psychological therapy: A multilevel meta-analysis and implicaations for science and practice. *American Psychologist, 72*, 79–117. https://doi.org/10.1037/a0040360

Wettig, H. H. G., Coleman, A. R., & Geider, F. J. (2011). Evaluating the effectiveness of Theraplay in treating shy, socially withdrawn children. *International Journal of Play Therapy, 20*(1), 26–37. https://doi.org/10.1037/a0022666

Wolraich, M. L., Hagan, J. F., Allan, C., Chan, E., Davison, D., Earls, M., Evans, S. W., Flinn, S. K., Froehlich, T., Frost, J., Holbrook, J. R., Lehmann, C. U., Lessin, H. R., Okechukwu, K., Pierce, K. L., Winner, J. D., & Zurhellen, W. . (2019). Clinical practice guidelines for the diagnosis, evaluation, and treatment of attention-deficit/hyperactivity Disorder in children and adolescents. *Pediatrics, 144*, e20192528.Subcommittee on Children and Adolescents with Attention-Deficit/Hyperactive Disorder

Yaholkoski, A., Hurl, K., & Theule, J. (2016). Efficacy of the circle of security intervention: A meta-analysis. *Journal of Infant Child and Adolescent Psychotherapy, 15*(2), 95–103.

Zimmer-Gembeck, M. J., Rudolph, J., Edwards, E. J., Swan, K., Campbell, S. M., Hawes, T., & Webb, H. J. (2022). The circle of security parenting program (COS-P): A randomized controlled trial of a low intensity, individualized attachment-based program with at-risk caregivers. *Behavior Therapy, 53*(2), 208–232. https://doi.org/10.1016/j.beth.2021.07.003

Zisser, A., & Eyberg, S. M. (2010). Parent-child interaction therapy and the treatment of disruptive behavior disorders. In J. R. Weisz & A. E. Kazdin (Eds.), *Evidence-based psychotherapies for children and adolescents* (2nd ed., pp. 179–193).

Chapter 11
Assessment and Treatment Recommendations: A Paradigm Shift?

The previous chapter provides a review of current treatments for both externalizing and internalizing disorders in young children and describes some of the issues associated with these treatments. In this chapter, we focus on assessment and treatment recommendations based on what we have learned from the PACT research program. First, we briefly comment on the "take-home message" from this research program, which is described in detail in Chaps. 7, 8, and 9. Taken together, these studies have increased our knowledge about models of externalizing (ODD and ADHD) and internalizing (depression and anxiety) psychopathology, as well as general psychopathology in young children. The findings reveal that, in keeping with the multilevel and systems principles in developmental psychopathology, risk factors from different domains at different levels increase the risk for each of these disorders. Furthermore, while no single risk factor emerged as paramount, three temperament risk factors (effortful control, negative affect, sensory regulation) showed significant direct effects on two or more symptom types and were mediators of the pathways to higher symptom levels for numerous paths from contextual, parent, and parenting factors. The studies examining bi-directional effects between parenting and child symptoms show that, in line with the developmental psychopathology principle of reciprocity, there are transactional effects between parenting and child symptoms. Specifically, we found that several aspects of parenting at an earlier age impact subsequent child symptoms (e.g., parental hostility at age 5 is associated with an increase in age 6 child depression symptoms), and also that child symptoms at an earlier age affect subsequent parenting (e.g., age 5 child anxiety leads to an increase in hostile parenting at age 6). The latter finding is also in keeping with the agency principle since it shows that the child actively participates in their own development and directly affects other systems (e.g., parenting). Examining the temporal sequencing of anxiety and depression symptoms across the periods of preschool, kindergarten, and school entry reveals that symptoms of both anxiety and depression increase the risk of developing the other type of symptom at a later age (Chap. 8). Consistent with the principle of multifinality, the transdiagnostic model

K. R. Gouze et al., *Early Childhood Psychopathology*,
https://doi.org/10.1007/978-3-031-68877-5_11

(Chap. 9) shows that many of the same risk factors lead to both externalizing and internalizing disorders, as well as to general psychopathology, but that there are also symptom-specific risk factors. Finally, the multi-domain and transdiagnostic models of risk factors revealed that child self-regulation (EC) has a particularly important role in the development and maintenance of psychopathology symptoms in young children since this variable was significantly related to each type of symptom. Additionally, all the measured pathways to transdiagnostic first-order symptom types were funneled through EC.

In addition to their theoretical significance, the findings from this research program have major implications for the assessment and treatment of internalizing and externalizing disorders in young children and those who experience both types of symptoms. Thus, the remainder of this chapter focuses on the recommendations emanating from these findings.

Recommendations for Assessment

The PACT findings make it clear that many risk factors and pathways between them contribute to the development of psychopathology in young children, and these factors should be addressed in conducting diagnostic evaluations and formulating a treatment plan. Consistent with these findings, we recommend that the assessment process should be comprehensive and include an evaluation of all the multi-domain factors identified in PACT that *may* play a role in the development and maintenance of the child's symptoms, including the family's financial resources (i.e., SES), family conflict, parental hostility, parent support, parent functioning (i.e., if the parent is depressed), and the parent-child relationship. In some settings (i.e., academic medical centers), this is standard practice. Still, in many community-based clinics, clinicians are limited by time constraints or requirements to use brief questionnaires to render a diagnosis. What we learned from PACT is that the diagnostic process should *not* focus narrowly on the child's presenting symptoms or on questions solely designed to yield a differential diagnosis; rather, it is essential that it encompasses a broader assessment of the child and the world in which they live. Of course, not all these factors may play a role in a child's problems, so the clinician's task is to determine which factors are relevant for a specific child and family.

To do this, the clinician can use a range of evidence-based assessment (EBA) procedures (Roberts et al., 2017) that include strategies such as structured interviews, empirically validated questionnaires, and direct observation to gather information about each of the risk factors external to the child (i.e., contextual, parent and parenting), as well as information about the child's characteristics (i.e., temperament, attachment security). In addition to identifying the specific risk factors that play a role in the child's symptoms, this comprehensive approach to assessment should include an assessment of strengths in the various domains so that they can be capitalized on in treatment. For example, a child who lives in an under-resourced (i.e., low SES) community may still have a parent who is highly supportive, or a child with a depressed parent may have a secure attachment relationship.

Another PACT finding relevant to assessment is that the symptoms of each of the internalizing disorders (i.e., depression and anxiety) in young children increase the risk that the child will develop symptoms of the other type of internalizing disorder (e.g., higher levels of anxiety at age 4 predict higher levels of depression at age 5, and vice versa). This means that it is incumbent on clinicians to assess if the child is experiencing both types of internalizing symptoms to determine which symptoms to target in treatment. It is not sufficient to simply decide if the child meets the criteria for a particular internalizing disorder and then develop a treatment plan for that specific disorder. For example, a parent may refer a child because of several clear-cut symptoms of anxiety, such as extreme avoidance of new situations and hypervigilance, and a diagnostic interview indicates that the child meets the criteria for a DSM-5 diagnosis of generalized anxiety disorder. In this case, the PACT findings suggest that the clinician should determine if the child is also experiencing any depression symptoms that need to be addressed in treatment. This is particularly important since a parent may not notice and report if their child has symptoms of depression, such as a lack of interest in play, which are less obvious than the fearfulness and avoidance of new situations that are the hallmarks of anxiety.

The PACT transdiagnostic findings reveal that symptoms of externalizing and internalizing disorders in young children are significantly related, so it is important to keep in mind that a child who is referred for behaviors that typically are considered symptoms of an externalizing disorder such as ODD may be experiencing anxiety symptoms as well. That is, the child's oppositional, uncooperative behavior may be what prompts their parents to bring them for treatment, but careful assessment might reveal that their refusal to engage in activities is because those activities make them anxious. This is but one example of how symptoms of one disorder may "masquerade" as symptoms of another, again emphasizing the need for comprehensive assessment.

Finally, it is important to assess characteristics of the child and family that serve as strengths, since their particular strengths can be capitalized on in treatment. For example, a young child whose affect is sad and who is showing a lack of interest in play (i.e., symptoms of depression) may have well-developed skills in emotional regulation that can be used to help moderate their negative affect.

In sum, the most important recommendation for assessment is to conduct a comprehensive evaluation not only of the child but also of the factors at the various levels that envelop the child, including the parent-child relationship, the parent's (parents') functioning and type of parenting, and the family environment, including family conflict and resources. Moreover, it is important not only to identify the specific factors in each of these domains that play a role in a particular child's problems but also to identify areas of strength. Perhaps most importantly, the assessment of the child should not just focus on determining if they meet the criteria for a particular diagnosis (or diagnoses); rather, it should be used to identify all the behaviors and emotions that are problematic for the child and their family, as well as the relevant contextual factors that promote strengths or create barriers to improved functioning. This comprehensive assessment will serve as the guide for developing a treatment plan based on the recommendations described in the next section of this chapter.

Recommendations for Treatment

The review of current treatments for ODD, ADHD, depression, and anxiety in young children in Chap. 10 makes it clear that, although there are a number of effective interventions for these disorders, it is also the case that the effect sizes of these treatments only range from small to moderate (Hudson et al., 2023; Reyno & McGrath, 2006; Weisz et al., 2017a; Wuthrich et al., 2023), so there clearly is room for improvement.

Our primary recommendation to increase treatment effectiveness, based on the knowledge gained from PACT, parallels our recommendations for assessment. That is, treatment needs to be comprehensive and target each of the risk factors in the different domains that affect the child's functioning. As stated previously, the multi-domain models of psychopathology make it clear that symptoms in young children develop from a complex interplay of risk factors in different domains that affect the child via multiple pathways and that no single risk factor or pathway, by itself, accounts for poor mental health outcomes. Thus, to improve outcomes, treatments need to include strategies designed to address a wide range of risk factors related to the development and maintenance of a particular child's symptoms, rather than focusing on only one or two of these factors, as do most current treatments. For example, parent management programs target parenting primarily, and attachment-based treatments focus solely on improving the parent-child relationship. There are treatments that target both parenting and child factors, for example, Parent-Child Interaction Treatment-Emotional Development (PCIT-ED) (Eyberg & Funderburk, 2011), but none of the current treatments target as wide a range of factors as we are recommending in this chapter. To maximize treatment effectiveness, we recommend that in addition to strategies that target parenting, the parent-child relationship, and child emotion regulation, we develop interventions that address all of the factors relevant to a particular child's problems, including the family's financial resources (i.e., SES), family conflict, stress, and parent depression.

The comprehensive approach to treatment we recommend in this chapter may be a paradigm shift, but it is consistent with the recommendations proposed by leading child psychotherapy researchers to move the field forward. Specifically, these researchers (Chorpita et al., 2017; Fitzpatrick et al., 2023; Ng & Weisz, 2018; Weisz & Bearman, 2020; Weisz et al., 2017b) argue that it is time to move beyond manualized therapy protocols for specific disorders to a more personalized, principle-guided approach (Ng & Weisz, 2018). What is meant by a more personalized approach to treatment? This approach refers to using evidence-based strategies targeted at a particular child's specific problems and areas of strength rather than a manualized treatment for a specific disorder (e.g., Being Brave to treat child anxiety). It involves selecting strategies shown to be effective for each of the child's problems, for example, using exposure to target a child's avoidance of new situations and parenting strategies to address their oppositional behaviors. There are several treatments for older children and adolescents that incorporate this approach. A Modular Approach to Therapy for Children with Anxiety, Depression, Trauma, or Conduct Problems (MATCH) (Chorpita & Weisz, 2009) is one such treatment designed for youths ages 6–17. MATCH includes a "menu" of techniques from empirically supported treatments for anxiety, depression, trauma, and conduct disorders and consists of 33 specific treatment procedures embodied within modules. The FIRST program (Weisz & Bearman, 2020) is another transdiagnostic treatment approach co-designed by clinical practitioners and psychotherapy researchers (Weisz et al., 2017b) around five core principles of therapeutic change that incorporates treatment procedures derived from evidence-based treatments for anxiety, depression, and conduct problems. MATCH and FIRST share two basic common elements: a transdiagnostic approach and modular treatment strategies. However, unlike the recommendations we make emanating from the PACT research, the focus of these treatments is still exclusively on the child's symptoms and ignores the larger environment in which they live.

The approach we advocate expands the focus on symptoms found in most manualized treatments to address the multi-domain risk factors identified in PACT contributing to the child's behavioral or emotional problems. Although we also recommend incorporating a range of evidence-based strategies designed to target each of the factors relevant to the development and maintenance of the child's problems (i.e., a modular approach), we go one step further than the transdiagnostic modular approach for older children recommended by Weisz and colleagues (Ng & Weisz, 2018; Weisz et al., 2017a). Specifically, we recommend incorporating strategies aimed at risk factors in different domains (e.g., the child's environment and the parent's depression) that play a role in their problems. In other words, treatments that target the whole child and the family system within the context of their environment are more likely to be successful than the current treatments that focus on single symptom pictures or risk factors. The next section provides suggestions for specific strategies that can be used to target factors in each of these domains that may be contributing to the child's problems.

Contextual Factors: SES

The factor most distal to the child in the PACT models, SES, was not fully transdiagnostic, but it did have significant effects on each of the symptom types (ODD, ADHD, depression, and anxiety) via different pathways. Thus, it makes sense that strategies directed at reducing risk related to this factor could potentially contribute to the effectiveness of a comprehensive treatment plan. Addressing the family's level of resources (i.e., SES) is often considered to be beyond the scope of a mental health clinician. Still, this finding highlights the importance of clinical involvement in the development of empirically driven social policy initiatives and, where applicable, engagement of social services to assist the family (see Chap. 12). Collaboration with other professionals such as care coordinators and social workers can assist families in obtaining resources that they might not be aware of, such as Temporary Assistance for Needy Families (TANF) benefits, which can help ameliorate some of the stresses associated with financial insufficiency.

Another example of offsetting the risks imposed by limited financial resources can be found in another PACT study (Romero, 2016). Romero found that neighborhood quality predicted an important child outcome, child self-regulation, such that even after accounting for SES, poorer neighborhood quality was linked to more limited growth in child self-regulation across the ages of 4, 5, and 6. Since there are aspects of poorer neighborhood quality, such as a high level of exposure to community violence, that are modifiable, this suggests, for example, that psychoeducation to teach parents how to reduce their child's exposure to community violence is a potentially useful strategy to decrease some of the negative effects of living in a neighborhood with high levels of violence. Findings from another recent study using ecological momentary assessment (Gibson, 2021) indicated that greater exposure to community violence in young children, even exposure to violent events that the child did not witness but only *heard about,* was linked to an increase in externalizing and internalizing symptoms over one week. Furthermore, this study revealed that the mothers who participated were not aware of how often they talked about violent events in front of their young children until they had to record this type of exposure. They also reported that, now that they were aware, they planned to stop discussing these events within their young children's earshot. Although, unfortunately, it is not possible to reduce young children's exposure to other types of community violence, such as hearing gunshots, it does suggest that just reducing the child's exposure to hearing the adults around them talking about violence may be helpful for young children. Hence, one way to reduce exposure to this type of violence would be to provide psychoeducation to parents about the negative effects of hearing about violent events, as well as to suggest strategies to reduce this exposure, such as limiting conversations about violence. Other strategies include identifying places in the neighborhood where it is safe to engage in outdoor activities and participating in neighborhood events.

Clinicians might also work with parents to identify resources in their community that they might not be aware of that could help offset the negative effects of living in a historically marginalized neighborhood (e.g., community drop-in centers, government-funded preschool programs, and daycare centers). It also seems likely that including these strategies in a treatment plan would enhance the parent-therapist relationship, a significant factor in treatment success (Fluckiger et al., 2018), since it would make it clear to the parent that the therapist is aware of and empathizes with the stressors in their lives and can be helpful in addressing at least some of these seemingly unalterable realities.

Family Conflict

Family conflict, another contextual risk factor, was transdiagnostic and stable across ages 4, 5, and 6 in both the hierarchical and bifactor models. There were significant pathways from conflict to ODD, depression, and anxiety symptoms in the cascade models, indicating a relation between presence of family conflict and emergence of these symptoms in young children This suggests that in cases where there is a high level of conflict in the child's family (whether that is a two-parent or multi-generational family), incorporating strategies derived from family therapy approaches may contribute to the effectiveness of the child's treatment. For example, when disagreements arise during a session, the clinician can incorporate communication skills training to help family members resolve these issues in a positive way. Similarly, therapeutic interventions that address affect regulation in the family, the structure of the family, role differentiation, and alliances between family members, to mention just a few, might be helpful in managing the family context in which the child's symptoms emerge and are maintained; see Gouze and Wendel (2022) for a more comprehensive discussion of family assessment and treatment. Both the American Psychological Association and the American Psychiatric Association recommend incorporating family assessment and treatment into the psychological treatment of children (American Psychological Association Presidential Task Force on Evidence-Based Practice, 2006; Josephson, 2007). Although many treatments for externalizing disorders in young children involve parents in parent management training (see Chap. 10 for a review), the focus is directly on the parent's interactions with the child. It ignores other potential sources of stress for the child such as inter-parental conflict or conflict between parents and grandparents living in the home. Clearly, the PACT studies indicate that a broader lens is required to address the needs of many children and families struggling with symptoms that negatively impact child functioning.

Parent Factors: Parent Depression

The multi-domain models of risk factors for each symptom type, as well as the transdiagnostic model, make it clear that it is extremely important to address parent depression in treatment, since this risk factor has direct effects on child depression and anxiety, as well as indirect ones on all four symptom types, albeit via a number of different pathways including negative affect (NA), effortful control (EC), and sensory regulation (SR). Moreover, parent depression was a transdiagnostic risk factor across all three ages (4, 5, and 6) studied. The question then arises as to how best to address the parent's depression. In some cases, it may be feasible to refer them to another clinician for individual therapy (or medication). However, in many cases, this is likely to place too great a burden on the family in terms of time and cost. In these cases, it is important for the clinician to incorporate strategies known to be effective in treating depression in the child's treatment plan. There is extensive evidence that increasing positive activities (behavioral activation) is an effective strategy for treating depression (Cuijpers et al., 2007). Thus, developing a list of enjoyable activities for the parent and child to engage in together may be effective in decreasing the parent's level of depression. Furthermore, this strategy has the double benefit of enhancing the parent-child relationship. Connecting parents to resources in their community, as recommended in the section on strategies targeting SES, could also help the clinician explore positive activities or other forms of social support in their neighborhoods. Although research on the role of social support in ameliorating the effects of depression in young mothers experiencing high levels of stress is equivocal, there is some evidence that social support can be helpful (Manuel et al., 2012; O'Neill et al., 2014).

Stress

Since it is well known that stress is strongly related to depression (Bjorndal et al., 2023; Kendler et al., 1999), other ways to address the parents' depression would be to recommend stress reduction techniques such as mindfulness and relaxation training. There are several low-cost self-help books that teach mindfulness and relaxation strategies, as well as online videos that clinicians can recommend to parents.

In addition to strategies targeted directly to address the parent's depression, it is also likely that the parenting strategies included in a comprehensive treatment plan (see below) will be effective in decreasing parental depression. That is, in addition to the direct effects that positive parenting practices have on decreasing symptoms of both externalizing and internalizing problems (see Chap. 10), there is also evidence that the strategies taught in PMT interventions also lead to an increase in parental self-efficacy and a concomitant decrease in depression (Kazdin & Wassell, 2000).

Parenting Factors: Support and Hostility

The multi-domain models of risk factors for the two externalizing disorders, ODD and ADHD, showed that parent support and hostility (see Chap. 7) had direct and indirect effects on both symptom types. Parent support also had indirect effects on child depression. This indicates that strategies focused on parenting are a vital component of treatment. Thus, parenting strategies shown to be effective in various parent management training (PMT) programs (The Incredible Years, Parent-Child-Interaction Treatment, and Triple-P) (see Chap. 10) are also likely to be an important and effective component of the comprehensive approach to treatment that we are recommending. The parenting practices taught in different PMT programs share common features that can be incorporated into treatment, including modelling and coaching parents to use labelled praise and teaching positive discipline strategies such as extinction and time-out.

Scaffolding

In the multi-domain risk models, parental scaffolding had a direct effect only on ODD symptoms at age 6, but not on any of the other symptom types. In the hierarchical transdiagnostic model, however, scaffolding was transdiagnostic within the internalizing symptom group. Furthermore, examining the bi-directional relations between parenting and each of the symptom types revealed that better parental scaffolding when the child was age 5 led to decreases in anxiety symptoms at age 6. This suggests that coaching parents on how to increase specific parent behaviors included in scaffolding, particularly positive support and respect for the child's autonomy, can be an effective strategy for children who have both anxiety symptoms and ODD symptoms. In fact, it is often the case that highly anxious children also exhibit many oppositional, uncooperative behaviors due to their avoidance of situations that elicit anxiety. Thus, coaching parents on how to positively support their child's approach behaviors while not becoming too intrusive (i.e., respecting their autonomy) or reacting too intensely to their refusal is likely to be an effective strategy to reduce both their anxiety symptoms and their oppositional behavior.

In addition to the effects of parenting on child symptoms, the models examining bi-directional effects between parenting and each type of symptom also showed that, consistent with the developmental psychopathology principle of reciprocity, some of the symptom types had specific effects on parenting (see Chaps. 7 and 8). For example, higher levels of child anxiety and ADHD symptoms at age 5 led to decreased parental support at age 6. As explained in Chaps. 7 and 8, it seems that as time went on, their child's symptoms wore parents out, so they became less supportive. This suggests that providing psychoeducation to parents about how their parenting and their child's symptoms are affecting each other might be another potentially effective treatment strategy. That is, the empathy and support provided by the therapist regarding how difficult it is to be supportive in the face of the persistence of their child's symptoms and the encouragement that, over time, continuing support of their child is likely to be helpful, may enable parents to remain supportive of their child.

Child Factors: Attachment

The PACT findings reveal that attachment security is another risk factor for the development of child depression and anxiety and also plays a role in ODD and ADHD via a pathway mediated by child EC. Moreover, attachment security plays a role in the maintenance of depression and anxiety symptoms across the ages of 4 to 6 as revealed by the models that included each of these symptom types at each age. In those models, less secure attachment at age 5 was the only variable that predicted an increase in anxiety symptoms at age 6, and it was one of only two age 4 risk factors that had an indirect effect on an increase in age 6 depression symptoms. Thus, in cases where the comprehensive assessment indicates problems in the parent-child relationship, specifically, insecure attachment, we recommend implementing strategies to improve this relationship. As stated in Chap. 10, the parent-child attachment relationship is the focus of attachment-based treatments such as Circle of Security and Child-Parent Psychotherapy (CPP; see Chap. 10); additionally, all parent management (PMT) programs include a component focused on building positive parent-child relationships. Relationship-enhancing strategies from these approaches, such as teaching parents to be more sensitive and responsive to their child's emotional cues as is done in CPP, or coaching them to use praise, verbal reflection, and imitation (Parent-Child Interaction Treatment PRIDE skills), as is done in PMT are likely to increase the effectiveness of treatment when there are problems in the parent-child relationship.

Effortful Control

The PACT findings revealed that child self-regulation is a crucial factor in the development and maintenance of a wide range of child problems. Specifically, the multi-domain models of risk factors for ODD, ADHD, child depression, and anxiety showed that child EC was related to all four symptom types. In addition, EC served as a stable transdiagnostic risk factor across all three ages in its association with the second-order factors of internalizing, externalizing, and a hierarchical general p factor. Even more importantly, in the transdiagnostic cascade risk models, all measured pathways to first-order symptom types that were transdiagnostic were funneled through age 5 EC; no other parenting or child factor was *fully* transdiagnostic. This suggests that EC is a mechanism whereby risk factors from other domains contribute to child outcomes. Psychotherapy researchers (Hanisch et al., 2014; Kraemer et al., 2002; Ng et al., 2023) have recommended directing increased attention to examining the mechanisms of change in treatment since understanding how a treatment works will enable the strengthening of that specific component (i.e., the mediator) which will enhance overall treatment effectiveness. Thus, the PACT finding that EC is one such mechanism is particularly important and suggests that strategies designed to enhance child EC are an essential component of a comprehensive treatment plan. Some of the current PMT treatments for child disorders do include a component targeted at emotional development, including Parent-Child Interaction Treatment-Emotion Development (PCIT-ED) and Tuning Into Kids (see Chap. 10 for a description of these treatments). However, a recent review (England-Mason & Gonzalez, 2020) of parenting programs that included an emotion coaching component revealed that few of these programs included an assessment of child emotion regulation as an outcome measure. Thus, there is a need for future research to evaluate if the emotion socialization strategies included in these treatments are effective in enhancing child emotion regulation or EC.

Since the PACT research indicates that self-regulation (EC) is an important mechanism accounting for change, we developed a manual (Gouze et al., 2020) consisting of a set of strategies designed specifically to increase emotion regulation in young children. The efficacy of this intervention has not been examined, but as a recommended first step in the development of a novel treatment (American Psychological Association, 2002), a qualitative study (Lossia, 2020) was conducted to examine if stakeholders (i.e., parents of children referred to a child psychiatry clinic and expert child therapists) found these strategies feasible and acceptable. A qualitative thematic analysis of in-depth focus group discussions led to the conclusion that both therapists and parents considered the intervention feasible and supported the overall approach.

Several of the strategies included in the manual, such as teaching children to recognize emotions in themselves and others and practicing coping skills, are used in the PMT programs with an emotion socialization component, such as PCIT-ED and Tuning Into Kids (See Chap. 10). However, this intervention also includes a novel strategy that consists of intensive in vivo practice in emotion regulation strategies in typical situations that elicit child dysregulation. Since ER strategies are not as well-known as behavioral ones (e.g., praise, ignoring), a description of them is provided below to enable readers who are not familiar with them to learn what they entail. It is important, however, to state that, to date, this intervention has not been examined in an RCT.

The first set of strategies includes one or two individual sessions with the parent to provide psychoeducation about the role of EC in their child's problematic behavior and emotions. These sessions are also used to gather information about specific situations that elicit the child's emotional distress and consequent behavioral dysregulation; managing these will be practiced in subsequent parent-child sessions.

The remaining sessions consist of parent-child sessions conducted in three phases. In the first phase, the clinician teaches the parent strategies similar to those included in PCIT-ED and Tuning Into Kids, which focus on helping the parent enhance their child's ability to recognize and label emotions in themselves and others. To accomplish this aim, the manual includes suggestions for a range of activities using props such as a feelings chart, dolls, puppets, stuffed animals, and pictures of people demonstrating various emotions. For example, one activity involves having the child decorate masks (using paper plates) or puppets with various facial expressions and then identifying the associated feelings. These activities first focus on having the child identify basic emotions (i.e., happy, sad, mad, and afraid), followed by more complex ones (e.g., disappointed, ashamed, jealous).

The second phase, also similar to the strategies included in PCIT-ED and Tuning Into Kids, consists of psychoeducation with the parent and child about different strategies that can be used to regulate distressing emotions. First, the parent is coached in helping the child identify signals that cue when they need to engage in an emotion regulation strategy. These cues include noticing and identifying their feelings, tuning into their bodily sensations, and recognizing specific situations that help them know they are becoming upset. The clinician then coaches the parent in a range of emotion regulation strategies they can use with their child, including distraction, physical soothing, relaxation, and visual imagery. The manual identifies many activities to assist parents and children in practicing each of these strategies. For example, to practice relaxation, the therapist coaches the parent to instruct the child in deep breathing by having them lie on their back with a stuffed animal on their stomach and then watching the toy move up and down as they take deep breaths.

The final phase, which is the novel component of this intervention, consists of in vivo practice of situations that the parent has identified as likely to lead to dysregulation. Consistent with the behavioral principle of shaping, these practice sessions begin with situations that the parent has rated as likely to elicit only mild emotional dysregulation. Then, as the sessions continue, the parents and child practice increasingly 'hot" situations. Situations that frequently elicit emotional dysregulation include asking the child to clean up after playing, interrupting an ongoing activity, and receiving a disappointing gift. Each session consists of setting up the activity likely to elicit distress, followed by the therapist coaching the parent to scaffold the child's use of an emotion regulation strategy if they become upset. In the qualitative feasibility study (Lossia, 2020), both therapist and parent groups expressed support for including the program's three main intervention components: psychoeducation, developing emotional knowledge, and in vivo practice. Nevertheless, an RCT to examine if this intervention is effective is needed before it can be disseminated.

Sensory Regulation

In addition to emotion regulation, PACT research revealed another aspect of self-regulation that was a risk factor for psychopathology in young children, specifically, sensory regulation (SR). As previously stated in Chap. 5, little attention has been paid to the role of SR in child psychopathology research. The findings from the PACT models thus contribute novel information since they reveal that this aspect of child self-regulation is related to ADHD, child depression, and anxiety symptom types. Additionally, SR was a transdiagnostic risk factor associated with the second-order factors of internalizing, externalizing, and a general p factor across the ages of 4, 5, and 6. SR also proved to be a mechanism whereby factors from other domains exerted their effects on child outcomes. Specifically, SR mediated two paths to the internalizing, externalizing and general p factors and also served as the mediator for pathways to symptoms of ADHD, child depression, and anxiety in the multi-domain transdiagnostic models. This suggests that if the comprehensive assessment reveals that the child has problems with SR, the treatment plan should include strategies to manage or enhance the child's SR, such as creating a sensory diet to provide needed sensory stimulation; see books by Biel and Peske (2009) and Smith and Gouze (2004) for additional strategies. Also, in some cases, a separate referral to an occupational therapist qualified to address SR might be needed.

Development of a Comprehensive, Personalized Treatment Plan

How does the clinician decide which strategies to include in their personalized modular treatment plan? First, the comprehensive assessment should provide a 'roadmap" indicating which risk factors play a role in developing and maintaining the child's problems. In some cases, there may only be a few relevant risk factors that operate in only a few domains. For example, in families with good financial resources and non-depressed parents, addressing a lack of resources and parental depression will not be necessary. However, strategies for parenting practices and increasing child self-regulation may be needed. In other cases, there may be a multiplicity of risk factors including a lack of resources, parental depression, less optimal parenting, and poor child EC. In those cases, the clinician will have to select strategies to address factors in each domain related to the child's problems. Of course, it is not feasible to include all the strategies recommended in each of these domains, so the clinician will need to choose those strategies most likely to ameliorate the problems causing the greatest impairment in the child's functioning and the most distress to the family. For example, in the case of a child who is at risk of being expelled from their daycare setting due to severe tantrums and aggression and who is living with a depressed mother struggling with parenting, it will be necessary to first implement strategies that are most likely to decrease the child's behavior problems in the shortest amount of time. Thus, the focus for this family's treatment might be on helping the mother with parenting and emotional regulation strategies; the mother's depression might best be attended to later. Importantly, though, the clinician will need to assess this choice as the treatment progresses and change course if other risk factors or the severity of the mother's depression are creating barriers to treatment success. Unfortunately, it is not possible to write a "prescription" for which strategies should be applied in which cases because the variations are endless. Rather, implementing a personalized, modular treatment approach depends on a well-trained clinician (see Chap. 12) conducting a comprehensive assessment to identify all the child's problems and then determining which strategies are appropriate to address the most pressing problems.

Summary

The key recommendation derived from the PACT research program is that a comprehensive approach to assessment and treatment is needed. Although many clinicians routinely assess a range of problematic behaviors and emotions, not just those that are the basis of the referral question, the PACT findings emphasize the importance of keeping this important principle in mind. Furthermore, PACT research suggests that this approach should be adopted in settings where such a comprehensive approach is not routine.

The comprehensive treatment recommendations in this chapter are consistent with those proposed by leading child psychotherapy researchers (Chorpita et al., 2017; Fitzpatrick et al., 2023; Ng & Weisz, 2018; Weisz & Bearman, 2020; Weisz et al., 2017a) to move the field forward by adopting a personalized modular transdiagnostic approach, which involves selecting effective strategies for each of the child's problems. We go one step further than the transdiagnostic modular approach for older children recommended by Weisz and colleagues (Ng & Weisz, 2018; Weisz et al., 2017a) in that we also recommend incorporating strategies aimed at risk factors in different domains that play a role in the child's problems including contextual factors, parental psychopathology, parenting practices, and the child's own characteristics (i.e., temperament and attachment security). To that end, this chapter provides specific examples of potentially effective strategies in each domain. In the contextual domain, an area not typically addressed in treatment, we recommended a simple strategy to reduce a young child's exposure to community violence, which may be effective in decreasing some of the negative effects of living in an under-resourced community. If the child's environment includes living with a depressed parent, we recommended incorporating strategies effective in treating adult depression in the treatment plan. Strategies from various PMT programs are also recommended since these strategies have been shown to be effective in increasing positive parenting practices and decreasing negative ones, which frequently play a role in the child's problematic behavior and emotions. If there are problems in the parent-child relationship, our recommendations include applying strategies used in attachment-based treatment programs shown to be effective in increasing attachment security. The PACT findings revealed the important role of EC as a mechanism accounting for change; thus, this chapter also provides a detailed description of strategies designed to enhance child self-regulation. Finally, we also recommend addressing another aspect of child self-regulation, child SR, which has been largely overlooked in developmental psychopathology research. The PACT findings show that SR is a risk factor for internalizing and externalizing symptom types and a transdiagnostic risk factor; thus, strategies designed to enhance child SR may need to be included in a comprehensive modular treatment approach.

This approach to treatment is likely to require a change in the training of child clinicians. Chapter 12 provides recommendations for changes in training to enable future clinicians to develop competencies that address the broad range of risk factors contributing to early childhood mental health problems. Chapter 12 also addresses the PACT findings' public policy implications and recommendations for future research.

References

American Psychological Association. (2002). Criteria for evaluating treatment guidelines. *American Psychologist, 57*(112), 1053–1059.

American Psychological Association Presidential Task Force on Evidence-Based Practice. (2006). Evidence based practice in psychology. *American Psychologist, 61*, 271–285. https://doi.org/10.1037/0003-066X.61.4.271

Biel, L., & Peske, N. (2009). *Raising a sensory smart child: The definitive handbook for helping your child with sensory processing issues*. Penguin Books.

Bjorndal, L. D., Kendler, K. S., Reichborn-Kjennerud, T., & Ystrom, E. (2023). Stressful life events increase the risk of major depressive episodes: A population-based twin study. *Psychological Medicine, 53*(11), 5194–5202. https://doi.org/10.1017/S0033291722002227

Chorpita, B. F., & Weisz, J. R. (2009). *MATCH-ADTC: Modular approach to therapy for children with anxiety, depression, trauma, or conduct problems*. PracticeWise.

Chorpita, B. F., Daleiden, E. L., Park, A. L., Ward, A. M., Levy, M. C., Cromley, T., Chiu, A. W., Letamendi, A. M., Tsai, K. H., & Krull, J. L. (2017). Child STEPS in California: A cluster randomized effectiveness trial comparing modular treatment with community implement treatment for youth with anxiety, depression, conduct problems, or traumatic stress. *Journal of Consulting and Clinical Psychology, 85*(1), 13–25. https://doi.org/10.1037/ccp0000133

Cuijpers, P., van Straten, A., & Warmerdam, L. (2007). Behavioral activation treatments of depression: A meta-analysis. *Clinical Psychology Review, 27*(3), 318–326. https://doi.org/10.1016/j.cpr.2006.11.001

England-Mason, G., & Gonzalez, A. (2020). Intervening to shape children's emotion regulation: A review of emotion socialization parenting programs for young children. *Emotion, 20*(1), 98–104. https://doi.org/10.1037/emo0000638

Eyberg, S. M., & Funderburk, B. W. (2011). *Parent-child interaction therapy protocol*. PCIT International.

Fitzpatrick, O. M., Cho, E., Venturo-Conerly, K. E., Ugueto, A. M., Ng, M. Y., & Weisz, J. R. (2023). Empirically supported principles of change in youth psychotherapy: Exploring codability, frequency of use, and meta-analytic findings. *Clinical Psychological Science, 11*(2), 326–344. https://doi.org/10.1177/21677026221120230

Fluckiger, D., Del Re, A. C., Wampold, B. E., & Horvath, A. O. (2018). The alliance in adult psychotherapy: A meta-analytic synthesis. *Psychotherapy, 55*(4), 316–340. https://doi.org/10.1037/pst0000172

Gibson, L. L. (2021). *The relation between community violence exposure and young children's psychopathology symptoms* [ProQuest Information and Learning].

Gouze, K. R., & Wendel, R. (2022). Family based assessement and treatment. In M. K. Dulcan (Ed.), *Dulcan's textbook of child and adolescent psychiatry* (pp. 933–954). American Psychiatric Publishing. https://doi.org/10.1176/appi.books.9781615374809

Gouze, K. R., Hopkins, J., & Lossia, A. K. (2020). *Relationship-Based emotion regulation manual* [unpublished manuscript].

Hanisch, C., Hautmann, C., Pluck, J., Eichelberger, I., & Dopfner, M. (2014). The prevention program for externalizing problem behavior (PEP) improves child behavior by reducing negative parenting: Analysis of mediating processes in a randomized controlled trial. *Journal of Child Psychology and Psychiatry, 55*(5), 473–484. https://doi.org/10.1111/jcpp.12177

Hudson, J. L., Minihan, S., Chen, W., Carl, T., Fu, M., Tully, L., Kangas, M., Rosewell, L., McDermott, E. A., Wang, Y., Stubbs, T., & Martiniuk, A. (2023). Interventions for young children's mental health: A review of reviews. *Clinical Child & Family Psychology Review, 26*(3), 593–641. https://doi.org/10.1007/s10567-023-00443-6

Josephson, A. M. (2007). Practice parameter for the assessment of the family. *Journal of the American Academy of Child and Adolescent Psychiatry, 46*(7), 922–937. https://doi.org/10.1097/chi.0b013e318054e713

Kazdin, A. E., & Wassell, G. (2000). Therapeutic changes in children, parents, and families resulting from treatment of children with conduct problems. *Journal of the American Academy of Child and Adolescent Psychiatry, 39*(4), 414–420. https://doi.org/10.1097/00004583-2000040000-00009

Kendler, K. S., Karkowski, L. M., & Prescott, C. A. (1999). Causal relationshp between stressful life events and the onset of major depression. *The American Journal of Psychiatry, 156*, 837–841. https://doi.org/10.1176/ajp.156.6.837

Kraemer, H. C., Wilson, G. T., Fairburn, C. G., & Agras, W. S. (2002). Mediators and moderators of treatment effects in randomized clinical trials. *Archives of General Psychiatry, 59*(10), 877–880.

Lossia, A. K. (2020). Stakeholder feedback on a novel emotion regulation intervention for preschool-age children with disruptive behavior problems: A thematic analysis. *Dissertation Abstracts International: The Sciences and Engineering (Vol. 81, issue 9-B).*

Manuel, J. J., Martinson, M. L., Bledsoe-Mansori, S. E., & Bellamy, J. L. (2012). The influence of stress and social support on depressive symptoms in mothers with young chilren. *Social Science and Medicine, 75*(11), 2013–2020. https://doi.org/10.1016/j.socscimed.2012.07.034

Ng, M. Y., & Weisz, J. R. (2018). Personalizing evidence-based psychotherapy for children and adolescents in clinical care. In J. R. Weisz & A. E. Kazdin (Eds.), *Evidence-based psychotherapies for children and adolescents* (pp. 501–519). Guilford Press.

Ng, M. Y., DiVasto, K. A., Cootner, S., Gonzalez, N., & Weisz, J. R. (2023). What do 30 years of randomized trials tell us about how psychotherapy improves youth depression? A systematic review of candidate mediators. *Clinical Psychology: Science and Practice, 30*(4), 396–419. https://doi.org/10.1111/cpsp.12367

O'Neill, S., Schneiderman, R. L., Rajendran, K., Marks, D. J., & Halperin, J. M. (2014). Reliable ratings or reading tealeaves: Can parent, teacher, and clinical behavior ratings of preschoolers predict ADHD at age six? *Journal of Abnormal Child Psychology, 43*, 623–634. https://doi.org/10.1007/s10802-013-9802-4

Reyno, S. M., & McGrath, P. J. (2006). Predictors of parent training efficacy for child externalizing behavior problems-a meta-analytic review. *Journal of Child Psychology and Psychiatry, 47*(1), 99–111.

Roberts, M. C., Blossom, J. B., Evans, S. C., Amaro, C. M., & Kanine, R. M. (2017). Advancing the scientific foundation for evidence-based practice in clinical child and adolescent psychology. *Journal of Clinical Child & Adolescent Psychology, 46*, 915–928. https://doi.org/10.1080/15374416.2016.1152554

Romero, E. Y. (2016). The role of neighborhood and parenting in the development of effortful control and subsequent social competence during early childhood. *Dissertation Abstracts International: The Sciences and Engineering (Vol. 77, Issue 1-B(E).*

Smith, K. A., & Gouze, K. R. (2004). *The sensory-sensitive child: Practical solutions for out-of-bounds behavior*. Harper Collins.

Weisz, J. R., & Bearman, S. K. (2020). *Principle-guided psychotherapy for children and adolescents: The FIRST program for behavioral and emotional problems*. Guilford Press.

Weisz, J. R., Bearman, S. K., Santucci, J. C., & Jensen-Doss, A. (2017a). Initial test of a principle-guided approach to transdiagnostic psychotherapy with children and adolescents. *Journal of Clinical Child & Adolescent Psychology, 46*(1), 44–58. https://doi.org/10.1080/15374416.2016.11

Weisz, J. R., Kuppens, S., Ng, M. Y., Eckshtain, D., Uqueto, A. M., Vaughn-Coaxum, R., Jensen-Doss, A., Hawley, K. M., Krumholz Marchette, L. S., Chu, B. C., Weersing, V. R., & Fordwood, S. R. (2017b). What five decades of research tells us about the effects of youth psychological therapy: A multilevel meta-analysis and implicaations for science and practice. *American Psychologist, 72*, 79–117. https://doi.org/10.1037/a0040360

Wuthrich, V. M., Zagic, D., Dickson, S. J., McLellan, L. F., Chen, J. T.-H., Jones, M. P., & Rapee, R. M. (2023). Effectiveness of psychotherapy for internalising symptoms in children and adolescents when delivered in routine settings: A systematic review and meta-analysis. *Clinical Child & Family Psychology Review, 26*(3), 824–848. https://doi.org/10.1007/s10567-023-00433-8

Chapter 12
New Directions for Early Childhood Clinical Training, Public Policy, and Research: Lessons Learned From PACT

Across the lifespan, mental health problems are among the most common and debilitating health concerns worldwide (GBD Mental Disorders Collaborators, 2022). As noted in Chap. 1, currently these rates are increasing (World Health Organization, 2022), particularly for children and adolescents (Lebrun-Harris et al., 2022), with between 25% and 33% of youth meeting DSM criteria for a disorder sometime during their lifetime (Merikangas et al., 2009). With over 50% of adult mental disorders beginning in childhood and adolescence, the importance of early prevention and intervention efforts is obvious (Kazdin, 2019; Merikangas et al., 2009). Prevalence rates based on community samples of young children indicate that as many as 5% of preschool children suffer from some form of anxiety, 13.4% from ODD, and up to 15% from ADHD (Lavigne et al., 2009). Based on the PACT studies (see Chaps. 7 and 8), as well as earlier research, it is clear that these symptoms remain fairly stable throughout the preschool years (Campbell et al., 2000; Gaffrey et al., 2018; Gouze et al., 2021; Hopkins et al., 2020; Lavigne et al., 1998), with co-morbidity increasing over time (Egger & Angold, 2006; Lavigne et al., 2001). This is particularly true for children who show early emotional or behavioral sub-clinical symptoms that cut across internalizing and externalizing disorders (Basten et al., 2016). Estimates of children with subthreshold behavioral problems, i.e., those not meeting full diagnostic criteria, run as high as 40% (Oppenheim et al., 2016), and many children exhibiting subthreshold conditions are likely to meet full diagnostic criteria in the future (Lavigne et al., 2001). This suggests that an even larger number of young children are at risk for developing poor mental health outcomes than are captured in studies using diagnostic criteria to establish prevalence rates.

Despite the prevalence and persistence of externalizing and internalizing symptoms in early childhood, identification of these problems remains woefully inadequate, with estimates revealing that only about 50% of these children are identified in pediatric or community settings (Lavigne et al., 1993; Merikangas et al., 2009; Weitzman & Wegner, 2015). Of those who are identified, access to services, i.e., finding a clinician, getting to appointments, and being able to pay for the available

K. R. Gouze et al., *Early Childhood Psychopathology*,
https://doi.org/10.1007/978-3-031-68877-5_12

care, is a further barrier to treatment (Owens et al., 2002; Yu-Lefler et al., 2023). Thus, problems with early identification and lack of access to care hinder current treatment efforts and prevent escalating problems over time.

What we have learned from the PACT research program, along with a large body of extant research, is that the many risk factors contributing to the development and maintenance of internalizing and externalizing symptoms present during the early years of children's lives are extremely complex, operate at multiple levels, consist of long causal chains that implicate risk factors both more distal and more proximal to the child, and have cascading effects on development over time. Given this complexity, many questions remain regarding the best points of identification, prevention, and intervention.

This chapter addresses three areas that hold promise for yielding fruitful advances in the development and delivery of mental health services for young children. In Chap. 11, we discussed specific recommendations for assessment and treatment by mental health practitioners. This chapter delves further into what we learned from the PACT research regarding needed changes in the training of mental health professionals, particularly child and adolescent psychologists, including the need for increasing role identification and involvement in advocacy and public policy. We then address public policy changes that can have an impact on the cascading effects resulting from contextual risk factors that influence healthy child development. Finally, we discuss future research areas needed to understand how risk factors operate over time and potential protective buffers that can promote more positive developmental outcomes.

Clinical Child Training: Does It Meet the Need?

The PACT studies, along with a large body of research in developmental psychopathology, suggest that training of child clinicians requires a broad-based understanding of typical development and developmental psychopathology, including the mechanisms and processes that place children at risk for developing externalizing and internalizing symptoms. Over the past 30 years, training in clinical child psychology has moved from a focus on laboratory-based research that establishes the efficacy of manual-based treatments (many of which are reviewed in Chap. 10) to effectiveness studies that document the applicability of these treatments for multiple populations in community settings. Although laudable for establishing a range of empirically based treatments that yield small to moderate effect sizes for particular disorders, this approach to training only partially prepares clinicians for the vast array of clinical problems and presentations they will encounter in practice. In other words, this reliance on training in empirically based, manualized treatments is "useful, but not sufficient" to address the expanding mental health crisis that begins with our youngest children.

In contrast, the science of developmental psychopathology offers an ideal approach for developing more appropriate ways to ameliorate child mental health problems by applying a multi-domain, multi-level lifespan approach to understanding the development and maintenance of mental health risk and protective factors. Specifically, the PACT studies (see Chaps. 7, 8, and 9) suggest that externalizing and internalizing symptoms emerge over time as a function of long chains of risk factors, some of which are specific to particular diagnoses but many of which are transdiagnostic. Thus, it is unlikely that focusing primarily, for example, on training emerging clinicians to identify specific symptom patterns, to apply taxonomically derived DSM diagnoses to those symptoms, and to implement the relevant empirically based manualized treatments will suffice for them to understand how to assess and treat the vast majority of children that they encounter in clinical practice. As many researchers have noted, training needs to move away from the "one size fits all" approach to child psychopathology and move towards training that emphasizes personalized, patient-centered care (Levenson, 2014; Shoham et al., 2014; Weisz et al., 2013), with a greater emphasis on how children develop and function in real-world settings (Ng & Weisz, 2018; Weisz et al., 2017). Often, this will lead to the successful application of a well-established and well-researched empirically based treatment, such as the Incredible Years Program or PCIT; but, more often, it will require the clinician to apply a broader understanding of risk and protective factors to develop an effective treatment plan. Training students to attend to developmental psychopathology research, such as the PACT findings, as well as to broader principles of scientific inquiry (Atkins et al., 2014; Heatherington et al., 2012) will equip them with a deeper understanding of these processes. More importantly, it will provide direction for assessment and treatment that includes, for example, greater attention to contextual issues (e.g., family conflict) and to the impact that risk factors in one domain might have on risk factors in other domains, which, in turn, lead to particular child outcomes (e.g., the importance of parental depression in contributing to poorer child effortful control which, in turn, contributes to multiple symptom manifestations). Until child clinicians are taught to think in terms of these models, they are at risk for asking the wrong questions during assessment or ignoring important aspects of children's lives and restricting treatment in such a way as to lead to only moderate success (see Chap. 11 for an elaborated discussion). Palermo and colleagues (Palermo et al., 2014) argue for such training when they recommend that all child clinicians receive a strong foundation in normative, adaptive, and maladaptive development in all areas—cognitive, social, emotional, and behavioral—and that this foundation be framed in the context of the norms and expectations of the larger environment. Effective training must also include attention to differences in families' lived experiences as a function of their culture, race, social class, or other aspects of diversity. Understanding the impact of these factors on child development and the potential cascading effects resulting from risk or protective factors related to diversity requires training that includes didactics and supervision related to these issues. Additionally, immersion experiences and ongoing discussion of cultural issues and differences are required to enhance students' understanding of these contextual variables (Benuto et al., 2019).

Adhering to the tenets of developmental psychopathology clearly requires training that moves away from a singular focus on the child and considers the environment in which the child lives, plays, and learns. Although many treatments for child externalizing and internalizing disorders include parents, such as parent management training, the emphasis remains on changing parenting behaviors to alter "what is wrong" with the child, with less attention paid to the dyadic relationship, parent psychopathology, or relevant contextual variables (see Chap. 10 for a description of these treatments, and Chap. 11 for specific strategies to target these domains). Training needs to go beyond this focus, which still has as its sole goal the elimination of the child's symptoms. For example, for a child presenting with symptoms who is living in a highly conflictual family with a depressed parent, utilizing one of the manual-based treatments in which students are trained is likely to be ineffective or only partially effective. Thus, students require training to broaden their lens in assessing and treating early childhood internalizing and externalizing symptoms.

The PACT research supports the need for clinical training in more complex models that view externalizing and internalizing symptoms dimensionally, rather than categorically, and considers multi-level, multi-domain approaches to the development and treatment of psychopathology. Training primarily in empirically supported, manual-based treatment of discrete diagnostic presentations has many problems in addition to the narrowness of its focus. For one thing, there is not enough time to train child clinicians in all the manual-based treatments they need to learn to treat children in community-based clinics that serve children and families with a range of presenting problems (Weisz et al., 2014). Additionally, treatments shown to be efficacious in research settings are frequently ineffective when administered in community-based clinic settings (Weisz et al., 2013). Among other difficulties, they suffer from having to contend with shifting patient concerns from session to session and poor attendance, both of which interfere with implementing pre-set manual-based protocols with fidelity (Lyon & Budd, 2010; Weisz et al., 2017). Clinicians who have training experiences only in applying manual-based treatments find themselves at a loss when confronted with the more typical child patient in a clinic, who might reside in a neighborhood plagued by violence, have a depressed parent, live in a family with high levels of conflict, and lack the effortful control (EC) skills required to manage their own behavior. Training students in the medical model, in diagnosis-based clinics that assign a primary diagnosis to this child (in this case it might be ADHD or anxiety, for example) and implementing the EBTs associated with that disorder does not prepare them for actual practice. As Atkins and colleagues (Atkins et al., 2016) note, over-reliance on evidence-based treatments (EBTs) does not account for knowledge of settings and individuals being served in such a way as to optimize effectiveness. Training must move away from this model and adhere more closely to the tenets of developmental psychopathology outlined in Chap. 1, which are exemplified in the PACT research findings, showing that child problems arise from a complex array of factors in different domains. In fact, despite the emphasis on the development of empirically supported treatments, clinical outcomes have not improved dramatically over the past decades (Weisz et al., 2019) and outcome studies show only small to moderate effects (Weisz et al., 2013), with some researchers noting that these effects are even smaller when one considers the "file drawer" or unpublished studies problem (McLeod & Weisz, 2004). As noted in Chap. 11, there is an increasing need for treatment that is transdiagnostic and that can address multiple diagnoses that might emanate from similar (e.g., poor EC) and also multiple risk factors (e.g., family conflict, parent depression, hostile parenting) that contribute to this more generalized symptom picture. Training that encourages students to assess and treat risk factors from multiple domains leading to co-morbidities and cascading effects are more likely to equip them to treat children in real world settings. As Chorpita (2019) notes, it is time for clinical psychology to move away from clinical approaches that focus on the "products" of research (e.g., manual-based interventions) and move towards a greater understanding of the knowledge underlying these products, that is, an understanding of the mechanisms and processes that contribute to the development, maintenance, and prevention of emotional and behavioral disorders. Our recommendations for a greater adherence to the principles of developmental psychopathology and the research presented in this book are consistent with this call for a shift in focus.

Expansion of Clinical Psychology Training

As noted in Chap. 10, most current clinical interventions directed towards the remediation of externalizing and internalizing disorders in young children focus on providing treatment in which the child is the focus of that treatment and, most often, is seen in conjunction with parents or other caretakers, or, in some cases, parents are seen alone. In both approaches, dyadic and parent alone, the treatment focuses on reducing symptoms in the child. The PACT studies, and the extant literature, reveal that many factors external to the child, such as family conflict, parent psychopathology, parenting practices, and other environmental variables, significantly contribute to the development and maintenance of symptoms in young children. As such, training for child clinicians *must* include training that enhances their understanding of these relations and promotes the use of interventions that address these larger contextual factors, in addition to more focused training on the reduction of child symptoms. Focusing on the child's symptoms alone is likely to result in large numbers of children showing only small-to-moderate improvements in mental health following treatment and reduced sustainability of positive outcomes. This problem is particularly exacerbated during the preschool years, as this is a time when symptom pictures shift, frequently changing or inconsistently meeting criteria for clinical intervention, thereby making it hard to know what specific symptoms should be addressed in treatment (Basten et al., 2016). Nevertheless, the relatively high stability of problems for those children experiencing both externalizing and internalizing symptoms (see Chaps. 7 and 8 and Basten et al.) suggests that early prevention and intervention efforts at this age are critically important. Therefore, broadening the training of clinical child psychologists to expand reach, scalability, affordability, and flexibility in who, when, where, and how prevention and intervention are provided is a necessary mandate for the coming decades for more children to experience positive developmental trajectories (Atkins et al., 2014; Berenbaum et al., 2021; Kazdin, 2019; Kazdin & Blasé, 2011; Kazdin & Rabbitt, 2013).

One means for improving the training of child clinicians with the requisite skills for addressing mental health problems as they present in real-world settings is to introduce modalities of training that allow for movement away from current models that require highly trained professionals to provide services in person in particular settings (e.g., clinics, medical centers, private offices); such settings significantly limit accessibility, increase cost, and ignore parents' reluctance to access services due to stigma (Berenbaum et al., 2021; Kazdin, 2019). An example of a shift in these models means training clinical psychology students to work with the other adults in children's lives, specifically teachers, youth workers, and paraprofessionals, to provide prevention and early intervention services. One such program is the Ready To Learn Through Relationships Program (Center for Child Resilience, 2019a, b) in which experienced psychologists and social workers train coaches in early childhood education settings to instruct teachers in providing social-emotional learning and trauma-informed care in preschool classrooms (Goldenthal et al., 2023). Kazdin (2019) further recommends increased use of technology and integrated care approaches to address these issues and suggests that training in these modalities is required to expand the reach of mental health services for children and adolescents. Berenbaum and colleagues (Berenbaum et al., 2021) advocate for a complete revision of training in clinical psychology that promotes a two-stage training model in which the first stage includes foundational training critical to acquiring the needed knowledge base for all clinical psychologists (we would argue for strong training in developmental psychology and developmental psychopathology). The second stage consists of specialized training geared towards a wide range of activities that might include direct clinical care for some students, but based on interest, would prepare other trainees for targeted work in one or more of the following activities—the development, dissemination, and implementation of new programs, community-based prevention activities, integration of mental health into primary health care, and designing public policy. Specialized training in both prevention and intervention that promotes a public health approach to mental health promises to create a psychology workforce that is more flexible and better equipped to address all three tiers—universal prevention, targeted treatment, and intensive intervention—needed for the promotion of mental health and well-being in children (Atkins et al., 2014, 2016).

Several community settings provide an ideal opportunity to integrate prevention and intervention strategies that can contribute to child mental health and well-being (So et al., 2019). Specialized training for psychology students to prepare them for work in these settings provides options for expanding service implementation that can enhance the mental health of young children. The two most promising places for early prevention and intervention efforts include primary care settings (Asarnow et al., 2015; Oppenheim et al., 2016; Talmi et al., 2016) and early childhood education settings (Bartlett & Smith, 2019; Martin et al., 2021; Stein et al., 2022).

There is clear evidence that increases in parent and child mental health challenges result in increased healthcare use (Lavigne & Meyers, 2019), increasing the burden on the healthcare system and on society resulting from childhood mental health problems, but also suggesting that primary care provides a promising route for early prevention and intervention. The PACT studies suggest several routes for the education of pediatric staff that might be fruitful for the early identification of symptoms that contribute to the development of more serious externalizing or internalizing behaviors. Recognizing the stresses associated both with certain social conditions such as poverty and trauma, and with other circumstances, such as family conflict, checking for signs of parental depression, and attending more carefully to parent concerns about problematic behaviors are all areas that hold promise for helping children progress towards healthier development. Psychology training programs should train students to integrate their knowledge, research, and the most easily transferred intervention skills into primary care settings to facilitate pediatric involvement in early identification and prevention efforts. Involving primary pediatric care professionals in understanding and addressing early mental health concerns has been shown to be effective in ameliorating problems (Asarnow et al., 2015; Lavigne et al., 2008; Molnar et al., 2018; Oppenheim et al., 2016) and is a fruitful area for expansion of training efforts in clinical child psychology. Early detection in pediatric practices holds promise for the expansion of both prevention efforts (Berenbaum et al., 2021) and early intervention as well as triage to more intensive care as recommended in a 3-tiered public health approach (Atkins et al., 2016). Psychologists are in a unique position to train pediatricians, pediatric nurse practitioners, and other professionals in pediatric offices to recognize and appropriately take action to promote mental health in young children, but only if they receive appropriate training in theories and empirical studies in developmental psychopathology and integrative and collaborative care models of service delivery. Unfortunately, current demands on pediatricians are such that they can only add one to two minutes to their regular visits with a child to deal with mental health concerns, so radical changes would be needed in the reimbursement system to enable pediatricians to have the time to do this. Nevertheless, since they are the first avenue of contact for most parents, it seems that this would be a fruitful avenue to pursue in advocating for public policy changes.

Schools are another community space in which a three-tiered approach that includes universal prevention, targeted intervention, and referral for intensive intervention can have a significant impact on the current mental health crisis. Training clinical child psychology students to provide mental health services in early childhood education settings (ECEs), not just directly but through a "train the trainer" model in which they teach prevention and intervention strategies to ECE personnel to ensure sustainability is a promising avenue for preventing the cascading effects of early symptoms and related factors, such as poor effortful control that lead to later difficulties. Universal interventions designed to improve ECE teachers' implementation of social-emotional skills have shown positive effects on teacher practice (Goldenthal et al., 2023) and child social-emotional skills (Bierman et al., 2008; Yang et al., 2018). In one study (Reyes & Gilliam, 2021), which evaluated the benefits of mental health consultation in early childhood education settings, moderate to strong effects were found for the kinds of risk factors that the PACT research program revealed to be especially important for early childhood outcomes. Effect sizes for improvement in self-regulation were moderate (0.29), while those for teacher-child attachment were even higher (0.42), suggesting that mental health supports in early childhood settings can have a significant impact on child socio-emotional developmental outcomes. Furthermore, concerns regarding child behavior decreased (effect size −0.27), as did teacher ratings of child aggressive behavior (effect size −0.25) and anxiety (effect size −0.35). Other studies have obtained similar results (Heckman et al., 2010). Currently, approximately 54% of all 3- and 4-year-old children are enrolled in early childhood education settings (National Center for Education Statistics, 2023). Research has shown that mental health consultation in these settings can decrease the impact of many of the risk factors identified in the PACT studies, e.g., insecure attachment and poor effortful control (Heckman et al., 2010; Reyes & Gilliam, 2021). Furthermore, it can help reduce teacher stress, thereby resulting in lower levels of staff turnover and greater attention to children's emotional needs and socioemotional skill development (Brennan et al., 2008; Conners-Burrow et al., 2013; Stein et al., 2022). Thus, it follows that training child psychologists to consult in these settings, both directly and through a train-the-trainer model, is particularly important for the future promotion of child mental health.

Lastly, training future child clinical psychologists in both developmental psychopathology and dissemination and implementation science will provide opportunities for the creation, promotion, and adoption of new programs that adhere to the multi-domain, multi-level, longitudinal tenets that hold promise for promoting improved mental health and early intervention (see the section below on research). In short, it is time for a scientist-practitioner-advocacy training model that creates a public psychology that applies research and practice in psychological science to advance social justice and enhance children's life chances (Miles & Fassinger, 2021).

Public Policy

Many of the PACT findings have implications for the generation of public policies that can enhance the well-being of young children and provide fruitful avenues for addressing the current mental health crisis among them. It is clear that emotional and behavioral difficulties start at an extremely young age, are relatively persistent across the preschool years, and are related to characteristics such as effortful control that have lifelong implications for academic and job success and financial and partnership stability. Additionally, they result from long causal chains that begin with the larger context in which children live and result in cascading effects over time that can profoundly affect their life trajectories. As noted in Chap. 11, these findings have many implications for the direct treatment of externalizing and internalizing behaviors in children. They also have implications for public policy initiatives that have the potential for exponential expansion, thereby reaching an even larger number of children and shifting the needle on mental health more dramatically at a population level.

SES

The PACT studies revealed that SES contributed to long causal chains leading to both externalizing (see Chap. 7) and internalizing (see Chap. 8) outcomes in young children. The relationship between poverty, often assessed by SES measures, and a range of child outcomes including externalizing and internalizing behaviors has been well documented (Bradley & Corwyn, 2002; Brooks-Gunn & Duncan, 1997; Chaudry & Wimer, 2016; Gleason, 2024; Thomas, 2024) particularly when experienced during early childhood (Brooks-Gunn & Duncan, 1997; Duncan et al., 1998; Ratcliffe & McKernan, 2012) and persisting over time (Duncan et al., 1994; Ratcliffe & McKernan, 2012). Several differing theoretical explanations have been offered for these associations (see Chap. 3). To briefly reiterate, the downward drift explanation assumes that adults with mental health difficulties drift downward socioeconomically due to the challenges they face from their mental illness, and transmission to their children might be a function of genetic influences. In contrast, social explanations suggest that families with fewer financial means lack resources, including food, housing, health-related, and enrichment resources, thereby contributing to poorer child mental health outcomes. Additionally, these parents experience greater stress, depression, family conflict, and resulting parenting challenges that contribute to poorer child outcomes (the family stress model). The PACT studies can be applied to this last theory. For example, the long pathways between SES and externalizing and internalizing symptoms in young children operated through parent depression for internalizing disorders (see Chap. 8) and through family conflict and parenting for externalizing disorders (see Chap. 7). Understanding the mechanisms through which these effects are transmitted is important for generating public policy and programming that is effective in preventing or ameliorating negative outcomes. Although large-scale policies that lift children out of poverty are likely to be most impactful (Costello et al., 2003), programming that alters other risk factors in these long causal chains, such as preventive programs that address parent depression for those living in poverty or teach effective parenting approaches (Haskins et al., 2014) are likely to have greater impact than individual treatment applied once problems have been identified. Important points of early identification and prevention efforts must shift to pediatric practices (Gitterman et al., 2016) and to school and community settings (Atkins et al., 2010, 2016; Kazdin, 2019; Martin et al., 2021) With over 21% of all American children living in poverty (Gitterman et al., 2016) and the long-term negative impact of poverty on child mental health being incontrovertible, it is essential that we both develop policies that lift children out of poverty and that research, such as the PACT studies, be designed to identify effective points of prevention and intervention. Specifically, dissemination and implementation research is needed to understand the most effective implementation strategies for public policy and where the highest cost-benefit lies for such policies (Hoagwood et al., 2020). Hoagwood and colleagues point out that, as a society, we have not directed serious public policy initiatives to address child mental health outcomes. The continued focus on empirically supported specific interventions and discrete psychosocial programs is unlikely to shift the needle significantly on child well-being. The American Academy of Pediatrics Council on Community Pediatrics (Gitterman et al., 2016) notes that studies from 1967 to 2012 document the positive effects that government programs can have on lifting children out of poverty. They cite many examples, including the earned income tax credit, increases in minimum wages, Temporary Assistance for Needy Families (TANF), and government-funded quality childcare and early childhood education programs (Gitterman et al., 2016). Clearly other solutions to eliminating or reducing child poverty exist as well, but they require a concerted effort by all adults and professionals working with children to advocate for large scale public policy changes that will potentiate these changes. Programs such as the Society for Research in Child Development Public Policy Fellowship is just one example of a professional program for child psychologists that provides training in advocacy and public policy.

Neighborhood Effects

A risk factor often associated with SES, although not isomorphic with it, is neighborhood residence (Butler et al., 2012; Dahal et al., 2018; Leventhal & Brooks-Gunn, 2000; Xue et al., 2005). In a study of over 2000 children ages 5 to 11 years old, Xue and colleagues found that 21.5% and 18.3% of children in low and medium SES neighborhoods scored above clinical levels on the Child Behavior Checklist compared to 11.5% of children in high SES neighborhoods. These effects were independent of family demographics and maternal depression. In one of the PACT studies, Romero (2016) found that neighborhood quality in historically marginalized communities was related to lower effortful control (EC) at age 4 and less growth in EC from age 4 to age 6. This neighborhood variable, assessed via social composition, economic composition, social processes, and physical composition contributed additionally to child EC, even after accounting for SES. In a study following children from birth through 32 years of age, Moffitt and colleagues (Moffitt et al., 2011) found a direct relation between better self-control and fewer negative adult outcomes in physical health, mental health, substance use, and criminal outcomes. Given the strong findings for the association between poor self-regulation in the form of EC (as well as sensory regulation, SR), and all the PACT mental health outcome measures, this study suggests that one explanation for the consistent relations found between neighborhood quality and mental health outcomes (Butler et al., 2012; Dahal et al., 2018; Leventhal & Brooks-Gunn, 2000; Singh & Ghandour, 2012; Visser et al., 2021) might be that children from historically marginalized neighborhoods are less likely to develop the self-regulatory skills that are critical to better outcomes (Heckman et al., 2013; Heckman & Kautz, 2012; Moffitt et al., 2011). Other studies suggest that it is the social organization of the neighborhood, lack of social support, and poor relationship quality that contribute to neighborhood effects rather than SES per se (Dahal et al., 2018; Visser et al., 2021; Xue et al., 2005). Further research is needed to determine the specific aspects of low SES neighborhoods that contribute to poorer development of self-regulatory skills in young children, as well as to the general effects of neighborhood on mental health outcomes. A better understanding of these variables will contribute to psychologists' efforts to promote public policy (Hoagwood et al., 2020) that shores up neighborhoods in ways that can have an impact on child outcomes.

Early Identification and Preventive Care

Public policy directed towards earlier identification of symptoms, as well as risk factors, is critical to alter the current trajectory towards increasing mental health problems in the United States and worldwide. The PACT studies clearly indicate that both early occurring symptoms and a range of risk factors that impact children during early childhood lead to more negative developmental outcomes. In fact, when early symptoms were added to many of the PACT models, they accounted for a large degree of the variance in outcome (see Chaps. 7 and 8), leading the PACT researchers in several papers (Gouze et al., 2022; Hopkins et al., 2020; Lavigne et al., 2016) to recommend that risk factor research on these outcomes needs to begin even earlier than age 4, the youngest age of the PACT participants. Economists have long argued for the benefits of early prevention and intervention efforts as a cost-effective approach to child well-being and mental health that can positively impact a host of adult outcomes that are costly to individuals and society such as lack of employment, substance use, and physical health problems, to mention just a few (Goodman et al., 2011; Heckman, 2006; Karoly et al., 1998). Similarly, psychologists and public health advocates have long advocated that it is easier to prevent a negative outcome than to fix it (Costello, 2016) and have recognized, as the PACT studies indicate, that contextual variables, the circumstances in which children live, learn, and play, have a strong impact on their developmental outcomes. In addition to addressing these contextual variables through programs that can impact SES and deleterious neighborhood effects described above, early identification of risk and symptoms, and early prevention and intervention efforts are essential. To accomplish this, some advocate for better pediatric screening and early intervention in pediatric offices and "medical homes" (Conti & Heckman, 2012; Foy et al., 2019; Molnar et al., 2018; Oppenheim et al., 2016; Weitzman et al., 2015). When it works, integrated primary care can promote accessibility and family engagement, reduce barriers to mental health care, reach more families, and lead to improved outcomes (Njoroge et al., 2016), thereby heeding Kazdin and colleagues' (Kazdin, 2019; Kazdin & Rabbitt, 2013) call for increasing reach, scalability, affordability, and expansion of child mental health prevention and intervention services. Before this potential can fully be realized, however, a range of problems need to be solved. These include difficulties with effective screening (Charach et al., 2020), lack of agreement between physicians and mental health clinicians on mental health presentation (Lavigne et al., 1993), and inadequate referral follow-up, with most parents indicating that they spoke first to their physicians regarding an emotional or behavioral problem, but less than half reported receiving referrals to mental health practitioners (Charach et al., 2020). Nevertheless, integrated primary care programs hold promise for addressing the population level increases in mental health problems because pediatricians see children at least annually for well-child check-ups, are already the "de facto" mental health providers for young children, do not carry the stigma of mental health professionals, and have extant relationships with parents that allow them to provide feedback in non-threatening ways (Lines, 2022). Given the promise that it holds for the future of child mental health, further exploration of various models of integrative and collaborative care are critically needed to determine the most effective means for addressing the mental health needs of our youngest citizens.

As noted in the section on training, another setting that potentially provides extensive access and de-stigmatized care for children with early risk factors and symptoms of emotional and behavioral problems is early care and early childhood education settings. Social-emotional programming in these settings, as well as mental health consultation, is effective in providing protective benefits in the form of better social skills, improved self-regulatory skills, and better cognitive performance (Conners-Burrow et al., 2013; Heckman et al., 2013; Jones et al., 2015; Martinsone et al., 2022; Reyes & Gilliam, 2021). Advocates for implementing social-emotional programs in early childhood education argue that acquiring these skills promotes long-term positive outcomes well into adulthood (Heckman et al., 2013; Jones et al., 2015). Data from the Perry Preschool Program (Heckman et al., 2013) revealed that implementing a preschool curriculum that strongly supported the development of self-regulatory and planning skills significantly decreased externalizing behaviors and improved later adult outcomes, including education level, employment, earnings, and health. Preschool teachers are already focused on teaching social-emotional skills, but studies reveal that few feel qualified to address mental health problems or child exposure to potentially traumatic experiences (Goldenthal et al., 2023; Walter et al., 2006). Mental health consultation models show good outcomes (Conners-Burrow et al., 2013; Reyes & Gilliam, 2021) but do not address the need for universal programming and training of non-mental health professionals to recognize early risk factors and implement effective preventive programming. The number of trained mental health professionals is insufficient to meet the current mental health needs of children (Kazdin, 2019), and this imbalance is expected to grow over the next few years (Berenbaum et al., 2021). As such, programs that are preventive in nature and train the adults who already work with children (e.g., daycare providers and preschool teachers) hold the most promise for changing the current trajectories toward increasing mental health needs.

Costello (2016) makes a compelling argument for the early detection and prevention of mental illness as the most effective means for combatting it. He argues both that epidemiological studies, which help us understand the patterns whereby certain groups of children are more likely to evidence poor mental health, and studies examining long chains of risk factors are needed to implement prevention and early identification programs. Epidemiological studies contribute to understanding the cost and benefits of different approaches to childhood behavioral and emotional disorders. Is it more cost-effective, for example, to provide support for foundational life needs or to implement interventions when unmet needs result in functional impairment and emotional distress? The long causal chains contributing to risk that were revealed in the PACT research indicate that a two-pronged approach is likely to be most effective. Specifically, this approach must include prevention efforts oriented towards ameliorating the larger structural impacts of race and class along with universal programming geared towards enhancing the well-being of all children. The PACT studies suggest that multi-level prevention programs that address adult mental health, parenting practices, and the factors that contribute to the evolution of fundamental developmental tasks such as self-regulation are most likely to be effective. Costello maintains that effective implementation of prevention programs requires an understanding of timing, as well as duration and intensity, that is, at what point do persistent problems begin, how severe does the risk factor have to be (e.g., how severely depressed does a depressed mother have to be to impact child well-being?), and how important is the persistence of that risk factor? Although the PACT studies cannot answer all these questions, they make clear that these long causal chains of risk begin extremely early in life, and many are persistent over time. Thus, it is evident that the earlier prevention programs are put into place, the more effective they are likely to be. The idea that "earlier is better" is also supported by economic analysis of prevention programs (Conti & Heckman, 2012). Early home visiting programs, universal prevention in early childhood care settings and early childhood education settings, and engagement of pediatric primary care practitioners all hold promise for effective prevention. Unfortunately, many of these settings focus exclusively on the child, thereby missing several of the major contributing risk factors to poor child outcomes, including living in an under-resourced community (Costello et al., 2003; Dahal et al., 2018; Duncan et al., 1998), poor parental mental health (Leijdesdorff et al., 2017; Wolicki et al., 2021), and less supportive and more hostile parenting (Barrios et al., 2017; Callahan et al., 2011; Campbell et al., 2000; Rose et al., 2018; Waller et al., 2012) (see Chaps. 3, 4, and 5 and the PACT findings in Chaps. 7, 8, and 9 for a review). Early prevention programs need to target children and their parents, as well as contextual factors, to have the most impact. Importantly, research is needed to further understand the long causal chains and mechanisms contributing to child outcomes and the elements needed for effective prevention and early intervention program implementation.

Future Research

As with most research, the PACT studies raise as many questions as they answer. What other factors, besides those examined in the PACT studies, are important to the development of child well-being? How do protective factors interact with risk factors? How does risk vary in different population groups? How can the multigenerational effects of race and class be dissected to increase our understanding of their impact? The questions go on and on. Clearly, good developmental psychopathology research is needed to further our understanding of when, how, and in what settings to intervene to alter the life chances of children who are at risk. Over a decade ago, Kazdin and Blasé (2011) called for research that could promote greater integration of prevention and treatment, enhance understanding of the contextual factors that influence health behaviors and health care, and increase knowledge regarding the who, what, and where of effective treatment intervention.

Research in developmental psychopathology and the risk and protective factors contributing to poor mental health outcomes can help inform public policy initiatives and the lawmakers and decision-makers who mandate the implementation of such policies. This pipeline for research to policy is needed to generate large-scale programs and policies that promote healthy development and protect the population against risks contributing to negative mental health outcomes (Hoagwood et al., 2020; NASEM, 2019; Williamson et al., 2015). Hoagwood and colleagues write eloquently of the need to move dissemination and implementation research into new areas that inform policy development and implementation. Indeed, despite two decades of research on EBTs to ensure research-based treatment of children and families, the mental health needs of youth have increased over that time and treatment effect sizes remain moderate at best. This failure is due to the difficulty of translating psychosocial EBTs into general practice settings, the ineffectiveness of many of these treatments applied in community settings (Weisz et al., 2013), the high rate of co-morbidities in real-world settings (Bearman & Weisz, 2015), the difficulty in accessing behavioral health care resources (Chien et al., 2022; Hansen et al., 2021), and the ineffectiveness of most treatments in addressing the larger structural factors that determine mental health outcomes in children (Bradley & Corwyn, 2002; Conti & Heckman, 2012; Costello, 2016). The call for dissemination and implementation of research that prioritizes the needs and resources of the settings in which children and families live, learn, work, and play (Atkins et al., 2016), that expands reach, scalability, affordability, the use of a nonprofessional workforce (Kazdin & Rabbitt, 2013), and that prioritizes research that can inform policymakers (Frazier et al., 2014; Hoagwood et al., 2020) and supports the move towards public psychology (Eaton et al., 2021) is one that must be heeded by those who train students of clinical child and developmental psychopathology as well as by those who fund research.

As child clinicians and researchers, the authors of this book support intensive investment in research to support a myriad of efforts, both those that address population-level risk factors and those that can be effectively applied to children and families who are already suffering from a range of mental health problems. It will take a concerted investment of resources to shift development towards healthier trajectories in our children and to alter the current trends towards increasingly poor mental health documented worldwide. The investment is well worth it. As Frederick Douglass so eloquently stated over a century ago, "It is easier to build strong children than to repair broken adults."

References

Asarnow, J. R., Rozenman, M., Wiblin, J., & Zeltzer, L. (2015). Integrated medical-behavioral care compared with usual primary care for chid and adolescent behavioral health: A meta-analysis. *JAMA Pediatrics, 169*, 929–937. https://doi.org/10.1001/jamapediatrics.2015.1141

Atkins, M. S., Hoagwood, K. E., Kutash, K., & Seidman, E. (2010). Toward the integration of education and mental health in schools. *Administration and Policy in Mental Health, 37*(1–2), 40–47. https://doi.org/10.1007/S1048-010-0299-7

Atkins, M. S., Strauman, T. J., Cyranowski, J. M., & Kolden, G. G. (2014). Reconceptualizing internship training within the evolving clincial science training model. *Clinical Psychological Science, 2*(1), 46–57. https://doi.org/10.1177/2167702613501308

Atkins, M. S., Rusch, D., Mehta, T. G., & Lakind, D. (2016). Future directions for dissemination and implementation science: Aligning ecological theory and public health to close the research to pratice gap. *Journal of Clinical Child & Adolescent Psychology, 45*(2), 215–226. https://doi.org/10.1080/15374416.2015.1050724

Barrios, C., Bufferd, S. J., Klein, D. N., & Dougherty, L. (2017). The interaction between parenting and children's cortisol reactivity at age 3 predicts increases in children's internalizing and externalizing symptoms at age 6. *Development and Psychopathology, 29*(1–13), 1319. https://doi.org/10.1017/S0954579417000293

Bartlett, J. D., & Smith, S. (2019). The role of early care and education in addresing early childhood trauma. *American Journal of Community Psychology, 64*(3–4), 359–372. https://doi.org/10.1002/ajcp.12380

Basten, M., Tiemeier, H., Althoff, R. R., van de Schoot, R., Jaddoe, V. W. V., Hofman, A., Hudziak, J. J., Verhulst, F. C., & van der Ende, J. (2016). The stability of problem behavior across the preschool years: An empirical approach in the general ppulation. *Journal of Abnormal Child Psychology, 44*(2), 393–404. https://doi.org/10.1007/s10802-015-9993-y

Bearman, S. K., & Weisz, J. R. (2015). Review: comprehensive treatments for youth co-morbidity – Evidence-guided approaches to a complicated problem. *Child and Adolescent Mental Health, 20*(3), 131–141. https://doi.org/10.1111/camh.12092

Benuto, L. T., Singer, J., Newlands, R. T., & Casas, J. B. (2019). Training culturally competent psychologists: Where are we and where do we need to go? *Training and Education in Professional Psychology, 13*(1), 56–63. https://doi.org/10.1037/tep0000214

Berenbaum, H., Washburn, J. J., Sbarra, D., Reardon, K. W., Schuler, T., Teachman, B. A., Hollon, S. D., Atkins, M. S., Hamilton, J. L., Hetrick, W. P., Tackett, J. L., Cody, M. W., Klepac, R. K., & Lee, S. S. (2021). Accelerating the rate of progress in reducing mental health burdens: Recommendations for training the next generarion of clinical psychologists. *Clinical Psychology: Science and Practice, 28*(2), 107–123. https://doi.org/10.1037/cps0000007

Bierman, K. L., Domitrovich, C. E., Nix, R. L., Gest, S. D., Welsh, J. A., Greenberg, M. T., Blair, C., Nelson, K. E., & Gill, S. (2008). Promoting academic and social-emotional school readiness: The Head Start REDI program. *Child Development, 79*(6), 1802–1817. https://doi.org/10.1111/j.1467-8624.2008.01227.x

Bradley, R. H., & Corwyn, R. F. (2002). Socioeconomic status and child development. *Annual Review of Psychology, 53*, 371–399. https://doi.org/10.1146/annurev.psych.53.100901.135233

Brennan, E. M., Bradley, J. R., Allen, M. D., & Perry, D. F. (2008). The evidence base for mental health consultation in early childhood settings. *Early Education and Development, 19*(6), 982–1022. https://doi.org/10.1080/10409280801975834

Brooks-Gunn, J., & Duncan, G. J. (1997). The effects of poverty on children. *Future of Children, 7*(2), 55–71.

Butler, A. M., Kowalkowski, M., Jones, H. A., & Raphael, J. L. (2012). The relationship of reported neighborhood conditions with child mental health. *Academic Pediatrics, 12*(6), 523–531. https://doi.org/10.1016/j.acap.2012.06.005

Callahan, K. L., Scaramella, L. V., Laird, R. D., & Sohr-Preston, S. L. (2011). Neighborhood disadvantage as a moderator of the association between harsh parenting and toddler-aged children's internalizing and externalizing problems. *Journal of Family Psychology, 25*(1), 68–76. https://doi.org/10.1037/a0022448

Campbell, S. B., Shaw, D. S., & Gilliom, M. (2000). Early externalizing behavior problems: Toddlers and preschoolers at risk for later maladjustment. *Development and Psychopathology, 12*(03), 467–488.

Center for Child Resilience. (2019a). *Ready to learn through relationships: A trauma-informed framework for early childhood educators* [Unpublished manual].

Center for Child Resilience. (2019b). *Ready to learn through relationships: A trauma-informed toolkit for early childhood educators* [Unpublished toolkit].

Charach, A., Mohammedzadeh, F., Belanger, S. A., Easson, A., Lipman, E. L., McLennan, J. D., Parkin, P., & Szatmari, P. (2020). Identification of preschool children with mental health problems in primary care: Systematic review and meta-analysis. *Journal of Canadian Child and Adolescent Psychiatry, 20*(2), 76–105.

Chaudry, A., & Wimer, C. (2016). The relationhp between income, poverty, and child well-being. *Academic Pediatrics, 16*(3 Suppl), S23–S29. https://doi.org/10.1016/j.acap.2015.12.010

Chien, A. T., Leyenaar, J., Tomaino, M., Woolshin, S., Leininger, L., Barnett, E. R., McLaren, J. L., & Meara, E. (2022). Difficulty obtaining behavioral health services for children: A national survey of multiphysician practices. *Annals of Family Medicine, 20*(1), 42–50. https://doi.org/10.1370/afm.2759

Chorpita, B. F. (2019). Commentary: metaknowledge is power: Envisioning models to address unmet mental health needs: Reflections on Kazdin (2019). *Journal of Child Psychology and Psychiatry, 60*(4), 473–476. https://doi.org/10.1111/jcpp.13034

Conners-Burrow, N. A., McKelvey, L., Sockwell, L., Ehrentraut, J. H., Adams, S., & Whiteside-Mansell, L. (2013). Beginning to "unpack" early child mental health consultation: Types of consultation services and their impact on teachers. *Infant Mental Health Journal, 34*(4), 280–289. https://doi.org/10.1002/imhj.21387

Conti, G., & Heckman, J. (2012). The developmental approach to child and adult health. *Pediatrics, 131*, S133. https://doi.org/10.1542/peds.2013-0252d

Costello, E. J. (2016). Early detection and prevention of mental health problems: Developmental epidemiology and systems of support. *Journal of Clinical Child and Adolescent Psychology, 45*(6), 710–717. https://doi.org/10.1080/15374416.2016.1236728

Costello, E. J., Compton, S. N., Keeler, G., & Angold, A. (2003). Relationships between poverty and psychopathology: A natural experiment. *JAMA, 290*(15), 2023–2029. https://doi.org/10.1001/jama.290.15.2023

Dahal, S., Swahn, M. H., & Hayat, M. J. (2018). Association between neighborhood conditions and mental disorders among children in the US: Evidence from the National Survey of Children's Health 2011/12. *Psychiatry Journal, 2018*, 1. https://doi.org/10.1155/2018/5914315

Duncan, G. J., Brooks-Gunn, J., & Klebanov, P. K. (1994). Economic deprivation and early childhood development. *Child Development*, 65(2 Spec No), 296–318.

Duncan, G., Yeung, W., Brooks-Gunn, J., & Smith, J. (1998). How much does childhood poverty affect the life chances of children? *American Sociological Review, 63*, 406–423. https://doi.org/10.2307/2657556

Eaton, A. A., Grzanka, P. R., Schlehofer, M. M., & Silka, L. (2021). Public psychology: Introduction to the special issue. *American Psychologist, 76*(8), 1209–1216. https://doi.org/10.1037/amp0000933

Egger, H. E., & Angold, A. (2006). Common emotional and behavioral disorders in preschool children: Presentation, nosology, and epidemiology. *Journal of Child Psychology and Psychiatry, 47*, 313–337.

Foy, J. M., Green, C. M., Earls, M. F., & Committee on Psychosocial Aspects of Child and Family Mental Health-Mental Health Leadership Work Group. (2019). Mental health competencies for pediatric practice. *Pediatrics, 144*(5), e20192757.

Frazier, S. L., Bearman, S. K., Garland, A., & Atkins, M. S. (2014). Dissemination and implementation in children's mental health: Closing the research to training gap. In R. S. Beidas &

P. C. Kendall (Eds.), *Dissemination and implementation of evidence based practices in child and adolescent mental health* (pp. 98–123). Oxford University Press.

Gaffrey, M. S., Tillman, R., Barch, D. M., & Luby, J. L. (2018). Continuity and stability of preschool depression from childhood through adolescence and following the onset of puberty. *Comprehensive Psychiatry, 89*, 39–46. https://doi.org/10.1016/j.comppsych.2018.07.010

GBD Mental Disorders Collaborators. (2022). Global, regional, and national burden of 12 mental disorders in 204 countries and territories, 1990–2019: a systematic analysis for the Global Burden of Disease Study 2019. *Lancet Psychiatry, 9*(2), 137–150. https://doi.org/10.1016/S2215-0366(21)00395-3

Gitterman, B. A., Flanagan, P. J., Cotton, W. H., Dilley, K. J., Duffee, J. H., Green, A. E., Keane, V. A., Krugman, S. D., Linton, J. M., McKelvey, C. D., & Nelson, J. L. (2016). Poverty and child health in the United States. *Pediatrics, 137*(4), 1098–4275.

Gleason, M. M. H. (2024). Mental Health Promotion and Problem Prevention [Podcast] In *Promotion and problem prevention.*

Goldenthal, H. J., Gouze, K. R., Raviv, T., Tragoudas, G., Holley, C., & Cicchetti, C. (2023). The ready to learn through relationships (RLR) program: Development feasibility, and acceptability. *Early Childhood Education Journal, 52*(3), 587–601. https://doi.org/10.1007/s10643-023-01472-0

Goodman, S. H., Rouse, M. H., Connell, A. M., Broth, M. R., Hall, C. M., & Heyward, D. (2011). Maternal depression and child psychopathology: a meta-analytic review. *Clinical Child and Family Psychology Review, 14*, 1–27. https://doi.org/10.1003/sl10567-010-0080-1

Gouze, K. R., Hopkins, J., Lavigne, J. V., & Bryant, F. B. (2021). A multi-level longitudinal model of risk factors for generalized and separation anxiety symptoms in a community sample of 6-year-olds. *Child Psychiatry and Human Development, 53*(3), 405–417. https://doi.org/10.1007/s10578-021-01132-7

Gouze, K. R., Lavigne, J. V., & Bryant, F. B. (2022). A multi-level longitudinal model of risk factors for generalized and separation anxiety symptoms in a community sample of 6-year-olds. *Child Psychiatry and Human Development, 53*(3), 405–417. https://doi.org/10.1007/s10578-021-01132-7

Hansen, A. S., Telleus, G. K., Mohr-Jensen, C., & Lauritsen, M. B. (2021). Parent-perceived barriers to accessing services for their child's mental health probems. *Child and Adolescent Psychiatry and Mental Health, 15*, Article 4. https://doi.org/10.1186/s13034-021-00357-7

Haskins, R., Garfinkel, I., & McLanahan, S. (2014). Helping parents, helping children: Two-generation mechanisms. *Future of Children, 24*(1), 3–12. https://doi.org/10.1353/foc.2014.0001

Heatherington, L., Messer, S. B., Angus, L., Strauman, T. J., Friedlander, M. L., & Kolden, G. G. (2012). The narrowing of theoretical orientations in clinical psychology doctoral training. *Clinical Psychology: Science and Practice, 19*(4), 364–374. https://doi.org/10.1111/cpsp.12012

Heckman, J. J. (2006). Skill formation and the economics of investing in disadvantaged children. *Science, 30*(312(5782)), 1900–1902. https://doi.org/10.1026/science.1128898

Heckman, J. J., & Kautz, T. (2012). Hard evidence on soft skills. *Labour Economics, 19*(4), 451–464. https://doi.org/10.1016/j.labeco.2012.05.014

Heckman, J. J., Moon, S. H., Pinto, R., Savalyev, P. A., & Yavitz, A. (2010). The rate of return to the HighScope Perry Preschool Program. *Journal of Public Economics, 94*(1–2), 114–128. https://doi.org/10.1016/j.jpubeco.2009.11.001

Heckman, J., Rodrigo, P., & Savelyev, P. (2013). Understanding the mechanisms through which an influential early childhood program boosted adult outcomes. *American Economic Review, 103*(6), 2052–2086. https://doi.org/10.1257/aer.103.6.2052

Hoagwood, K. E., Purtle, J., Spandorfer, J., Peth-Pierce, R., & Horowitz, S. M. (2020). Aligning dissemination and implementation science with health policies to improve children's mental health. *American Psychologist, 75*(8), 1130–1145. https://doi.org/10.1037/amp0000706

Hopkins, J., Gouze, K. R., Lavigne, J. V., & Bryant, F. B. (2020). Multidomain risk factors in early childhood and depression symptoms in 6-year-year-olds: A longitudinal pathway model. *Develoment and Psychopathology, 32*(1), 57–71. https://doi.org/10.1017/S0954579418001426

Jones, D. E., Greenberg, M., & Crowley, M. (2015). Early social-emotional functioning and public health: the relationship between kindergarten social competence and future wellness. *American Journal of Public Health, 105*(11), 2283–2290. https://doi.org/10.2105/AJPH.2015.302630

Karoly, L. A., Greenwood, P. W., Everingham, S. S., Hoube, J., Kilburn, M. R., Rydell, C. P., Sanders, M., & Chiesa, J. (1998). *Investing in our children: What we know and don't know about the costs and benefits of early childhood interventions*. Rand Corporation.

Kazdin, A. E. (2019). Annual research review: Expanding mental health services through novel models of intervention delivery. *Journal of Child Psychology and Psychiatry, 60*(4), 455–472. https://doi.org/10.1111/jcpp.12937

Kazdin, A. E., & Blase, S. L. (2011). Rebooting psychotherapy research and practice to reduce the burden of mental illness. *Perspectives on Psychological Science, 6*(1), 21–37. https://doi.org/10.1177/1745691610393527

Kazdin, A. E., & Rabbitt, S. M. (2013). Novel models for delivering mental health services and reducing the burdens of mental illness. *Clinical Psychological Science, 1*(2), 170–191. https://doi.org/10.1177/2167702612463566

Lavigne, J. V., & Meyers, K. M. (2019). Meta-analysis: Association of parent and child mental health with pediatric health care utilization. *Journal of Pediatric Psychology, 44*(9), 1097–1110. https://doi.org/10.1093/jpepsy/jsz049

Lavigne, J. V., Binns, H. J., Christoffel, K. K., Rosenbaum, D., Arend, R., Smith, K., Hayford, J. R., & McGuire, P. (1993). Behavioral and emotional problems among preschool children in pediatric primary care: Prevalence and pediatricians' recognition. *Pediatrics, 91*, 649–655.

Lavigne, J. V., Arend, R., Rosenbaum, D., Binns, H. J., Christoffel, K. K., & Gibbons, R. D. (1998). Psychiatric disorders with onset in the preschool years: I. Stability of diagnosis. *Journal of the American Academy of Child and Adolescent Psychiatry, 37*(12), 1246–1254.

Lavigne, J. V., Cicchetti, C., Gibbons, R. D., Binns, H. J., Larsen, L., & DeVito, C. (2001). Oppositional defiant disorder with onset in preschool years: Longitudinal stability and pathways to other disorders. *Journal of the American Academy of Child and Adolescent Psychiatry, 40*, 1393–1400.

Lavigne, J. V., LeBailly, S. A., Gouze, K. R., Cicchetti, C., Pochyly, J., Arend, R., Jessup, B. W., & Binns, H. J. (2008). Treating Oppositional Defiant Disorder in primary care: A comparison of three models. *Journal of Pediatric Psychology, 33*(5), 449–461.

Lavigne, J. V., LeBailly, S. A., Hopkins, J., Gouze, K. R., & Binns, H. J. (2009). The prevalence of ADHD, ODD, depression and anxiety in a community sample of 4-year-olds. *Journal of Clinical Child and Adolescent Psychology, 38*, 315–328. https://doi.org/10.1080/15374410902851382

Lavigne, J. V., Gouze, K. R., Hopkins, J., & Bryant, F. B. (2016). Multi-domain predictors of attention deficit/hyperactivity disorder symptoms in preschool children: cross-informant differences. *Child Psychiatry and Human Development, 47*(6), 841–856. https://doi.org/10.1007/s10578-015-0616-1

Lebrun-Harris, L. A., Ghandour, R. M., Kogan, M. D., & Warren, M. D. (2022). Five-year trends in US children's health and well-being. *JAMA Pediatrics, 176*(7), e22056. https://doi.org/10.1011/jamapediatrics.2022.0056

Leijdesdorff, S., Doesum, K., Popma, A., Klaasen, R., & van Amelsvoort, T. (2017). Prevalence of psychopathology in children of parents with mental illness and/or addiction: An up to date narrative review. *Current Opinion in Psychiatry, 30*(4), 312–317. https://doi.org/10.1097/YCO.0000000000000341

Levenson, R. W. (2014). The future of clinical science training: New challenges and opportunities. *Clinical Psychological Science, 2*(1), 312–317. https://doi.org/10.1177/2167702613499330

Leventhal, T., & Brooks-Gunn, J. (2000). The neighborhoods they live in: The effects of neighborhood residence on child and adolescent outcomes. *Psychological Bulletin, 126*(2), 309–337. https://doi.org/10.1037/0033-2909.126.2.309

Lines, M. M. (2022). Pediatric integrated primary care: a population health approach to meeting the behavioral health needs of children and families. *Delaware Journal of Public Health, 8*(2), 6–9. https://doi.org/10.32481/djph.2022.05.002

Lyon, A. R., & Budd, K. S. (2010). A community mental health implementation of Parent-Child Interaction Therapy (PCIT). *Journal of Child and Family Studies, 19*(5), 654–668. https://doi.org/10.1007/s10826-010-9353-z

Martin, C. P., Russo, J., Goldenthal, H. J., Holley, C., Gouze, K. R., & Williford, A. (2021). Supporting young children exposed to potentially traumatic events: Implications for early care and education policy. *Policy Insights from the Brain and Behavioral Sciences, 8*(2), 119–126. https://doi.org/10.1177/23727322211103388

Martinsone, B., Supe, I., Stokenberga, I., Damberga, I., Cefai, C., Camilleri, L., Bartolo, P., O'Riordan, M. R., & Grazzani, I. (2022). Social emotional competence, learning outcomes, emotional and behavioral difficulties of preschool children: Parent and teacher evaluations. *Frontiers in Psychiatry, 12*, 760782. https://doi.org/10.3389/fpsyg.2021.760782

McLeod, B. D., & Weisz, J. R. (2004). Using dissertations to examine potential bias in child and adolescent clinical trials. *Journal of Consulting and Clinical Psychology, 72*(2), 235–251. https://doi.org/10.1037/0022-006X.72.2.235

Merikangas, K. R., Nakamura, E. F., & Kessler, R. C. (2009). Epidemiology of mental disorders in children and adolescents. *Dialogues in Clinical Neuroscience, 11*(1), 7–20. https://doi.org/10.31887/DCNS.2009.11.1/krmerikangas

Miles, J. R., & Fassinger, R. E. (2021). Creating a public psychology through a scientist-practitioner-advocate training model. *American Psychologist, 76*(8), 1232–1247. https://doi.org/10.1037/amp0000855

Moffitt, T. E., Arsenault, L., Belsky, D., Dickson, N., Hancox, R. J., Harrington, H., Houts, R., Poulton, R., Roberts, B. W., Ross, S., Sears, M. R., Thomson, W. M., & Caspi, A. (2011). A gradient of childhood self-control predicts health, wealth, and public safety. *Proceedings of the National Academy of Sciences of the United States of America, 108*(7), 2693–2698. https://doi.org/10.1073/pnas.1010076108

Molnar, B. E., Lees, K. E., Roper, K., Byars, N., Mendez-Penate, L., Moulin, C., McMullen, W., Wolfe, J., & Allen, D. (2018). Enhancing early childhood mental health primary care services: evaluation of MA Project Launch. *Maternal and Child Health Journal, 22*(10), 1502–1510. https://doi.org/10.1007/s10995-018-2548-4

NASEM. (2019). *Fostering healthy mental, emotional, and behavioral development in children and youth: A national agenda*. The National Academies Press.

National Center for Education Statistics. (2023). *Enrollment rates of young chilren*. U.S. Department of Educatin, Institute of Eduation Sciences.

Ng, M. Y., & Weisz, J. R. (2018). Personalizing evidence-based psychotherapy for children and adolescents in clinical care. In J. R. Weisz & A. E. Kazdin (Eds.), *Evidence-based psychotherapies for children and adolescents* (3rd ed., pp. 501–509). Guilford Press.

Njoroge, W. F., Hostutler, C. A., Schwartz, B. S., & Mautone, J. A. (2016). Integrated behavioral health in pediatric primary care. *Current Psychiatry Reports, 18*(12), 106. https://doi.org/10.1007/s11920-016-0745-7

Oppenheim, J., Stewart, W., Zoubak, E., Donato, I., Huang, L., & Hudock, W. (2016). Launching forward: The integration of behavioral health in primary care as a key strategy for promoting young child wellness. *American Journal of Orthopsychiatry, 86*(2), 124–131. https://doi.org/10.1037/ort0000149

Owens, P. L., Hoagwood, K. E., Horwitz, S. M., Leaf, P. J., Poduska, J. M., Kellam, S. G., & Ialongo, N. S. (2002). Barriers to children's mental health services. *Journal of the American Academy of Child and Adolescent Psychiatry, 41*(6), 731–738. https://doi.org/10.1097/00004583-200206000-00013

Palermo, T. M., Janicke, D. M., McQuaid, E. L., Mullins, L. L., Robins, P. M., & Wu, Y. P. (2014). Recommendations for training in pediatric psychology: defining core competencies across training levels. *Pediatric Psychology, 39*(9), 965–984. https://doi.org/10.1093/jpepsy/jsu015

Ratcliffe, C. E., & McKernan, S.-M. (2012). *Child poverty and its lasting consequence*. (Urban Institute Low-Income Working Families working paper no. 21).

Reyes, C. R., & Gilliam, W. S. (2021). Addressing challenging behaviors in challenging environments: Findings from Ohio's early childhood mental health consultation system. *Development and Psychopathology, 33*, 634–646. https://doi.org/10.1017/S09545794200001790

Romero, E. Y. (2016). The role of neighborhood and parenting in the development of effortful control and subsequent social competence during early childhood. *Dissertation Abstracts International: The Sciences and Engineering (Vol. 77, Issue 1-B(E))*.

Rose, J. S., Roman, N., Mwaba, K., & Ismail, K. (2018). The relationship between parenting and internalizing behaviours of children: A systematic review. *Early Childhood Development and Care, 188*(10), 1468–1486. https://doi.org/10.1080/03004430.2016.1269762

Shoham, V., Roghbaugh, M. J., Onken, L. S., Cuthbert, B. N., Beveridge, R. M., & Fowles, T. R. (2014). Redifining clinical science training: Purpose and products of the Delaware Project. *Clinical Psychological Science, 2*(1), 8–21. https://doi.org/10.1177/2167702613497931

Singh, G. K., & Ghandour, R. M. (2012). Impact of neighborhood social conditions and household socioeconomic status on behavioral problems among US chldren. *Maternal Child Health Journal, apr, 16*, S158–S169. https://doi.org/10.1007/s10995-012-1005-z

So, M., McCord, R. F., & Kaminski, J. W. (2019). Policy levers to promote access to and utilization of children's mental health services: A systematic review. *Administration and Policy in Mental Health, 46*, 334–351. https://doi.org/10.1007/s10488-018-00916-9

Stein, R., Garay, M., & Nguyen, A. (2022). It matters: Early childhood mental health, educator stress, and burnout. *Early Child Education Journal, Dec, 30*, 1–12. https://doi.org/10.1007/s10643-022-01438-8

Talmi, A., Muther, E. F., Margolis, K., Buchholz, M., Asherin, R., & Bunik, M. (2016). The scope of behavioral health integration in a pediatric primary care setting. *Journal of Pediatric Psychology, 41*(10), 1120–1132. https://doi.org/10.1093/jpepsy/jsw065

Thomas, M. M. C. (2024). Latent classes and longitudinal patterns of material hardship as predictors of child well-being. *Child and Society, 38*(2), 253–276. https://doi.org/10.1111/chso.12687

Visser, K., Bolt, G., Finkenauer, C., Jonker, M., Weinberg, D., & Stevens, G. W. J. M. (2021). Neighbourhood deprivation effects on young people's mental health and well-being: A systematic review of the literature. *Social Science and Medicine, 270*, 113542. https://doi.org/10.1016/j.socscimed.2020.113542

Waller, R., Gardner, F., Hyde, L. W., Shaw, D. S., Dishion, T. J., & Wilson, M. N. (2012). Do harsh and positive parenting predict parent reports of deceitful-callous behavior in early childhood? *Journal of Child Psychology and Psychiatry, 53*(9), 946–953. https://doi.org/10.1111/j.1469-7610.2012.02550.x

Walter, H., Gouze, K. R., & Lim, K. (2006). Teacher's beliefs about mental health needs in inner city elementary schools. *Journal of the American Academy of Child and Adolescent Psychiatry, 45*, 61–68. https://doi.org/10.1097/01.chi.0000187243.17824.6c

Weisz, J. R., Kuppens, S., Eckshtain, D., Hawley, K. M., & Jensen-Doss, A. (2013). Performance of evidence-based youth psychotherapies compared with usual clinical care: A multilevel meta-analysis. *JAMA Psychiatry, 70*(7), 750–761. https://doi.org/10.1001/jamapsychiatry.2013.1176

Weisz, J. R., Ng, M. Y., & Bearman, S. K. (2014). Odd couple? Reenvisioning the relation between science and practice in the dissemination-implementation era. *Clinical Psychological Science, 2*(1), 58–74. https://doi.org/10.1177/2167702613501307

Weisz, J. R., Bearman, S. K., Santucci, J. C., & Jensen-Doss, A. (2017). Initial test of a principle-guided approach to transdiagnostic psychotherapy with children and adolescents. *Journal of Clinical Child & Adolescent Psychology, 46*(1), 44–58. https://doi.org/10.1080/15374416.2016.11

Weisz, J. R., Kuppens, S., Ng, M. Y., Vaughn-Coaxum, R. A., Ugueto, A. M., Eckshtain, D., & Cortesellil, K. A. (2019). Are psychotherapies for young people growing stronger? Tracking trends over tme for youth anxiety, depression, attention-deficit/hyperactivity disorders, and conduct problems. *Perspectives on Psychological Science, 14*(2), 216–237. https://doi.org/10.1177/1745691618805436

Weitzman, C., & Wegner, L. (2015). Promoting optimal development: Screening for behavioral and emotional problems. *Pediatrics, 135*(2), 384–395. https://doi.org/10.1542/peds.2014-3716

Weitzman, C. D., Wegner, L., & Section On Developmental And Behavioral Pediatrics. (2015). Promoting optimal development: Screening for behavioral and emotional problems. *Pediatrics, 135*, 384–395. https://doi.org/10.1542/peds.2014-3716

Williamson, A., Makkar, S. R., McGrath, C., & Redman, S. (2015). How can the use of evidence in mental health policy be increased? A systematic review. *Psychiatric Services, 66*(8), 783–797. https://doi.org/10.1176/appi.ps.201400329

Wolicki, S. B., Bitsko, R. H., Cree, R. A., Danielson, M. L., Ko, J. Y., Warner, L., & Robinson, L. R. (2021). Mental health of parents and primary caregivers by sex and associated child health indicators. *Adversity and Resilience Science, 2*(2), 125–139. https://doi.org/10.1007/s42844-021-00037-7

World Health Organization. (2022). *Mental disorders*.

Xue, Y., Leventhal, T., Brooks-Gunn, J., & Early, F. J. (2005). Neighborhood residence and mental health problems of 5- to 11-year-olds. *Archives of General Psychiatry, 62*(5), 554–563. https://doi.org/10.1001/archpsyc.62.5.554

Yang, W., Datu, J. A. D., Lau, M. M., & Lin, X. (2018). Can early childhood curriculum enhance social-emotional competence in low-income children? A meta-analysis of the educational effects. *Early Education and Development, 30*(3), 36–59. https://doi.org/10.1080/10409289.2018.1539557

Yu-Lefler, H. F., Hsu, Y. J., Sen, A., & Marsteller, J. (2023). Service utilization for parent management of early childhood behavior problems in a private outpatient behavioral clinic: The impact of out-of-pocket cost, travel distance, and initial treatment progress. *Administration and Policy in Mental Health, 50*(5), 834–847. https://doi.org/10.1007/s10488-023-01282-x

Appendices

Appendix A

Study Measures: Description and Psychometric Characteristics

This appendix elaborates on the measures and procedures described in Chap. 6.

Demographics and Screening

Family Background Questionnaire

A parent completed a demographic questionnaire including information on the child's age, sex, race, family size, parents' marital status, and with whom the child lives. Parent education and employment information, also collected in this questionnaire, was coded for socioeconomic status using the Hollingshead Four-Factor Index of Social Status (Hollingshead, 1975).

Peabody Picture Vocabulary Test (PPVT)

The PPVT (Dunn & Dunn, 1997) is an individually administered, norm-referenced measure of single-word receptive language skills widely used as a language screening instrument for persons ranging from 2½ years to adulthood. It is an individually administered test in which the respondent chooses a pictorial response that best matches the vocabulary word verbally presented by the examiner. It takes approximately 10–15 min to administer. Internal consistency (alpha) is 0.94, and test-retest reliability is 0.89. Validity correlations with other vocabulary tests range from 0.67

K. R. Gouze et al., *Early Childhood Psychopathology*,
https://doi.org/10.1007/978-3-031-68877-5

(CELF) to 0.82 (EVT-2). The PPVT in this study was used to establish exclusion criteria; those children achieving scores equivalent to an IQ below 70 were eliminated from further study.

Risk Factors

Life Stress

Parenting Stress—Parenting Stress Index, Short Form (PSI-SF).

The PSI-SF (Abidin, 1995) is a 36-item self-report measure designed to identify parenting competence, parenting stress, and maladaptive parent-child relationship styles. Items are rated on a Likert scale with response options ranging from 1 (strongly disagree) to 5 (strongly agree). Higher scores indicate greater stress. The total stress score was used for analyses in this study. Total scores have demonstrated acceptable internal consistency (i.e., alphas >0.9) and test–retest reliability coefficients between 0.65 and 0.96 (Lessenberry & Rehfeldt, 2004). The PSI-SF was completed by caregivers at each wave of data collection. Sample items: "Divorce," "separation," "pregnancy," "went deeply into debt."

Perceived Stress Scale (PSS)

The PSS (Cohen et al., 1983) is a 14-item measure of perceived global stress designed to assess the degree to which respondents found their lives unpredictable, uncontrollable, and overwhelming. The measure correlates well with other measures of life stress, is distinct from ratings of depression, and has high internal reliability (0.84–0.84) and test-retest reliability (0.86). Sample items: "In the last month, how often have you been upset because of something that happened unexpectedly?;" "In the last month, how often have you found that you could not cope with all the things that you had to do?"

McCubbin Family Changes & Strains Scale

The Family Changes & Strains scale (McCubbin & Patterson, 1996) is a 15-item measure assessing life stresses affecting a family (e.g., spouse became ill, close friend of family died, etc.), with an alpha of 0.79. Sample items: "Remarried and/or added a child to the family;" "Incurred financial debts due to the use of credit cards/loans/more expenses; "Death of husband's or wife's parents or close relative."

Family Conflict

Family Environment Scale (FES)

The FES (Moos & Moos, 1986) is a 90-item measure that assesses the family's social environment. Principal components analysis with varimax rotation of factors yielded two factors, one of which is family conflict, which was used in this study, alpha = 0.78 (Moos & Moos, 1986). Sample items: "Family members criticize each other often;" "Fight a lot in family;" "Family members rarely become openly angry (reverse scored)."

McCubbin Family Distress Index

This 8-item scale (McCubbin et al., 1996a) assesses conflict in a family (e.g., increase in arguments between parent(s) and children; increase in conflict among children in the family), with an alpha of 0.87, and is related to family pressures, communication problems, and a lack of social support. Sample items: "Increase in the number of problems or issues which don't get resolved;" "Increase in conflict between adults in the house;" "Increased disagreement about a member's friends or activities."

McCubbin Family Problem Solving/Communication scales. This is a 10-item scale (McCubbin et al., 1996b) assessing conflict-related communication, alpha = 0.89 Sample items: "We talk things through till we reach a solution;" "We make matters more difficult by fighting and bring up old matters;" " We work hard to be sure family members were not hurt, emotionally or physically."

The FES, McCubbin Family Distress Index and the McCubbin Family Problem Solving/Communication scales were used to derive a composite family conflict measure (composite reliability = 0.71).

Maternal Depression

Beck Depression Inventory (BDI)

The BDI (Beck et al., 1996) is a 21-item self-report measure of depression symptoms. Respondents are forced to choose between several response options for each item, which are scored on a 4-point Likert scale. The sum of these scores is used as an index of depression severity. The BDI is widely used as a screening tool for depression, and the psychometric properties of this measure have been well documented, with an average internal consistency (alpha) of 0.86 in clinical samples (Beck et al., 1988). The BDI is completed by caregivers at each wave of data collection. Sample items: "Feeling Sad;" "Self-Dislike;" "Guilty Feelings."

Center for Epidemiologic Studies-Depression Scale (CES-D)

The CES-D (Radloff, 1977) is a widely-used, 20-item scale designed to measure depression in adults, with high internal consistency (>0.85), moderate reliability (0.45–0.70 across several weeks), and validity as reflected in correlations with other depression scales and ability to differentiate depressed adult patients from the general population (Radloff, 1977). Sample items: "Could not shake off the blues, even with help from friends/family;" "Thought life had been a failure;" "Hopeful about future (reverse scored)."

A composite measure of depression was derived from the BDI and CES-D. The composite reliability for parental depression was 0.89 at age 4 and 0.88 at age 5.

Parent-Child Interaction

Parent Behavior Inventory (PBI)

The PBI (Lovejoy et al., 1999), a 20-item parent-report measure of parenting behavior for parents of preschool and school-age children, was used as the questionnaire measure of parenting behavior. It has two factor-analytically derived subscales, Support/Engagement and Hostility/Coercion. Internal consistency indices for the Support/Engagement and Hostility/Coercion scales are 0.90 and 0.87, respectively. Test-retest reliabilities are 0.74 and 0.69 respectively. Sample items for support/engagement: "Pleasant conversations with child;" "Laugh with child;" "Listen and try to understand child's feelings." Sample items for hostility/coercion: "Lose temper when a child doesn't do something requested;" "Demand child does something right away;" "Threaten child."

NICHD Three Boxes Task

The Three Boxes Task (NICHD Early Childhood Research Network, 1999a), which consists of a 15-minute semi-structured videotaped parent-child interaction paradigm, was used as the observational measure of parenting. It includes two activities designed to be too difficult for the child to accomplish without assistance, as well as a free-play activity. Parental behavior was rated on 7-point qualitative scales that included ratings of supportive presence, respect for autonomy, quality of assistance, cognitive stimulation, confidence, and hostility (reverse coded). Inter-rater reliability for these scales has been demonstrated to be good to excellent (NICHD Early Child Care Research Network, 2002; NICHD Early Childhood Research Network, 1999a, b). Composite ratings of the scales have significantly predicted children's attachment security and social competencies (NICHD Early Child Care Research Network, 2002; NICHD Early Childhood Research Network, 1997).

Coders were trained to a criterion of 80% reliability with two master coders, who were trained by Margaret Tresh-Owen, Ph.D. of the NICHD EECRN study. A random sample of 20% of the tapes was double-coded to assess inter-rater reliability. Coders were blind to the other measures of child and parent functioning.

The six parent ratings were factor-analyzed using a maximum likelihood method to create a composite measure of parenting behavior. The factor analysis indicated that a one-factor solution provided the best fit for the data. All parenting variables loaded positively on this factor, except for hostility, which had a negative loading. Thus, a composite measure that we labeled parental scaffolding was calculated by summing the ratings for supportive presence, respect for autonomy, cognitive stimulation, quality of assistance and confidence and subtracting the hostility rating.

Child Variables

Attachment

Attachment Q-Sort (AQS)

The AQS (Waters, 1987), a Q-sort which provides a continuous measure of attachment security, was used to assess attachment. The AQS consists of 90 behavioral descriptions that are sorted into nine piles according to similarity with the target child's behavior. A security score (between -1 and 1) is calculated by correlating the child's sort with the sort of a prototypically secure child. Interrater reliability for the AQS has been reported to range between 0.58 and 0.72 (Pederson et al., 1990; Vaughn & Waters, 1990). A meta-analysis (van IJzendoorn et al., 2004) indicated that the AQS showed convergent validity with the Strange Situation Paradigm and excellent predictive validity with measures of sensitivity.

The AQS was selected over alternative methods (i.e., the Strange Situation Paradigm) because it was designed specifically to assess differences in attachment quality beyond infancy, does not require a lab visit, and yields continuous measures of attachment. Graduate research assistants trained to a criterion of 90% reliability with two master coders (trained by German Posada, Ph.D.) completed the AQS after the 2-hour home visit. Inter-rater reliability was assessed by randomly selecting (in blocks of 10) 20% of the home visits to be double-coded by two graduate research assistants. Mean inter-rater reliability was 0.77. Observers were blind to study hypotheses and all other measures of child and family functioning.

Child Temperament

Negative Affect (NA) and Effortful Control (EC)

Children's Behavior Questionnaire (CBQ) The CBQ (Rothbart et al., 2001) is a 195-item parent report questionnaire designed to assess temperament in 3- to 7-year-old children. Authors of the CBQ define temperament as constitutionally-based personality traits assessing individual differences in reactivity and self-regulation. Two of the three CBQ temperament factors were used in this study: NA (discomfort, fear, anger/frustration, and sadness, with soothability negatively loaded; and EC (inhibitory control, attentional focusing, low-intensity pleasure, and perceptual sensitivity). Item-total correlations for the CBQ range from 0.64–0.92 for 4-year-olds; stability over two years (age 5- age 7) is 0.69; and validity has been determined by establishing significant relationships between the CBQ temperament dimensions and other socialization-relevant dimensions (Rothbart et al., 2001). The questionnaire is self-administered; parents respond to questions on a 7-point scale ranging from "extremely untrue of your child" (low scores) to "extremely true of your child" (high scores). Sample items for inhibitory control include "Approaches places s/he has been told are dangerous slowly and cautiously;" "Has a hard time following instructions;" "Is usually able to resist temptation when told s/he is not supposed to do something." Sample items for attention focus include "shifts from one uncompleted activity to another;" "is forgetful in daily activities;" "has difficulty paying attention to tasks or play activities (looking at picture books, etc.)."

Sensory Regulation

The Short Sensory Profile (SSP) The SSP (McIntosh et al., 1999) is a 38-item parent-report questionnaire designed to screen for sensory processing difficulties in children between the ages of 3 and 10. The seven scales, derived from factor analysis, include tactile sensitivity, taste/smell sensitivity, movement sensitivity, under-responsive/seeks sensation, auditory filtering, low energy/weak, visual/auditory sensitivity. Intercorrelations of the total score with the scale scores range from 0.48–0.80; validity was established both by correlating sensory profile scores with physiological measures of sensory processing and by reliably demonstrating differences between groups of children with and without sensory processing difficulties. The questionnaire is self-administered; parents respond to questions on a 5-point scale stating whether the item "always" (low scores) or "never" (high scores) characterizes their child. The higher the score, the better the child's sensory regulation. Sample items for movement: "Dislikes activities where the head is upside down (for example, somersaults, roughhousing);" "Becomes anxious or distressed when feet leave the ground.: Sample items for tactile: "Expresses distress during grooming (for example, fights or cries during haircutting, face washing, fingernail cutting);" "Avoids going barefoot, especially in sand or grass;" "Prefers long-sleeved clothing when it is warm or short sleeves when it is cold." Sample items for low energy: "Tires easily, especially when standing or holding a particular body position;" "Props to support self (even during activity);" "Seems to have weak muscles."

Assessing Child Symptom Types

ODD Symptoms

Diagnostic Interview Schedule for Children-Parent Scale—Young Child Version (DISC-YC)

The DISC-YC (Fisher & Lucas, 2006) is a developmentally appropriate adaptation of the DISC-C (Shaffer et al., 2000), a DSM-IV-based structured parent interview that yields information about the child's overall level of symptoms, the presence or absence of a psychiatric disorder, and the type of diagnosis. High levels of agreement are obtained for concrete, observable symptoms, and test-retest reliabilities for the DISC-YC are high. Overall reliability of symptom scales is acceptable to high (test-retest reliability for ADHD scales = 0.67; for ODD, test- retest reliability = 0.88; for anxiety and depression scales = 57–0.81) (Lucas, personal communication).

Child Symptom Inventory (CSI)

The CSI-Parent (Gadow & Sprafkin, 1997, 2000a) is a problem behavior checklist with items derived from DSM-IV diagnostic criteria. The checklist provides response categories so parents can rate the extent to which a symptom is present from "never" to "very often." Algorithms based upon DSM-IV criteria are used to determine if the child meets the criteria for various psychiatric disorders without regard to impairment. In addition, each scale can be treated as a continuous measure yielding T-scores. Overall reliability of symptom scales is acceptable to high for ADHD scales (Inattention, hyperactivity-impulsivity: alpha, 0.91; test-retest, 0.67); ODD (alpha, 0.7 ; test-retest , 0.9); depression (alpha, 70–0.74; test-retest, 0.51–0.53) and anxiety scales (alpha, 0.70–0.83; test-retest, 65–0.77). For purposes of the PACT studies the continuous scores were used. . Sample items for ODD: "loses temper;" "argues with adults;" "Defies or refuses what you tell him/her to do."

Eyberg Child Behavior Inventory (ECBI)

The ECBI (Eyberg & Pincus, 1999) is designed to assess parental reports of behavioral problems in children and adolescents ages 2–16. The ECBI is suitable for assessing symptoms of oppositional behavior and has been widely used in parent training studies for ODD symptoms. Norms obtained from a sample of 1526 children and adolescents are available for the measure. Criterion validity for the ECBI has been assessed and found to be acceptable; test-retest reliability ranges from 0.86 to 0.88, inter-rater reliability ranges from 0.86–0.79, and internal consistency for the Eyberg subscales ranges from 0.88 to 0.95 (Eyberg & Pincus, 1999). The ECBI is completed by caregivers at each wave of data collection. Sample items: "Doesn't obey house rules;" "defiant when told to do something;" "Argues with parents about rules."

Attention Deficit/Hyperactivity Disorder

Attentional focus/attention problems. Child attention problems were assessed with three parent-rated measures of attention control problems (Child Symptom Inventory (CSI) ADHD rating scale; DISC-YC-P ADHD severity scale; DuPaul ADHD Rating Scale). The DuPaul scales are one of two measures of ADHD recommended by the American Academy of Pediatrics.

ADHD Rating Scale. The ADHD Rating Scale was developed for parent and teacher ratings for children ages 4 to 18. It includes a scale for the inattentive type (ADHD-I), hyperactive-impulsive type (ADHD-HI), and combined type (ADHD-C). In this sample, alphas were: ADHD-I, 77–0.87; ADHD-HI, 85–0.91.

Anxiety

Anxiety was assessed using the CSI generalized anxiety and separation anxiety scales; the CSI does not include a measure of social anxiety at this age, so no social anxiety scale for use in this study was identified. The generalized anxiety scale of the DISC-YC was also used. All of these measures are described above.

Depression

The DISC-YC described above was also used to assess depression. Scales of symptom severity for dysthymia and major depression were used in the same manner as the ODD scale. While conceptually distinct, there is a sufficiently high correlation that these scales can be used to measure a common, latent construct for the SEM analyses.

The CSI is a problem behavior checklist with items derived from DSM-IV diagnostic criteria. There are two depression scales, dysthymia, and major depression; quantitative ratings were used for SEM analyses and qualitative ratings for secondary analyses described later. As with the DISC, major depression and dysthymia are discussed as being conceptually distinct but often co-occur. The MDD and depression scales correlated highly (0.9).

Procedures

Recruitment Recruitment occurred through schools and pediatric practices to obtain an ethnically and racially diverse sample, as discussed above. School recruitment occurred at 13 Chicago public schools' preschool programs, with parents approached through multiple venues (e.g., drop-off/pickup times; at school conferences/report card pickups, social events). Pediatric practice recruitment is accomplished through 21 city and suburban practices affiliated with our institution's Pediatric Practice Research Group. In both venues, data were collected on the number of parents approached and refusals. Parents of 3- and 4-year-old children were approached by a research assistant, the study was explained to them, and their agreement was elicited to contact them to schedule an appointment (parents of 3-year-olds were contacted after the child's fourth birthday). For those agreeing to participate, phone numbers and addresses were obtained; subsequent phone contacts (or contacts through the schools if parents lacked a phone number) were used to schedule the first annual visit. Data were obtained for use in tracking families to ensure high retention at subsequent waves of data collection (e.g., getting names and numbers of relatives, and permission to call to track families through relatives, etc.). Quarterly telephone calls, birthday cards for the children, etc., were used to maintain rapport with families and to aid in retention. Recruitment data were entered into a database and formatted on an Excel spreadsheet to monitor progress toward achieving the desired ethnic/racial distribution of study families.

Collecting Annual Visit Data: Parents When an annual appointment was scheduled, a research assistant mailed questionnaires (Family Background Questionnaire, Beck Depression Inventory, Parent Behavior Inventory, Parenting Stress Inventory, Family Conflict Scale, Child Behavior Checklist, Child Behavior Inventory) to the parent prior to the home visit. At the home visit, the research assistant did the following: (a) assisted the parent in completing unfinished questionnaires; (b) observed the parent and child for about an hour (for the AQS ratings); (c) administered the NICHD 3-Boxes Task, and the child inhibitory control tasks; and conducted the DISC-YC interview. The NICHD 3-Boxes Task was videotaped during the home visit for later scoring. Immediately after the visit, the research assistant completed the AQS, and interrater reliability scores were calculated for 20% of visits; these were found to be reliable. Each annual visit took approximately 2.5 h (Tables 1 and 2).

Table 1 Measures

Category	Variable	Measure(s)
Demography	Demographics	Family Background Questionnaire (study created)
Screening	Language	Peabody Picture Vocabulary Test (Dunn & Dunn, 1997)
Risk factors	Socioeconomic status (SES)	Hollingshead-Redlich Four-Factor Index of Social Status (A. B. Hollingshead, 1975)
	Stress	Parenting Stress Inventory (Abidin, 1995) Cohen Life Stress Scale (Cohen et al., 1983) McCubbin Stress scale (Family Strains and Changes) (McCubbin & Patterson, 1996)
	Conflict	Family Environment Scale (Moos & Moos, 1986) McCubbin Family Distress (H. I. McCubbin et al., 1996) McCubbin Family Problem Solving/Communication (M. A. McCubbin, H. I. McCubbin, & A. Thompson, 1996)

(continued)

Table 1 (continued)

Category	Variable	Measure(s)
	Maternal depression	Beck Depression Inventory (Beck et al., 1996) Center for Epidemiologic Studies-Depression Scale (CES-D) (Radloff, 1977)
	Parental support-engagement	Parent Behavior Inventory: support-engagement scale (Lovejoy et al., 1999)
	Parental hostility	Parent Behavior Inventory: hostility/coercion scale (Lovejoy et al., 1999)
	Parental scaffolding skills	Three Boxes Task (NICHD Early Childhood Research Network, 1999a)
	Temperament: negative affect	Child Behavior Questionnaire (CBQ): Negative Affectivity Scale (Rothbart et al., 2001)
	Temperament: effortful control	Child Behavior Questionnaire: Effortful Control Scale (Rothbart et al., 2001)
	Temperament: sensory regulation	Short Sensory Profile (McIntosh et al., 1999)
	Attachment security	Attachment Q-Sort (Waters, 1987)
Outcomes	Opposition defiant disorder (ODD)	DISC-YC ODD (Fisher & Lucas, 2006) Eyberg Scale (Eyberg & Pincus, 1999) CSI-ODD (Gadow & Sprafkin, 2000b)
	Attention deficit/ hyperactivity disorder	CSI ADHD inattention scale (Gadow & Sprafkin, 2000b) CSI ADHD hyperactive- impulsive scale (Gadow & Sprafkin, 2000b) DuPaul ADHD Scales (inattentive and hyperactive-impulsive scales) (DuPaul et al., 1998)
	Anxiety	DISC-YC GAD (Fisher & Lucas, 2006) CSI-GAD (Gadow & Sprafkin, 2000b) CSI-SAD (Gadow & Sprafkin, 2000b)
	Depression	DISC-YC dysthymia (Fisher & Lucas, 2006) DISC-YC MDD (Fisher & Lucas, 2006) CSI-Dysthymia (Gadow & Sprafkin, 2000b) CSI-MDD (Gadow & Sprafkin, 2000b)

Table 2 Reliability coefficients

Demographics (age, gender, etc.)	Family background questionnaire	Mother	Wave 1
Language screen	Peabody Picture Vocabulary Test (A: 0.94; TR: 0.91)[191]	Child	Wave 1
Life stress	Parenting Stress Inventory (A: 0.70–0.93; TR: 0.69–0.91)[175]; Cohen Life Stress Scale (A: 0.84–0.85; TR: 0.86)[176]; McCubbin Stress Scale (A: 0.72; TR: 0.77) [177]	Mother	Wave 1–3
Family conflict	Family Environment Scale-conflict Subscale (A: 0.75; TR: 0.85) [178]; McCubbin Family Strains and Family Problem Solving/Communications Scale (A:0.89; TR: 0.86) [179–180]	Mother	Wave 1–3
Maternal depression	Beck Depression Inventory (A: 0.92.; TR: 0.93) [168]; CES-D (A: 0.85–0.90; TR: 0.51–0.57) [169]	Mother	Wave 1–3
Temperament: negative	Children's Behavior Questionnaire (Rothbart) (A: 0.66–0.81; TR: 0.50–0.73 at 2 years)[81]	Mother	Wave 1
Temperament: effortful control	Children's Behavior Questionnaire (Rothbart) (A: 0.64–0.78; TR: 0.52–0.77 at 2 years)[81]	Mother	Wave 1
Attachment security	Attachment Q-Sort (IR: 0.92) [191]	Observer	Wave 1
Mother-child support/engagement	Parent Behavior Inventory (support/ engagement) (A: 0.90; TR: 0.74)[173] Play interaction (maternal sensitivity, positive affect) (IR: 0.83–0.87) [192]	Mother; observer	Wave 1–3
Parental hostile/ coercion	Parent Behavior Inventory (hostile/coercion) (A: 0.87; TR: 0.69) [173] Play Interaction (overcontrol, NA) (IR: 83–0.87) [192]	Mother; Observer	Wave 1–3
Attention problems/ effortful control	Child Symptom Inventory: ADHD scales (Inattention, hyperactivity-impulsivity) (A: 0.907[182]; TR: 0.67) [183] DuPaul Scales: (TR: Parent, 0.88; Teacher, 0.89) [184] Statue, boxes, delay tasks (A: 0.71–0.85)[194]	Mother, Teacher Child	Wave 1–3
ODD symptoms Parent outcome model	DISC-YC ODD scale: [183] (TR: 0.88) Child Symptom inventory: ODD scale (A: 0.92; TR: 0.65) [182] Eyberg Scale (A: 0.94–0.95; TR: 0.75) [188]	Mother Mother Mother	Wave 1–3 1–3 1–3
Depressive symptoms /anxiety symptoms Parent outcome model Teacher outcome model	DISC-YC Depression and Anxiety Scales:[183] (TR: 0.57–0.81) Child Symptom Inventory Depression (A: 0.70–0.74[182]; TR: 0.51–0.53) and Anxiety Scales (A: 0.70–0.8374[192]; TR: 0.65–0.77) [182] Child Symptom Inventory Depression and Anxiety scales[182]	Mother Mother Teacher	Wave 1–3 1–3 1–3 1–3

References

Abidin, R. R. (1995). *Manual for the parenting stress index*. Psychological Assessment Resources.

Beck, A., Steer, R. A., & Brown, G. K. (1996). *Manual for the beck depression inventory-2*. Psychological Corporation.

Beck, A. T., Steer, R. A., & Carbin, M. G. (1988). Psychometric properties of the beck depression inventory: Twenty-five years of evaluation. *Clinical Psychology Review, 8*(1), 77–100.

Cohen, S., Kamarck, T., & Mermelstein, R. (1983). A global measure of perceived stress. *Journal of Health and Social Behavior, 24* 385–396.

Dunn, L., & Dunn, L. (1997). *The Peabody picture vocabulary test,* 3rd edn. American Guidance Service.

DuPaul, G. J., Anastopoulos, A. D., Power, T. J., Reid, R., Ikeda, M. J., & McGoey, K. E. (1998). Parent ratings of attention-deficit/hyperactivity disorder symptoms: factor structure and normative data *Psychopathology and Behavioral Assessment, 20*, 83–102.

Eyberg, S., & Pincus, D. (1999). *Eyberg child behavior inventory manual*. Psychological Assessment Resources.

Fisher, P., & Lucas, C. (2006). *Diagnostic interview schedule for children (DISC-IV)-young child*. Columbia University.

Gadow, K. D., & Sprafkin, J. (1997). *Early childhood inventory 4 norms manual*. Checkmate Plus.

Gadow, K. D., & Sprafkin, J. (2000a). *Early childhood inventory 4 screening manual*. Checkmate Plus.

Gadow, K. D., & Sprafkin, J. (2000b). *Early childhood symptom inventory-4. screening manual*. Checkmate Plus.

Hollingshead, A. B. (1975). *Four-factor index of social position*. Yale University Department of Sociology.

Lessenberry, B., & Rehfeldt, R. (2004). Evaluating stress levels of parents of children with disabilities *Exceptional Children, 70*, 231–244.

Lovejoy, M. C., Weis, R., O'Hare, E., & Rubin, E. C. (1999). Development and initial validation of the Parent Behavior Inventory. *Psychological Assessment, 11*(4), 1–12. https://doi.org/10.1037/1040-3590.11.4.534

McCubbin, H. I., & Patterson, J. (1996). Family member well-being. *Family assessment: Resiliency, coping and adaptation*, 735–782.

McCubbin, H. I., Thompson, A., & Elver, K. M. (1996a). Family distress index. In H. I. McCubbin, A. Thompson, & M. A. McCubbin (Eds.), *Family assessment: Resiliency, coping, and adaptation-Inventories for research and practice* (pp. 783–788). University of Wisconsin.

McCubbin, M. A., McCubbin, H. I., & Thompson, A. I. (1996b). Family problem solving and communication (FPSC) In H. I. McCubbin, A. Thompson, & M. A. McCubbin (Eds.), *Family assessment: Resiliency, coping, and adaptation-Inventories for research and practice* (pp. 639–686). University of Wisconsin System.

McIntosh, D., Miller, L., Shyu, V., & Dunn, W. (1999). Overview of the short sensory profile (SSP). In W. Dunn (Ed.), *The sensory profile: Examiner's manual* (pp. 59–73).

Moos, R. H., & Moos, B. S. (1986). *Family environment scale manual*. Consulting Psychologists Press.

NICHD Early Child Care Research Network. (2002). Early child care and children's development prior to school entry: Results from the NICHD study of early child care. *American Education Research Journal, 39*, 133–164.

NICHD Early Childhood Research Network. (1997). The effects of infant child care on infant-mother attachment security: Results of the NICHD study of early child care. *Child Development, 68*, 860–879.

NICHD Early Childhood Research Network. (1999a). Child care and mother-child interaction in the first three years of life. *Developmental Psychology, 35*, 1399–1413.

NICHD Early Childhood Research Network. (1999b). Chronicity of maternal depressive symptoms, maternal sensitivity, and child functioning at 36 months. *Developmental Psychology, 35*(5), 1297–1310.

Pederson, D. R., Moran, G., Sitko, C., Campbell, K., Ghesquire, K., & Acton, H. (1990). Maternal sensitivity and the security of infant-mother attachment: A Q-Sort study. *Child Development, 61*, 1974–1983.

Radloff, L. A. (1977). The CES-D Scale: A self-report depression scale for research in the general population. *Applied Psychological Measurement, 1*, 385–401.

Rothbart, M. K., Ahadi, S. A., Hershey, K. L., & Fisher, P. (2001). Investigations of temperament at three to seven years: The Children's behavior questionnaire. *Child Development, 72*(5), 1394–1408.

Shaffer, D., Fisher, P., Lucas, C. P., Dulcan, M. K., & Schwab-Stone, M. E. (2000). NIMH diagnostic interview schedule for children version IV (NIMH DISC-IV): Description, differences from previous versions, and reliability of some common diagnoses *Journal of the American Academy of Child and Adolescent Psychiatry, 39*, 28–38.

van IJzendoorn, M., Vereijken, C., Bakermans-Kranenburg, M., & Riksen-Walraven, J. (2004). Assessing attachment security with the attachment Q-sort: Meta-analytic evidence for the validity of the observer AQS. *Child Development, 75*, 1188–1213. https://doi.org/10.1111/j.1467-8624.2004.00733.x

Vaughn, B. E., & Waters, E. (1990). Attachment behavior at home and in the laboratory: Q-Sort observations and Strange Situation classifications of one-year-olds. *Child Development, 61*, 1965–1973.

Waters, E. (1987). *Attachment Q-set (version 3.0)*. State University of New York at Stony Brook.

Appendix B

Fit Indices for Structural Equation Modeling

Researchers vary considerably in the choice of model fit indices they choose to examine in deciding whether a structural equation model shows good fit. Furthermore, the standards for what threshold to adopt in deciding whether a model fits well have varied over time.

As stated in Chap. 6, Brown (2006) notes no single fit index is sufficient; rather he emphasizes the importance of looking at multiple fit indices from multiple fit categories (measures of absolute fit, comparative fit, etc.) before making a judgment about model fit.

For the guidelines we used in determining the way to describe model fit, we used the following standards for the root mean square error of approximation (RMSEA), the standardized root mean square residual (SRMR), the normed fit index (NFI), and the non-normed fit index (NNFI):

Good fit: RMSEA < approximately 0.06, NNFI >0.95, CFI >0.95, and SRMR of <0.08 as good fitting models.

Moderately good fit: If RMSEA is >0.06 but <0.08, NNFI >0.90 but <0.95, CFI >0.90 but <0.95, and SRMR <0.08, as moderately good fitting models.

Poor fit: We described models whose fit indices do not reach these thresholds as poor fitting models.

Significant indirect effects: Joint significance testing (JST) is based on each segment of a long chain path (e.g., at least two segments with at least one mediator) being significant. If each segment is significant, the indirect path is considered significant. If any segment is not significant, then the long-chain path is not significant. For JST see the following references (Taylor & MacKinnon, 2012; Taylor et al., 2008). While bootstrapping procedures as described by Mallinckrodt et al. (2006) are often preferred, JST often performs better with regard to Type 1 error (Mallinckrodt et al., 2006; Taylor & MacKinnon, 2012).

References

Brown, T. A. (2006). *Confirmatory factor analysis for applied research*. Guilford.

Mallinckrodt, B., Abraham, W. T., Wei, M., & Russell, D. W. (2006). Advances in testing the statistical significance of mediation effects. *Journal of Counseling Psychology*, *53*, 372–378. https://doi.org/10.1037/0022-0167.53.3.372

Taylor, A. B., & MacKinnon, D. P. (2012). Four applications of permutation methods to testing a single-mediator model. *Behavior Research Methods*, *44*, 806–844.

Taylor, A. B., MacKinnon, D. P., & Tein, J. Y. (2008). Tests of the three-path mediated effect. *Organizational Research Methods*, *11*, 241–269. https://doi.org/10.1177/1094428107300344

Appendix C

Suppression Effects in the PACT Study

Suppression occurs when the relation between two variables (e.g., between Predictor variable A and outcome variable C) is affected by the addition of another predictor variable (e.g., predictor variable B (Kline, 1998, 2011). To determine if a relation between two variables is affected by suppression, the following strategies are used: (a) comparing the beta weights of equations including only one predictor (e.g., A→C) with those including both predictors (A and B → C); or (b) by comparing the direction of effects of the beta weight in the equation with two predictors to the Pearson correlation between the predictor and outcome variable e.g., comparing the beta weight for A →C in the equation including both predictors to the Pearson correlation of A with C. If the beta weight is considerably different than the Pearson correlation or even has the opposite sign, then suppression is occurring.

One form of suppression is called negative suppression. When negative suppression occurs, the correlations of the predictors and outcomes change from a positive to a negative correlation, or vice versa. In the PACT study, as described in Chap. 7, we were concerned that suppression may have occurred regarding the scaffolding variable and the ODD symptom level variable because there was a negative association between the two, which was unexpected. To examine this possibility, the correlations of the three manifest indicators for scaffolding with ODD were examined. Because there was no change in the signs of the correlations and the signs of those bivariate correlations and the path coefficients were the same, we determined that negative suppression was not occurring.

When we examined the correlations between the parenting risk factors, we found that supportive parenting was correlated with scaffolding. As a result, it was possible that including both support and scaffolding in the ODD model may have resulted in a second kind of suppression effect, cooperative suppression. When cooperative suppression occurs, the addition of a second predictor results in an increase in the strength of the relation between the predictor and outcome measure. That is, the inclusion of support in the model and scaffolding may have increased the predictive value of scaffolding by partialing out or "suppressing" error variance in ODD symptoms, leading to an otherwise nonsignificant bivariate finding to be significant. This possibility led to the examination of two additional models in the PACT study. In one model, the path from age 5 support to age 6 ODD symptoms was retained, while the path from age 5 scaffolding to age 6 ODD symptoms was eliminated. In the original model, the age 5 support → age 6 ODD symptoms model was not significant, and it continued to be nonsignificant when the path from age 5 scaffolding to age 6 ODD symptoms was removed. Next, a second model was tested in which the path from age 5 scaffolding to age 6 ODD symptoms was retained while the path from age 5 support to age 6 ODD symptoms was eliminated. Because that model continued to show a significant relationship between age 5 scaffolding and age 6 ODD symptoms (PC = 0.12, $p < 0.01$), it is unlikely that suppression was occurring, so the possibility that better parent scaffolding skills actually are associated with higher subsequent ODD symptoms had to be considered.

References

Kline, R. B. (1998). *Principles and practice of structural equation modeling*. Guilford.
Kline, R. B. (2011). *Principles and practice of structural equation modeling*, 3rd edn. Guilford.

Appendix D

Bifactor Models and Their Anomalies

In Chap. 9, we discussed how bifactor models are structured and how they differ from hierarchical models. In this appendix, we expand on the discussion of the S-1 version of the bifactor model and the role of suppression effects in understanding anomalous findings that sometimes arise in these models.

Bifactor S-1 Models

Critics argue for abandoning the standard approach to modeling bifactors and replacing it with a theory-driven bifactor S-1 model (Burns et al., 2020; Eid et al., 2017). In this approach, one of the latent factors is designated as primary. This factor loads on all the first-order factors; thus, it replaces the general p factor in the standard bifactor model. Each of the other latent factors continues to load on a subgroup of symptoms (or symptom types). For example, in a model with two second-order factors representing internalizing and externalizing disorders (or symptom types), the internalizing factor could be designated as primary and allowed to load on all the first-order symptom types (i.e., anxiety, depression, ODD, ADHD, etc.). In contrast, the externalizing factor continues to load only on the ODD and ADHD symptom types. With the internalizing factor designated as primary, the externalizing factor would be interpreted as the residual of the new primary factor. Similarly, if there were several second-order factors, one would be designated as primary and the others as its residuals. Figure 1 illustrates such a model, with the internalizing factor defined as the reference factor.

Proponents of the S-1 model note that it is best if the choice of the reference factor is based on theory. If, for example, there were compelling theoretical reasons to argue that internalizing factors developed first and then externalizing symptoms emerged subsequently, then the model depicted in Figure 1 would be appropriate.

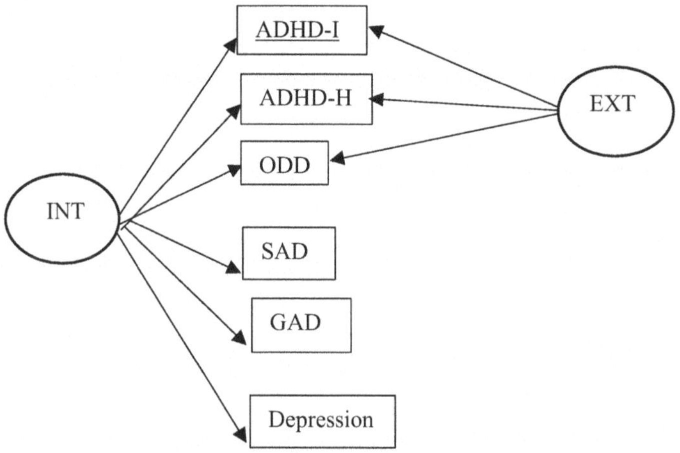

Fig. 1 A bifactor S-1 model for second-order internalizing and externalizing factors

Similarly, if there were reasons to believe that externalizing factors preceded internalizing ones, then a model with externalizing symptoms loading on each symptom with internalizing symptoms as the residual would be appropriate. Researchers are less clear on how to decide on a reference factor when the theory guiding that choice is unavailable. We know of no theory of the structure of psychopathology supporting the choice of internalizing as the reference factor in a bifactor model (or for choosing externalizing to be the reference factor, either). As critics of the S-1 model have argued (Burke & Johnston, 2020), the S-1 model may merely shift the problem of anomalous findings in the standard bifactor model to the problem of finding a meaningful rationale for the structure of the resulting S-1 model. It is not clear that this is really an advantage.

Suppression and Bifactor Model Anomalies

Anomalies identified in bifactor models are based on differences in factor loadings between those in the bifactor model and those that are found in similar models that do not have a bifactor structure. For example, if the factor loadings of a hierarchical model for a second-order internalizing factor onto first-order anxiety factors and depression factors were all positive, but one or more were negative for the loadings of the internalizing factors in the bifactor model, that finding would be anomalous. Similarly, if the factor loadings were moderate in the hierarchical model (e.g., a loading of 0.4 onto depression and 0.6 onto anxiety symptom types), and their magnitude increased or decreased considerably in the bifactor model, that also would be anomalous. Critics of standard bifactor models argue that these anomalies make the bifactor models uninterpretable.

We argue that it may be better to seek a way of interpreting the negative factor loadings. The low or negative factor loadings in a bifactor model, but not in a corresponding hierarchical model, may be due to positive or negative suppression. Both types of suppression may help clarify important relations between variables, and their interpretation may be useful, as described by Gaylord-Harden et al. (2010). For that reason, it may be important to consider whether a bifactor model yielding such "anomalous" or "contrast" effects (Scopel Hoffmann et al., 2022) is useful. Ultimately both types of models may serve a different purpose, e.g., one model may be more effective for determining the utility of risk factors and another may be more useful for predicting impairment, etc.

Other critics have raised concerns about the low reliability of some of the factors derived from the bifactor model. Lahey et al. (2021) raise the possibility that the reliability coefficients, measured by a reliability statistic known as coefficient H, may be low. Still, in some studies such factors appear to be stable at different ages or developmental periods.

References

Burke, J. D., & Johnston, O. G. (2020). The bifactor S-1 model: A psychometrically sounder alternative to test the structure of ADHD and ODD? *Journal of Abnormal Child Psychology*, *48*, 911–915. https://doi.org/10.1007/s10802-020-00645-4

Burns, G. L., Geiser, C., Servera, M., Becker, S. P., & Beauchaine, T. P. (2020). Application of the bifactor S-1 model to multisource ratnigs of ADHD/ODD symptoms: An appropriate bifactor model for symptom ratings. *Journal of Abnormal Child Psychology*, *48*, 881–894. https://doi.org/10.10007/s10802-019-00608-4

Eid, M., Geiser, C., Koch, T., & Heene, M. (2017). Anomalous results in G-factor models: Explanations and alternatives. *Psychological Methods*, *22*(3), 541–562. https://doi.org/1.01037/me0000083

Gaylord-Harden, N. K., Cunningham, J. A., Grant, K. E., & Holmbeck, G. N. (2010). Suppressor effects in coping research with African American adolescents from low-income communities. *Journal of Consulting and Clinical Psychology*, *78*, 843–855. https://doi.org/10.1037/a0020063

Lahey, B. B., Moore, T. M., Kaczkurkin, A. N., & Zaid, D. H. (2021). Hierarchical models of psychopathology: Empirical support, implications, and remaining issues. *World Psychiatry*, *20*(1), 57–63.

Scopel Hoffmann, M., Moore, T. M., Axelrud, L. K., Tottenham, N., Zuo, X. N., Rohde, L. A., Milham, M. P., Satterthwaite, T. D., & Salum, G. A. (2022). Reliability and validity of bifactor models of dimensional psychopathology in youth. *Journal of Psychopathology and Clinical Science*, *131*(4), 407–421. https://doi.org/10.1037/abn0000749

Index

K. R. Gouze et al., *Early Childhood Psychopathology*,
https://doi.org/10.1007/978-3-031-68877-5

SPRINGER NATURE

GPSR Compliance

The European Union's (EU) General Product Safety Regulation (GPSR) is a set of rules that requires consumer products to be safe and our obligations to ensure this.

If you have any concerns about our products, you can contact us on ProductSafety@springernature.com

In case Publisher is established outside the EU, the EU authorized representative is:

Springer Nature Customer Service Center GmbH
Europaplatz 3
69115 Heidelberg, Germany

The manufacturer's authorised representative in the EU is Springer Nature Customer Service Centre GmbH, Europaplatz 3, 69115 Heidelberg, Germany. If you have any concerns regarding our products, please contact ProductSafety@springernature.com

Printed and bound by CPI Group (UK) Ltd, Croydon, CR0 4YY
01/10/2026
02225897-0007